DATE DUE

The American

Photographs by

Ansel Adams
Eliot Porter
Philip Hyde
Bill Ratcliffe
Josef Muench
Don Worth
Bob Clemenz
Ruth Kirk
and others

WEST

A Natural History

Ann and Myron Sutton

Maps by Walter Hortens and Kenneth Thompson

Photographs on the half-title, title and
contents pages are respectively by Ansel Adams,
Rondal Partridge and Don Worth.

All rights reserved under International
and Pan-American Copyright Conventions
Library of Congress Catalog Card Number: 76–1418
ISBN 0–88394–042–6
Planned and produced by Chanticleer Press, New York
Printed in Japan
Published by arrangement with Random House, Inc.,
New York.

Contents

Foreword

From southern Texas to northern and western Alaska, the American West has a span of fifty degrees in latitude and nearly a hundred degrees in longitude. It is the country of the Big Sky, a land of "room enough and time enough," of great mountain ranges, deserts, rivers, seashores, forests, muskeg and Arctic tundra. To some persons the West begins at a boundary such as the hundredth meridian, the north-south line that passes through western Kansas. For the naturalist it may begin less precisely, perhaps where prairie grass and deciduous forest meet, or at the ramparts of the Rocky Mountains, or on the broad sweeps of the Staked Plains. For Mexicans the West never really begins; it is the North, *El Norte,* and the surface expressions of it are subtle changes in vegetation over expanses of Chihuahua or Sonora or Colorado Desert. For the traveler flying in from Hawaii, North America rises out of the Pacific as a low gray mountain range, enclosed with fog, or dim in the softness of a coastal haze.

Some of the early explorers, once beyond the point where they thought of the West as a land of desolation, scarcely knew how to praise what they saw. Ordinary superlatives were quickly exhausted. Often they entered in their journals such phrases as "the scenery here becomes colossal." They talked of startling forms, of mighty avenues hewn in stone, of optical illusions, of the grand and the sublime. The explorers regretted that such "wonderful and instructive subjects" should receive so brief a notice by them; and nearly all returned to seek a scientific explanation for transcendent scenic wonders. The legacy they left is a treasury of hundreds of reports on the West as it was.

Today, the West is a gallery of natural masterpieces as well as a living laboratory of science. To be sure, a considerable part of it has changed under the hand of man, but the laws of nature in all their fascinating diversity still operate with predictable precision, and there are some encouraging signs that the damage done by men in the past is being repaired.

The real excitement is natural change, the only constant in all the West's environments. To review the transformation of the West from past into future this book uses chiefly geology and ecology, the master sciences to which many others contribute. By ecology is meant not only plant and animal interrelationships, but the relation of all organisms to the world in which they live—a complex network of climate, topography, soil, and the works of man.

Another aspect of this review is the change in human attitudes toward the West, and the development of new ways to measure its wonders. Fresh discoveries are being made with instruments undreamed of in the days of John Wesley Powell. For example, the United States Geological Survey, which he headed for thirteen years, has under way a program that includes isotope and nuclear studies, infrared investigations of fault systems, geothermal resources reviews, and programs in geophysics, geochemistry, hydraulics, hydrology, limnology, sedimentation, minerals, water resources and contamination. Especially interesting is astrogeologic research that helps to determine where men land on the moon and how techniques of lunar exploration can be applied to terrestrial studies. This brings us to the new technology being used by research and resource management agencies: P-wave velocities, K-Ar ages, and dynamics of ungulate populations, and such instrumentation as FM data telemetry systems, airborne multispectral photography, and remote sensing and recording apparatus.

Behind the scientific understanding of western natural history lies something equally essential but far less measurable. The call of a marmot in the Sierra Nevada; the hush of centuries in a redwood vale; a night full of stars that seem to have multiplied and grown to twice their regular size; the shining gold of the morning sun on Mount McKinley; the bark of a prairie dog in the badlands; a horizon of desert flowers after a rain; the song of a canyon wren echoing along a cliff—such things are the ultimate measure of the West today, and are likely to be so tomorrow. For there has risen within this century a continental conscience of conservation, nourished by an appreciation of geologic and biologic processes that make the West so wonderful in human eyes. Most Americans no longer measure the value of the West exclusively in tons of ore, barrels of oil, or acres of grazing land. The modern traveler is a new breed of explorer, stirred by discovering and understanding the wild panoramas and hidden canyons, the secretive animals, and the drama of life itself beside a road or trail.

To help make such discoveries a little more meaningful, we have tried in these pages to review the background of tectonic activity and erosional history of the land, the shifting equilibrium between man and wildlife, and some places where the West is still wild and wonderful.

We have had the help of many companions in the field and many instructors in the literature. In fundamental principles we have been guided by Eardley on structural geology, Thornbury on geomorphology, King and Shelton on the general geologic evolution of North America, Hunt on physiography, Odum, Woodbury, and Shelford on ecology, and Gleason and Cronquist on plant geography—all listed in our bibliography. Geologic terminology is standardized in accordance with that of the American Geological Institute, and all scientific (Latin) names have been reviewed with specialists at the Smithsonian Institution.

Dozens of experts in the field—too many to fit into these introductory pages—have advised us on parts of the manuscript according to their regional or specialized knowledge. Likewise, the assistance we have received for many years in the West, and in the course of a twenty-thousand-mile journey through all the western states and Canadian provinces during preparation of this book is so large that pages would be required to catalog it. Allow us rather to honor the institutions these specialists serve so devotedly: Utah State University at Logan, Northern Arizona University, San Francisco State College, California Academy of Sciences, Arizona-Sonora Desert Museum, Museum of Northern Arizona, Navajo Tribal Parks Service, British Columbia Department of Recreation and Conservation, Yukon Forest Service, National and Historic Parks Branch of the Canadian Department of Indian Affairs and Northern Development, Forest Service, United States Department of Agriculture, and the Smithsonian Institution. To the United States Department of the Interior we pay special honor and acknowledge the help of specialists in the Geological Survey, Bureau of Sports Fisheries and Wildlife, and National Park Service who read the manuscript and offered extremely valuable suggestions. Without the work of such public agencies, of universities spearheading investigations, and of institutions that present this material to the public, the West would not today contain unimpaired as many of the "wonderful and instructive subjects" that so deeply moved the explorers of yesteryear.

Ann and Myron Sutton

1. Sun, Sand and Saguaros: The Hospitable Desert

*This giant cactus was a very strange thing.
It was just a tall, thick, soft green thing
growing out of the ground. All the Indians and
all the animals came to look at it.*

Papago Indian legend

Almost without warning, a clap of thunder burst over the mountain peaks and sent reverberations down through the canyons. The balanced rocks and thin gray pinnacles of rhyolite in the heart of the Chiricahua Mountains seemed to shake under the onslaught. Cumulonimbus clouds had expanded quietly, almost unnoticed, in the morning sky; while we had hiked, they had been born of heat from the valley floor and cooled by currents of air that had traveled to Arizona from as far away as the Gulf of Mexico. The sun was blotted out. A strong wind blew into the grove of ponderosa pines and lifted a mass of dust and needles and leaves. The trees bent and swayed as if about to break from their moorings. Birds flew almost out of control, gusts propelling them like rockets into and out of the canyons below. White-tailed deer stood their ground as best they could, ears alert at the sudden violence of nature. The landscape darkened. We scarcely had time to retreat beneath an overhang before lightning struck the rocks and rain poured down.

Deluge was the word for it—but not surprise. Thunderstorms are the pattern of life in this land of two rainy seasons—one in summer, one in winter. Summer rains result primarily from moisture entering the Southwest around a high-pressure air mass thrusting into the central United States from the Atlantic Ocean. Most summer precipitation is of convective origin, where air flows over land much warmer than itself, creating atmospheric instability. The rise of heated air may be at the rate of fifty feet per second. Strong updrafts in a thunderstorm produce intensive downward-flowing winds as well, which are propelled at velocities high enough to stir up clouds of sand and dust.

In a few Southwest locations there may be eighty to ninety thunderstorms during the two summer months of July and August. If conditions are right, and an Atlantic hurricane sweeps across Mexico into the Pacific, as happened in 1951, the backlash can bring a record storm. Winter rains are important, and tropical storms, or *chubascos,* occasionally travel up the west coast of Mexico into the Sonoran and Mojave deserts. Even where there are not especially heavy storms, certain weather stations report precipitation as great as five inches in a single day.

That much seems to fall in a single hour when you are caught in the midst of it on a desert mountain peak. By the time the sky had cleared and the downpour had diminished to a drizzle, the Chiricahua forest was alive with a surging flood. A hundred types of music filled the woods as the waters plunged downward in rivulets that joined other rivulets to become silt-laden streams. Through the chaparral of oak and manzanita, into groves of Arizona cypress, the waters flowed in a roiling mass. One after another the muddy torrents gathered into steep stream courses, or fell in cascades over the edges of cliffs and down the sheer canyon walls. This drama did not end as quickly as it began. All afternoon, as we hiked down the Rhyolite Trail, we were almost

The desert's floral wonders depend on brilliant sun and nourishing soil. But water determines when, whether and how grand the display will be. (Josef Muench)

Above: The cactus wren (Campylorhynchus brunnei-capillus), *largest of North American wrens and predominantly insectivorous, nests amid the protection of numerous cholla spines. (Allan D. Cruickshank: National Audubon Society)*
Left: A land of little rain nurtures an abundant and varied flora. In southwestern Arizona, cholla, saguaro and organ pipe cactus predominate. (Steve Crouch)

surrounded by falling water and the roar of countless streams.

The following day, as we left the Chiricahuas, we saw streams pouring out of the mountains where no streams seemed ever to have existed. Grass- and cactus-covered flats lay soaked in water. Roads were washed out. Gullies filled with mud and debris had begun to dry in the heat of the morning sun. Before many hours had passed, we knew, the water would disappear. Below, on the bajadas, bolsons, and playas, we could see that erosion and deposition had been swift and extensive. Now, for a while, the desert would have new life.

A Variety of Deserts

Such thundering cascades seem utterly out of place in an environment that endures long periods of dryness and extremes of temperature. One of the longest dry spells in the West occurred in Bagdad, California, in 1912 when a drought lasted 767 days. Drought is the key to explaining this land. Deserts may be diverse—hot or cold, high or low, black or white, vegetated or nonvegetated—but they all have one thing in common: they are generally dry.

On nearly every continent, at a latitude of approximately thirty degrees, the persistent descent of dry winds leaves certain areas deficient in rainfall, endowed with cloudless skies and subject to a burning sun. North America is no exception, and on it, as on other continents, extensive deserts have developed. No American desert is as large as that which stretches from the African Sahara to the Asian Gobi, but in variety of vegetation, animal life, habitats, and natural wonders, the deserts of North America take their place among the most remarkable in the world.

It is a common misconception that North American deserts have a predominance of cactus. There are hot deserts and cold, and the leading characteristic of all of them is not cactus, nor even heat, but aridity. Wide variations in precipitation guide the destiny of desert life. In some places there is very little life, but for the most part the North American deserts have specific groups of flora and fauna by which they can be distinguished from one another. These are the Chihuahuan Desert in the basin of the Rio Grande, the Sonoran and Yuman deserts from the Gila River basin south, the Colorado Desert of southern California, and the Mojave, Great Basin, and Painted deserts along the Colorado River and in the Basin and Range Province.

The Chihuahuan Desert, lying mostly in Mexico but with its northern end extending into Texas and New Mexico, is an area of rolling grasslands and tracts of creosote bush. Stretching from the Mexican state of Sonora north into Arizona is the Sonoran Desert, spotted with giant saguaro cactus. The western part of it, along the lower Gila River drainage system to the Colorado River, is sometimes called the Yuman Desert; it is extremely arid but it still has a cover of creosote bush, mesquite and associated shrubs.

The Colorado Desert of southern California and Baja California is notable for its lack of saguaro, but it possesses familiar shrubs and occasional smoke trees (*Asagraea spinosa*), desert willow, and ironwood (*Olneya tesota*). In all these southern deserts, the creosote bush is common, and mesquites grow along dry watercourses.

Parts of the high plateaus of Utah and Arizona are desert, too, and so colorful that the name of Painted Desert is sometimes applied to them. That name, however, seems better restricted to certain parts of the Little Colorado River basin in Arizona, where the vivid badlands topography is sparsely clad in herbs.

In the Mojave Desert of southern Nevada and adjacent California creosote bush is abundant. Yuccas, and in particular the larger form called Joshua tree, are also prominent.

Finally, to the north, is the largest desert of all, the Great Basin Desert, land of sagebrush (*Artemisia tridentata*) and saltbush. This region rests in the shelter of the Sierra Nevada, Cascades, and Coast ranges, which interrupt the eastward flow of moisture from the Pacific Ocean and thus rob parts of Nevada, Utah, Idaho, and Oregon of moisture.

Nearly all of these deserts fall into a single physiographic subdivision, the Basin and Range Province, which constitutes a sizeable segment of the American West. We shall examine it in sections; the present chapter emphasizes basins and ranges in southern Arizona, New Mexico and Texas.

Desert Life

Springs are few and far between. Nor are there many natural lakes, even in the mountains. Few major rivers flow all year; and countless thousands of washes run only when there is sufficient rain.

The last thing one might expect in such an outwardly harsh and inhospitable land is life. But though arid regions may lack the biomass, that is, the total weight of living organisms, of tropical forests, they have an abundance of life, ranging from forms that are dependent upon available moisture to those almost completely independent of it.

Plants, of course, derive their basic energy from the sun, and through the process of photosynthesis produce and store complex organic compounds in ratio to available moisture, soil minerals, and other environmental factors. These organic compounds are an enormous food product manufactured when the engine of life becomes active every spring. Even in the wide extremes of the desert, the circle or chain of life goes on: fixation of light energy, use of simple inorganic substances to produce complex ones, consumption, decay, release of simple substances again.

In the desert community, as anywhere else, the products of growth are broken down by microorganisms into organic detritus. Normally, the process has no end, for the detritus is fed upon by organisms that are in turn fed upon. Each community such as this is in effect a closed system analogous to an electronic network; each part has its function, established by ages of evolution. Such an interconnected biotic and physical environment is known as an ecosystem, and the study of relations between life forms and their environment is called ecology. The community of life does not long endure without a cycling of materials and flow of energy through the ecosystem, no more than a fox can function without mice, or a mouse without grass, or grass without water. In the desert, or on grasslands, or in the densest forest, the circle of life is a symbol of time that never ends.

Instead of leading to monotonous biological communities, this arid climate, combined with elevation, results in distinctive plant and animal associations—perhaps because, as ecologists suggest, the diversity of habitats may be greater than that of any other region. When we consider the sunny and shady canyon walls, springs, streams, open flats, rocky foothills, and grassy uplands, this is not surprising. It is difficult to contrive a single definition to cover so diverse an environment. One authority says that a desert is a tract of bush-covered land with much bare ground exposed; but some deserts are scarcely bush-covered at all and others have very little bare ground exposed.

Another authority, after years of study and observation, describes the desert as a region of low and

Right above: The hedgehog cactuses (Echinocereus) *are usually low-growing and have spiny, more or less columnar stems.   Right: Wild four-o'clocks grow in clumps with many flowers. At dusk they open their petals and, like the evening primrose, stand vigil through the night. (Both by Bill Ratcliffe)   Far right: Pincushion or fishhook cactuses* (Mammillaria), *of which there are hundreds of varieties—mostly native to Mexico—have global or cylindrical bodies and numerous spines. (Richard F. Dyson)*

The great horned owl (Bubo virginianus) *is one of several predatory owls in the cactus country.* *(Ruth and Louie Kirk)*

unevenly distributed rainfall, poor drainage, sporadic streamflow, low humidity, high air and ground temperature, great daily and seasonal ranges, strong winds, violent erosion, and soil with a high content of mineral salts.

Desert organisms, like all forms of life, must have the materials for growth and reproduction. Their survival may depend not so much on necessities that are abundant around them, but on those that are scarce. This is an ecological truism: an organism is no stronger than the weakest link in its chain of requirements. Thus the desert may have an abundance of nutrients in the soil, but without water there is no mass dispersion of water-loving plants. With sufficient rain the desert blossoms like a giant garden. The greatest populations of plants and animals, therefore, are those that have become adapted to a lack of water and to wide extremes of temperature.

Some organisms have a substantial range of tolerance for certain factors—for example, they may never drink water—and a narrow range for others—they may be unable to endure high temperatures. Thus organisms most tolerant of all factors ought to be widely distributed. Of this, no better example can be cited than the creosote bush *(Larrea tridentata)*.

Nearly all of the arid Southwest has a covering, though sparse, of this extremely successful species. Sometimes erroneously called greasewood, which applies more accurately to plants of the genus *Sarcobatus,* the creosote bush can survive on the driest and poorest

of soils. It has an extensive root system and often is evenly and widely spaced for optimum water absorption. Rarely does it grow alone, however, associating in some localities with white bur-sage *(Franseria dumosa)*, in others with tar bush *(Flourensia cernua)*, and in the more heavily vegetated parts of hot deserts with salt-bush *(Atriplex)*, brittlebush *(Encelia farinosa)*, and numerous other species. The shrub gives off a creosote-like, though pleasant, odor, especially noticeable after rains. It is host to such insects as grasshoppers, katydids, and shield-bearers.

The Cactuses

Cactuses, of course, are symbols of the desert, though they grow naturally not only in nearly every state of the Union but as far north as Canada and as far south as the Strait of Magellan. On the colorful deserts of southern Arizona, the species are chiefly saguaro, organ pipe, night-blooming cereus, the hedgehogs, strawberry and rainbow cactuses *(Echinocereus)*, barrel cactuses *(Echinocactus)*, fishhooks and pincushions *(Mammillaria)*, and the largest genus and most common of all, the *Opuntia,* which includes prickly pears, cane cactuses, and chollas.

Most spectacular is the saguaro *(Cereus giganteus)*, which may reach fifty feet in height, have as many as fifty branching arms, and weigh up to fifteen tons, ranking it as the largest succulent in the United States. Arizonans have made the saguaro blossom their state flower, and for complexity, few flowers match it: one blossom had 3480 stamens. It blooms at night, and thus attracts the longnose bat and other night-flying animals, but the blooms usually persist until the following afternoon before withering. They offer food for the white-winged dove and other birds as well as hordes of insects.

The flowers ultimately develop into abundant fruit with a high sugar content attractive to men, wild mammals, and birds. But so drawn-out is the process of growth (saguaros live up to 250 years), and so beset by disturbances that nearly all the seeds perish. Because the seedlings need shelter, they get started best beneath nurse plants or in rocky foothills; but then they are usually obliterated by wood rats and other rodents, ground squirrels, insects, birds, freezing, and drought. It has been estimated that of every twelve million seeds produced, only one will grow into a mature saguaro.

Because of its size, the saguaro may soak up a ton or more of water, and thus is not as susceptible to drought as most of its neighboring plants. Accordion-like folds in the trunk permit the saguaro to expand or contract, depending on the amount of water available to its wide-spreading but shallow roots.

Low temperature is another matter. Saguaros are influenced by climate, and do not tolerate severe cold snaps. One evening in January, 1962, temperatures fell below freezing in the Santa Catalina Mountains of southern Arizona. Small saguaros sheltered from cool breezes suffered few or no ill effects. Saguaros also survived among rocks that, during the night, gave off heat absorbed in daylight. Large saguaros, massive and able to retain some warmth, lived through the night unharmed. But small saguaros exposed on open slopes

began to freeze. All next day the temperature remained below freezing and during the following night as well. With this, cells in the cactus tissue lost their firmness and the tissues collapsed. Bacterial decay set in, and only afterwards could the full extent of damage be observed. A grove of cactus had turned into a scene of destruction. On upper slopes more than seventy percent of the tall saguaros died. Sturdy individuals survived, in accordance with laws of natural selection, and the net effect was to thin the forest and reduce the density of stems rather than to wipe out the grove entirely.

Very likely this unusual combination of circumstances had been a limiting factor before. That hot deserts can get cold is well known; snow occasionally falls in the desert, even in Death Valley.

The Desert in Bloom

With such heat and moisture extremes, the evolution of desert plants has been a response to special environmental requirements. Some plants, such as the sycamores and cottonwoods, have few obvious adaptations, but they germinate and grow where moisture is present and so have become established along stream courses. Such habitats are alive with quail, Abert's towhees, Bewick's wrens, black phoebes, and other creatures of moist to semiarid riverbanks.

Out on the dry flats and hillsides vegetation is far more dependent on the timing and amount of rain that falls. Sometimes the desert floor becomes so thoroughly covered with poppies or composites that it is hard to see the ground beneath. Yet this happens only after sufficient rain at the proper time. The inception of life in certain desert plants has become such a sophisticated process that seeds germinate primarily under conditions that assure prompt completion of growth and development of new seeds without any additional moisture. There are seeds that do not even respond to wetting. They must be cracked open. Hard-coated seeds, such as those of paloverde, smoke tree, and ironwood, are scratched and scarred as they roll with gravel down the course of a flooding stream. After that their embryos begin to sprout.

One shrub to be found in many localities is mesquite *(Prosopis)*, a legume that reaches heights of forty feet with roots to depths of sixty feet. Swarms of bees and butterflies seem to be ever present around its pendant yellow flowers, which are produced by some trees at a rate of three crops a year. Mesquite seeds are an important segment of the desert food economy; as many as 142,000 have been counted on a single tree. The seeds can remain dormant for three years or more, and one-hundred-percent germination is not uncommon. They may also pass unharmed through the alimentary tracts of animals, and be scattered with the feces.

For naturalists it is a pleasure to investigate thickets of mesquite, for something always seems astir in them. If it isn't vermilion flycatchers hunting insects, it is

A century plant stands on a grassy knoll in southeastern Arizona. The giant stalk grows only once; the plant then blooms and dies. (Don Worth)

ladder-backed woodpeckers drilling into the trunks. Quail hide and roost in the branches, and wood rats pile up enormous collections of mesquite beans in front of their burrows.

Other desert plants have been endowed with true endurance, and are in a class by themselves. Such is the ocotillo *(Fouquieria splendens)*. Its scarlet flowers grow in panicles at the ends of elongated curling stems—an arrangement that resembles a cluster of coach whips. Leaf petioles and lower midribs during the first season of growth harden to form spines, and from an axillary bud above each spine the leaves of succeeding seasons are produced. In dry or cold weather ocotillos remain leafless, but during wet seasons the leaves become well developed. With this kind of adaptation, the ocotillo has no trouble thriving in the desert—which it does from sea level to 6500 feet.

Associated with the ocotillo in rocky uplands is the yellow paloverde *(Cercidium microphyllum)*. Another paloverde, *C. floridum*, sinks its roots deep into dry watercourses to tap as much subterranean water as it can and bursts into spectacular flower in the spring. Although it loses its leaves in winter, the plant is still conspicuous because of its green trunk and branches, which carry on photosynthetic processes and manufacture chlorophyll as necessary.

What the ubiquitous heaths are to eastern North America, the yuccas are to the West. They are found nearly everywhere, from the hottest and lowest deserts to altitudes above eight thousand feet. That they belong in the lily family is evidenced by showy clusters of white to creamy blossoms. Nearly all parts of the plant—leaves, fibers, roots, fruits, buds, and flowers—were used in dozens of ways by western Indians. Yucca supplied them with food and drink, soap, the raw materials for making clothing and baskets, and the mystic, even sacred, ingredients of medical and religious concoctions. This plant also gives us several signal examples of close ecological relationships, the best known of which is that of the yucca moth *(Tegeticula yuccasella)*. These moths gather pollen from the anthers of one yucca flower and push it onto the stigma of another, thus pollinating the second plant. The female then lays one or two eggs in the ovary of the flower. As these hatch, the larvae eat a few of the seeds that have developed. It is a mutually beneficial relationship, with neither plant nor insect able to do without the other.

Yuccas reach giant proportions in the West and have developed into some unusual and picturesque forests. One is a forest of giant daggers in the Big Bend

Left above: Along desert washes grows the paloverde, a member of the legume family. Green trunk and limbs continue the tree's food-making process even during the absence of leaves. (Josef Muench) Left: The desert grasshopper (Taeniopoda eques) *often congregates in large numbers beneath mesquite and other vegetation. Far left: Grasshoppers and locusts* (Acrididae) *normally feed on vegetable matter but can become carnivorous and cannibalistic when plants are unavailable. (Both by Edward S. Ross)*

region of Texas. Another extensive tract is that of Joshua trees located in northwestern Arizona near Lake Mead. The most famous group has been preserved in Joshua Tree National Monument in southern California, where some plants attain a height of forty feet.

Hiding From Heat

Almost as close to the yucca as the moth is the yucca night lizard *(Xantusia vigilis)*. When a plant topples over, it becomes a home for the lizard and for a host of arthropods—spiders, insects, crustaceans—on which the lizard feeds. As far as the lizard is concerned, the yucca provides excellent insulation from the sun and a splendid fortress in which to hide from predators. The yucca also retains a little moisture, which preserves the lizard from total desiccation in times of drought. The arrangement is a harmonious one and might seem to be a general rule of the desert, but this night lizard is one of the few reptiles known to be closely associated with a specific plant.

For all their lack of water, apparent dearth of food, and temperatures that rise close to two hundred degrees on the surface, deserts are remarkably well populated. Most of the animals are shy and nocturnal, for nature long ago favored them with sense enough to move into shade or to go underground and avoid the heat of midday. Kangaroo rats rarely venture out on the desert surface in the heat of day. Their burrows, even when the rats are at home, never get much hotter than eighty-five degrees. These behavioral adjustments to environment enable the kangaroo rat to live in the hottest and driest deserts far from water.

Animals That Never Drink

Two primary processes of animal life in so dry a land are to get water and to conserve it. A few animals, including birds and amphibians, take water directly from springs, rivers, ponds, and the like. Others depend on the succulent leaves of plants or the flesh of cactus. Some plants gather and store moisture in times of rainfall and have special devices for restricting the loss of it by transpiration, i.e., evaporation from their exposed surfaces. The creosote bush simply drops its leaves in prolonged drought. Still another source of moisture is to be found in the insects. Because of a hard and dry external skeleton, insects can retain moisture taken from plants; they are thus important water sources to insectivorous bats, birds, and reptiles. The grasshopper mouse is an example of this: if insects are plentiful it seldom has to rely on other sources of water. Likewise, in the endless chain of who eats what, small mammals, birds, and reptiles themselves are moisture-filled and become a supply of water for the larger predators—snakes, bobcats, foxes, and coyotes, to name a few.

One of the most ingenious evolutionary adaptations of animals in the quest for water is that of simply manufacturing it within their bodies. "There is hardly a more intriguing problem in the physiology of desert animals," points out Knut Schmidt-Nielsen, a longtime student of the biological problems of heat and water, "than the water balance of the many small rodents that live on air-dried food and never drink

The growing point of a saguaro cactus is a symmetric mass of fibers and burgeoning spines. (Ann and Myron Sutton)

water. The best known of these are the kangaroo rats *(Dipodomys)* which live in the deserts of the southwestern United States, but all the major deserts of the world have a variety of small rodents that fill the same ecological niche and have the same striking ability to live without water."

In using up nutrients, all animals maintain chemical processes whereby natural foods, dry or not, are converted to energy plus carbon dioxide and water. The amount of such "metabolic water" may be minute, but animals such as kangaroo rats are able to use that water effectively; they seldom, if ever, need a drink.

Once water has been ingested, or manufactured, conserving it is just as complex a process, and varies from animal to animal. A basic water-conserving mechanism important to desert reptiles is precipitation of uric acid from the urine, then expulsion of the urine in an almost solid mass. In desert birds, urinary and fecal discharges are combined, and are also so concentrated that they are relatively dry. The urine of kangaroo rats is four times as heavily concentrated as that of man. Water may also be resorbed from undigested food residue in the large intestine. Numerous animals eat their own feces, thereby reusing not only nutrients that passed through, but moisture as well.

Another technique is reduction of evaporation from skin and lungs. To slow down loss of moisture in the respiratory process, some desert animals, such as reptiles, bats, pocket mice, poorwills, and swifts, enter periods of quiescence in which physical activity, and hence water loss, are reduced. For certain species this period of torpidity is in the summer, so that they are said to estivate. While the antelope ground squirrel neither estivates nor hibernates, one of its neighbors, the Mojave ground squirrel *(Spermophilus mohavensis)*, does both. In the middle of summer, with the approaching dry season, this ground squirrel retires underground, its body temperature falls, and it enters a state of lethargy in which heartbeat, breathing, and all body processes are reduced to a very slow rate.

The Poisonous Ones

It is fashionable to talk of the poisonous inhabitants of the desert in terms of terror, as if each step into this environment were fraught with peril. On the contrary, naturalists who know the desert well are inclined to believe that it, like any other wilderness, is safer than many an urban environment. As a precaution anywhere in the out-of-doors, human visitors should watch where they step and where they put their hands, especially at night. All animals, desert creatures included, protect themselves with whatever means are at their disposal.

This defense takes the form of poison in the stinging apparatus of the deadly yellow slender-tailed scorpion *(Centruroides sculpturatus)*; the bite of the black widow spider; the fangs of the rattlesnake; and the jaw glands of the Gila monster, largest lizard native to the United States and the only poisonous one. Thus a few desert inhabitants are poisonous to man, but so exaggerated are the tales about them that some of the reputation for being dangerous rubs off on innocent creatures. Certain large scorpions, for example, as well as tarantulas, ants, wasps, hornets, kissing bugs, solpugids, and vinegarones are not fatal to man, unless perhaps the victim has an allergy.

The truly poisonous desert dwellers deserve respect. There are excellent books about them, with descriptions of first-aid treatment for their bites, but an effort should be made to avoid the attitude that anything ugly must be poisonous. The majority of desert life is harmless as well as fascinating. One seldom forgets the sight of a gila woodpecker flying among the cactuses, a phainopepla or black silky flycatcher perched atop a mesquite, the cactus wren singing at dawn from the highest saguaro, white-winged doves gathering at a spring, locusts filling the cottonwood groves with waves of sound, a hognose skunk rooting in the desert soil for larvae, peccaries running among the graythorn, or a jackrabbit sitting beneath a cactus with its ears backlighted in the morning sun. Such sights and sounds make the desert one of the most exhilarating environments on earth.

Desert Mammals

Piglike collared peccaries *(Tayassu tajacu)* roam the wild washes and rocky foothills of the desert. They range from Mexico into the southernmost parts of the southwestern United States; once they extended

In Big Bend National Park, the "giant daggers," a species of yucca, approach twenty-five feet in height. Each plant may lift hundreds of lily-white blooms to the Texas sun. (Josef Muench)

to Arkansas but were reduced by man and are now protected within their limited area of distribution. For the most part they are shy, nervous, and wary, but can put up a vigorous, slashing fight if cornered. They rove in bands, leaving behind a pronounced musky scent, and are fair game for larger predators such as the rare jaguars—if any survive in the mountain forests.

Kit foxes *(Vulpes)* inhabit mountain and desert regions of the West, though not as abundantly as in the past. They are small and shy, but all too susceptible to the traps and poisons set by men. They have large ears, bushy tail, and buff-colored fur, and make their homes in underground burrows.

Above-ground burrows are characteristic of the desert, too. The wood rat *(Neotoma lepida)* is at home among cactuses, usually moving about without difficulty in a thorny environment; it often builds runways in cactuses and nesting burrows in the trunks of yuccas.

Mule deer are common among desert inhabitants.

wildlife were rounded out by introduction of the animal best adapted to the desert—the camel. Ironically, paleontological evidence suggests that camels, like horses, originated in North America. The first camels, living in the early part of the Cenozoic Era, were no larger than hares. Those of the Oligocene were about as big as sheep. Prehistoric camels lived as far north as Alaska, and at some point in their evolution migrated across the Bering Strait to the Old World, where they appear in the early stories and legends of man. Camels ultimately declined and disappeared in North America, and the only survivors of the group in the Western Hemisphere are the humpless camels of South America—llamas, vicuñas, and guanacos.

A few early explorers, prospectors, and military men who entered the southwestern deserts in the middle of the nineteenth century must have longed for animals that could carry a thousand pounds of cargo and go for ten days or more without water. After the Gold Rush began, Navy Lieutenant Edward F. Beale had such

Left: If temperatures are not too low, ocotillos burst into leaf with sufficient rain. When drought returns, the leaves fall away. (Don Worth)
Above left: Not all scorpions are deadly to man. But crickets caught in their embrace have little defense against the potent sting. (Ruth and Louie Kirk)
Above right: They call it Gila monster, but Gila lizard would be better. Handsome, sluggish, unique, it inhabits the deserts of the Southwest and Mexico. (Ruth Kirk)

The white-tailed deer *(Odocoileus virginianus)*, a species typical of eastern North America, lives in western desert woodlands.

When the Camels Came

There used to be persons who thought that the American desert would be more habitable and usable if its

thoughts as he crossed the desert to deliver dispatches between California and the East. He persuaded Jefferson Davis, then Secretary of War, to support the idea, and in due course, Congress appropriated $30,000 to purchase and deliver camels to the Southwest. More than 130 camels were imported, and Lieutenant Beale himself led the first camel caravan across the great American desert.

The War between the States soon dashed all hopes of enlarging the experiment. Besides, cowboys never quite adapted themselves to the rolling, swaying gait, and mules and horses stampeded whenever they saw or smelled a camel. Turned loose along the lower Gila River, the camels multiplied and eventually grew wild, foraging by night and sleeping by day. Some were shot on sight by white and red men alike; some were even eaten. At last the slaughter became so great that the deaths exceeded births, and camels were not seen in the

Equally at home in cactuses or hardwoods, the Gila woodpecker leaves a legacy of abandoned holes that may be used by snakes, lizards, owls, wrens and flycatchers. (Harry Crockett: National Audubon Society)

Southwest after 1905. By then, the railroads had proven to be a more dependable—and acceptable—means of desert transportation.

The American Pronghorn

No creature of the American West has a more curious past than the pronghorn *(Antilocapra americana)*. It is not an antelope, and never was, being today a lone species in a lone family. Its branched and deciduous horns are annually shed and replaced, which separates it from deer, whose antlers are bone, not horn, and cattle and goats, which keep their horns for life. Pronghorns hold the distinction of being the only living hoofed mammal completely native to North America.

They apparently evolved not much longer ago than the Pliocene, making them geological newcomers. They roamed the ancient plains of the Southwest, the Great Basin, the Pacific Coast region, and what is now Mexico. One group had spirally twisted horn cores. Others, of which entire skeletons have been recovered from tar pits in California, had four horns. A pygmy pronghorn less than two feet high had parallel horns.

Today, the one remaining species is perhaps the most graceful mammal in the American West. It certainly is the fastest. We clocked one once at forty-five miles per hour, but it speeded up and left us behind, bursting through a barbed-wire fence and taking off across country. (Pronghorns usually go through, not over, obstacles.) Forty million are said to have existed when Coronado and, later, Lewis and Clark saw them, but then the hunting began and because of their innate curiosity they often ventured within range of man's weapons. The slaughter was stopped before it was too late and the pronghorn has since made a remarkable comeback. Two subspecies, however, fared less well— the Sonoran pronghorn is now endangered, and the Baja California pronghorn is probably extinct.

White Sands, White Mice

There are only a few sand dunes in western North America, but they are truly picturesque. The Pacific Coast has 55,000 acres of dunes; Colorado has its Great Sand Dunes, which reach seven hundred feet in height; and southern California has the Algodones, which seem like displaced parts of Arabia. The strangest, and certainly the brightest, are the White Sands of the Tularosa Valley of New Mexico.

Lying east of the Rio Grande, the Tularosa Valley is a basin as strong in contrasts, literally, as black and white. It is what geologists call a *graben*, that is, a depression broken by faults on either side which has no external drainage. The Tularosa Valley therefore has for thousands of years received the desert's scanty rains and either absorbed their waters, or collected them in ephemeral lakes where they evaporated and precipitated various kinds of salts. Such is Lake Lucero, thirty miles from Alamogordo, where the salts are chiefly gypsum (calcium sulfate) weathered out of ridges of Permian rocks. Prevailing winds pick up the gypsum crystals and carry them northeastward, where they collect in pure white dunes covering four hundred square miles. From the flat valley floor the dunes rise gently in billows of white, their shadows deep blue, their rolling crests presenting a spectacle that in the full light of the desert sun is dazzling, almost blinding.

On these sands certain species of mice and lizards exhibit a classical case of adaptive coloration. When a race of ancestral pocket mice with darker fur ventured out on the dunes, they must have been easily seen by hawks, and even by owls at night, and so were readily annihilated. Paler forms, not as easy to see, survived, so that after numerous generations a race of white mice evolved. Similarly, a species of *Sceloporus* lizard has become much paler on these sands.

The Tularosa Basin also contains extraordinary lava flows, one of which is more than forty miles long; and these are almost as black as the sand dunes are white. Pocket mice, rock squirrels, and wood rats living on this black rock have developed a protective coloration to match their background. Light-colored animals were no doubt easily detected against the dark volcanic rock and so were attacked by predators. Those with darker fur survived. A species of *Uta* lizard is also dark enough to blend with the lava on which it lives. Similarly, in the red-colored hills not far away are pocket mice of reddish color. Color adaptation is, of course, not unusual, and we shall note other instances of it.

Southern Basins and Ranges

In the language of the American West, *sierra* denotes

The white-winged dove is a warm-weather bird, moving to the northern parts of deserts in summer and retiring to Mexico in winter. (Capt. P.E. Huth: Western Ways Photo)

a rugged, serrated mountain range of any length, although in this southern portion of the Basin and Range Province the ranges are shorter and lower in elevation than farther west. We see only the tops of them. The lower elevations of New Mexico, Arizona, and southern California have seldom more than ten inches of rain a year, often only five, and sometimes none. What water does pour from a mountain carries silt and gravel, and deposits sediment around the base of the mountain in alluvial fans, spreading out like the flaring skirt of a squaw dress. This results in long and gentle lower slopes called pediments, or *bajadas*. Additional waters, if any, flow on into a wide intermountain basin, called a *bolson,* and there create a temporary lake, or *playa*.

These terms of Spanish derivation describe the fundamental physical character of the southern basins and ranges, a region that is some seven hundred miles wide and extends southward far into Mexico. Many of the basins have no outlet and internal drainage is typical. The mountains are isolated, seemingly truncated, often parallel, and spectacular in the way they rise abruptly, like islands, from the gently sloping pediments and plains around them. They seem, in fact, to be buried in their own debris. To look at these mountains, one would think that the only movement in this hot

and desiccated land, the only possible erosional force, is wind. But while playing a role in modifying the surface of the land, wind is not the major force in erosion. Ironically, it is water.

The Chihuahuan Desert

But to visitors approaching the Chihuahuan Desert from the east, there doesn't appear to be any water at all, only open and endless plains as big as Texas. It all seems, as the saying goes, "a place where you saw a visitor coming at sunup and watched him all day, and then he didn't get to your place until half an hour late for supper."

The auto traveler heading west across Texas finds himself on the great Staked Plains (or Llano Estacado, as the Mexicans called them). The origin of this name is obscure. Some historians think that the Spanish explorer Coronado staked his route across these featureless flats in order to find his way back to Mexico. Others believe that staked should be regarded in the sense of palisaded, in which case the term refers to escarpments in New Mexico. In any case, the traveler may be impatient to reach the mountains because the open land through which he drives seems devoid of interest: mile after mile of wide flats of brush, a few arroyos, some hills, a vulture. But this is clearly a deception, a penalty he pays for speeding by. Were he to pause, he could explore the region embracing western Texas and southeastern New Mexico and find gigantic gypsum crystals, underground passages sparkling with red and white crystals and cubes of blue salt, dazzling caverns with chambers half a mile long and twenty-eight stories high, wells of oil and artesian water, "bottomless pits," twisted trees with white, orange or red bark, giant yuccas, drooping junipers....

It takes a while to cross, for despite the relatively high elevation, it is, as J. Russell Smith, the geographer, points out, the largest tract of nearly level land in the United States. It is windy in spring, hot in the summer, and occasionally covered with dust or, in winter, glaze and snow. But there are subtle beauties and mysteries in it withal. There is the delicate odor of creosote bush and a chance to hear the call of the kingbird. And there are basins, marine reefs and lagoons that reveal, almost as much as any part of the West, the grand changes that have taken place in the earth and the immensity of time.

Ancient Reefs and Seas

Eventually the traveler comes to mountains—the Guadalupe Mountains—four hundred miles west of San Antonio, and catches the gleaming reflection of the sun off their most southerly point, El Capitan. This uplift greatly differs from those of the Black Hills and the Rocky Mountains; here we find scant indication of volcanic eruptions or terrestrial rock strata. In the great Permian basins of Texas nearly everything is marine, and the center of interest is a barrier reef which crops out with lordly magnificence in the cliffs of the Guadalupes.

The casual observer may see in those walls little evidence of a tropical reef. He expects a reef at the margin of some warm sea, with waves breaking on shoals and, to landward, clear lagoons. None of this seems even remotely related to the Guadalupe Mountains.

But it is. An informed eye recognizes the ordered limestones of back-reef lagoonal deposits, the massive rock of the reef, and the fallen debris of organic formations on the fore-reef seaward side. The reef is no longer active, of course, but back in Permian time it grew so big and was afterwards uplifted so high that it became a circle of Texas and New Mexico mountains— the Guadalupe, Glass, Apache, and Sierra Diablo. Among the towering crags is clear-cut evidence of life and death at the edge of marine embayments.

Such an embayment was the Delaware Basin, which is estimated to have been 10,000 square miles in extent. With the Midland and Marfa basins, it makes up what is now a notable series of fossil channels, bays, reefs, and shelves. Most of the sediments deposited in these basins—crystalline limestones, salt, gypsum, potash— still lie beneath the earth, their revelations buried with them. But earth forces have lifted the Guadalupe section to its present commanding position and have exposed enough other parts of the basins and reefs to yield a few of the grandest secrets of the history of this area.

While Guadalupe Peak, at 8751 feet, is now the highest point in Texas, the sediments of which the range is composed were accumulated just below sea level. Into the great embayments settled sediments from as far away as the ancestral Ouachita Mountains of Oklahoma and Arkansas. Around the margins of the embayments, secretions, and remains of countless billions of aquatic plants and animals collected. On the reef, warmed by the rays of the sun and nourished by the waters of the sea, green and blue-green algae thrived. Through the chemistry of calcium metabolism, these minute aquatic plants converted solar energy and bottom nutrients into calcium carbonate, which they secreted in deposits on the reef. As with modern reefs, these algae and other organisms were at work encrusting and binding loose material into a solid frame, a process proceeding year after year, century after century.

In this way the reef grew and expanded, and other reefs formed until they virtually lined the margin of the embayment. Millions of organisms found the waters a highly suitable environment. The reef fauna, as is clear from abundant fossil remains, included fusilines and other foraminifera (unicellular animals that secrete calcium carbonate), bryozoa, brachiopods, hydrocorallines, sponges, and the ubiquitous crinoids. Of the latter, known as sea lilies, fossil fragments of "cross sections" are encountered by the millions in various parts of these limestones, and in many parts of the West. Clams, however, were not too common, and how abundant fishes were on this reef is not well known, for their remains are exceedingly scarce.

Out in the basin, where the waters attained an estimated depth of 1800 feet, there was far less life because the waters were much less aerated. The Delaware Basin may have been stagnant part of the time, as to some extent the waters of the Black Sea are today. Being hemmed in by land, the waters in all probability circulated poorly, and the lower layers may have contained lethal amounts of hydrogen sulfide. Near the edge of the sea lived brachiopods, clams, and snails, but life in other parts of the basin seems to have been rare, or at least less capable of fossilization.

Change followed change; the underwater scene grew more and more complex. Sands and muds from the mainland worked through the reefs and washed into the basin. So did bioclastic materials, the washed-away skeletons and fragmented debris of reef-building organisms. Broken bits of reef limestone, algae, coral and other calcareous remains, together with millions of tons of debris from shore, poured into the basin.

Back of the reef, on a shelf connected to the mainland, lay lagoonal basins shallow enough to serve as gigantic evaporating pans. The evaporation in these back-reef pools produced waters that were hypersaline. If circulation took place, it must have been a result of interchange with the sea beyond the reef, which brought in additional salt. This led to fluctuations in salinity, which certain marine organisms cannot tolerate. Hence there is not the same kind or the abundance of life in lagoonal deposits as on the reef or in front of it. At the same time, oxidation and evaporation in back-reef lagoons, mud flats, and stagnant ponds caused the deposit of salt and gypsum. Some idea of the immensity of these deposits and the time required for their precipitation may be gained from an estimate of the volume of Permian salt in western Texas and eastern New Mexico: 25,000 cubic miles.

Eventually the reef grew upward a total of eighteen hundred to two thousand feet. Lagoonal deposits like-

As predators and tunnellers, badgers play multiple roles in subsurface ecology. Their diet consists of rabbits, squirrels and mice. Few desert fighters are more fierce. (Robert L. Leatherman)

wise thickened. In time, the reef became a barrier to the interchange of waters between lagoon and basin. The basin became more stagnant and received increasing deposits of anhydrite, a form of calcium sulfate akin to gypsum. These changes of time and circumstance made living conditions intolerable around the margins of the great embayments, and reef organisms were killed in droves. At last the great reef died.

So ended an era, but there seems to be no end to the variety of features left above and below the surface as a geologic legacy from this ancient seascape. Erosion has stripped away subsequent deposits above the reef, and crustal movements have gently raised the surrounding land and the Guadalupe Mountains high enough to expose a catalog of Permian geology. It is as though a classic text, well illustrated, were laid open. Little vegetation obscures it; bright sun through clear desert air illuminates it.

For example, evidence of submarine landslides is readily visible at a number of exposures. Embedded in the walls are giant boulders weighing many tons, part of a mass of clastic (i.e. transported fragmental) material that fell from the reef and skidded on mud for as much as ten miles into the basin. The most extensive, a slide that may have had a volume of 600 million cubic yards or more, is found along both sides of Trew Canyon at the southern edge of the Delaware Mountains.

Much of the original sediment, largely composed of plant and animal remains, has been recrystallized into fine-grained rocks similar to limestone, with a marble-like texture that ranks them among the most handsome strata of the Southwest. Included fossils may still be evident, though somewhat ghostlike.

The hiker in these dry, rocky parts of the Guadalupes discovers other unusual structures in the Permian reef complex—ripple marks, wavy bedding, cut-and-fill channels, tepee structures, and others. Out on the plains to the east, oil wells tap accumulations of petroleum. There are giant transparent crystals of selenite, a form of gypsum, which is used in making plaster of Paris. Deposits of potash—crystal clear, red, white, and blue—so valuable in the fertilizer industry, glitter by the light of miners' lamps more than a thousand feet beneath the surface. One such deposit underlying an area of two hundred square miles is 3800 feet thick.

Yet always the mind and the eye return to that massive escarpment overlooking the plains of Texas and New Mexico, the reef itself. The Capitan Reef, as it has been named, curves gently northeastward from its promontory in Texas until it disappears underground near Carlsbad, New Mexico. It has undergone natural modifications in texture since it was deposited, and has been cracked by earth movements, making it permeable to ground water. Thus began the great disintegration. What nature had taken so many millions of years to build was now broken and opened to solution. Underground water, charged with a slight amount of carbonic acid, circulated through the reef for thousands of years and dissolved an unknown number of cavities. Some are of gigantic size, and many, if not

25

most, have been ornamented with secondary limestone deposits precipitated from dripping water. Of all such cavities and their associated dripstone phenomena, the largest known to man are in the Capitan Reef some twenty miles southwest of Carlsbad.

Carlsbad Caverns

Although entering Carlsbad Caverns might seem like leaving the sunlit world of the living for a gloomy, lifeless underworld, it is simply not so. During hundreds of trips into these caverns, including exploration in passages rarely visited or seen, we have always found something new and exciting to see each time.

In Bat Cave, the first large chamber, the fascination and complexity of cavern phenomena are immediately apparent; there is enough to keep scientific researchers busy for years, for this is the home of a colony of Mexican freetail bats *(Tadarida mexicana),* one of about eighteen species of bats within this and adjacent caves. After the caverns were opened (by natural processes) an unknown number of years ago, Mexican freetails established a permanent colony there. Each summer evening, just before dusk, the bats begin flying out of the entrance, spiralling upward as they go, in a funnel-shaped flight pattern. Sometimes the flight takes hours. Pouring out of the cave as smoke pours from an Indian fire pit, the bats spread out to the south and east along the river bottoms in search of night-flying insects. In a good night's search for food they may consume as much as seventy tons of insects. By dawn, the colony returns, one by one, into Bat Cave, where they spend the day suspended upside down on the ceiling and in crevices along the walls. When autumn frosts begin to reduce the supply of food, some of the bats migrate southward eight hundred miles into Mexico. A few thousand may remain and hibernate in Bat Cave. In a good year, as many as eight million bats may reside here for the summer.

The bat flight very likely revealed the location of the caverns to cowboys in the 1880's, and little time was required for commercial interests to attach themselves to the enormous deposits of guano, a nitrogen-rich fertilizer, in Bat Cave. During the first twenty years of the present century, 100,000 tons were removed. Fortunately, the land was in the public domain, and by 1923, it was established as a national monument; in 1930 its establishment as a national park was authorized.

Most visitors into Bat Cave go no farther than a quarter of a mile before turning and heading down to lower chambers. But the park naturalist on a mission of observation lights a lantern and climbs over fallen limestone boulders, proceeding into the part of the cave occupied by the bats. It is a very active habitat: he sinks up to his ankles in twenty-foot-deep deposits of guano, beetles, larvae, bat bones and hair. The bats, perhaps hundreds of thousands of them, seem never to rest. With high-pitched shrieks and other sounds they whirl by the thousands in circles around the chamber. The stench of ammonia fumes is almost overpowering, for urine falls in a light but steady drizzle. Also from overhead come dead and dying bats, fresh feces, mites, flies, and other objects of a world that only a naturalist—or a bat—could love.

Stalactites and Stalagmites

In Bat Cave the ceiling is flat, typical of back-reef layering, whereas down through a vertical passageway called the Devil's Den, the ceiling is a natural arch, characteristic of the massive limestone of the Capitan Reef. Totally without layers, the reef had no openings for the passage of ground water. Its arching therefore supports much weight and permits chambers to enlarge considerably before the ceiling collapses.

By the time the visitor has descended 650 feet he has penetrated the heart of the Capitan Reef, which is about two and a half miles wide and four hundred miles long. Cracks and crevices in the ceiling reveal the extent to which the limestone has been fractured since it was first deposited. This permitted ground water to enter and dissolve and thus hollow out the first subterranean chambers. Over the centuries, pockets became larger, merged with other cavities, and eventually formed a system of underground corridors, galleries, and passageways. When the limestone was uplifted, the water within the cave drained away, but cracks permitted surface water charged with calcium carbonate to percolate, drip, and flow through the cavern system. This "hard water" oozed from cracks and fell free, or ran along the ceilings and walls. Upon emergence into the cave atmosphere there occurred a "pressure release" of carbon dioxide which forced the remaining calcium carbonate in the water to precipitate. The result has been various deposits of dripstone: stalactites, ribbons, and draperies hanging from the ceiling, and stalagmites and other deposits on the cavern floor.

In addition, fragments of limestone have fallen from the ceiling. The passage below the Devil's Den leads over a concentration of fallen rubble. The largest block that separated from the ceiling—probably thousands of years ago—and settled into the rubble is estimated to weigh over 200,000 tons.

The caverns have been explored to a depth of eleven hundred feet. Some of the rarest formations in the lower chambers are the branched and twisted helictites, which grow in nearly every direction, resembling frozen roots. They defy explanation as well as gravity; one theory holds that water seeps by hydrostatic pressure through a minute canal to the tip of the helictite where it evaporates; the process is so slow that drops of water do not form and therefore gravity has little effect. In some chambers are quantities of bat remains. That any life could survive this far beneath the surface of the earth seems incredible. But life is not unknown in

Right above: Vermilion flycatchers are relatively abundant where moisture occurs and insects gather. Other red birds of deserts include cardinals, pyrrhuloxias and tanagers. (Eliot Porter) Right: The leopard frog (Rana pipiens), most widely distributed of North American amphibians, is ready to spawn whenever the desert rains arrive. (Edward R. Degginger) Far right: Named for markings on its head, the lyre snake (Trimorphodon lambda) feeds mostly at night and injects venom into its victims by a chewing process. (Willis Peterson)

caves; indeed, speleologists estimate that the caves of the Edwards Plateau, in south-central Texas, have as many as two hundred species of troglobites—animals living entirely in caves. None of it is as spectacular as the glowworm grottoes of Waitomo and Te Anau in New Zealand, where thousands of glowworms illuminate the ceilings; and Carlsbad Caverns lack, as far as is known, blind fish and other species of more moist cavern systems, but they do have mice, crickets, spiders, and insect larvae.

Bats have no problem reaching these lower chambers, for their powers of echo location usually save them from flying into walls or other obstacles. They may be seen sleeping singly or in small groups, and their bones are abundant at these depths.

Now that man has introduced light—and himself—into the caverns, there are also mold, algae, and mushrooms, all growing more or less near sources of illumination. Actually, conditions are fairly favorable for growth. The caverns are near a constant fifty-six degrees in temperature and have ninety percent humidity. Air circulation is so good that there is a complete change of air about every twenty-four hours.

Passing "boneyards," grottoes, gypsum deposits, pillars, rimstone dams, masses of flowstone, and deposits of rubble, the trail reaches the Big Room, largest single cavern known. Roughly in the form of a cross, it measures two thousand feet in one direction and eleven hundred feet in the other. At the so-called Bottomless Pit, itself dropping 138 feet below the trail, the ceiling of the Big Room rises 232 feet above the trail. An abundance of reddish-brown decomposed guano suggests occupation by bats in the distant past. Since few bats now venture this far back, we assume that there were once cracks or crevices through which the bats could enter.

In places the walls are adorned with aragonite, thousands of white crystal needles so fragile that it seems as though a breath of air would destroy what took centuries to make. In another chamber hangs a stalactite five feet long and as thin as a pencil. Elsewhere, shafts and crevices disappear in the fading light of the lantern, falling away inaccessibly below. In the silence one may hear the dripping of water into some adjacent pool which no man has ever seen.

Life on the Surface

Outside, in the clear air and warm sun of the desert, plants and animals flourish in a land regarded by the uninformed as hostile and barren. This is the Chihuahuan Desert, one of a half-dozen arid regions of the West with a distinctive vegetation. It lacks the giant cactus of other deserts, but from where it begins deep in Mexico to its upper limit in central New Mexico, it is a shimmeringly beautiful expanse of yucca, creosote bush *(Larrea divaricata),* smaller cactus, dry lakes, brownish-purple mountains, and rolling grassland.

The rainfall amounts each year, with luck, to ten inches. There are extremes. On stifling 100° summer days one looks from the Capitan Reef escarpment out over the basin sediments and a scene where images are often strangely transposed. On cold and wind-whipped winter nights the temperature sinks almost to zero.

Sometimes there are dust storms when, as local residents say, Texas leaves for Oklahoma. Sky, horizon, and foreground merge into a brownish, almost foglike pall. The dust is so fine that there are few places it does not penetrate; ripple-marked mounds on window sills, inside and outside, are customary.

But dust is characteristic of the Chihuahuan Desert, and while it may sometimes be unpleasant to man, much of the time the sun shines from a clear blue sky, gentle breezes carry the scent of creosote bush or of wildflowers in bloom, and the vastness and solitude stir in man's soul the urge to see as many parts of this land as possible and discover the secrets of its hidden canyons.

Out over the plains, where the Pecos River flows to its junction with the Rio Grande, one may meander across flats of creosote bush and saltbush, a desert shrub community. Harsh as it may seem, there is a functional stability about this land. Natural systems, large and small, wet and dry, tend to resist any disturbance; they have self-regulating mechanisms that work to restore a state of constancy. This seems especially true as we walk along the banks of the Pecos River and hear the world alive about us. Fundamentally, the desert is as changeable and delicate as any other natural area. Its biomass, the total weight of the organisms present, may not be as great, say, as that of a deciduous forest, but biomass does not determine the richness of a land; productivity does. As in other places, productivity is continuous here, but its rate is variable, dependent upon that most important natural limiting factor in the West—water.

Badgers are at work underground, and coyotes and reptiles above ground, controlling flourishing populations of jackrabbits, kangaroo rats, and pocket mice. In pools and ponds along the Pecos are microenvironments with aquatic and shore species. Higher areas of broken rock, in the foothills of the Guadalupes and on up to the summits clad with forests of pine and juniper, have abundant life. Within the sheltered canyons grow walnut trees, desert willow (*Chilopsis saligna,* not a true willow but a member of the Bignonia family), hackberry, and mesquite. On the drive up Walnut Canyon, or back to hidden mountain caverns in Lincoln National Forest, New Mexico, one is likely to encounter mule deer, gray foxes, raccoons, and the ubiquitous skunk.

South to the Rio Grande are deserts in which, as the saying goes, there are more streams and less water than anywhere else. The region is not dominated by cactus, although there is plenty of prickly pear, cholla, and barrel cactus *(Echinocactus wislizeni).* Creosote bush is most abundant, turning the light plains green and harboring insects that are in turn a source of food for birds and other organisms. Innumerable circles of life revolve even where temperature and moisture extremes are so pronounced. Flowers bloom when sufficient water falls, and grass is by no means absent.

Of the plants that do grow in this region, three impart to it a special character simply by their abundance or beauty or both. So common is the Texas sotol *(Dasylirion texanum)* on rocky slopes that the region sometimes goes by the name of sotol desert. It is a member of the lily family, and graces the hillsides with its burst of spiny-margined, elongated leaves and a fifteen-foot stalk thrusting up a cluster of handsome cream-colored blooms. Second is the lechuguilla (*Agave heteracantha*), generically related to the century plant and sisal. It is small as Agaves go, but handsome with yellow flowers, and often grows in colonies. Like other Agaves it lives not a century but considerably less, perhaps twenty years, sending up a multiflowered stalk at the rate of five to seven inches daily, after which it dies. The lechuguilla pocket gopher burrows beneath the plant and eats its roots. Indians roasted the stalk to make "mescal," a liquor, hence the name Mescalero Apache.

Third of the indicative plants in this region is the colorful Texas madrone (*Arbutus menziesii*). That it is related to manzanita (*Arctostaphylos*) is readily suggested by its smooth, thin, exfoliating bark; whereas the bark of manzanita is red or maroon, that of the madrone is orange, almost a copper color, which brightens the landscape along the pale brown cliffs where it grows.

Beside the Rio Grande

Down in Big Bend country, beyond the Chisos Mountains where the Rio Grande makes a turn of ninety degrees from southeast to northeast, Texas lives up to many of the tales about it. Cowboys thought that the plants were all designed to stick or sting, and when you consider the assorted cactuses, the barbs of ocotillo, the spiny allthorn, the Agaves, catclaw, mesquite, and the giant dagger (*Yucca carnerosana*), there was something to what they said.

The Big Bend country is made up of soaring mountains and remote canyons, and hence a variety of environments and biological associations. We are never far from the influence of Mexico, nearly always in sight; several forms of life come over the border to establish themselves as the northernmost representatives of their kind and the only place where the species occur in the United States. Such, for example, is the Colima warbler (*Vermivora crissalis*), of which about four dozen pairs are resident. The drooping juniper (*Juniperus flaccida*), which may be seen on trails in the high country, was once in the same category, but has recently been found in the upper reaches of the Guadalupe Mountains.

One of these trails ascends through belts of pine and Douglas fir in the Chisos Mountains to an elevation of 7200 feet where panoramic views into Mexico reveal the Chihuahuan Desert in all its wildness. It is a rugged land, made so by complex geologic activity. The Big Bend region is a sunken fault block, a mass of rock bounded on several sides by fracture zones. One side is the great escarpment of the Sierra del Carmen, and the other the cliffs at Santa Elena Canyon. Between them, igneous action has raised the Mariscal, Chisos, and Christmas mountains. The Chisos are composed of rocks in such diversity as to compare with the Terlingua-Solitario region not far to the west, which has several hundred intruded masses of igneous rocks—plugs, dikes, sills, laccoliths, and lava flows. Add to this a mosaic of fossil limestones, coal deposits, dino-

Stalactites, built downward from the ceiling by deposits of carbonate-laden water, sometimes touch or coalesce with stalagmites being built up from the floor in the Queen's Chamber, Carlsbad Caverns, New Mexico. (Josef Muench)

saur bones, and petrified trees, and we have an area of great geologic interest.

Varmints Protected

Some of what nature put together so painstakingly over millions of years, man has put asunder in less than a hundred. Overgrazing by cattle so thoroughly upset the ecologic balance of this country that stock-growers did not complain when part of the region was withdrawn in 1944 to establish Big Bend National Park.

Sunset silhouettes a yucca on the white gypsum sands of New Mexico. (Edward R. Degginger)

The wolf, which used to be fairly common, is only a legend now. The bighorn was also extirpated, but has been reintroduced. With luck we may see eagles and mountain lions, those much maligned predators, so vital a part of the natural scene. They are still subjected to vilification by modern ranchers who would like nothing better than to kill "those varmints raised in the park."

The National Park Service hopes to restore to some degree the original natural scene that existed here. The progress has been encouraging. According to reports by rangers and biologists, the park has more or less stable populations as follows: 3500 peccaries, three thousand mule deer, five hundred white-tailed deer, and four hundred coyotes, as well as an abundance of smaller mammals. But as far as is known, there are only about fifteen mountain lions. Nevertheless, restoring the natural scene will not be easy, and bringing back a landscape damaged so severely requires both patience and time. There are still, for example, approximately

thirty horses and 125 burros remaining as exotics in the wild.

Meanwhile, the visitor may stroll between the massive natural limestone gates of Santa Elena Canyon and be surprised by sudden rugged beauty after all the miles of flat and open land. Or if fully prepared, he may descend the Rio Grande by boat and feel his insignificance beneath the two-thousand-foot walls of Mariscal and Boquillas canyons. High cliffs of sharply tilted strata shut out the sun. The river boat slides into whirling, churning rapids, or through waters laden with silt that originated somewhere between there and Colorado. In a tributary canyon may be seen remains of a pilo, or vat in which plants are boiled commercially. The candelilla plant *(Euphorbia antisyphilitica)* is gathered widely in this region, loaded on burros, brought to the pilos, boiled, and made into wax.

Past Mexican villages and haciendas, the river flows into Boquillas Canyon, longest on the Rio Grande. At the base of imposing columns and towering pinnacles, the river winds beside willows, cottonwoods, mesquite and Baccharis that appear to thrive in this secluded environment. In places the wind has picked up sands from the river bank and driven them against the walls.

The canyons and the mountains are a contrast to the open deserts and high plateaus of Mexico and Texas. But then that is the fascination of this segment of the West, a land of contrasts, of the unexpected, of reefs and caverns, and of plant and animal communities that flourish in a land of little rain.

Will the Desert Vanish?

As we know it today, the desert is a stable, fertile environment which, when supplied with water, has high agricultural value. A good part of it is already under irrigation. But at the moment it appears that cultivation may not be the final destiny of the desert. The prediction has been made, in a report published by the American Association for the Advancement of Science, that if only two million more retired citizens transfer their fixed incomes to the arid West, the added income would total more than the present value of all irrigated crops. A great deal of the land may then become more highly valued for its natural qualities and the native Indian tribes that occupy it than for crop production. On the other hand, if too many persons enter the region to build retirement homes, we may have all homes and no desert.

In the meantime, the desert is changing in other ways. The overriding impact on the ecology of this region is apparently climatic, though man's studies of this long-range influence are still not old enough to be conclusive. A number of factors have most certainly been at work, man included, and complex changes have been wrought. These are evident in comparison of photographs taken decades ago with photographs of the same places today.

For one thing, the ranges of mesquite and paloverde seem to be slowly moving upward, away from the low, hot, dry environments where these plants approach the limits of their tolerance. Grass on desert grasslands is apparently declining and being replaced by woody species—mesquite, ocotillo, juniper, cottonwood, and others. In oak woodlands at higher elevations, oaks are dying faster than they have been replaced, and mesquite, ocotillo, beargrass, cottonwood and other species have invaded.

All this suggests that an enormous change is going on. Taken as a whole, according to one study, the changes suggest a shift in the regional vegetation so striking that it might better be associated with the

Kangaroo rats, obedient to the laws of evolution and adaptation, have developed a capacity to do without water on even the hottest deserts. They venture to the surface in hours of coolness. (Robert L. Leatherman)

oscillations of Pleistocene time than with the "stable" present. What is behind it and where it will lead are subjects for further study. Speculations are that climate, fire and overgrazing during the past eighty years have united to produce the "new vegetation," that the desert grassland is disappearing, and that the shrubs are there to stay. This means that runoff will increasingly exceed infiltration of water into the ground, and that arroyo cutting could continue to increase—as it has ever since man came. But these are still speculations, even though they have about them a certain urgency and a warning to man to go slow, lest he do some irreparable harm to the fragile desert.

2. The Southwestern Plateaus: High, Wide and Lonesome

There is an eloquence to their form which stirs the imagination.

Clarence E. Dutton, Geologist on
the Powell Survey, 1875

With our desire to see what is on the other bodies of the solar system, we can readily understand the determination of nineteenth-century Americans to explore their western territories. The West seemed as far away as the moon, and from the first reports of trappers and scouts, it appeared to possess a topography and structure like that of the moon. In due course, pioneer surveyors were dispatched on horseback, foot, and boat to fill in the scanty knowledge of mountain and plateau country. A study of at least the two principal expeditions is inevitable in any perspective view of the natural history of the Far West.

Stairway to the Clouds

The first serious geological exploration was undertaken during the scouting of railroad routes to California, shortly before the War between the States. The second was a group of coordinated surveys between 1867 and 1879, centering largely on the Colorado Plateau. These came to be called the "Great Surveys," and included expeditions led by Clarence King, George M. Wheeler and F. V. Hayden. But the one that first explored the scientific aspects of the heart of the Colorado Plateau was the so-called Geographical and Geological Survey of the Rocky Mountain Region, directed by John Wesley Powell.

Powell's pioneer voyages down the Colorado River by boat in 1869 and 1871 revealed a region more widely stripped of overlying sediments than perhaps any other, yet with an almost unsurpassed sequence of rock layers that recorded the history of the earth. In one short section, between the southern part of the Grand Canyon and the Dirty Devil River, a distance of 160 miles, the strata dip slightly to the north and expose more than 25,000 feet of sediments in sequence. "Each cliff," wrote Clarence E. Dutton, an Army captain and geologist who joined Powell's survey in 1875, "marks the boundary of a geographical terrace and....the termination of some geological series of strata.... In the distance may be seen the spectacle of cliff rising above and beyond cliff, like a colossal stairway leading from the torrid plains below to the domain of the clouds above."

Scientists have since then corrected and expanded the work of the Great Surveys, and found even more to be amazed about. As one leading geologist, A. J. Eardley, says, the Colorado Plateau is one of the world's show places, not only for the tourist but for the geologist.

This segment of the earth's crust is not one plateau but many. It is an uneven upland of 150,000 square miles, the size of Pennsylvania, New York, and New England combined, and in elevation ranges from five thousand to thirteen thousand feet. Its two most arresting aspects are form and color, and in the extent of these it is unique. There are localities in Argentina that approach it; Australia has parallel scenery; Jordan and parts of Africa compare; but no semiarid land equals it in structural magnitude and visual impact. One

Rain and wind have sculptured into various shapes the soft sandstones of Utah's Bryce Canyon, on the edge of the Paunsaugunt Plateau. (Byron S. Crader)

measure of all this is that there are more national parks and monuments on the Colorado Plateau than in any other comparable geomorphic region of the United States. Another is that the record of the rocks can be read almost as easily as one reads a book.

The sediments of which the plateau is comprised were deposited on or adjacent to a continental shelf. Vast beds of limestone accumulated in the sea. Masses of sediment settled and compacted on floodplains, river deltas, and stream banks, sometimes to a considerable thickness; Cretaceous strata in the San Juan Basin alone are ten thousand feet thick.

The uplifting of so wide an area with such a weight of sediments, contemporaneously with Rocky Mountain uplifts, was caused by several forces at somewhat different periods. This subjected the strata to uneven stresses and strains. Despite the impression that the plateau country possesses a marvelous horizontality and seemingly undisturbed rock layers, many a fold and flexure has bent the strata, and faults have broken them repeatedly. It is a wonder that so much still remains horizontal.

The Colorado Plateau has at least seven major types of "architecture." These include fault blocks, folds, salt structures, domes and basins, and upwarps and downwarps of the earth's crust. Each of these structures takes some form of surface expression and, thanks to erosion and a minimum of concealing vegetation, is often clearly exposed, or even cross-sectioned, by natural processes.

A Desert Clown

Such an up-and-down landscape was bound to have brought on differences in climate, and thereby fauna and flora. To say that the Colorado Plateau has a minimum of concealing vegetation is thus not true for all parts of the plateau. In places it is maximum and very concealing.

If you start at the lowest edges, at the bases of some of the southern escarpments in Arizona, or at the mouths of sheltered canyons, you are very definitely surrounded by cactus, mesquite, catclaw *(Acacia greggii)* and other plants of the Sonora or Mojave deserts. In this thorny domain you may hear a curious rattling noise that resembles a rubber hose run along a picket fence, and that will be your introduction to *Geococcyx californianus,* literally the California ground cuckoo, more popularly known as the roadrunner. You will see it sitting in the uppermost branches of a mesquite as it gives this call, and you can consider yourself fortunate; the roadrunner spends little time in trees. Ground cuckoo is a fitting name, for the bird is a wanderer extraordinary and is a member of the cuckoo family—as is indicated by two toes pointing forward and two pointing backward. For a bird pushed to the edge of extinction, it has made a remarkable comeback and now may be found in arid regions from Kansas to

On the Colorado Plateau is the world's greatest collection of erosional land forms, including canyons, cliffs and towering spires like these in Monument Valley. (Hans W. Silvester: Bavaria Verlag)

35

California and south into Mexico. It is protected under international law and has been made the state bird of New Mexico.

In some ways the roadrunner seems like a desert buffoon, for its build appears ill adapted to speed and its actions awkward in a community where one misstep might mean impalement. But evolution, as always, has done about the right thing, and the roadrunner's physiological accoutrements are all assets. That broad black tail, for example, serves as a signal, brake, and gyro-stabilizer. The long legs and gripper feet are used far more habitually for locomotion than are the wings, and give the bird a maximum thrust of at least twenty-five miles an hour. The young look like something out of delirium tremens, and grow up with the same intense devotion to grasshoppers, snakes and lizards as their elders.

From the Sonora Desert environment one rises into the middle elevations of the Colorado Plateau, around five thousand feet, where a transition forest of pinyon, juniper and ponderosa pine grows. There are bears and mountain lions at this and higher levels, and thousands of deer and elk, plus all of the smaller residents—ring-tail, skunk, fox, coyote and others.

Winters on the high plateaus, nine thousand to eleven thousand feet up, can be as severe as Canadian winters, but the sight of mountain meadows strewn with flowers of nearly every color attests to the rich productivity of the plateau and mountain ecosystems. Dense coniferous forests of spruce, fir, and pine prevail, enlivened with groves of quaking aspen *(Populus tremuloides)*. And finally, at close to thirteen thousand feet, the highest peaks are reached, a number of them volcanic cones with the Colorado Plateau as a base. These environments lie above tree line, in a tundra zone where snow patches remain the greater part of the year, and where in a few places the cony, or pika, a relative of the rabbits, manages an exciting and probably rather trouble-free existence.

The Great Upheavals

But this biological stairway to the clouds, in reality a kind of vegetative zonation, is not exactly what Captain Dutton had in mind. You have a choice of geological stairways. At its western edge the Colorado Plateau is a series of bold escarpments thousands of feet high, generally oriented north-south, rising from one fault block to another. The Grand Wash Cliffs, in northwestern Arizona, have been eroded along the Grand Wash Fault, of which the two sides have slipped past each other almost seven thousand feet. The platform elevated by this movement is locally known as the Shivwits Plateau (*shivwits* is a Paiute Indian word meaning coyote spring); it fills a great bend of the Colorado River in the lesser-known western section of the Grand Canyon region. Next toward the east is the Hurricane Fault, which extends 170 miles from the Grand Canyon and well into Utah. One fracture after

Sand dock, or wild rhubarb (Rumex), *gets a roothold that is almost as temporary as the shifting dunes. (Bill Ratcliffe)*

another marks this zone of crustal breakage, and the result is Hurricane Ledge, a promontory reaching fourteen hundred feet in height. This is the western border of the Uinkaret Plateau (*uinkaret* means pine mountain).

Continuing this arrangement *en echelon,* the Toroweap fault begins far south of the Grand Canyon, follows the Toroweap Valley and the edge of the Kanab Plateau, and joins the Sevier fault which continues into Utah—one of the longest fault systems in the Southwest. The Kaibab upwarp lifts the plateau country to its peak in Arizona at an elevation of 9300 feet north of the Grand Canyon. The uplift is gentle and inconspicuous, so that the word *kaibab* applies exceedingly well—"mountain lying down." Finally, in Utah, the easternmost line of disturbance, the Paunsaugunt fault, borders on the Aquarius Plateau, where elevations exceed eleven thousand feet.

Such is the giant stairway that forms the western edge of the Colorado Plateau. Sometimes it is difficult to believe that so many fractures took place, because most are hidden or hard to see. But one look at the United States Geological Survey map of Grand Canyon—the geologic map, not the topographic—erases all doubt. The region is crossed with fault lines in a network as complex as the veins in a hackberry leaf.

On the other side, the eastern half of the Colorado Plateau is not so distinctly fractured, but there is a great deal of crustal breakage just the same. From the Book Cliffs of northern Utah, down through the Canyonlands into the Navajo Indian Reservation, a remarkable collection of geologic structures is on display: sharp ridges called cuestas and hogbacks, rock layers folded upward and downward, gentle flexures and those sharply bent or broken in every conceivable fashion, normal faults and thrust faults, grabens (structural valleys), horsts (structural uplifts), and broad domes.

Grove K. Gilbert, a geologist with the Powell survey who came into the region a century ago, called this an area of comparative calm, but it hardly seems so. In Utah, the San Rafael Swell is a ruggedly eroded crustal upwarp fifty miles wide and a hundred long. The 150-mile Waterpocket fold, an elongated bend of the rock strata in southern Utah, remains one of the longest and best-known folds in the Colorado Plateau. It is now eroded into great cliffs with colorful rock layers, such as in Capitol Reef National Monument, where one may see a thousand-foot canyon only sixteen feet wide. The Monument and Defiance upwarps have exposed their red strata to the artistic hand of nature, and one finds in them the celebrated Monument Valley and Canyon de Chelly.

The Colorado Plateau is engraved imperishably upon the memory of many persons as red rock country, but on its eastern border the rocks are frequently more yellowish. In the San Juan Basin and the Mesa Verde Plateau, ancient Indians used these rocks to construct cliff dwellings and elaborate pueblos, as on the Mesa Verde and in Chaco Canyon. The Uinta Basin, a broad downwarp of the earth's crust near the base of the Uinta Mountains, holds sediments that have developed extensively into badlands. Others possess some of the

The Gambel quail is restricted to the Southwest, where it thrives in high and low arid regions, preferring shrubby tangles of mesquite. (Ruth and Louie Kirk)

largest known reserves of oil shale, a laminated sedimentary rock containing hydrocarbons.

Red Rivers and Colorful Cliffs

And then, as if incidental to all the basic structural features of the southwest plateaus, come the rivers. Master of all, the Colorado rises in the snow-covered heights of the Rocky Mountains and flows 1440 miles to the Gulf of California. Along the way, seven major tributaries join it—the Gunnison, Dolores, Green, San Juan, Little Colorado, Virgin, and Gila. This drainage system receives an annual average of fifteen inches of precipitation. Together with an untold number of dry creek beds that intermittently carry the waters of floods, the Colorado and its tributaries have for millenniums scoured, cut, carved, and carried away the sediments of the plateaus. This job of removal is more or less half finished. If at every stage the erosional features continue to be as striking as those exhibited today, then the entire history of the river has as a by-product the manufacture of extraordinary scenic beauty.

The Colorado River itself has carved high cliffs and gorges, and flows through deep canyons for no less than a thousand miles of its total length. Almost all of the major tributaries have cut spectacular gorges as well—Split Mountain and Flaming Gorge on the Green; the Black Canyon of the Gunnison; the Great Goosenecks of the San Juan; and Zion Canyon on the Virgin.

It is perhaps in the region of Zion Canyon that the Colorado Plateau achieves its greatest display of color. In the thousands, or even millions, of years that erosion has been digging into northern Arizona and southern Utah, great thicknesses of slightly tilted strata have been worn into cliffs, slopes and terraces. This erosional process contrasts with the tectonic or upthrusting process characteristic of the Shivwits, Uinkaret, and Kaibab plateaus farther south. The great uncovering, as it might be called, has unveiled formations of contrasting color.

First of the outstanding promontories are the Chocolate Cliffs, composed of brown Triassic strata known as the Moenkopi formation, Shinarump conglomerate, and Chinle formation. Second are the Vermilion Cliffs, a series of red sandstones deposited during Jurassic time. Third are the White Cliffs, made up of massive, bright-colored Navajo sandstone and other Jurassic formations, and above that the Gray Cliffs, composed of Cretaceous rocks.

Finally, and for us the most brilliantly colored formations in all the West, are the Pink Cliffs, composed of Tertiary lacustrine, or lake-deposited, sediments outcropping most spectacularly at Bryce Canyon and Cedar Breaks. In Bryce Canyon, especially, these easily eroded sediments resemble man-made spires, temples, pyramids—whole "silent cities"—in red, orange and white.

By contrast, fully ten percent of the Colorado Plateau has been overspread by eruptive volcanic rocks. Moreover, molten matter from beneath the earth has pushed up mountains such as the La Sal, Abajo, Navajo, Carrizo, El Late, and Henry. Indeed, it was in an early study of the Henry Mountains that G. K. Gilbert introduced the term *laccolite,* since modified to laccolith, to denote a mountain formed by the pushing up of igneous material from below. As late as the twelfth century A.D., Sunset Crater, near Flagstaff, Arizona, erupted, destroying early Indian habitations.

Life on the Southern Fringes

Thus the Colorado Plateau is a wide, high, chromatic country, complex but exposed to view like illustrations for a text. It is indeed earth's best history book, with pages from virtually every episode. To man it may seem forbidding and impenetrable; it is no such thing to the varied populations of plants and animals in it. The fact is that communities of living things operate on the high plateaus and cold deserts as efficiently as elsewhere. Life has developed substantially in two major types of environments in this region—mountains and canyons. In the next few chapters, we shall concentrate on the canyons and their abundant fauna and flora.

This abundance becomes apparent on the approaches

Dry flats of lower Oak Creek Canyon, Arizona, nourish the clumps of yucca (Yucca elata) *that once supplied Indians with essentials and comforts of life. (Josef Muench)*

to the uplands, for life at the edges of the plateaus—in the fringing cliffs, canyons and foothills—moves into adjoining valleys, and vice versa, in a natural interchange. Let us take an example and bring into sharper focus the complexity of the various ecosystems.

The Verde Valley of central Arizona, a basin bounded on two sides by structural uplifts, is strongly influenced by the adjacent plateau, and that influence begins with water. Rainfall on the porous lava capping of the Coconino Plateau sinks into the ground and percolates downward to an impermeable layer of rock, then laterally along this until it pours out in seeps and sinks in the valley. Because the plateau is, in effect, an enormous reservoir that is seasonally replenished, the springs are dependable—so much so that power is generated, fish are cultured, and crops are irrigated from them.

Montezuma Well, a natural spring in a limestone sink 470 feet in diameter, contains a lake some sixty-five feet deep, supplied by a thousand gallons of water a minute, day after day, year after year. That it has been thus supplied for nearly a thousand years—and probably a good deal longer—is evidenced by the remains of irrigation canals built by early Indians and lined by lime precipitated from the water. Like most oases in semiarid uplands, Montezuma Well is a site of wildlife concentration, a crossroads where desert and plateau species meet. Mule deer often wander down from the mountains. Lewis woodpeckers *(Asyndesmus lewis)* and Steller jays *(Cyanocitta stelleri),* both pine country species, fly into the valley on occasion. The white-breasted nuthatch *(Sitta carolinensis)* and several juncos descend from the uplands during winter.

From the other direction come desert species, the most obvious and vociferous being the Gila woodpecker *(Centurus uropygialis).* Two of the most interesting birds, with unusual markings and especially pleasing songs, are the desert or black-throated sparrow *(Amphispiza bilineata)* and vermilion flycatcher *(Pyrocephalus rubinus).* Desert reptiles such as rattlesnakes are here, and back in the cool, moist places grow maidenhair fern *(Adiantum capillus-veneris),* monkey flower *(Mimulus luteus),* and the yellow columbine *(Aquilegia chrysantha).*

Volumes would be needed to describe the animal species in this one locality, so attractive is it to wildlife. Take the insects, for example. Man has barely touched the subject, but one review of butterflies in the Verde Valley listed 132 distinct species. In late summer the insects, inconspicuous at other times, dominate the orchestra of sounds along the river bottoms. In groves of cottonwood, sycamore, ash, and willow, the cicadas *(Tibicen cultriformis),* or seventeen-year "locusts," set up a high-pitched buzzing that drowns out nearly every other creature. By vibration of membranes over sounding chambers underneath the abdomen, each cicada sustains a steady note. It turns this note off and on, in

In the semi-arid plant community of lower Oak Creek Canyon, Arizona, a group of century plants (Agave) *presents its once-in-a-lifetime flower display. (Josef Muench)*

Along desert washes, life often resembles that of more humid regions, as exemplified by the ubiquitous raccoon. (Ed Park)

cadence with its companions, until October, or until it is dashed to pieces on a limb by a hungry yellow-billed cuckoo *(Coccyzus americanus)* or some other predator.

Some insects are large and some are vividly marked. Verde Valley specimens of the rhinoceros or unicorn beetle *(Dynastes granti)* measure not quite three inches. One of the most brilliant species is a light green scarab beetle *(Plusiotis gloriosa)* marked with golden stripes. Sometimes seen feeding on milkweed (both *Asclepias* and *Funastrum*) and goldenrod is a wasp *(Triscolia ardens)* with blue anterior, red posterior, and iridescent blue and purple wings. Another insect that often feeds on milkweed and goldenrod, and that is equally colorful, as well as extraordinarily interesting in its habits, is the tarantula hawk (both *Pepsis formosa pattoni* and *P. mildei* occur here). This solitary wasp will eat virtually any spider, but the tarantula is its main meal. It plunges its stinger into a nerve center on the underside of the tarantula's body, inducing paralysis. It then drags the tarantula across the limestone, occasionally leaving its prey in order to reconnoiter, and stuffs it into a crevice. It then deposits an egg on

the tarantula's body, and when this hatches, the wasp larva has the tarantula as an immediate source of living food.

When a hundred or so painted lady butterflies *(Vanessa cardui)* congregate on blooming seepwillow *(Baccharis)* in the autumn, it is a dazzling sight. More nocturnal and less conspicuous are the moths, but a few of them are beautifully patterned, such as the leopard moth *(Callarctia)* and the delicately colored *Cisthene* and *Pygarctia*.

Among the least conspicuous insects are the midges, or no-see-ums *(Culicoides)*. Collections made at Montezuma Well some years ago included not only species new to science but some known from nowhere else but Texas and California. There are plainly many discoveries yet to be made in the natural science of this region.

The Ever-Changing Scene

Now that wildlife observations in many parts of the West are close to or more than a century old, it is interesting to note the changes constantly under way in the distribution of animals. Some of the earliest records in the Verde Valley were made by Dr. Edgar Mearns, a surgeon at old Fort Verde in the 1880's. Although Mearns traveled about northern Arizona for four years and collected thousands of birds and mammals, he evidently did not see either the Gila woodpecker or the white-winged dove *(Zenaida asiatica)*; both are very common in the valley now. Other birds, such as white-throated sparrows, are occasionally wanderers. Factors behind such changes are no doubt many and complex, as in the case of the uphill movement of mesquite in other desert grasslands, and man may be at the root of some of them. Still, we are reminded that even in deserts nothing is static.

Life on the Colorado Plateau and its fringes is an often intricate and unusual mixture. To a considerable degree, this life is related to the topography of the land, to the structure of these "stairways to the clouds," and to the canyons slashed across them. Because of contrasts in natural features and in precipitation, temperature, and other factors, there is a large assortment of climates, called microclimates, within the prevailing general climate. They sustain pockets of life that are quite often distinctive, and frequently in sharp contrast to the life of adjacent habitats. An understanding of this principle of the microenvironment is essential if we are to understand the nature of plant and animal distribution in the West. There are few better places in which to examine such an environment than along one of the tributaries of the Verde River, for example, in what some persons have called the most beautiful place in North America—Oak Creek Canyon.

Exploring Oak Creek Canyon

Approaching the lower reaches of the canyon, where it broadens out into the Verde Valley, one sees a vivid layering of rocks—bright red shales, yellow sandstones, and a white limestone cap—all Permian in age and similar to layers outcropping in the upper walls of the Grand Canyon. Changes in vegetation are subtle and not always apparent to the untrained eye, for the pinyon and juniper seem to be everywhere. But as we progress up the canyon its walls grow higher and come closer together, more than a thousand feet overhead, and changes become sharply apparent.

The sun's heat, of course, is the most important element in this habitat, for that is the source of the energy that causes the circulation of atmosphere and runs the great engine of life on earth. In desert and canyon country, where the air is clear and dry, solar radiation is most intense because its path through the upper air layers is rarely obstructed by droplets of moisture, as is often the case in humid climates. Radiation consists of electromagnetic waves, and the quality and intensity of these has a bearing on the biological community, each plant and animal responding to different wave lengths.

In the lower parts of Oak Creek Canyon, where the red rock country is wide and relatively open, desert conditions prevail, and we find cactus, ocotillo, mesquite, catclaw, and the false paloverde *(Canotia holocantha)*. As the canyon floor rises and the multicolored walls begin to close in, there is a greater dominance of juniper and pinyon *(Pinus edulis)*.

But at the mouth of the canyon, we begin to notice peculiar changes in the distribution of plants. Out on the open and unprotected slopes hardy plants grow in dense and thorny thickets called chaparral. These stiff-limbed growths make hard going for man or horse,

Horned lizards (Phrynosoma) *are active by day, searching for insects. If disturbed, they can readily bury themselves in sand. (Rondal Partridge)*

being composed chiefly of the sharp-leaved live or scrub oak *(Quercus undulata)*, and the magnificent red-trunked manzanita *(Arctostaphylos pungens)*, kin to the orange-trunked Texas madrone. To make passage even more difficult there are also sharp-spined century plants *(Agave parryi)* and barberry *(Berberis fremontii)*. Mountain mahogany *(Cercocarpus montanus)* begins its empire here, in association with silktassel *(Garrya flavescens)*, buckthorn *(Rhamnus californica)* and sugarbush *(Rhus ovata)*, the latter sometimes known as sumac or mountain-laurel. At times the narrow-leaved yucca puts on a profusion of blooms. All these are plants more or less of open slopes, where the sun is hotter and where moisture vanishes faster.

On the shaded slopes of side gullies and back in secluded box canyons is an environment of more moisture, richer soil, and denser greenery. Hardy ridge-top plants, growing in sheltered spots, reach larger proportions. But more significantly, other groups of plants appear, for example, the Arizona cypress *(Cupressus arizonica)*. These handsome trees, with globular cones and thin outer bark, grow in gray-green thickets usually in fairly inaccessible locations. Sometimes they reach a height of seventy feet, but they seldom do this on ridges open to drying winds sweeping up from the desert.

But cypresses are only a first indication of life in relatively confined conditions, the first of the canyon microenvironments.

North and South Slopes

Both in number and in species, organisms become adjusted to differences in climate. Whether the slope on which they grow faces south or north makes a great deal of difference. On north-facing slopes, the moisture remains longer since it is seldom dried out by the sun. This means more vegetation and hence less runoff and overall erosion.

On south-facing slopes, which are drier and have less vegetation, the rains can do more erosional damage to rocks, terraces and soils. Perhaps this is partly why south-facing walls of certain canyons are cut more deeply into the plateau—that side is simply eroded faster. Studies have shown that south-facing slopes undergo cycles of winter freezing and thawing, and summer wetting and drying, which do not occur, or are much reduced, on north-facing slopes. There is less humus and litter on sunnier slopes, and many steep surfaces where the soil is gone altogether.

The climate difference between two slopes of a canyon, then, is basically a difference in the radiation they receive. This is true even of the north and south sides of a tree or cactus, and in some cases a plant has greater concentration of sap on the southwest side, or blooms on that side first, such as the saguaro cactus.

Investigators have found that for similar reasons twice as many seedlings appear on north-facing as on south-facing slopes. And humidity is of all environmental factors most able to modify the effects of temperature. Inside a canyon, the average daily temperatures are lower and the relative humidity is higher than outside the canyon. Average daily air movements are lower inside, and hence so is the rate of evaporation. Inside a canyon soil temperatures remain lower and during drought the soil moisture tends to diminish more slowly. All of this explains why environmental conditions within a canyon are generally milder than those outside and why plant life is richer.

A Canyon Stream

The crucial factor is the amount of sunlight that falls on any given area. There is less and less of it as we proceed up canyon. The walls close in, the cliffs become more sheer, the slopes more steep. In this sheltered environment, twilight ends later in the morning and begins earlier in the afternoon. When the sun does come over the rim, an immense and sudden change occurs and the intensity of illumination received by all living organisms changes from weak to strong. Were it not for the equalizing influence of rising and falling air masses—up canyon by day, down by night—the differences would be even sharper. Of course, variations in temperature are very important in an ecosystem; they have different effects on different organisms. Constant temperature tends to depress, in the lower animals as well as in human beings.

Extremes of temperature are also mitigated by Oak Creek, a crystal-clear stream that issues from springs at the head of the canyon, and flows from pool to pool, rapid to rapid. In this idyllic setting we first become aware of the sudden and enormous change from dry desert flats below. You can smell it in the air—the delicious fragrance of river moisture, of fresh green cottonwood and willow, and the decaying litter of leaves—long before you arrive at the bank of the stream. Instead of the catclaw and cactus of a few steps back, we now walk under alder, sycamore, and walnut. In patches of red osier dogwood *(Cornus stolonifera),* and in wild grape, we see birds in search of fruit, seeds, and insects.

On the shelf between stream and base of the cliff are also magnificent specimens of box elder *(Acer negundo)* and netleaf hackberry *(Celtis reticulata),* as well as

beds of horsetail *(Equisetum).* With all the rich soil brought down by the creek and deposited on narrow terraces, the streamside trees are bound to get a good start.

But there is another factor—what is called incident radiation. Tests have shown that radiation from a nearby wall varies with the color of the wall and has a definite, sometimes pronounced, influence upon the growth and yield of adjacent plants. The intensity of this incident radiation, the state of the sky, slope of the land, moisture and similar factors all have a bearing, and suggest that plants and animals exist in an environment which is more profoundly complex than man realizes.

And more yet: the soil of the stream terrace is almost a mosaic, with its roots, tunnels, stones, water, air, and dead and decaying organic matter. To some extent it is porous and not capable of holding a great deal of moisture, but it is often well sorted by stream action and supports many herbaceous plants. The microclimate becomes milder as the grass grows taller. Conditions for growth are more favorable in dense stands, possibly because a heavier cover lowers evaporation from the top layer of soil and thus tends to prevent temperature and humidity extremes.

At the edge of the stream grow watercress *(Rorippa nasturtium-aquaticum),* naturalized throughout North America from Europe; monkey flower *(Mimulus),* dock *(Rumex);* sedges *(Carex);* rushes, spiderwort, and others, imparting to this hidden canyon a feeling of luxuriance that seems anomalous in desert country. Such are the contrasts of microenvironments.

The Upper Canyon

Climbing toward six and seven thousand feet, one gets the feeling of entering a boreal forest, one characteristic of the northern regions of the world. This is not far from true, for the plant life is distinctly of a zone more moist and cool. Canyons often harbor species from far away, and Oak Creek is no exception. In its upper reaches, clinging to the nearly vertical slopes of limestone overlain with basaltic lava flows, are Douglas fir and white fir on the cooler slopes, and ponderosa pine on the warmer. Conspicuous, too, are plants of the northern mountains, such as columbine, anemone, and golden-pea *(Thermopsis).* An occasional big-toothed maple *(Acer grandidentata)* brightens the coniferous forest with bursts of color every autumn.

From the rims above, cold air flows like water down into the canyons, increasing the frequency of nights with frost, and sustaining a climate more typical of northern environments. If the air is trapped it forms in a "lake" or "pool" at the lowest elevation and at night

Right above: Roadrunners, with omnivorous appetites, must keep on the move to supply their average brood of half a dozen chicks. (Eliot Porter) Right: The tarantula hawk (Pepsis), *actually a wasp, paralyzes its prey and deposits eggs in the huge spider's body. Far right:* Plusiotis gloriosa *is regarded as one of the most brilliant of North American scarab beetles. (Both by Edward S. Ross)*

The grinding process of erosion has reduced vast layers of the Colorado Plateau to sand. The region seems durable and everlasting to men, but all of its configurations are temporary. (Josef Muench)

may deal a withering blow to blooming plants unless they are hardy. The old rule holds: at night concave land surfaces are cold, convex surfaces warm.

In some parts of the West, the different microenvironments within canyons and steep-walled valleys lead to the presence of species isolated from their normal range, separated by several hundred or even several thousand miles from a more abundant and widespread population. Eastern deciduous maples, for example, are found in Oklahoma, miles from their nearest relatives. Douglas fir *(Pseudotsuga menziesii)* occurs throughout the plateau country as a prominent species in cool canyons where solar radiation is restricted, or on high mountain slopes. That is why it is abundant just over the edge of the south rim of Grand Canyon, and may be found widespread along and back from the edge of the canyon's north rim, a thousand feet higher.

In the Purisima Hills of Santa Barbara County, California, is a small isolated stand of Douglas fir

within a forest of Bishop's pine *(Pinus muricata)*. The relict population is ninety miles southeast of the general southern limit of the species in California and survives in a deep, narrow canyon on the north aspect of a main ridge.

Such relict groups may have been separated from their parent populations by long-term climatic changes, but at least in canyons they still find the kind of environment they need.

Canyon Animals

Among these ever-changing clusters of canyon microenvironments there is a constant interchange of living organisms. The simplest is exchange of pollen and airborne seeds on transfers of air. Cones fall from trees. Seeds roll downhill. Squirrels transport seeds both down and up. Mule deer follow old animal trails up and down the slopes.

Animal distribution is often a consequence of adjustment to the most desired microenvironment. Vultures have become adapted to life in the open sky above the rims. Ravens and cliff swallows nest on the canyon walls. Rock wrens seldom inhabit forest or stream or flat; they stick to open cliffs and talus slopes and spend their lives among the sun-drenched boulders of desert and canyon country. Water ouzels, water thrushes, and various amphibians stay near streams. White-footed mice and other small rodents live beneath the earth and among the clumps of grass.

Soil type and density of vegetation strongly influence the location and habits of burrowing animals. Canyons may serve as physical and biological barriers to animal movements; or warm air currents and cold air drainage may make them a channel for migratory movements. Along such corridors are dispersed not only food in the form of air plankton (spiders, spores, seeds and the like), but creatures such as butterflies.

Back in remote tributary canyons, along the rims, and roaming the high pine lands, are mountain lions *(Felis concolor)*, also called cougars or pumas. Though hunters with hounds have persistently tracked, treed, and killed them in the Southwest, severely reducing their numbers, mountain lions still occupy wild habitats from mountains to prairies to deserts—indeed nearly all parts of the Americas. They travel widely, and have been seen at elevations between sea level and 13,000 feet. The jaguar is larger, but mountain lions are faster and may grow to a respectable weight—Theodore Roosevelt once captured one weighing 227 pounds. They breed every two or three years and produce litters of one to six kittens. The life span is something less than ten years. What is most important, however, at least to the national conscience, is retention of this animal as an integral part of canyon and mountain systems, such as at Oak Creek Canyon and on the Colorado Plateau. It is strong and patient, clean, and graceful; in some ways it is a symbol of the changing mores of men from the days of eradication to the days of protection. In wilderness areas such as those along tributaries of Oak Creek Canyon and in Sycamore Canyon, farther west, are habitats where deer and mountain lion may roam, to their mutual benefit as predator and prey.

Another inhabitant of these canyon rims is the wild turkey *(Meleagris gallopavo merriami)*, at the western edge of its original range. Before the coming of Columbus, an estimated ten million wild turkeys inhabited a region now covered by thirty-nine states. The average weight of the bird seems to be less than twenty pounds, though males over that size have been taken. But for all their weight, they can, when necessary, move very rapidly. Professor A. W. Schorger of the University of Wisconsin, an authority on this bird, points out that none of our native animals is more wary than the "educated" wild turkeys. They are curious and suspicious, have keen eyesight, and are strong on the wing.

Very often all you will see of them is a blur of black wings that vanishes as you look up. The flight speed of wild turkeys has been estimated to be as high as sixty miles per hour. But they prefer to run, and can do a good twenty miles or more per hour in short sprints. Pinyon nuts seem to be a favorite food of theirs, but acorns, grass, and various seeds are regularly consumed.

We have watched them for hours as they flew from rim to rim along these plateau edges, working their way down to lower canyon depths, their call note amplified and made resonant by the canyon walls.

Few animals, however, leave a more enduring impression of the canyon environment than the canyon wren *(Catherpes mexicanus)*, a small brown-and-white bird characteristic of chasms and gorges throughout the West. Not many birds are endowed with such a heroic voice in such dramatic settings. The Argentine chucao, a small brown bird of Andean forests, is one, but its song, though powerful, does not have the ringing cascade of whistles of the canyon wren. No song is like it, and once heard, it is not likely to be forgotten. Arthur Cleveland Bent, an outstanding ornithologist who wrote a twenty-volume series on the life histories of North American birds, made a trip into the mountains of southern Arizona and afterwards wrote: "We saw or heard a long list of interesting birds, but the gem of them all was the canyon wren.... We are astonished to connect such a volume of sound with such a tiny bird." Sometimes the song is reduced to less than half a dozen notes; sometimes it starts and stops abruptly, incomplete. Mostly it is a series of more than a dozen notes, each lower in pitch than that preceding, trailing away at a gradually slower rate.

Insectivorous, cliff-nesting, perpetually energetic, the canyon wren holds its tail high and bobs vigorously as it hunts for food in its complex, vertical habitat. Although it visits the dwellings of man and may even nest in them, it is essentially a wild bird, detached and uninhibited, concerned only with its voracious appetite and its vocal delivery. Of all the sounds of the West, this bird's song seems to have captured the attention of men as much as any. In some ways, the canyon wren symbolizes the self-sufficient, rugged, well-adapted, yet often fragile, life in western canyon and mountain ecosystems.

It is also part of the complicated laws of the very universe itself. "In the vocabulary of nature," said George Perkins Marsh, who wrote *Man and Nature,* in 1864, "little and great are terms of comparison only; she knows no trifles, and her laws are as inflexible in dealing with an atom as with a continent or a planet."

3. The Hundred Worlds of the Grand Canyon

All about me are interesting geologic records.
The book is open and I can read as I run.
All about me are grand views, too, for the
clouds are playing again in the gorges.

John Wesley Powell,
Canyons of the Colorado, 1895

Although naturalists as well as artists and writers agree that the immensity of the Grand Canyon, both in space and time, and the cosmic unrealities it represents, are stunning, naturalists are willing to attempt a description of its complex make-up and to speculate with considerable authority upon its origin. "It is not to be comprehended in a day or a week, nor even in a month," said Captain Dutton, the pioneer geologist. "It must be dwelt upon and studied, and the study must comprise the slow acquisitions of the meaning and spirit of that marvellous scenery which characterizes the Plateau Country, and of which the great chasm is the superlative manifestation."

A great deal is unknown about it, as about the earth and moon, and scientists are as diligent now as they were a century ago in trying to decipher the secrets of the canyon walls. But for how long shall we enjoy the privilege of knowing this gorge as intimately as Dutton did? So many people are visiting or entering the canyon that a genuine and dangerous threat is beginning to be posed to its values as wilderness and place of solitude.

If the canyon has a single dominant quality, it is its immensity. Color may be subdued or wanting and life is in places missing, or nearly so. But not size or vastness. The canyon's length and width and depth have a biological as well as esthetic significance. Its boldness and bigness confront a visitor in high cliffs, great depths, broad platforms, abyssal side canyons, and vistas disappearing in the natural haze. The canyon is so big in fact that it contains a hundred worlds, microenvironments within the climatic and topographic framework of the Colorado Plateau. Such vastness may overwhelm visitors, and a fair number of them profess a preference for Oak Creek or Zion canyons because the latter are smaller and can be studied on more familiar terms. "Zion Canyon is man's size," said a wrangler years ago, "and the Grand Canyon is God's size."

Following the initial shock on seeing Grand Canyon, one may achieve an understanding and appreciation of the size of the canyon by stages. We have gone to the bottom twenty-five times or more in the past forty years, and have slowly become accustomed to the size and space; yet each trip has been a renewal of respect for the work of wind and water which, over extensive periods of time, have widened and deepened the canyon system.

To a large degree the determining factors of canyon erosion and topography have been structural. Breakage and slippage of the rock formations, readily visible on a geologic map as profuse, often intersecting fault lines, have resulted in elongated zones of weakness that have been attacked by the agents of erosion. Water falls into cracks, freezes, expands, breaks off pieces of rock. Soil begins to form. Seeds drop into the soil, sprout, grow, push their roots into every possible crevice, expand, and break off more rock. Wind-borne dust and sand smooth off the ridges. Then the work of disintegration

The Colorado River seems insignificant but its erosive action has opened the way for other streams and agents of weathering to work. [*Joseph Hall*]

and transportation begins in earnest. Summer cloud-bursts pick up the debris in cascading floods and take it away, carrying it eventually to the Colorado River for final removal to the sea.

"It rains!" wrote John Wesley Powell on one of his river voyages. "Rapidly little rills are formed above, and these soon grow into brooks, and the brooks grow into creeks and tumble over the walls in innumerable cascades, adding their wild music to the roar of the river. When the rain ceases the rills, brooks, and creeks run dry. The waters that fall during a rain on these steep rocks are gathered at once into the river; they could scarcely be poured in more suddenly if some vast spout ran from the clouds to the stream itself."

The Colorado River

During Powell's time, in the 1870's, the average daily load of sediment transported by the river past any given point was probably about 550,000 tons. How long the river has carried its cutting and carving ingre-dients—sand, gravel, boulders—through the center of the canyon, and how long its numerous tributaries have been widening the system, is slowly being disclosed by research and investigation on a plateau-wide scale.

Some scientists favor the theory that the Colorado's present course is the result of what is called stream cap-ture, which took place during the latter part of Pliocene time, more than ten million years ago. The ancestral Colorado flowed southeastward then, perhaps into the drainage of the Rio Grande and thence to the Gulf of Mexico. There is also evidence that the Colorado may have emptied into a nearer body of water, possibly a lake, in the Bidahochi Basin of the Navajo Indian Reservation. In the opposite direction, another stream system flowed north, slowly eroding and working its way back into the Kaibab highland; in time, these headward eroding tributaries ate their way through to the banks of the Colorado and captured the river. A reversal of the drainage pattern was thus forced, and Colorado River waters were diverted toward the west. For the first time, the Colorado flowed from the Rockies to the Southwest. But, as geologist Charles B. Hunt says, where the Colorado River went during the several million years it was in the vicinity and awaiting capture is still not clear. "The problem of the origin of the canyon," he points out, "remains with us."

That the river system during this action removed a tremendous weight of rock from the region is evident no matter how one approaches the canyon. Cedar Mountain and Red Butte, on the east and south ap-proaches respectively, as well as the Echo and Ver-milion Cliffs, stand as prominent remnants of some five thousand feet of Mesozoic beds that covered the canyon region and are now gone. "The Great Denu-dation," it was called. This stripping away, combined with cutting of the canyon and its gorges, suggests that it took vast periods of time—perhaps ten million years—to wear down the strata and sculpture the walls, grain by grain, rock by rock, century after century.

The cutting has revealed an extraordinary sequence of earth history and the gradual development of life forms and microenvironments. The canyon can be looked at today not as a barren, forbidding and un-changing enigma but a delicate and fragile wilderness that has slowly been fashioned into complex and pro-foundly interrelated ecosystems. Within this canyon are deserts, prairies, forests, streams, ponds, marshes, and mountains.

The South Rim Forest

Like all the land approaches to the canyon rims, the two leading to the south rim rise. The traveler enters a vegetational transition zone where elements of pinyon-juniper woodland mix with open forests of ponderosa pine. Patches of light green aromatic sagebrush (Arte-misia tridentata) spread out to grace whole valleys with such a density that passage is restricted. This shrub, valuable to mule deer as browse, occurs in nearly pure stands over much of the West, and is a sign of fertile, nonsaline soil. Climate at the south rim elevation of 7000 feet varies from winter days of snow and tempera-tures well below freezing, or even below zero, to sum-mer days in which the temperature has occasionally reached a hundred degrees. The presence of pinyon and juniper attests to the aridity of the climate—an average sixteen inches of precipitation annually—but summer cloudbursts may temporarily transform the surface of the land into a network of ponds and streams.

This climate is highly suitable to the growth of the familiar yellow pine (Pinus ponderosa), tallest and broadest of canyon trees, and largest of western pines except for the sugar pine. Though in youth the bark is black, as the tree matures and lower branches fall away, the bark turns a golden orange, unblemished for per-haps as far up as sixty feet. Ponderosa needles grow nearly a foot in length, most often in bundles of three, and sparkle in the clear sun of the plateau country.

Every part of the ponderosa pine has a significant func-tion in the forest system: the bark is home for insects sought by birds, its twigs and needles furnish food for squirrels, and its nuts nourish both birds and mammals.

Characteristic of this forest community is the Abert squirrel (Sciurus aberti), known for its tasseled ears. The range of the species is a continuous but irregular band that includes the mountains of northern Arizona, western and northern New Mexico and central Colo-rado, with isolated groups in Utah. Abert squirrels dine on yellow pine and pinyon seeds, acorns of Gam-bel's oak, and mushrooms. Their penchant for twigs of ponderosa pine account for "clippings" seen under especially desirable trees. Twig ends are bitten off and discarded, leaving the succulent inner cambium ready for chewing. The outer bark is also sometimes con-sumed and apparently provides bulk in the diet.

Holes in trees make excellent homesites, though the squirrels more often build their nests among the top-most branches of a pine. On sticks and twigs laid loosely the animal places a lining of grass and fibers. Juniper fibers are preferable but they peel in such long strips that an Abert with a mouthful may tip over back-wards and have a difficult time righting itself; but they manage to make their way through the forest and up the tree with fibers protruding like giant whiskers. The Abert squirrel is normally an agile climber, but cau-tion is thrown aside at mating time, when the male embarks upon skirmishes or pursuits that carry it up and down tree after tree and that sometimes ends, at least temporarily, in a flight through the air to land flat on its stomach fifty feet below.

The south rim forest possesses an abundance of animal life. The noisiest and most conspicuous inhabitant is the Steller jay *(Cyanocitta stelleri)*, a flashing blue species with a large black crest, discovered in Alaska by the pioneer naturalist of Bering's last expedition, Georg Wilhelm Steller. No other bird stirs up western forests quite as this one; the pioneer ornithologist Elliott Coues maintained that the bird scolded about trifles, quarreled about nothing, and constantly kept the neighborhood in ferment. It was a filibusterer, he added, and a coward at heart. "But withal, our jay has his good points, and I confess to a sneaking sort of regard for him." It occurs throughout western North America, but rarely in desert regions, relying on acorns and other vegetable matter for the bulk of its diet. At Grand Canyon, the Steller jay presides over a less conspicuous bird life, chiefly pygmy and white-breasted nuthatches, mountain chickadees, robins, chipping sparrows, and red-shafted flickers.

Best known and most often observed of the canyon fauna is the ubiquitous mule deer. A common sight for summer visitors is a doe and her twin fawns, the latter born as a rule in June. Because of its dominance and the ever-present possibility of irruptions in population, care has to be taken in the management of this species—as will be seen in our discussion of the north rim forest. Mule deer will eat almost any natural vegetation. Their preference is for fresh grass and other herbaceous plants, but they can be seen browsing on fernbush, sagebrush, buckbrush, cliffrose, mountain mahogany, oak, aspen, and manzanita, to name a few. Thus an overabundance of deer means a sustained attack on the vegetation to the point where natural recovery cannot offset the consumption. This incidentally demonstrates the importance of such natural predators as coyote and mountain lion to keep the deer in check and thus conserve the habitat.

Edge of the Canyon

Approaching the edge of the canyon, we notice a greater variety of plants, which seems surprising since the soils are very shallow and a great deal of bare limestone is exposed. The bedrock is cracked, however, and broken into an uneven surface that permits plant roots to penetrate deeply. The variety of plants is not haphazard, but rather a result of evolutionary development inseparably linked both to climate and animal life. Mountain mahogany and serviceberry, members of the rose family, provide a source of food for animals. The long-tubed flower of the gilia is fed upon by hummingbirds. Tall verbenas and thistles receive constant visits from butterflies. Bees make honey from the bee plant *(Cleome integrifolia)*.

Insects also cluster abundantly around the blooms of the century plant *(Agave utahensis)*, most bizarre of the rim flora, standing like a sentinel at the edge of the forest. One July we measured the rise of a burgeoning stalk by erecting a long stick beside it and recording the daily position of the growing tip. The growth was as much as ten inches a day.

Equally tall and conspicuous, and as attractive to flying insects, is the fragrant cliffrose *(Cowania mexicana)*, whose persistent petals remain well after the blooming season. Though flowers so profuse offer sore temptation to human visitors to break off a branch, the regulations at Grand Canyon reserve the flowers and foliage for wild animals.

The fernbush *(Spiraea millefolium)* is also abundant and is notable for its finely notched leaves and conspicuous flowers. This shrub is almost perpetually attended by nectar-loving insects, which in turn are the sustenance of flycatchers, swallows, and swifts. Indeed, the air over Grand Canyon is an integral part of the environment. On buoyant updrafts the raven soars and the turkey vulture circles in search of food. Two other birds are especially worthy of note for their role in insect predation. The violet-green swallow *(Tachycineta thalassina)*, a nearly iridescent flash of color as it flutters over and into the abyss, twitters almost perpetually, scooping up flying insects. White-throated swifts *(Aeronautes saxatalis)* are far more slender and obviously constructed for speed—a short body and long narrow wings that are flapped alternately in flight. Swifts are among the fastest animals on earth, which is easy to believe when you hear a rush of air and see the bird speeding effortlessly in a long curving arc into the void below. All day is spent on the wing, in the perpetual search for airborne ants, beetles and treehoppers—another link in the endless and fragile chain of predation.

Down the Trail

Starting into the canyon from the south rim, the visitor on foot enters a cool and shaded pocket of life, a sheltered slope or steep side canyon that faces away from the sun. In this microenvironment the vegetation contrasts sharply with the pinyon-juniper-ponderosa pine woodland back from the rims. In moist and virtually sunless locations grow plants such as Douglas fir and white fir that indicate a cooler and more northerly climate. The spring display of locoweed *(Astragalus lentiginosus)* is attractive along the trail just below the rim. Deer may often be seen near the trail, for they are known to range to the bottom and on occasion to the other side. This vertical environment is also a home for the cliff chipmunk *(Eutamias dorsalis)*.

There is not a dull moment on an inner canyon descent by foot. A leisurely hike of seven and a half miles to the bottom requires about five hours and is a continuous sequence of discoveries, large and small. For example, not far down the Kaibab Trail is a classic demonstration of the work of faulting. Two rock masses have slipped and ground against each other with sufficient force and heat to polish their respective surfaces, a friction phenomenon known colloquially as "slickensides."

Engulfed within the canyon, the hiker begins to appreciate its immensity. With himself as the unit of

Overleaf: A scraggly pinyon (left) and juniper stand temporary guard on the south rim of the Grand Canyon. (Esther Henderson: Rapho Guillumette)

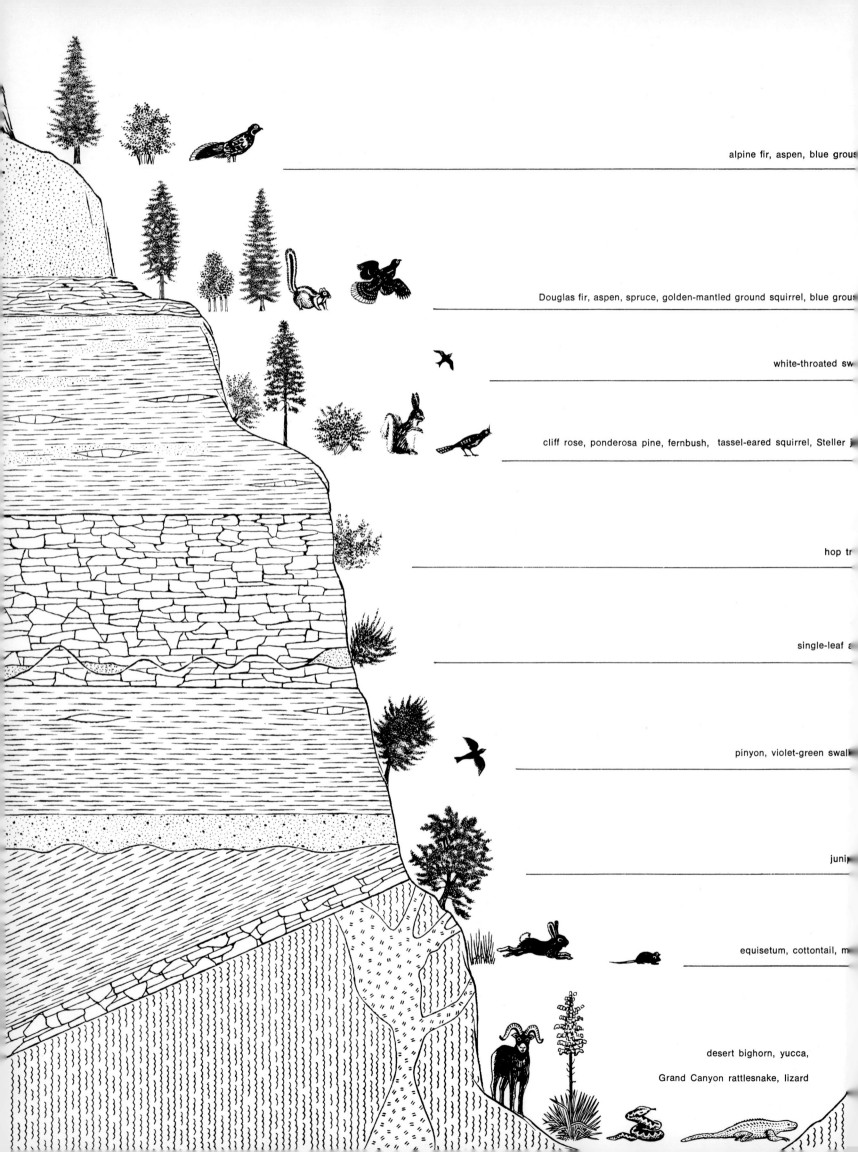

alpine fir, aspen, blue grous

Douglas fir, aspen, spruce, golden-mantled ground squirrel, blue grous

white-throated sw

cliff rose, ponderosa pine, fernbush, tassel-eared squirrel, Steller j

hop tr

single-leaf a

pinyon, violet-green swall

junip

equisetum, cottontail, m

desert bighorn, yucca,

Grand Canyon rattlesnake, lizard

measure, the whole environment takes on a new dimension. Buttes and ridges within the gorge are separated from their backgrounds and stand out in relief against the sky. Forms and shapes emerge. The canyon begins to show a profile.

The layered white Kaibab limestone overhangs the trail in a three-hundred-foot cliff, and there are few formations in the West with a more interesting or visible fossil assemblage. Both the Kaibab limestone and the lower half, the Toroweap formation, probably represent shallow deposits laid down during several advances and retreats of Permian seas. Of the eighty genera of invertebrates identified in them, the brachiopods, or "lamp shells," with their two unequal but bilaterally symmetrical valves, are the most commonly seen *(Productus, Derbya, Meekella)*. Some of these brachiopods have assumed the form of a geode, containing a hollow inner cavity lined with white or transparent crystals of quartz. In addition there are abundant nodules of chert, a variety of quartz that in some specimens takes on jasper-like characteristics.

The Coconino sandstone, an outstanding light yellow cliff of three hundred feet, is visible in all directions and on all walls beneath the Toroweap. Once a barren Permian desert of shifting dunes, on which little more than reptiles walked, this formation varies from zero to one thousand feet in thickness and 32,000 square miles in area. It is classic for its cross-bedded structure; the successive surfaces of ancient dunes have hardened into interlocked planes. Several outcrops, such as that near Drake, Arizona, seventy miles to the south, possess rock whose bedding planes may be split into slabs and commercially extracted as "flagstone." Exceptional slabs contain the tracks of Permian reptiles, of which more than two dozen types have been recognized, as well as impressions of raindrops and ripple marks.

A sharp change occurs at the base of the Coconino, where cream-colored cliffs of former desert sands rest directly upon red siltstones of the Hermit shale. This dark red coloration suggests that it was deposited in a terrestrial environment conducive to oxidation, such as an ancient delta or floodplain. Borings of worms, impressions of fern leaves, and the footprints of amphibians seem to bear this out. The fossil flora of the Hermit shale is particularly notable, consisting of at least thirty-five species, mainly ferns and cone-bearing plants.

Below this point, the beds of the canyon walls change somewhat in structure and composition. They are still largely red and primarily deposits from ancient delta or near-shore environments; but alternating soft and resistant beds weather into a distinctive slope-and-terrace topography. Some eight hundred feet thick, this is called the Supai formation and along with the Hermit shale is responsible for the predominant reds in canyon coloration. Waters wash these reds down over the prominent gray limestone cliff immediately below, staining it red; hence the name Redwall limestone.

Plant and animal associations in the Grand Canyon reflect the changing climates of different elevations and exposures.

We are now half way down the trail, and in this surface of cliff and bench, niche and alcove we may observe characteristic microenvironments. Inclined slopes facing south toward the sun may receive more than twice the solar radiation received on level terraces. Gone are the ponderosa pines of the rim and the Douglas firs of the alcoves above. On these inner-canyon red beds the smaller and shrubbier species predominate—pinyon, juniper, yucca, agave, and cliff fendlerbush *(Fendlera rupicola)*. In sunny places are the paperflower *(Psilostrophe sparsiflora)*, prince's plume *(Stanleya pinnata)*, an indicator of selenium-bearing soil, and snakeweed *(Gutierrezia euthamiae)*, all a contrasting yellow against the red rock of the canyon walls.

In more sheltered locations grow the windflower *(Anemone tuberosa)*, sego lily *(Calochortus nuttallii)*, and the single leaf ash *(Fraxinus anomala)*. Catching a faint aromatic scent in a protected alcove, the hiker comes upon the hoptree *(Ptelea pallida)*, whose lanceolate leaves produce a strong, familiar pungence.

Reptiles and amphibians are not too commonly seen in the canyon, though some are abundant. Various kinds of lizards—scaly, swift, horned, whiptail, and others—appear, searching for ants, flies, or perhaps soft-bodied larvae. Other reptiles are nocturnal or they seek the undersides of rocks or cliffs when daytime temperatures rise.

In this canyon, largely on the Supai, may be seen an interesting example of evolutionary adaptation to color, the Grand Canyon rattlesnake *(Crotalus viridis abyssus)*. It is exclusively a Grand Canyon form, but it is fairly widely distributed within the canyon, feeding chiefly on lizards and small mammals. Over the centuries it has inhabited these red rock talus slopes and developed a coloration that ranges from vermilion to salmon to orange. According to Laurence Klauber, a consulting curator of reptiles at the San Diego Zoo and author of a two-volume work on rattlesnakes, these reptiles are far less quarrelsome than the western diamondback *(Crotalus atrox)*, which he describes as dangerous, resolute in defense, and possessed of a hair-trigger readiness to strike. Russell K. Grater, a distinguished western naturalist, tells of leaning over to drink from a stream and realizing that one of the Grand Canyon rattlers was coiled under his chest, less than a foot from his chin. As Grater moved very carefully away, the only movement of the snake was the flicking of its tongue. It gave no warning sound and made no attempt to strike. "After my nerves had settled a bit," Grater adds, "I teased this rattler to see what he would do. His only reaction was to try to get under the rock by which he was coiled."

Red Cliffs and Blue Water

The Supai formation outcrops spectacularly in Oak Creek and Sycamore canyons, south of Flagstaff, and in other localities in the Grand Canyon region. But few places in the West have the beauty and charm of Havasu Canyon, some forty miles west of the Kaibab Trail. Here the Supai has been eroded into sheer walls and red monoliths along Havasu Creek, one of the few major tributaries on the south side of Grand Canyon.

Home of the Havasupai Indians, this side gorge is enhanced by a rich vegetation and scenic cataracts of which the highest are 110, 180, and 210 feet. The main part of the canyon is reached by two trails, the shortest about seven miles long. One of the most breathtaking experiences in the West is to round a bend in these narrow defiles and come suddenly upon a full-flowering western redbud *(Cercis occidentalis)*. Its large magenta flowers literally cover the tree, and when backlighted provide a brilliant view for the photographer. Penstemons and buckwheats of several species are abundant in the drier portions of this botanical paradise, and among them may be seen the colorful carnivorous collared lizard *(Crotaphytus collaris baileyi)* pausing on a rock in its search for smaller lizards, spiders, and insects.

Along the crystal clear stream are natural travertine dams, and behind them quiet pools that become a rich blue-green with depth. At the bases of the waterfalls grow patches of stream orchid and a delicious wild celery. In these places, as around the springs adjacent to the creek, is another of the Grand Canyon's worlds within a world, a microenvironment of streamside plants and animals, made luxurious with maidenhair fern and masses of watercress brightened by the crimson monkey flower *(Mimulus cardinalis)*.

The Red Wall

Beneath the Supai formation, the largest, sheerest cliff in the canyon falls away—the Redwall limestone. It is also the purest formation, containing less than one percent of sand and mud. Yet the Redwall is a complex formation because of its discontinuous lenses of chert and the millions, or probably billions, of fossils it contains. Directly at waist and shoulder level along the Kaibab Trail, down a series of switchbacks, the Redwall exhibits some of its striking properties. Among these are the crystalline structure of the limestone and the beds of fossil crinoids and other animals deposited in clear and quiet Mississippian seas, three hundred million years ago. These fossils are particularly well viewed with a simple hand lens or other small magnifying eyepiece that brings into view their detailed structure.

Below the Redwall lies the Temple Butte formation of the Devonian age. Though lacking the height and grandeur of the Redwall, it carries the geologic story back through the times when early armor-plated fish, ancestors of the common fishes of today, evolved in the seas. The bony plates of these fish, together with corals,

Far left above: Alongside trails to the inner gorges, hikers may observe a high percentage of the hundreds of species of plants within the Canyon. Shown here is prince's or desert plume, a wild mustard. Left above: The fragrant and persistent flowers of cliff rose help support a community of nectar- and pollen-loving insects. (Both by Bill Ratcliffe) Far left: The Abert squirrel finds in ponderosa pine forests its sources of food and sites for nesting. (Floyd R. Getsinger) Left: Few canyons have no collared lizards. Colors of this reptile vary among green, yellow, olive and brown, depending on locality and color phases. (James R. Simon)

snails, and brachiopods, have been found in this formation, an impressive physical link to the life of some 400 million years ago.

One of the rarest spectacles in the canyon country is associated with the Redwall across the canyon. One winter day, when the temperature on the rim was zero and fresh snow lay three feet deep, we hiked down the trail to the bottom, where there was no snow at all, and east to Clear Creek, nineteen miles from the rim. Not many hikers make this trip, especially in winter, though the scenery makes every step worthwhile. What we saw, however, was Cheyava Falls, a usually inconspicuous cascade issuing from the top of the Redwall and descending more than a thousand feet—now completely frozen. The temperature had been ideal for the formation of tons of icicles, which clung in gleaming white banks to the red face of the limestone. With warming weather the ice soon melted and fell, but the frozen wall of Cheyava is a sight never to be forgotten.

Above the Redwall and below the Muav formation are broad natural platforms. While they appear from the rims to be devoid of life, the hiker going out on them finds himself in a desert garden. The dominant plant of these well-warmed inner-canyon plateaus is a rose, the blackbrush *(Coleogyne ramosissima)*. Its yellow flowers are borne on rigid sharp-tipped branches up to six feet high, and the small but abundant deciduous leaves provide forage for bighorn and other animals. Like the creosote bush of the desert, blackbrush is a highly successful shrub that grows over vast high prairies almost to the exclusion of other shrubs. Along the Kaibab Trail are exceptionally fine specimens mixed with Mormon tea *(Ephedra)* and numerous stems of the century plant. Farther on, saltbush is prominent along the trail, and patches of diminutive rockmat *(Petrophytum caespitosum)* are found directly on limestone surfaces.

The Inner Gorge

It is not until we approach and cross the gently sloping Tonto Platform that we begin to grasp the antiquity of the canyon, for here are Cambrian layers—Muav formation, green micaceous Bright Angel shale, and brown Tapeats sandstone—that were deposited when life was at an exceedingly primitive stage. All three formations possess the remains of trilobites, extinct crustaceans with bodies longitudinally trilobed.

The Tapeats, lowest of these strata, extends to the brink of the Inner Gorge, a canyon within a canyon, which is fifteen hundred feet deep and would be spectacular in its own right were it not overwhelmed by the rest of the canyon. The geologic structure through which the trail passes becomes more complex. No longer do the rocks lie horizontally like the layers of a cake; the dark and twisted Vishnu schist of the Inner Gorge forms massive walls, patternless, and shot through with light-colored granite and pegmatite. Set within this chaotic arrangement is a more or less isolated fragment of layered formations that once aggregated 12,000 feet in thickness—the so-called Grand Canyon series. They are Precambrian in age and not much of them remains after ancient erosion; they are no longer horizontal, and their tilted position clearly marks them from level layers above and non-layered levels below. They are also conspicuous from a fossil standpoint, for the life they contain is the simplest known, with none of the advanced species found in upper rock layers, and contrasting with the absence of fossils in the underlying rocks.

The Grand Canyon series can be best observed along the Kaibab Trail, where Shinumo quartzite, a hard, banded purple-and-white rock, forms an enormous cliff overhead. The Hakatai shale surrounds the hiker with some of the brightest orange-red rocks within the canyon. The Bass limestone exhibits algae-like structures that may represent the oldest life on earth.

At the bottom of the canyon, we are about as far back in time as we can get on earth, for radiometric measurements suggest an age of as much as two billion years for the Vishnu schist. After so much time, and so much evident folding, crushing, contorting, and chemical change it is difficult to determine what the rock originally was, but bits of evidence indicate that parts of it were sedimentary and parts volcanic.

To some the Inner Gorge may seem lacking in color and beauty, but the perceptive visitor finds it a treasure both geologically and biologically. In places the river has crystals of quartz and feldspar polished almost to a mirror finish, and the veins or bedding planes would be admired in any museum of modern art. Mica flakes in the schist shine like diamonds.

The temperature at this low point (2400 feet) and in this confined environment may approach 130 degrees, but there is life on the steeply pitching slopes. Cactus, brittlebush, and Mormon tea are three principal species; snakeweed also thrives, as do grasses, composites, yucca, and catclaw. Life along the river and the lower portions of the tributaries that drain into it is precarious at best. Floods like that of December, 1966, in Bright Angel Canyon, remove large deposits of soil and rock, taking out even the tallest and most deeply rooted trees; giant cottonwoods, for example, are deposited on sandbanks miles downstream, their mangled trunks lacerated by passing boulders. The Colorado River today, though altered by dams upstream, still gets muddy, still receives silt and boulders, still flows occasionally at twenty to thirty miles per hour, and crashes against the pegmatite cliffs. One can hear the grating, grinding roar of the rocks beneath, and realize the enormous erosional force that has helped to scour the channel and deepen the gorge.

Yet within this sometimes hot, sometimes violent domain are secret places where pools of emerald waters gather, where ribbon falls pour down over moss-covered embankments into cave lakes lined with ferns, and where the leaves in groves of cottonwood rustle at the demand of the wind. At dawn, or at evening, it is a cool, almost unreal world, where broad white blossoms of the sacred datura, or Jimson weed (*Datura meteloides*), unfold, later to be transformed into giant seed pods covered with spines.

Plants of the open slopes are adapted to heat and aridity, but those around springs are sheltered from the sun and supplied with water. In the margin of moist sand grow willows (*Salix*), seepwillows, and the ever-present *Tamarix gallica*. Within the pools and behind the spray we find mosses, liverworts, and algae, and in a few places the habitat is so cool that nettles common to much higher elevations manage to thrive. Amid boulder-strewn patches the delicate orange flower of the globemallow (*Sphaeralcea*) or the evening primrose seem almost out of place; a number of species *are* anomalous, such as ash, maple, and columbine, possibly relics of prairie and other mesophytic flora, that is, plants growing where rainfall is moderate rather than arid. Steep slopes of fallen rock, unstable and fit only for pioneer plants, support various cactuses and grasses, four-o'clocks, buckwheats, bur-sages, thickets of mesquite and catclaw, and occasional century plants.

Such distribution is the result of seeds borne by landslides, flood, wind, gravity, and animals. Mule deer come down the side canyons, browsing on what they can and depositing dung containing unharmed seeds. Bands of bighorn wander along the ledges above the river and feral burros roam the platforms, competing with deer and bighorn for the limited supply of vegetation. Beavers work the willow and cottonwood groves. Pocket mice range from canyon floor to rim, carrying and storing seeds, and the exchange is furthered by wood and kangaroo rats, antelope and rock squirrels, and numerous birds. With all this inner-canyon traffic, it is small wonder that plant life flourishes and animal life with it. Life within Grand Canyon is complex, interdependent and fragile, easily subject to change if even a part is disturbed, as witness the introduction of burros. Large numbers of human beings brought in by the increasingly popular boat trips may also bring about changes in inner-canyon ecosystems. How rapid the changes will be, and how profound the consequences, are questions which may well arouse anxiety.

North Rim

On the other hand, one of the most celebrated answers to how much man can disturb the whole environment by altering part of it was discovered on the north rim of the canyon fifty years ago. More than a thousand feet higher than the south rim, the north rim has a Canadian climate, with fifteen feet of snow each year and temperatures as low as forty-two degrees below zero. Abundance of moisture, together with delightful summers, produces an exceptionally rich montane forest of Engelmann spruce, white and alpine fir, ponderosa pine, aspen, and a ground cover ranging from bracken fern to the rare calypso orchid. Such a richness in vegetation naturally supports a healthy population of animals, including deer and mountain lion.

Or did. Man's first of a series of mistakes in tampering with this balanced ecosystem was to pasture too many thousands of cattle, sheep, and horses on the plateau, which by 1906 was denuded of protective grasses and laid open to erosion. His second mistake was to destroy as many predators as he could—moun-

So heavily does snow accumulate on the Kaibab Plateau that trunks of less sturdy trees like aspen may be deformed into "crooked forests." (Union Pacific Railroad)

In House Rock Valley, Arizona, bison refuges protect the descendants of great herds that once roamed freely through the West. (Leland J. Prater)

tain lions, coyotes, wolves—in the vain hope that this would improve the deer herd. It certainly increased the numbers, for without any natural culling the herd doubled and redoubled. With forage gone, livestock began to feed on woody plants, directly in competition with deer.

The shock of such a double attack was more than the forest could bear. Range conditions deteriorated and deer began starving by the thousands. Established plants were stripped of their leaves so fast that they began to die off, and a seedling with succulent leaves had hardly a chance at all. Efforts to round up the deer and drive them off the plateau in order to disperse them failed. At first, hunting efforts failed. Finally, through federal-state cooperative programs of more enlightened wildlife management, hunters harvested the surplus deer, and officials tightened grazing regulations. As the habitat began to improve, deer came back toward a balance with available forage. Regulated hunting came to be accepted as a management tool more "humane" than nature's throes of starvation.

In some of the larger reserves, such as Grand Canyon National Park, established in 1919, deer are not hunted and all predators are protected. The Kaibab experience has been a profound lesson to the whole world, and because of it men have saved other environments from similar destruction.

The White-Tailed Squirrel

Worldwide attention has also been focused on the shy, tufted-eared, white-tailed Kaibab squirrel *(Sciurus kaibabensis),* the range of which is limited to this plateau, and specifically to about 220,000 acres of pure ponderosa pine. The Grand Canyon is one of the West's prime examples of an area demonstrating speciation resulting from isolation. The canyon, widening and deepening over the millenniums, has served to split original populations of several animal species into isolated groups, one on the north rim and one on the south. Each group has gone its separate evolutionary way, until today the results of speciation are pairs of distinctive populations. Among the pairs that have been identified are the Utah cliff chipmunk on the north rim and the Gila cliff chipmunk on the south; the yellow-haired porcupine on the north and the Arizona porcupine on the south; the Rocky Mountain meadow mouse and the Mogollon meadow mouse; the Utah gopher snake and the Arizona gopher snake; and the Kaibab and Abert squirrels.

The depth of the canyon and the distance across it are not the only barriers separating these races. Vegetation zones within the canyon are alien to many rim species, and the absence of familiar food can discourage individuals from venturing beyond their customary habitat. Thus the Kaibab squirrel is so closely adapted to the ponderosa pine community because of its specialized feeding habits that it will go nowhere else. It lives on terminal twigs of the ponderosa and eats the red phloem, or "inner bark," much as we would eat corn on the cob. When the cone crop is good, pine seeds are also an important part of the diet of the squirrel and it is even addicted to mushrooms *(Gautieria)* that grow only in the immediate vicinity of ponderosa pine roots. Thus tied to its specific environment—as is the Abert squirrel on the south rim—the Kaibab form has been unable to mingle with its closest relatives for at least several thousand years. Consequently the Abert, developing independently, has come to possess light undersides and a gray tail, whereas the Kaibab has gray undersides and a light tail.

Joseph G. Hall, of San Francisco State College, who has studied the Kaibab squirrel, believes that there are even sub-populations isolated from the main rim group, especially on the Powell Plateau. To reach the latter, an elongated tableland detached from the rim and standing alone out in the canyon, animal traffic must descend nearly a thousand feet from the rim and then ascend a like elevation. That is a sufficient physical and vegetational barrier to prevent contact between plateau squirrels and rim squirrels. Hall sees a distinct possibility that the white-tails of the Powell Plateau may eventually become recognizably different from the rest, a reenactment on a smaller scale of what seems to have occurred on the Kaibab Plateau as a whole.

Hall's studies have advanced man's knowledge of white-tail behavior, but there is still a great deal to be learned about variations in population density of the squirrels and it may be that the decline in the health of ponderosa pines is directly related to the decline in white-tail population. The evidence points to a greater abundance formerly than the estimated three thousand Kaibab squirrels living there today. Certainly highway mortality is substantial, and there are also natural controls, chiefly goshawks. But the welfare of the squirrels, says Hall, is tied to the welfare of the forests as surely as the Australian koala is tied to its eucalyptus trees. Like other species strictly adapted to life in a climax community, the Kaibab squirrel has lean days whenever stability of the ponderosa pine community is upset or forest vigor diminished. Too many lean days, too many epidemics of bark beetles or wood borers, or a disease that would wipe out the pines, might well eliminate the handsome white-tail—another proof of the delicate balance of the Grand Canyon wilderness. With radio-telemetry and other wildlife management techniques, man hopefully will soon gain sufficient understanding of animal behavior and habitat improvement to forestall extinction of species such as the Kaibab squirrel.

The Enchanted Vista

Standing at Cape Royal or Point Sublime or the Vista Encantada, one sees in this grand panorama a nearly complete geologic history of the earth, back almost to the beginning of time. If somewhat overwhelming, the canyon is not incomprehensible, and in it a hundred small worlds stand as a challenge to ecological research during the decades ahead.

Inevitably there are schemes to penetrate the canyon's hidden corners by means other than foot, to introduce into its abyssal depths and fragile environments such mechanisms as helicopters, tramways, roads, and elevators. But man has promised himself and his heirs to keep the canyon unsullied, and the prevailing attitude today seems to be as Theodore Roosevelt phrased it in 1903: "Leave it as it is. You can not improve on it. The ages have been at work on it, and man can only mar it. What you can do is to keep it for your children, your children's children, and for all who come after you...."

4. Enchanted Circle: The Four Corners Country

Our mother is Earth, our father Sky Man.

Navajo Indian legend

East of the Grand Canyon two major tributaries to the Colorado River drain an open, colorful region variously known as Indian Country because it is the home of the Hopis, Utes, and Navajos, and Four Corners Country because one point of it is common to four states (Arizona, New Mexico, Colorado, Utah). Northernmost of these tributaries is the San Juan, which flows from upland meadows of the San Juan Mountains down through meandering canyons to its junction with the Colorado River not far from Rainbow, Owl, and Hawkeye Natural Bridges.

The southern tributary of this region is the Little Colorado, a wild and intermittent stream that responds to the vagaries of weather. High cliffs, in certain places, shut out the sun and imprison the river. In other places, across wide flats, it flows like mud or sinks beneath the sand. Only once is the channel blocked, and that by a natural lava flow which forces the river to detour around the lip of the lava and return to its channel over a 185-foot cliff. When snowmelt raises the volume of water, the Little Colorado thunders into this chasm in a muddy but ephemeral spectacle named Grand Falls.

Meteor Crater

Upstream along the Little Colorado the landscape seems to have been fashioned with gentle grace. But thousands of years ago a mass of rock and iron weighing 12,000 tons or more penetrated the atmosphere and plunged into the earth at an estimated 21,000 miles per hour. So great was the impact and so enormous the pressure generated by the subsequent explosion, that quartz grains of the Coconino sandstone were fused into natural silica glass. Two rare silica minerals—coesite and stishovite—their production requiring the kind of pressure found tens of miles beneath the surface, or in an explosion, were formed. Coesite is especially convincing evidence of shock conditions because it represents a transformation of quartz that is possible only under high pressure. How long ago the impact occurred is still conjectural; perhaps it was 5000 years ago, perhaps 50,000. The resultant depression, known today as Meteor Crater, measures six hundred feet in depth and four thousand feet in diameter.

Painted Desert and Petrified Forest

Quiet characterizes the Four Corners Country. Quiet and color. We climb vermilion plateaus that stretch away into the solitude, or hike into polychrome canyons inhabited only by creatures of the wild. And along the upper reaches of the Little Colorado and its tributaries, in the heart of the Painted Desert, lie badlands with a rich diversity of color. This spectrum-tinted region, a part of the Triassic Chinle formation, extends as far west as the Grand Canyon, nearly two hundred miles away. The banding and layering result from stratification of water-deposited volcanic ash, shale, sandstone and gravel. Oxides of manganese

Water is life in the arid wonderland of Monument Valley. The great monoliths represent eroded remnants of once continuous rock layers. (Bob Clemenz)

Spires and ridges of the Four Corners Country surrender slowly to the erosive power of summer storms and floods. (Rondal Partridge)

and iron, in various quantities and combinations, account for the yellows, oranges, reds, pinks, and blues of the desert. A great deal of the ash has been converted to bentonitic clay, which crumbles into a loose, friable material that weathers into rounded and rolling terrain.

On and within these hills lie jumbled, silicified logs, of which the heaviest remaining concentrations have been preserved in Petrified Forest National Park. The park encloses six separate "forests" containing fragments and even whole logs of ancient pines, chiefly

Araucarioxylon. While the logs lay buried, cellular cavities and interstitial spaces were filled with silica precipitated from percolating ground water. By this means, the wood was transformed into various forms of quartz, such as amethyst, opal, agate, jasper, and chalcedony. The logs and associated fossils are evidence of Triassic swamps where horsetails, ferns, clubmosses and the great pines grew, where amphibians and lungfishes thrashed among the plants and in the waters, and where carnivorous crocodile-like reptiles, known as phytosaurs, hunted their prey and perhaps engaged in savage duels.

Natural World of the Navajo

In addition to badlands, the Four Corners Country contains broad valleys and mesas, sprinkled with lone sedimentary buttes and the remains of volcanic necks, cones, and lava flows. No single type of vegetation is typical of it; variety is the rule. Much of it is desert, but the cactus is not as common as on the Sonoran desert. Grass is abundant, mingled on the broad plateaus with saltbush, Mormon tea, and sagebrush. Willows and cottonwoods, as might be expected, proliferate in the sandy bottoms of canyons. Patches of pinyon-juniper woodland clothe the red rock slopes and undulating uplifts, while in higher mountains the ponderosa pine community prevails. For the most part the Four Corners Country is arid to semiarid, making it necessary for many water-loving plants and animals to rely on springs or seeps as a source of moisture. Summer cloudbursts can produce substantial floods; winter snows are occasionally deep and the

climate at times is severely cold and quite windy.

The Navajo Indians are never very far from this natural world, physically or spiritually. The essence of their traditions, even their language, is natural beauty. In contrast to other societies, they have no great desire to conquer nature even if they could. They have traditionally felt that nature will take care of them if they adapt themselves to it, become a part of it, and follow its laws.

Certain mountains are sacred to the Navajos. Legends tell how a blanket was laid on the ground and the stars placed upon it, named, and told in what season to come and in what month. Navajos tell about making the moon and dressing it in white shell, pollen, and rainbows. The first fire, they say, was made of four woods brought from the four directions—

pinyon, juniper, spruce, and fir. Characters of Navajo legends include Coyote, the hunter's helper, White Squirrel People, Gopher People, Spider Woman, Bat Woman, Thunder Men, Bad Wind, and Monster Eagle.

Today the Navajos are taking special pains to promote in another way the natural values of their reservation, which at sixteen million acres is the largest in the United States. They know that tourism is a way of using this land and these natural treasures without using them up and almost without disturbance. The treasures include spectacular mesas and canyons, dinosaur tracks, lava beds, ice caves, springs, and lakes. Navajo Mountain, one of the sacred peaks, rises to 10,388 feet, almost certainly domed by the intrusion of igneous, i.e., molten rocks that have not broken through the crust in large masses. On the flanks of this mountain, dwarfed in its surroundings, is Rainbow Bridge, largest natural bridge in the world; its 278-foot span, curving to a height of 309 feet, would easily straddle the Capitol in Washington. Such height and span indicate tremendous weight, which could not be supported were it not for the strength of the massive Navajo sandstone.

Besides scenic qualities, nature favors the Navajo portion of the Four Corners Country in different ways. An extensive forest of ponderosa pine supplies raw materials for tribal forest products industries. Coal, the most developed resource on the Colorado Plateau, occurs plentifully on the reservation, especially near Gallup, New Mexico. Helium was formerly taken from wells near Shiprock and oil and gas come from both sides of the San Juan River. The Navajos point out that the first major uranium discovery in the United States was made on their reservation, in a place that happens also to be their greatest natural attraction. This land of natural marvels is a cluster of red mesas, alcoves, buttes, pinnacles, arches, dunes, and rocky washes known collectively as Monument Valley. So highly do the Navajos prize Monument Valley as a scenic and scientific attraction that it was established in 1960 as the first unit of their tribal park system. In jeeps or broad-tired vehicles travelers may visit such features as the Mittens, Mystery Valley, and the Totem Pole.

Monument Valley

The Monument upwarp, an asymmetric structure one hundred miles long and fifty wide, dips steeply on its eastern flank. It resembles the Kaibab uplift in this respect, and also in the exposure of Permian strata by streams that have cut across it. The San Juan River has deeply entrenched itself in a set of meanders, or sharp ox-bow bends, called the Great Goosenecks of the San Juan. Erosion has exposed upturned strata in hogback ridges, most prominent of which, Comb Ridge, rises as much as a thousand feet in height, and sweeps in a broad, hundred-mile arc from Blanding, Utah, to Kayenta, Arizona.

The cliffs and monoliths of Monument Valley are remnants of thick sandstones and shales progressively eroded by wind and water. Most rise from a floor of Cedar Mesa sandstone, Permian in age and exposed

in steep-walled tributaries of the San Juan River to the north. The lower portion of the great buttes is a series of red beds that form a gentle slope. The cliff-forming stratum that gives to Monument Valley its special grandness and dimensions is the massive, cross-bedded De Chelly sandstone. Ordinarily a tan or pinkish brown color, as at Canyon de Chelly, its type locality, in Monument Valley it is overlain by the deep red Moenkopi formation, source of dark crimson stains. Curiously, the De Chelly sandstone rarely erodes into isolated spires but takes the shape of rounded domes and crests. What gives it grandeur in Monument Valley is the protective cap of younger beds; under these it forms sheer walls that are usually marked by numerous vertical joints.

Atop the dark brown formation rests the resistant cap itself—Shinarump conglomerate of Triassic age. Nowhere is it very thick, not much over two hundred feet, but it covers thousands of square miles in Arizona and Utah. That the Shinarump was deposited in the beds of shifting streams is suggested by the materials of which it is composed: poorly sorted sandstones; boulders and pebbles of quartz, quartzite, and vari-colored chert; and silicified logs twenty or thirty feet long and two to three feet in diameter. In certain places these Shinarump gravels are extremely colorful, the pebbles and other fragments lying strewn like gems on the plateau.

Thus we can deduce one outstanding fact from Monument Valley and the Four Corners Country: resistance of rock to erosion determines the shape of the land. Whereas faults were so significant in the structure of the Grand Canyon, they are far less important here. The Navajo country is a region of tablelands less dissected than other parts of the Colorado Plateau, a landscape of brilliant sedimentary beds in different stages of disintegration. Added to the scene are some 250 volcanic necks and buttes, such as Shiprock, seventy miles east of Monument Valley, and Agathla Peak, fifteen miles south of it.

Hopi Indians and Their Land

In the heart of Navajo Indian country is the reservation of the Hopi Indians, people of a racial stock, Shoshonean, that antedates all other inhabitants of the region. Their village of Oraibi is believed to be the oldest continuously inhabited community in the United States. The secret of their survival in this sparsely vegetated land has been an extremely careful use of its natural resources. Without water for agriculture, which supplemented the supply of natural food, the early Hopis could not have lasted long, so they located their villages on Black Mesa. This broad sandstone block gathers rain water like a reservoir and releases it in springs from which the Hopis secure their domestic and agricultural water supply.

Of wild plants they made considerable use, and in some ways still do, despite, or perhaps in preference to,

One night's winds will alter the shapes of the dunes; the next day's rains may carry the sands a little closer to the distant sea. (Don Worth)

The restless dunes of Monument Valley are partially anchored by scattered patches of rabbitbrush. (Philip Hyde)

modern packaged foods. Even though the match long ago replaced the fire spindle, the natural flora still affords certain aids toward better living. In the past, wild grass seeds of the genus *Sporobolus*, plus seed pods of the bee plant and yucca, and nuts of pinyon pine were staples. Roots of the wild potato *(Solanum jamesii)* were cooked with a saline clay. Mustards served for greens as well as seasoning. Bundles of wild onion *(Allium)*, mint *(Mentha canadensis)*, and cactus fruits were stored away for seasoning. A "lemonade" was made from sumac *(Rhus trilobata)*, a "coffee" from berries of mistletoe *(Phoradendron juniperinum)*, and a tea from dried and boiled leaves of *Thelesperma megapotamicum*.

This is but a sampling of useful wild foods. In addition, both Hopi and Navajo gathered the plants around them for the manufacture of utilitarian goods. The juniper, its hard red wood aromatic and insect resistant, had scores of uses, including firewood, tea, medicine, ceremonies and the construction of dwell-

ings, corrals, and fences. Oak branches were bent into boomerangs, yucca fibers woven into twine, gourds filled with gravel and seeds for musical accompaniment, cottonwood root carved into figures of spiritual significance, cotton *(Gossypium hopi)* woven with mountain mahogany battens, and rug dyes extracted from several plants. Medicines were legion, and the Hopis had a wild plant cure for nearly every ailment: leaves of groundsel for pimples, bladderpod *(Lesquerella)* for snake bite, thistle for itch, mullein for fits, sagebrush for indigestion, mallow for diarrhea, fermented cooked beans for constipation, dock for colds, and Jimson weed "to cure a person of his meanness." Other plants served the Indians for construction, ceremonial, and magical purposes.

Indeed, so highly regarded were plants and animals that the Hopis named clans and phratries (groups of clans) after them. Alfred F. Whiting, in his classic *Ethnobotany of the Hopi*, points out that while other people sometimes distinguish individuals by some activity of their ancestors, such as Smith, Cook, or

Ancient dunes, now solidified and preserved as sandstone, are weathering out of cliffs at the bottom of Canyon de Chelly, Arizona. (Hans W. Silvester: Bavaria Verlag)

Baker, Hopi society submerges the individual in the group and uses as a group symbol some object related to it. Thus we have the Eagle-Sun Phratry containing reed and greasewood clans; the Fire-Coyote Phratry containing mescal, juniper and pinyon clans; the Tansy Mustard Phratry, Snake-Lizard Phratry, and so on. The Hopis, like the Papagos to the south and the Navajos around them, became an integral element of the natural environment in which they lived.

The Indians of the Four Corners Country are still mindful of the consequences of lost plant and animal life, and to an increasing degree are conserving their natural resources. The Navajos, for example, protect deer, pronghorn, and turkey in natural habitats, and have stocked beaver along high mountain streams in order to improve sport fishing. But underneath this ethic toward the land lies a longtime fundamental reverence of wilderness values and wilderness life, stressed in their religion and sung in their chants.

Coyote

Sung in the chants of many a tribe as hunter, brother, friend, and nemesis, the coyote *(Canis latrans)* has had more friends among early American Indians than among latter-day immigrants. To the Indians, coyotes were cultural heroes. To pioneer settlers and stockmen, they were enemies. To both groups they were tricksters—agile, clever, fast-moving, and, most humiliating of all, able to outrun dogs; as Mark Twain wrote in *Roughing It,* the coyote would lead a dog on a wild chase and then depart with a "rushing sound, and the sudden splitting of a long crack through the atmosphere, and behold that dog is solitary and alone in the midst of a vast solitude!"

Coyotes are indeed good runners and hunters, which they have to be in their business of trying to find sustenance, the most delectable of which inhabits burrows. Rabbits and rodents are their most common fare, but coyotes are well known for their broad appetites. They will eat almost anything from carrion to fish and fruit.

Few other animals have a range as extensive in North America, and few others have prospered so well in the face of human settlement. Perhaps this is because of the increased availability of lambs and chickens, the taking of which has given the whole race a bad reputation in agricultural circles. Coyotes have for years been poisoned, trapped, and shot, but the awareness is slowly spreading that despite minor depredations on commercial stock, the coyote's control of rodent population and thereby protection of forage resources makes it more valuable alive. In the natural world it is, to quote Victor Cahalane, "the garbage man, the health officer, the sanitary engineer and the exterminator.... Throughout the ages it has helped to weed out the unfit and keep survivors alert. Largely due to it and other predators, the deer, the antelope and other hoofed mammals have evolved

The Painted Desert of Arizona is colored by differing amounts of iron oxide in the bentonitic clay. (Bob Clemenz)

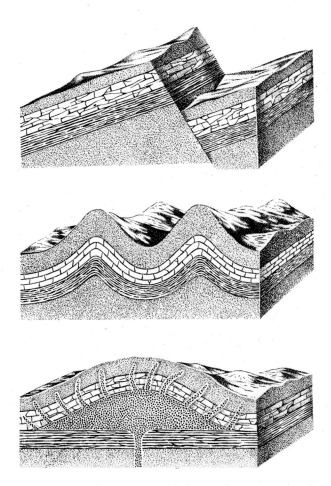

Some types of movement of the earth's crust: (top) Block faulting: breakage and uplift of crustal masses. (center) Folding: compression of horizontal strata into upfolds and downfolds. (bottom) Doming: intrusion and expansion of igneous rock beneath surface rock layers.

into swift, graceful, efficient animals. Were it not for the coyote, they would ... overpopulate their ranges."

Today the Navajo country or almost any western natural community is incomplete without a coyote loping across the prairie or barking in the mountains on a moonlit night, and obviously without this "common denominator" the ecosystem is out of balance.

San Juan and Mesa Verde

Like the Colorado and other western rivers, the San Juan's course bears little relation to underlying rocks; it crosses hard and soft alike, and is not deflected by belts of resistant strata. Meanders that must have developed on the freedom of wider plains were long ago entrenched and the river trapped. As the land was lifted, the river in its fixed position cut meandering canyons deeper. This ability of the rivers and their abrasive contents to cut through even the hardest formations was demonstrated by the violence of a San Juan River flood in 1911. The maximum depth of raging waters in narrower parts of the canyon was estimated at fifty feet. Such massive scouring is capable of removing accumulated alluvial debris down to the level of bedrock—and even deeper.

Above the San Juan Basin, beyond Shiprock and up into the southern Ute country of Colorado, rises a tilted plateau of buff-colored sandstone and shale that has been broken and fractured by earth movements. Dissected by streams into a maze of canyons, the plateau reaches an elevation of 8572 feet. Its dense cover of oak, pinyon and juniper, a transitional forest between desert below and mountains above, makes it a green tableland, a term that is rendered in Spanish as *mesa verde*. Through an unusually favorable set of circumstances, this plateau is enriched with fertile red soil that has for milleniums been blown in from the south and west. The porous sandstone of the surface absorbs the water from rain and melting snow and conveys it down to impermeable shales on which the sandstone rests. It is then carried along this contact zone to outpourings in seeps and springs. Thus little is lost of the eighteen inches of annual precipitation received on the mesa surface.

In the process, the sandstone erodes into shallow caves and overhangs which, with the arable soil nearby, appealed to early men. In these canyon walls and on the surface prehistoric Indians constructed hundreds of dwellings—hence the name applied much later to the surface rock formation, Cliff House sandstone.

Experts have determined that the Pueblo Indians flourished until a severe drought in the late 1200's drove them to lower and more moist locales, but while it lasted, life on the Mesa Verde must have been very good indeed. More than fifty species of mammals inhabit the region today—including mule deer, bighorn, black bear, mountain lion, coyote, fox, and cottontail. Of the nearly two hundred species of birds recorded in this upland, the cliff dwellers must have captured and utilized several; the turkey was evidently domesticated, for bones of it are numerous in the ruins.

From the commanding heights of the Mesa Verde today we obtain a splendid view in all directions, across the wide plateaus and basins of Navajo country to the south, the La Plata and San Juan Mountains to the northeast, and to the northwest the intricate, colorful canyon lands. Perhaps in the long run it does have a special orderliness, as Gilbert suggested, and as the Navajos sing in their chant:

For ages and ages the plans have been made.
For ages and ages the plans of the Holy Mountains have been made.

The San Juan River lies trapped and entrenched in deep incisions of its own making. These classic meanders are called goosenecks. (Hans W. Silvester: Bavaria Verlag)

5. Lesser Known Places of the Canyonlands

To roll, jostle, break, and finally grind up
and remove these bowlders is the task—
perhaps the chief task—of the river, and until
it removes them it can perform no work on
the solid rock which underlies.

Grove Karl Gilbert
in *Report upon Geographical and
Geological Explorations and Surveys
West of the 100th Meridian,* 1875

For most of the way, the road to Sleepy Hollow consists of a wide, wet, sandy river bed. The passage is so narrow in places that both sides of a vehicle nearly scrape the sandstone walls. The driver keeps his eyes on the texture of the sand lest a moment of careless judgment be a prelude to the gentle sinking and disappearance of the vehicle in quicksand. Only a jeep or its equivalent can make the trip, and even then there are places so steep that passengers have to walk.

Through clefts in the cliffs we have quick glimpses of the canyon lands of eastern Utah, red valleys and ridges studded with stone towers or balanced rocks. Obviously there are thousands of canyons like this one, but not all have a delightful stream along the bottom or such rich grass on the banks. As the canyon walls rise high and sheer, like a backdrop of some great drama, we round a bend and leave the stream bed to enter a grove of cottonwoods. We stop, dismount—and the canyon comes to life. A blur of black and white wings and a cackling call announce the departure of a pair of magpies.

Magpies, Mimulus, and Solitude

It is nearly impossible to visit the West without encountering black-billed magpies *(Pica pica)* or their California cousins, the yellow-billed *(P. nuttalli),* because they often fly beside a road or peck at the remains of animals slain on highways. So flexible are the appetites of these long-tailed members of the crow family that they take advantage of whatever food is in season. For black-bills this may be grasshoppers in the summer, which gives them status in the eyes of men, but when they have to take in refuse and manure, they lose a little of their glamor. In the days of roaming bison herds, magpies alighted on the backs of the beasts and rid them of parasitic insects and their larvae, or they picked ticks from the fur of deer, elk and bighorn. This habit, perhaps of benefit to wild animals, carried over to introduced livestock. Pecking at sores on horses, cattle or sheep, magpies plucked out not only larvae but flesh as well, resulting in the death of livestock if continued.

Like all creatures of ill repute, they were soon accused of more than they committed. Magpies were held accountable for stealing eggs and young from nests and thereby dooming other species to extinction. With a little thought, this thesis should not have led to severe condemnation, for even if nests were robbed, magpies and their neighbors had evolved together and occupied this territory long before men ever came to analyze and worry about it. Nevertheless, the undiscriminating magpies were hunted without mercy. They also often ate the poisoned bait put out for

Capitol Reef, in central Utah. Early explorers called such layered sedimentary cliffs "reefs" because of a fancied resemblance to coral formations. (Byron S. Crader)

Overleaf: The intricate spires in Bryce Canyon are eroding from hardened muds and sands deposited more than thirteen million years ago. (Hans W. Silvester: Bavaria Verlag)

coyotes—which of course killed hundreds of magpies.

Fortunately, as if to make up for all this, they pay a good deal of attention to reproduction. It takes quite a while, perhaps more than a month, to collect the sticks, twigs, plant fibers, animal hair, and other debris required to build their nest and then to line the inside with mud and more delicate padding. These efforts produce a nursery up to seven feet in vertical dimension, located high in cottonwoods, willows, oaks and other trees, and which in later years may be used by other birds. It all seems like a lot of trouble to protect a half-dozen to a dozen eggs, but the canyon country has severe spring winds and if theft of eggs or some other catastrophe interrupts the cycle, the magpies may have to use this same nest more than once in a season.

Like the roadrunner, magpies lay their eggs over a period of several days. In two or three weeks the young

marking the path of water that fell into one of the loveliest pools in the West. In the quiet, we heard each drop strike the surface with a sound like the ringing of a tiny bell in some great cave, a small sound magnified by acoustic properties of the cliff. Each drop broke the surface and immediately there were reflected streaks and blotches of sunlight against the shaded wall of the cliff.

To our minds this hidden vale held almost all of the fascinating natural characteristics of the canyon lands —contrast, color, water, dense thickets, life, and its own peculiar brand of solitude. Only a few persons who have been there know its whereabouts; and indeed its apt but not very original name exists entirely in their minds. But dozens of other "sleepy hollows" must exist in the canyon lands, secret, far-off, dreamlike, where men go not to defile but to enjoy, and where the greatest enjoyment comes from escaping

Running water fashions canyons in varied ways and produces numerous effects—terraced basins *that are broad and shallow,* deep clefts *that become V-shaped,* narrows *whose walls overlap,* fin canyons *where parallel cracks deepen through erosion,* wide valleys, *and precipitously walled* gorges, barrancas, *and* arroyos.

have hatched, and a few weeks after that can hardly be distinguished from their elders. They relish a diet of caterpillars, grasshoppers and fly larvae brought to them, and in due course leave the nest and seek for themselves the forage that sometimes brings them trouble.

However atrocious a few of their habits might be, they made quite a handsome sight when they broke away from a red rock cliff and swooped down into the canyon, their long tails streaming and their white wing patches flashing in front of the shadows. Possibly they had a nest somewhere in the thicket of cottonwood, alder, and willow through which we fought our way, but the tangle was so dense that we couldn't see, and as we came to Sleepy Hollow, the rest of the world was forgotten.

A hundred feet overhead curved the roof of a natural amphitheater in the red cliff, a rounded vale constructed by centuries of seep from springs and floods of rain water over the upper ledge. The temperature must have been twenty degrees cooler. Across the inner wall of the recess grew banks of maidenhair fern, mixed with deep red monkey flower *(Mimulus)*. Moss trailed downward from these hanging gardens,

temporarily a busy world and recapturing a little of the mood of nature among these remote canyons. Indeed, running water has scoured southern and eastern Utah into an infinite number of hollows and hidden vales, and has sculptured out of massive red rocks some of the most colorful bridges and canyons on earth. If you would find your own Sleepy Hollow there are many from which to choose.

Lost Canyons

As geologists postulate it, the Colorado Plateau was a coastal plain at the end of the Cretaceous period. Substantial deposits of earlier sediments had been completed and when the land emerged, the last of the Mesozoic seas retreated. This ushered in Cenozoic time, and the earth began to fold upward in a number of areas on the plain. Up came the San Rafael Swell and the Circle Cliffs. Up came the Uncompahgre region to the east, the Kaibab Plateau to the south, the Monument upwarp in the center. At the southern end rose the Defiance and Zuñi upwarps. In consequence the underlying Mesozoic rocks were exposed to weathering and disintegration, which led to the deposit of their sediments in lakes and streams between the upwarps.

Simultaneously, the whole plateau was lifted on a broad scale, parts of it warping gently, parts folding sharply, parts breaking into block faults. Uplifted sandstones were cracked in a complex pattern of jointing and faulting. Old stream systems were changed and new ones established. Canyons, bridges and arches formed. Molten igneous masses welled up in localities such as the Henry, La Sal, and Abajo mountains.

Degradation of the surface increased, and thousands of cubic miles of sediments were stripped away or redeposited by running water.

It would tax the credulity of their hearers, the early geologists felt, to describe the buttes and canyons of this land as works of nature and not of some race of Titans. Exploration had its perils, too, and Captain Dutton counseled all persons to exercise utmost caution in entering the deep gorges. Once in them, he warned, the explorer would have to possess rare craft to extricate himself—a statement still true today.

Perhaps the deepest and sheerest-walled canyons are the "narrows" of the Zion country, which G. K. Gilbert referred to as "the most wonderful defile it has been my fortune to behold." At the upstream end of Zion Canyon the walls come down to the banks of the Virgin River and public access ends, except for persons hardy enough to walk in the stream itself and knowl-

less the retarding effects of vegetation, if any. Little evidence of this downcutting is likely to be observed by man, for the increase in depth may be only a fraction of an inch per year; but over hundreds of thousands of years the abrasive sediments have lowered the canyon floors many hundreds or even thousands of feet.

Whatever the degree of erosion, the canyon lands display extraordinary evidence of planes of weakness resulting from jointing, that is, from joint cracks or fractures in which one side has not necessarily moved with respect to the other. These are not always true faults of the kind abundant in the Grand Canyon, but they accelerate erosion in much the same way because they are similarly vulnerable to weathering. Whole plateaus, as in the Arches country, have become a veritable network of such crevices. A picturesque phenomenon results when vertical joints cross horizontal bedding planes, as in the Navajo sandstone at Zion

edgeable enough to escape sudden floods that may result from cloudbursts. A trip through the narrows, however, is still the same kind of thrilling experience it was to Gilbert a century ago:

"As we entered and found our outlook of sky contracted—as we had never before seen it between cañon cliffs—I measured the aperture above, and found it 35°. We had thought this a minimum, but soon discovered our error. Nearer and nearer the walls approached, and our strip of blue narrowed down to 20°, then 10°, and at last was even intercepted by the overhanging rocks. There was, perhaps, no point from which, neither forward nor backward, could we discover a patch of sky, but many times our upward view was completely cut off by the interlocking of the walls, which, remaining nearly parallel to each other, warped in and out as they ascended.... The principle on which the cutting depends is almost identical with that of the marble-saw, but the sand grains, instead of being imbedded in rigid iron, are carried by a flexible stream of water. By gravity they have been held against the bottom of the cut, so that they should make it vertical, but the current has carried them, in places against one side or the other, and so far modified the influence of gravity, that the cut undulates somewhat in its vertical section, as well as in its horizontal."

This scouring process, aided by floods, continuously deepens and widens the canyons of the plateau country. Each grain of sand, each fragment of rock helps to wear away the bed of a channel. The rate of erosion is proportional to the volume and velocity of the stream

Canyon; the best evidence of it is seen in a prominent headland known as Checkerboard Mesa.

In this region, the explorer comes upon other unusual geologic phenomena. To Captain Dutton, parts of the canyon lands exemplified "in the most intelligible, compact, and complete manner" the broad facts and laws which engaged his attention. But he did not miss the esthetic values. In the Kolob Terrace, directly above Zion Canyon, he pointed out that one perceived rock forms of nameless shapes, often grotesque and ludicrous, starting up from the earth as isolated freaks of carving or standing in clusters and rows along the white walls of sandstone. "They tease the imagination," he wrote, "and many of them look farcical. The land here is full of comedy. It is a singular display of Nature's art mingled with nonsense."

The Hay Pilers

The Kolob Terrace is but the southern portion of the Markagunt Plateau, which rises to 11,307 feet. At these high elevations, meadows and slopes in spring become resplendent with wild flowers, principally paintbrush *(Castilleja)* and lupine, marsh marigold, mountain buttercup, fringed gentian, columbine, and mountain bluebells. Bristlecone pine *(Pinus balfouriana)*, famous in Nevada and California for its longevity, grows here, and one specimen has been dated at twelve hundred years in age. Most conspicuous of the fauna are mule deer and Clark's nutcrackers, but there is a less obvious population of marmots, ground squirrels and chipmunks, red squirrels which gather the cones of spruce and cache them for winter, porcupines that eat the bark

The magpie, resident of open country, flies through canyons, meadows and valleys in nearly all parts of the West, from north of the hot deserts all the way to Alaska. (Joe Van Wormer: National Audubon Society)

of conifers, and predators such as badgers and weasels.

Uppermost are the rock-dwelling pikas *(Ochotona)*, also known, though less correctly, as conies, behaviorally adapted to lands of high altitude, deep snow, and frigid temperatures. They spend their lives on barren western mountains without migrating, without hibernating, and without any special ability to tunnel through snow. They are even comparatively thin-skinned. They live in protected crevices or broken rock fields at the edge of forest or tundra, and when the cold of autumn covers their community, when other creatures sleep or flee, these tiny relatives of the rabbits gather herbs by the mouthful and deposit them in "hay piles" among the rocks. They gather a great variety of vegetation, from sagebrush to rock-mat, including roots, stems, twigs, leaves, and needles, and seldom venture very far from shelter.

It seems like an easy life—plenty of food during summer and winter, lots of rest, a new fur coat when needed, veritable rock catacombs in which to hide, and few other animals, even pikas, competing for existence. Nevertheless, pikas have their special lookouts, and it does not pay to relax their guard against hawks, or to let the deadly weasel and marten, which also live at high mountain elevations and have the ability to enter the tunnels, steal up on them. Pikas use their voices more than rabbits do, shouting an alarm if they think that danger is near, or advertising to other pikas that their domain is private. For that reason they have been called whistling hares. A month after mating, the females bear one to five young, usually in early summer. How the young grow and learn to live in their sometimes demanding environment is not as clearly known as is the case with animals more accessible to man or with those whose fur is more highly valued.

Canyons, Bridges, and Arches

The mountain-top environments are actually islands—someone has called them cony islands—in a sea of desert, the Great Basin on the west, the canyon-cut plateaus on the east. The Paunsaugunt Plateau is a similar island, the edge of which is eroding into the Pink Cliffs of Bryce Canyon National Park. It shares the same rich forest community as neighboring plateaus, a community that includes ponderosa, limber, and bristlecone pines, Douglas fir, white fir, blue spruce, quaking aspen, and manzanita. The Table Cliffs and Aquarius Plateau, together with the elongated Wasatch Plateau stretching to the north, are other "islands," overlooking the red rock country of the canyon lands.

Proceeding east, one crosses the drainage system of the Escalante River, its dry tributaries reaching up into the Straight Cliffs on one side and the Circle Cliffs on the other. Just beyond, the Waterpocket Fold, a down-warp in which corresponding rock layers have been offset as much as seven thousand feet, reaches eighty miles across the plateau west of the Henry Mountains. It is one of many such flexures on the Colorado Plateau, all examples of the folding of the earth's crust without breaking, the folds in some cases stretching a hundred and fifty miles and having a displacement of fourteen thousand feet.

Nearly everything is on a scale of hugeness. Before being inundated by a man-made reservoir, the southern portion of the Colorado River in Utah exhibited gigantic alcoves, sinuous canyons like those in the narrows of Zion, massive blocks of sandstone cleft in thousands of fascinating designs, and curving amphitheaters fit for academies of music. Yet it was a delicate land as well, its spring-wet seams alive with maiden-hair ferns, its sandy banks festooned with cane and willow and tamarisk, its shady glens enriched with redbud. Every mile had something to treasure, like a vast natural museum. John Wesley Powell called it a "curious *ensemble* of wonderful features—carved walls, royal arches, glens, alcove gulches, mounds, and monuments. From which of these features shall we select a name? We decide to call it Glen Canyon." In his little boats, Powell and his men glided, as he said, "hour after hour, stopping now and then, as our attention is arrested by some new wonder." Many individuals tried in vain to save the 186-mile gorge from inundation by a reservoir. A Glen Canyon, they felt, happens only once.

Other declivities and escarpments are named after the colors of the region: Red Canyon, White Canyon, Dark Canyon, Orange Cliffs. Not only colors but an infinite number of shapes are a scenic legacy of the erosion of sedimentary strata. Up White Canyon, a distance of about sixty miles northeast of Rainbow Bridge, are three other impressive bridges—Owachomo, 106 feet high with a span of 180 feet; Kachina, 210 feet high with a span of 206 feet; and Sipapu, 220 feet high with a span of 268 feet—all carved from the near-white, cross-bedded Cedar Mesa sandstone of Permian time.

This land abounds in both natural bridges and arches. They are quite distinct in formation. All natural bridges in the canyon lands result from running water,

Vertical cracks have cut across bedding planes in the Navajo sandstone to produce Checkerboard Mesa, in southern Utah. (Josef Muench)

at least initially. The original meandering courses of streams in this area were evidently developed on level surfaces, and the sharp meanders were later entrenched or trapped in canyons. Normally, the inside of a meander has a slow current and deposits sand and gravel, whereas the outside carries the main current which therefore grinds its load of sediments against the outer banks and erodes it. When only a knife-thin wall of sandstone remains between two curves of a meander loop, or between two meanders, the water will almost inevitably cut a hole or tunnel in the wall and flow through it, that is, beneath the bridge it has formed, and may abandon its oxbow loop. In time, additional weathering agents will enlarge the span.

With a natural arch, on the other hand, running water is not involved, except for the rare pothole arches, made by floodwaters drilling down through an overhanging cliff. The opening of most arches is simply a perforation in a vertical "fin," or slender canyon wall. So thoroughly have the massive sandstones of this region been cracked by jointing that many of the joints are close together. When erosive forces scour out these joint cracks they frequently leave thin walls, or fins, of high but narrow proportions standing between them. Alcoves on either side of these fins may be formed by collapse of rock, and at length more rapid weathering of softer spots results in a breakthrough. Over what is probably thousands of years, an arch is thus formed.

An Empire of Arches

Between the junction of the Green and Colorado rivers, just north of Moab, Utah, lies the greatest concentration of natural arches in the West—or in the world. So far, eighty-eight have been discovered in the drainage of Salt and Courthouse washes, and such is the maze of fin canyons in that area that no one knows how many more there may be. There are single, double, and triple arches, windows, tunnels, turret arches, pinholes, potholes, broken arches and fallen arches. Landscape Arch, believed to be the longest natural stone span in the world, measures 291 feet from buttress to buttress. Best known is Delicate Arch, nearly isolated by erosion, and so slender and cracked that collapse cannot be too far off—though hopefully thousands of years away.

A special set of conditions accounts for so impressive a collection of arches. The Entrada sandstone, measuring five hundred feet at its thickest, is ideally suited to the sculpture of arches by virtue of its strong and uniform character. Wind-deposited probably in a coastal desert environment of Jurassic time, its grains of sand were strongly cemented into a mass capable of bearing enormous structural weight. During subsequent uplift, the bed was jointed in a complex pattern seen to best advantage from the air. Great numbers of deep fin canyons have been eroded along the joints, and in the fins that separate these canyons the arches have developed. Some fins stand alone as isolated walls, like those along a canyon called Park Avenue. Some have been reduced to odd-shaped spires and pinnacles, and where the softer Carmel formation has eroded away beneath them, large blocks of Entrada remain as balanced rocks atop the spires.

The heart of the arches region is a labyrinth of fins and canyons known as the Fiery Furnace. Ropes give access into the depths but there is also a popular guided trail two miles long. Once on the silt-laden floor, the climber feels lost to civilization. The walls, scarcely a dozen feet apart, rise four hundred feet above him. The turns are sharp, the passageways circuitous and seemingly endless. Few persons dare to enter, unless they know this labyrinth thoroughly. Parts of it are about as "secret" and inaccessible as any locality in the canyon lands, and the climber comes away with a fresh appreciation of the geological forces that have fractured and carved this great plateau.

Salt Wash: A Plateau Community

Despite the claims of early geologists that this land was utterly barren of life, there was a considerable biologic community here. There still is, and an exploration of nearly any canyon, such as Salt Wash, west of Delicate Arch, reveals it. Salt Wash is a wide river bed flanked by sharp-edged cliffs of red sandstone. A trickling stream survives the searing summer, but it is too small to help the dust-covered saltbush or juniper that grow among the dry rocks above the bed of the creek. Like a thousand other streams in the canyon lands, it flows intermittently, at least at the surface, just wet enough to support riparian, or stream bank, vegetation—a winding green ribbon on the vast red plateau.

Water from a cold spring flows through grass, jointweed, and rabbitbrush to join the main stream, which is crystal clear except where algae have grown in eddy pools. On sandy and muddy narrow flats beside the stream, currents of water have engraved ripple marks in geometric patterns. Tracks of killdeer and heron, resembling mathematical equations, seem linked by worm trails and punctuated with the deep-set tracks of deer. Hundreds of annular ant hills line the drier mud bank, and the tracks of a wandering mountain lion lie between and beyond them.

In the heat of midday, Salt Wash animals, like all their desert brethren, practice the principle of withdrawal. Most remain in burrows or rock slides or under trees to escape the direct rays of the sun. But the evidence of their activity is plentiful. Farther on we see the skid marks of a cottonwood branch that was pulled across the sand, and beside them the tracks of a beaver.

The only motion is that of the horizon, made liquid by heat; or some grasshoppers; or a pair of magpies shuttling between the streambank and the red and yellow crags above; or a quiet flicker curious about something in the rushes. The wash abounds in tamarisk, gray-green or yellow-green, its lavender flower sprays swaying slightly. An old Russian thistle—the imported, ubiquitous tumbleweed *(Salsola kali)*—lies anchored in the mud, half covered with sediment. Driftwood and stream debris caught in a patch of cockleburs or among the rocks above the river bed attest to the occasional floods that roar down the canyon. Groves of seep-willow, more than head high, combine with cottonwood to indicate a substantial source of moisture, and upon investigation we find a pool from recent rains.

But the growth of white clover contrasts with the salt crust on the sun-dried mudflats, a high-temperature extreme and an almost lifeless environment only a few feet away. Beyond the bank, on and between the slick-rock slopes, grow lichen, rabbitbrush, and saltbush, cactus, oak, yucca, sumac, a little snakeweed, some straggling junipers, and perhaps half a dozen other dust-dry herbs and shrubs. Out there roam animals such as fox and deer and coyote, though they are bound more or less to seeps, springs, and streams for water supply. There, too, are kangaroo rats and other rodents entirely independent of such sources of water. Far from barren, the canyon and plateau ecosystems are, in fact, quite complex, and one finds in them squirrels, jackrabbits, cottontails, porcupines, and a host of other mammals, as well as birds.

If the moist stream bed and dry slopes are part of an arid environment considered hostile by men, they nevertheless support a variety of desert organisms, rarely observed by day but active during the evening, night, and morning. Salt Wash and other streams are highly important in the water economy of the region. To most human beings they are not only secret but forbidding, yet to visitors with perception they are

Delicate Arch, in Arches National Monument, Utah, casts an evening shadow over a natural red rock amphitheatre in the Entrada sandstone. The man in the foreground gives scale. (Western Ways Features)

among the most interesting and active parts of the canyon lands.

Paradox Basin: Valleys of Salt

What the early explorers never found, and perhaps never suspected, and what many visitors in east-central Utah and west-central Colorado do not suspect either, is that a great deal of this curious and exquisite scenery is underlain by the most unstable of rocks: common table salt. We now know, of course, that salt domes occur in many regions of the world. More than two hundred subterranean salt structures occur along the coast of the Gulf of Mexico, and some are associated with commercially important quantities of oil and sulfur. The salt structures of the Colorado Plateau, apart from limited oil and potash development, are not known to have such commercial value. But these salt structures have been responsible for numerous surface

features, including trenchlike valleys with imposing walls that are unique in the scenery of North America. They have produced eight long valleys that are the culmination of a series of events that began in late Pennsylvanian time.

Thick beds of saline rocks, chiefly salt and gypsum, were deposited in the Paradox formation, and were later covered by hundreds of feet of other sediments. Being viscous, unstable, and less dense than the rocks above, the salt masses responded to pressure differences and began to move. As the ages passed, salt surged upward repeatedly in plastic flows and broke out at the surface, only to be covered again by subsequent sedimentation. The Paradox Basin, a rectangular tract measuring seventy by one hundred and fifty miles, was arched and elevated as the Colorado Plateau rose in Tertiary time. Ground water then began to percolate down, dissolving great quantities of salt underground and thereby causing the collapse of adjacent and overlying strata. Today the ancient saline deposits are not visible at the surface, but dozens of deep wells have revealed an immense amount of halite and other salts beneath the ground. In places, these deposits are almost three miles thick.

The great upwarps and downwarps produced in overlying rock strata by the upwelling salt masses have been exposed to weathering. Their tops largely breached by erosion, they are now valleys—Salt Valley of the Arches country, Onion Creek, Castle Creek, Spanish and Lisbon valleys in Utah, and Sinbad, Paradox, and Gypsum valleys in Colorado. The mysterious Upheaval Dome, farther west near the Green River, is a structure resulting from a similar movement of salt.

Walking across these broken valleys the casual observer would little realize that they are structures without connection to hardrock underlying strata, that they are literally floating on beds of salt. Nor would he notice, perhaps, that the orientation of every one of these valleys is nearly parallel with the Uncompahgre uplift to the east. What this signifies is one of those mysteries that reminds man of the still-primitive state of his knowledge about the earth.

One can spend months or even years in these canyon lands and always find something new to see. There are the high cliffs, folds, and monoliths of the San Rafael Swell, an uplift of rock layers west of the Green River. There are scores of balanced rocks and hundreds of stone monoliths in the Goblin Valley, and handsome formations in Cathedral Valley. At Colorado National Monument, a scenic highway winds among brilliant cliffs and pinnacles.

Left above: Dry washes serve the Colorado River in collecting and transporting sediments toward the sea. (Darwin Van Campen) Far left: Desert asters and related members of the sunflower family (Compositae) *are common throughout the West. (Byron S. Crader) Left: Canyon tree frogs* (Hyla arenicolor) *cling to cliffs or trees by means of large expanded toe pads. (Marida Norgaard)*

Buried Treasure

The Uinta Basin represents an extensive downward sag in the earth's crust. It was filled with water during the early Tertiary period, and became a rich center of aquatic life, especially microorganisms such as algae. Over a long period of time, the remains of these organisms settled to the bottom of the lake, and sand and silt washed in from the nearby Uinta Mountains and other neighboring highlands. By the time this sedimentation ceased, some ten thousand feet of sandstone, marl, oolite, algal reefs, and organic-rich shale had been deposited. Remnants of this sedimentation, called the Green River formation, now underlie about sixteen thousand square miles in several basins in Utah, Colorado, and Wyoming. As early as a hundred years ago, F. V. Hayden, in the *Third Annual Report of the United States Geological Survey of the Territories,* remarked upon the "great amount of combustible or petroleum slates" in the region, and it now seems clear that the Green River formation is one of the richest deposits of petroleum shale in the world.

Oil shale is an organic-rich substance that yields substantial quantities of oil by conventional methods of distillation. Though worldwide deposits of oil shale have not been thoroughly appraised, many sources have been reported and a number utilized commercially. For more than a century, oil shale has been used to a limited extent as a solid fuel and as a source of oil and combustible gas where fuel is in short supply. In the United States, which may have almost as much as the rest of the world combined, oil shale has been reported not only in the Green River basins but in the central and eastern states, in southwestern Montana, in the Monterey shale of southern California, and in the northern foothills of the Brooks Range of Alaska. Other sources have been located and authorities predict that enormous additional quantities will be discovered.

Still, the largest known high-grade deposits in the United States are those of the Green River formation. Assays from rotary drill cuttings show that some of the better-grade shale would yield sixty-five gallons of oil per ton. The entire formation is estimated to contain more than two trillion barrels of oil equivalent. Altogether, the Uinta Basin deposits are said to contain fifty times as much oil as the total of all oil already produced and in reserve.

How much of this oil will be extracted is another question. At present the methods of extracting such oil are being refined to make production competitive with that from other sources of petroleum. But at the same time the use of nuclear energy is becoming increasingly sophisticated and consumer demands for electric vehicles are expected to expand. Another obstacle is public opposition to removal of underground minerals on a large scale, especially if the process threatens the value of the surface of the land. The lessons of stripmining, and the scars that it produced, have been well learned. The rapidly growing public respect for scenic resources calls for ingenious methods of extraction—perhaps through subterranean nuclear explosions—if the shale is ever to be mined.

85

On the Waterpocket Fold, and elsewhere in southern Utah, the Carmel formation erodes into spheroidal stone remnants perched on pedestals of relatively soft sediment. (Josef Muench)

Dinosaurs in Cliffs

Were it not for what is known to geologists as the Morrison formation, a great deal of the West would lack scenic and geologic interest. This rock formation is one of the most widespread and most varied in the West, outcropping as light yellow cliffs of sandstones in some places, and green, gray, lavender, pink or white shales and siltstones in others. It originally covered more than 100,000 square miles of the Rocky Mountain West, from Utah and New Mexico north to Montana. The sediments are never much thicker than four hundred feet, and were probably carried in shallow waters. They contain remains of freshwater mollusks, ostracods, mammals, crocodiles, calcareous algae, and rich vegetation, an abundance that suggests a subtropical environment during Jurassic time.

The Morrison is most famous, however, for its content of dinosaur bones. All the colossal dinosaurs of the American Jurassic—sixty-nine species in all—have come from this formation. And small ones, too, of course, including the *Hoplosuchus,* less than eight inches long. Dinosaurs have been taken from Como Bluff and along the Little Medicine River in Wyoming, and from the vicinity of Canon City, Colorado. Part of the first known skeleton of *Brachiosaurus* was excavated in 1900 from the Morrison formation at Riggs Hill, near Colorado National Monument—significant in paleontology as the first and only type of dinosaur with front legs longer than hind legs.

But the greatest concentration of dinosaurs in the world lies a few miles downstream from the junction of the Green and Yampa rivers in northeastern Utah. Three miles west of the mouth of Split Mountain Canyon, where "rainbow beds" of upturned Morrison strata have eroded into colorful undulating hills, is a ridge of sandstone known as Dinosaur Ledge. Powell missed seeing this on his river trips, and spoke only vaguely of "reptilian beds." The main ledge was not discovered, in fact, until 1909. For the next thirteen years, large numbers of bones and almost perfect skeletons were chipped out, boxed, and shipped to museums of natural history in the larger cities of the

When will it fall? Balanced rocks occur commonly where soft rock layers weather away more rapidly than durable overlying strata. (Hans W. Silvester: Bavaria Verlag)

Believed to be the world's longest natural span is Land-scape Arch, 291 feet between buttresses. Arches National Monument, Utah. (Josef Muench)

United States and Canada. So jumbled was the mass of bones that excavators could hardly distinguish one from another; all kinds and sizes were dug from the rock and near the end of the work the stripping was proceeding at a rate of about twenty thousand cubic feet per year. One museum took away parts of three hundred skeletons. At length the quarry and vicinity were established as Dinosaur National Monument and today a bone-rich surface, tilted sixty-seven degrees from horizontal, is slowly being etched and cut so as to outline permanently in high relief a group of skeletal fragments in their natural position.

One glance is enough to make a visitor believe the claim that this is the largest and best-preserved deposit of Jurassic dinosaurs. Arrangement of the remains suggests that the animals were stranded on a sandbar and tossed together like debris in a flood. The natural processes of decomposition and petrification have preserved large numbers of animal bones; more than twenty-three nearly complete skeletons and the bones of about three hundred other dinosaurs have been found. Most abundant were individuals of the genus *Diplodocus*—with one specimen measuring seventy-five and a half feet in length—and the armor-plated *Stegosaurus*. An *Apatosaurus (Brontosaurus)*, which must have had a length of seventy-five feet or so in life and a weight of close to forty tons, was unearthed; by contrast, a two-and-a-half-foot *Laosaurus* was also dug up. Here, too, were buried the remains of the plant-eating *Dryosaurus*, the flesh-eating *Antrodemus*, plus *Camptosaurus, Allosaurus, Camarasaurus,* two crocodiles, and a turtle—approximately fifteen reptilian species in all.

The Diamonds That Couldn't Be

In the days of western exploration and discovery, fossils were not the only treasures sought by men.

88

Riches of any sort, like gold and silver, were acceptable, but it was inevitable that search also be made for stones of the highest value. Although this region is not a natural setting, mineralogically speaking, for diamonds, a century ago a story of diamonds in this area made headlines from coast to coast, and maps still show Diamond Mountain Plateau, Diamond Gulch, and Diamond Peak as prominent features of the terrain. This was the great diamond swindle of 1872. Two prospectors named Philip Arnold and John Slack aroused a fever of expectations in San Francisco by distributing raw diamonds allegedly taken from a western locality. A group of prominent and wealthy men had the gems assayed and got an eminent geologist to verify the genuineness of the find at the location. With such assurances they paid Arnold and Slack more than $600,000 for the claim, then formed the New York and San Francisco Mining and Commercial Company to gather funds to work the diamond deposits.

By coincidence, Clarence King, one of the foremost geologists of the time, was conducting a geological survey along the fortieth parallel through what is now the northern parts of Colorado, Utah, Nevada, and California. King knew of no geological formation that was of the type in which diamonds were likely to occur, but in his capacity as a government geologist he felt professionally bound to check the claim. He did so, along with other geologists, locating the site near the point where Colorado, Utah, and Wyoming meet, and proving to the satisfaction of all that the diamonds had been salted, that is, planted there artificially. King became a public hero for having saved a number of small investors—and San Francisco as well—from financial calamity. Arnold and Slack disappeared, but Arnold was later found and forced to return a portion of the swindled funds.

This hoax has been called the greatest fraud ever perpetrated in the West. Perhaps it was symptomatic of the changing times that the fraud was uncovered by salaried government geologists with no monetary stake in the matter. Great riches of the West were later to be revealed systematically and impartially by such federal organizations as the United States Geological Survey—of which Clarence King, a few years after the diamond hoax, became the first director. And King, always sensitive to the wonders around him, must have felt that diamonds could never have compared with the treasure of arches, bridges, and hidden places of the canyon lands.

6. High Peaks and Fossil Beds: The Southern Rockies

*At two o'clock in the afternoon I thought
I could distinguish a mountain to our right,
which appeared like a small blue cloud.*

Lieutenant Zebulon Pike,
on the discovery of Pikes Peak

Going afoot in the Rockies is not only a high exhilaration but an intimate experience in a natural world that is endless and fascinating. Enos Mills, the great Rocky Mountain naturalist, said much the same in writing about his experiences alone, but never lonely, in these magic mountains. Not one of our own years there was ever long enough because each had a full four seasons in which the circle of life passed by with greater excitement and spectacle than a pageant, and with more complexity than any human being can keep track of.

It takes years to know these mountains well, but only minutes on a trail to realize how full of life and interest they are. The first revelation of this comes by way of the ears, for if a warbling vireo's song is not heard in the dense forest, the chatter of nuthatches is. A whole orchestra of sound fills the forest and if these can be identified, a naturalist's journey is greatly enriched. The red crossbill, for example, is worth searching out with binoculars, but it is usually up with the pine cones, its presence unsuspected unless we recognize its "cheep-cheep-cheep" call. Of course there are always the raucous notes of Clark nutcrackers, the singing of the chickadee, and the sharp call of the western flycatcher. But two birds in particular produce songs so pleasant to hear and in such dramatic environments that we remember them above all others. From the sheer Granite cliffs come the cascading notes of the canyon wren, previously described. In the loftiest forests may be heard the other, a flutelike note succeeded by rising and falling tones that resemble the ringing of bells. The melody is unmistakable, and belongs to no other than the hermit thrush *(Hylocichla guttata)*, thrilling accompaniment for our first steps into this mountain vastness.

Afoot in the Rockies

Only if you begin before dawn can you get a head start on the hermit thrush: it is the earliest and latest to sing each day. The bird is not conspicuous, being brownish and white with dark spots, but as its song emerges from the depths of spruce-fir groves, overspread with the colors of sunrise or of sunset, we recall the adjectives advanced by early ornithologists: soul-stirring, uplifting, serene, spiritual. To the thrush, such music most likely has meanings other than those expressive of joy, but if any joy is involved it could well be due to the abundance of berries and insects in this montane forest. When the thrush and its fellow migrants return each spring from their winters in Mexico or other subtropical environments their timing coincides with the production of enormous quantities of natural foods.

Along the trail the evidence is clear: rich vegetation sustains abundant animal life. The fruit of squaw currant is relished by birds and mammals, and the fresh tops of the shrub may be browsed by deer. Numerous birds join the thrushes in consuming service-

Autumn color in the Rocky Mountains is due in greatest measure to the dazzling shows of quaking aspen. (Darwin Van Campen)

berries, elderberries, mistletoe berries and similar natural fruit. Along the trail we see the trunks of ponderosa pines debarked and know that porcupines have been around. Or the trunks have been drilled by colorful Williamson's sapsuckers *(Sphyrapicus thyroideus)* who usurp the juices that ooze from the holes and pick off any insects that get caught there. Or we enter a grove of aspen and find that the bark has been recently chewed by elk, who use it as food in winter.

The trail passes clumps of blue spruce *(Picea pungens)* in a patch of yellow-flowered shrubby cinquefoil *(Potentilla fruticosa)*, crosses fields of grama, timothy, and needle grass, and rises into pockets of Douglas fir. As usual, woodlands on the northern slopes are much more dense than those with southern exposure. From time to time we glimpse the shining summit of Longs Peak in the distance, elevation 14,256 feet. Closer at hand we climb past granite boulders, miniature natural bridges, caves, overhangs, pillars and balanced rocks, vertical and horizontal joint cracks, and potholes opened by chemical decomposition combined with freezing and thawing. Pausing here, we see a world in itself; before they get choked with organic debris, the potholes are filled occasionally with water and such aquatic life as flatworms, beetles, and fairy shrimp. These latter, like the flowers of the desert, have a reproductive cycle that is delayed until sufficient moisture is available to complete the process; in this case, shrimp eggs stay dormant while the potholes are dry.

Along the streams we find ourselves in still a different world, cool, inviting, rich with the odors of growth and decay. The rocks are covered with moss, lichen, and liverwort; ferns grow in crevices; clusters of Engelmann spruce line the banks of the ravine; birch and aspen overhang the waterfalls; and wildflowers, including white bog orchid *(Habenaria dilatata)*, wild raspberry, rose, pink geranium, and shooting star abound along the stream course. The trail may pass a pond or lake whose surface is stabilized with water lilies and whose shore is lined with maples. These lakes are also favored by swifts, swallows and bats which sweep the air for insects.

There is in fact a continuing dynamic circle of life and death in these mountain forests and the hiker sees a great deal of it. He crosses old fire sites in abundance, where trees have been broken and burned by lightning, and finds a great many clumps of aspen and fireweed healing the scars and starting the cycle of regrowth. Certain trees are destroyed by beetles or by elk; others are damaged by a yellow-orange mistletoe that produces "witches brooms." Carpenter ants work briskly in fire-scarred stumps. The odor of rotting leaves mingles with that of mountain sagebrush. With robins, warblers, squirrels and cicadas in the trees, the Rockies are vibrant with a multiplicity of sounds that supplement the music of hermit thrushes.

Although above all is the cliff and tundra habitat, we have absorbed enough for a single walk. As we descend we are struck by unexpected impressions of colors, not only in wildflowers, but in the lichens that decorate granite outcrops with shades of orange, yellow and green. And, with good fortune, with the recognition of an avian chant in the treetops followed by a patient search, we see the most colorful of Rocky Mountain birds, the western tanager *(Piranga ludoviciana)*. Whenever a burst of yellow, red and black is sighted in the shadowed upper branches of the conifers, it is likely to be this species. Western tanagers breed high in the mountains of most of western North America, arriving in April or May, bursting into robin-like song, and raising three or four young on the abundant insects available, mostly bees and wasps caught in mid-air. Come August, western tanagers start down the mountains, gather in migratory flocks, and eventually find their way to Central America.

As the thrushes sing in the final stages of darkness we finish our hike, aware that we have merely begun to fathom the facts, the mysteries, the beauties of this great mountain ecosystem. Happily, for many years to come there will be new discoveries for the science-minded to unravel and continuing sources of stimulation to the senses of those who come only to wonder and enjoy.

When the Mountains Moved

Nature seems to have divided the mountains of western North America into convenient sections—the Rockies, the Basins and Ranges, the Plateaus, the Sierra Nevada, the Cascades, the Coast ranges—but the fact is that they are all part of one great mountain chain. They belong to a single north-south belt of crustal disturbance that extends from Alaska to Argentina. The Spanish term *cordillera,* meaning mountain chain, is applied to this system. But the mind boggles at having to grasp the whole system; and one unit, such as the Rocky Mountains, is enough to observe at a time.

Yet the Rockies can hardly be considered alone. Their ancestry is linked to that of the cordillera, and the cordillera to vast geologic periods of deposit and deformation. For millions of years a continental sea or trough persisted where the West is now located, a series of basins in which there accumulated some twenty thousand feet of sediments during Paleozoic time, plus additional deposits in Mesozoic. The weight of these contributed to unstable conditions. The result was excessive strain—an overload as it were—on one part of the earth's crust.

This kind of situation seems to be intolerable in the geologic course of events, for if nature reveals one overriding tendency it is to maintain balance in both geologic and biologic processes. So according to certain laws of crustal equilibrium action soon took place to counterbalance the overloading of the troughs. This resulted in a period of mountain-building called the Laramide Revolution. It began in early Mesozoic and continued into the Cenozoic; some geologists believe that this revolution may still be going on.

The underlying or basement rocks of the cordillera—

Few other trees in North America—perhaps none—are as widely distributed as quaking aspen. It springs up rapidly in the wake of forest fires, and often reproduces by root sprouts rather than seeds. (Don Worth)

Precambrian gneisses, granites, and schists—had been there a long time, and had been faulted and folded and sheared so long ago that the details of their past are obscure. Broken and weakened as they were, they readily yielded when new crustal unrest occurred. As the Laramide Revolution mounted in intensity, these old fault and shear zones of Precambrian time were reactivated.

It is tempting to think of this process as cataclysmic, but it must in fact have been rather slow and steady, with erosion stripping away the rocks as they were exposed to air. The building of the Rocky Mountains —indeed of the whole cordillera—is as much a product of gradual processes as of earth convulsions.

Elongated masses of Precambrian rock began to rise, pushing beds of sedimentary rock out of the sea. The Front Range of the Rockies rose, bending strata almost on end, as seen in the nearly vertical "flatirons" next to Boulder, Colorado, and the Garden of the Gods near Colorado Springs. For miles, parallel to the Front Range, extend the upturned edges of the well-known Dakota sandstone and similar resistant beds. In other places the strata buckled, forming structural traps where oil and gas accumulated.

So high did some of the core rocks rise that severe erosion sheared off the strata capping them; they now constitute the crests of several ranges. West of the Front Range rose the Sawatch Range, the summit of which, Mount Elbert (14,431 feet), is the highest mountain in Colorado. Farther west rose the White River Plateau, cut into majestic cliffs and canyons by the Colorado River. This western arm of the Rockies continues into Utah as the Uinta Mountains, which join perpendicularly the north-south Wasatch Mountains.

Meanwhile, streams attacking all this material filled the basins between the mountains with sediment, so that several mountain ranges were almost engulfed, as in the Wyoming basins. Lakes formed in other basins, possibly a western version of the present Great Lakes. Thick layers of sediment were formed in them, and in some, as we have seen, immense deposits of oil shale accumulated.

Pyrotechnics

The making of the cordillera may have been slow and persistent, but it was not without some pyrotechnics. Lava flows poured out, building up high plateaus of basalt, breccia, and tuff, such as the Yellowstone Plateau and Absaroka Mountains, where volcanic activity still goes on, as evidenced by thermal pools, geysers and steam vents. Lava burst up through cracks and crevices, catapulting fine debris high into the air and covering the land. Layers of volcanic mud and ash poured into surrounding basins.

Where igneous action was less explosive, it sometimes produced side effects that were to prove very valuable to man after millions of years. Rocks of diorite, quartz monzonite, and granite porphyry welled up in a belt diagonally transverse to the general north-south trend of the Rockies, and with them came hot mineral-laden gases and solutions that spread into fractures within the rocks. Out of these solutions were precipitated rich concentrations of minerals and in this zone occur most of the historic mining areas of Colorado—Central City, Leadville, Silverton and others. Gold was deposited, and a variety of other valuable metals as well, including the richest concentrations of molybdenum in North America. Precambrian crystalline rocks in the Black Hills area were similarly enriched, notably in the region of the Homestake Mine, largest gold producer in North America.

As broad-scale mountain building tapered off and the Mesozoic Era gave way to the Cenozoic, the cordilleran ranges continued to contribute sediments to adjacent lowlands. For a while the land lay subject to steady weathering under a moist, subtropical climate. The land was by no means lonely. Its animal life may well have been more exciting than it is today because it was the time of the camel, rhinoceros, saber-toothed cat, and a host of other mammalian species that reached the peak of their development in North America.

Finally, as the region rose again, mountain summits were thrust to new heights, and rivers of the Colorado Plateau entrenched themselves in cliffbound canyons. The land grew cooler. Tropical climates vanished, which helped to wipe out certain species of animals. The age of glaciation arrived. For a million years, masses of ice clung to the mountain summits and clawed at the ridges, pulling off bits of rock, transporting debris, scouring out huge amphitheaters and broad valleys. These actions left the highest ridges serrated. Then the climate warmed, melting many of the glaciers. The increase in stream runoff stepped up the rate of dissection on mountains and plateaus. And all these processes are still going on today.

Such is the Laramide Revolution, a mountain-making epoch of continental magnitude. Hardly a structural feature of western North America is not based on it, or has not been influenced by it. With the Laramide nature has fashioned and put on display a collection of geologic features that enables us to explore the fundamental mechanisms by which the earth was formed.

A Family of Mountains

Like the vast cordillera of which they are so large a part, the Rockies possess distinct divisions. Most of the higher ranges of New Mexico and Colorado are called the Southern Rockies. Ranges in and around Wyoming make up the Middle Rockies. Diverse uplifts in Idaho and Montana form the Northern Rockies. And finally there are chains of spectacularly folded beds in the Canadian Rockies.

The traveler moving west from Denver is soon surrounded by mountains. Since there are no extensive foothills, he may be unprepared for so sudden a change. He enters the mountains as if through a gate in a wall and finds himself climbing rapidly along steep slopes. Cliffs rise above. Gray-walled canyons fall away below. The rich vegetation is very different from what he saw on the plains. The immediate skyline is dominated by conifers and aspens, and with sharp ears or eyes he quickly discerns that the leading resident species is the Steller jay. Westerners sometimes

take this noisy bird for granted, but to the newcomer the large black crest—flaring when excited, lowered when thieving—is something to watch and the jay's song is something to hear, varying from a faint whisper song to a hawklike scream. The aggressive tactics help to provide omnivorous jays with an ample diet of insects, but apparently acorns are the favorite food. Steller jays are among the most adaptable of birds, nesting deep in the mountain wilds as well as close to human settlements. Time has taught them not to be so noisy and nervous during the nesting season, but when the young have grown and the birds wander through winter in family groups, discretion disappears. Along with their cousins, the crows and magpies, jays have been called the most intelligent and mentally alert of birds. Because of their curiosity they may be called into view by human beings who make some kind of a squeaking sound, perhaps like that of an animal in distress. This is apt to summon jays from several directions. But perhaps the most lasting impressions of these masters of the Rocky Mountain wilderness are the views of jays unfolding their wide blue wings

and, in a cascade of color, soaring through a grove of pines or into the shadowed depths of a canyon.

Far less noisy but just as common in or near the coniferous forest are the mule deer *(Odocoileus hemionus)*, stocky, big-eared, big-eyed, four hundred pounds at the heaviest. They are seen at higher elevations in summer, browsing on herbs, aspen and willow. Now and then a jay or magpie perches on their back to peck at ticks embedded in the flesh. With autumn the deer descend to lower slopes in their annual migration, but when spring brings back fresh leaves and grass they return to the mountain forests and meadows of home.

Above the forest and beyond the jays and deer, the traveler catches glimpses of bare rock and snow. Finally, upon rising to the passes he is thrust into a cold and treeless tundra where summer comes only briefly, and from which he can look out over a world of mountains piled on mountains. This is the Front Range, largest and highest section of the Southern Rockies: sixty miles across, more than three hundred miles in length, a mosaic of fault-bounded blocks of ancient granite, schist, and gneiss. Height marks all aspects of the Southern Rockies, and only in Alaska and California are the altitudes exceeded. Of the fifty highest summits in the United States, twenty-eight are in Colorado.

95

Between and around the ridges lie basins—often called parks—broad, high in elevation, filled with sediments, and in places interrupted by spurs from the main mountain masses. Southward the Rio Grande flows through a series of sharply downwarped basins known as the Rio Grande Depression. Much of New Mexico around it has been capped by volcanic deposits, from small cinder cones to great lava fields such as that of Mount Taylor. In Pleistocene time there was evidently a cataclysm of major proportions. In the western part of the Jemez Mountains, ten miles west of the present Los Alamos, a volcano ejected an estimated fifty cubic miles of rhyolitic material. With such a mass removed, the volcano collapsed to form a giant crater, also known as a caldera. The caldera floor was subsequently domed upward, and cinder cones exploded in a ring around it. The result today is the Valles Caldera, a circular basin eighteen miles in diameter.

Nature in Action

East of Santa Fe rise the tree-clad, snow-crowned Sangre de Cristo Mountains, a relatively slender but complex range extending north for 140 miles to Salida, Colorado. In both the Sangre de Cristos and San Juans, mobile masses of boulders and debris, known as rock glaciers and rock streams, illustrate an unusual form of erosional disintegration. These are actually slow-moving landslides which, when seen from the air, give the impression of mountains falling apart. On the ground they sometimes change the landscape, as the Slumgullion mudflow did in the northern San Juans when it blocked a branch of the Gunnison River and backed up Lake San Cristobal.

Very often western geologic features display interesting patterns. East of the Sangre de Cristos, not far from Trinidad, Colorado, is one of the few places in the world where radial dikes occur in large numbers. These dikes, actually ancient fissures filled with lava, are of a firmer texture than that of the rock into which the lava penetrated. Erosion has removed the softer surrounding rock more rapidly than the lava, which is left in walls.

Dike walls are common in volcanic regions, but the Spanish Peaks, one of which reaches 13,623 feet in altitude, have some five hundred of them radiating in all directions from their base. The dikes vary in width from one to more than a hundred feet, and in length up to twenty-five miles. Some stand exposed as walls a hundred feet in height; others are softer than adjacent rocks and thus have eroded into trenches. Several intersect at random, resembling junctions of the Great Wall of China.

Other interesting patterns may be seen near Montrose, Colorado. For verticality, few places exceed the 2700-foot depths of the Black Canyon of the Gunnison River. A few rivers of the Rockies have cut deep chasms into resistant rocks—the Colorado at Glenwood Canyon, the South Platte in the Front Range, the Arkansas at Royal Gorge—but none has produced a canyon as profound and sheer-walled as the Gunnison. Its mottled, striped, "painted," ribbed, and rugged sides show a remarkable complexity, yet also a subtle unity of design.

The Gunnison Uplift first appeared during the Laramide Revolution, and was later cut in cross-section by the Gunnison River. This opened to view rocks that radiometric analyses have dated as older than one and a quarter billion years. On viewing these rocks from the rim of Black Canyon, one marvels at the contorted veins of light-colored rock that crisscross the canyon walls. Dikes outcrop in bold relief or in nearly vertical groups. Zones of joints contain innumerable individual fractures, such as those seen from Cross Fissures View. The canyon is, in effect, a capsule summary of Laramide events, showing the sequence of upheaval and cracking, dislocating, folding, and intrusion that went into making of the Rocky Mountains.

Elsewhere, erosion is producing other new topographic features, and the Rockies, they say, have everything mountains should have—including deserts. In the San Luis Valley, in south-central Colorado, lies an accumulation of sand dunes covering an area of 150 square miles. Strong winds from the southwest pick up sediments from old abandoned oxbow curves of the Rio Grande and carry them toward the northeast, where they accumulate in fixed and active dunes as much as seven hundred feet high.

These sands have shifted for as long as man has known them, but their general location remains about the same. Normally the winds sweep upward and funnel through Mosca, Medano, and Music passes, and the dunes move toward the mountains at an average rate of three feet per week. But occasionally in winter the winds reverse themselves, and then the dunes move in the opposite direction at a speed of seven feet per day. In most places the Great Sand Dunes are barren. Only a few patches of grass, legumes and sunflowers are able to hold on and stabilize themselves in hollows among the dunes.

The Florissant Fossil Beds

Rare are the places on earth where man finds so remarkable a collection of evidence relating to life in the past that it seems as though he were looking through the porthole of a time machine. In the Florissant Lake Beds, thirty-five miles west of Colorado Springs, a spectacular "window" has been opened for viewing a cataclysmic episode in Oligocene time. Within these deposits lies an entire community of animals, a primitive ecosystem where life was suddenly stopped, trapped, buried, and solidified.

The Florissant beds are remnants of a lake that nestled in the crystalline Pikes Peak granite following the Laramide Revolution. This lake measured about eight miles long; how many others there were like it in this part of the ancestral Rockies is a detail vanished with time. That the shore communities were quiet and stable is suggested by fossilized standing stumps of

Rocky Mountain bighorns generally occupy themselves by feeding on grasses and sedges (right). But at mating time the autumn woods are filled with battle sounds as males assemble harems and fight to maintain them (right above). (John Crawford; William Bacon III)

Sequoia trees resembling the coast redwoods of California. No community could be more enduring. About thirty of these ancient Sequoia stumps remained when man arrived, the largest measurements being a height of nineteen feet and a diameter of thirteen feet. Vandals and fossil collectors soon tore them down, which is a special pity because their standing position showed they had been buried alive, fossilized while still rooted. If there was ever a true petrified forest, it is this, more so than that in Arizona, which is an assemblage of logs flood-borne from elsewhere and petrified in scattered concentrations.

Sudden burial and fossilization of trees so huge could mean but one thing—sudden catastrophe. And the paper-thin layers of volcanic ash that covered the trees suggests a Pompeii-style eruption that stopped the landscape in mid-growth. The extraordinary fauna in the thin white shales gives evidence of a luxuriant vegetative response to the mild, moist climate of Oligocene time. These deposits have yielded sixty thousand fossils of more than a thousand species of plants and animals.

The flora was principally that of a temperate upland—conifers and deciduous hardwoods. Leaves swept off the trees and sealed by ash against decay came from walnut, willow, oak, elm, maple, beech, alder, cottonwood, rose, hawthorn, serviceberry, holly, mesquite, catclaw, hackberry, and more than a hundred other species. Most mammals and birds may have fled at the first eruptions, but the remains of an oreodont, an opossum, a primitive horse, and some birds were found in the beds. Mollusks and freshwater fish were also discovered.

But the chief value of the bed is that it has supplied more finely preserved fossil plants and insects, rarely preserved because they are so fragile, than any other locality in the world. The beetle family, Coleoptera, was most abundantly represented, with approximately four hundred species, including scarabs, buprestids, and weevils. More than 230 species of the Hymenoptera (wasps and ants) were found; 140 Heteroptera (bugs); 80 Homoptera (aphids, cicadas); 60 Diptera (flies); 24 Orthoptera (locusts); and assorted mayflies, dobsonflies, and dragonflies. Nearly all the fossil butterflies of the New World have come from these lake beds. Of unusual interest was the discovery of four species of tsetse fly. Spiders were common, with at least thirty species uncovered.

Journey into Ice

Nearly everywhere in the West, the clear air magnifies and the peaks are farther away than they seem. Zebulon Pike discovered this in 1806 when he first saw the mountain that was to bear his name and tried to reach it in a day. "Marched early, with an expectation of ascending the mountain," he wrote in his journal, "but was only able to encamp at its base, after passing over many small hills covered with cedars and pitch pines."

Today Pikes Peak, which at 14,110 feet is twenty-eighth in altitude among the mountains of Colorado, has been scarred by road and railroad, but from its summit, or from any other summit in the Front Range, the gray mountain crags and white snow patches pre-

sent a dazzling sight. You may well feel that you are in the Alps, or the Cook Range of New Zealand, or the Chilean Andes. The sculptured forms are evidence of a familiar process: snow accumulates, drifts, freezes, collects into glacial masses and starts down the side of the mountain, tears rocks from the cliffs and embeds them in ice. Plucking, chattering, scratching, cutting and undercutting, grinding and polishing, the glacier utilizes embedded rocks as tools to scrape out a U-shaped valley. At lower and warmer levels, the ice front melts, depositing its boulder cargo in ridges known as moraines. From Longs Peak, one sees in Chasm Valley an elongated swale or depression that looks as though it were a bobsled run constructed for some race of giants.

Obviously the summits have survived prolonged assault by glaciers. Their very sharpness results from a gouging out of the ice beneath the crests to form Matterhorn-like peaks. Bowl-shaped amphitheaters, known as cirques, contain small lakes or ponds called tarns. In the valleys, morainal ridges lie clothed with dense forests, but their outline is unmistakable.

And yet, neither subzero temperatures of winter nor the crushing accumulation of snow and ice can prevent the burst of life on these mountains each year. Even before the bulk of snow has melted, alpine tundra vegetation has sprung into new life and graced the peaks with beds of brilliant color. Of course, the tundra zone is a limiting one, remindful of the salient fact about cordilleran vegetation: altitude and attendant climates make the difference. Tundra ecosystems thrive as far south as the Southern Rocky Mountains because summit climates are comparable to Arctic climates. Vertically down the mountains, just as horizontally south of the Arctic Circle, one enters and crosses zones of boreal forests, then mid-latitude forests, then semi-arid subtropical "pygmy" forests. Each association of plants and animals depends not alone on elevation but on exposure, soil, moisture and so on. Many mammals of lower slopes, for example, will migrate upslope in summer. The rock wren is seen at low elevations as well as on summits.

Nevertheless, it is obvious that the lower elevations belong to grasslands, pinyon and juniper; next above, the foothills are under command of the ponderosa pine; farther upslope the Douglas fir is dominant; approaching the limit of trees there is mostly Engelmann spruce and alpine fir *(Abies lasiocarpa)*; at the tree line the limber pine *(Pinus flexilis)* holds sway; and above the tree line the fields are given to hardy herbs and sedges.

As in the northern tundra, these high peaks possess a considerable population of mammals, most of which are seldom, if ever, seen by man, and whose activities remain to a large degree obscure. Streams, ponds, meadows, rocky cliffs, loose boulders, talus slopes, and dry patches of vegetation constitute the varied habitats.

Rocky Mountain Bighorn

Nearly all of these habitats are occupied at one time or another by the bighorn *(Ovis canadensis)*, whose skillful hoofwork in this dangerous domain is astonishing. Visitors who expect all sheep to graze in peace on level grasslands will be surprised, for this stout brownish-gray species—clad in hair, not wool—dashes or leaps with sureness of hoof across rugged slopes that seem too steep and too sheer to negotiate. Bighorn hooves have no hooks or gripper cleats and certainly are no more equipped with suction cups than those of other members of the cattle family—bison, musk oxen, and mountain goats. They do have traction, however, as a result of a pad on the underside of each hoof, and their feet are constructed to fit firmly to an uneven surface. They also have an excellent sense of balance, an almost unerring control, and a seemingly flagrant disregard of the consequences of one misstep. Not that they can't or don't fall; with the melee of mating, particularly, anything can happen. Obviously they are more concerned with enemies, which can lie in wait or creep up silently. These enemies include mountain lions, bobcats, coyotes and men.

A day in the life of the bighorn ordinarily revolves around the simple routine of eating grass, herbs or the tender leaves of trees and shrubs, chewing cud, and resting. In autumn, harmony disappears and the sounds of mating battles rend the air. Rams clash head-on in what seems a determined effort to smash an adversary off the mountain. It is at this time that we realize why the horns are so ruggedly constructed and the rams so sturdily built. Starting at twenty feet or so the males charge each other with all their might. The enormous impact of each collison does not seem to induce any permanent concussion or broken necks, though it does bring on a temporary dizziness. Fractured skulls are possible, though, and during the rutting season various wounds may be inflicted, even to the point of death.

A single lamb per ewe, rarely twins, is the customary result of all this furor. The mothers little fear that the lambs will fall from their precarious perches; what they may guard against more is the sudden strike of a golden eagle. But they are good mothers, and that counts more than ever now that the bighorn's natural range has been restricted by the gradual encroachment of man. In reserves such as Rocky Mountain National Park, bighorns can occasionally be seen and photographed by visitors, and in those places they may be able to survive the pressures against them.

Life on the Summits

Bighorns move up in summer to graze on grass and sedge of the tundra. So do elk. In these upper domains an abundance of mice and pocket gophers, as well as other small mammals, means food for coyotes and red foxes. The herbs support a population of invertebrates, such as leafhoppers *(Dikraneura)*, grasshoppers *(Melanoplus)*, beetles, bees, and flies. These bring the mountain bluebird and other insectivorous birds to what is a veritable feast. The white-tailed ptarmigan, American pipit, and brown-capped rosy finch are regular breeding species. Pine grosbeaks and white-crowned sparrows nest commonly, and on larger alpine meadows the horned lark may be seen.

In the mountain ecosystems of the West, each summit, each slope, each valley has its own specific complexity, produced under natural laws of succession and climax. The quaking aspen *(Populus tremuloides)* pioneers in fire-opened or landslide-opened tracts where it shelters the growth of conifers and in time gives up to them. Aspens group their slender trunks in groves, or clones, spreading underground by roots far more than by seed. Conifer colors are drab, but white-barked aspens light the gloom and their leaves radiate a fresh yellow-green. Conifers keep their leaves but the aspens, in such places as the highway between Ouray and Silverton, Colorado, and the Maroon Bells, present a remarkable autumn display. The yellow leaf, as close to golden coins as nature produces, stands out against the shadows of the conifers, and at times one notices leaves of a rare reddish color, as around Bear Lake, in Rocky Mountain National Park.

The aspen community also shelters chains of life and death, just as do the desert communities, the montane forests, or alpine tundra. Victor Shelford, the ecologist, points out that leafhoppers are the most conspicuous animals in aspen forests, and that they serve in turn as food for birds. Wildflowers grow in profusion. Alpine meadows are colored by blue and yellow forget-me-not *(Eritrichium elongatum)* and lavender sky pilot *(Polemonium viscosum)*. Below the limit of trees one finds hundreds of species, such as the blue penstemon *(Penstemon confertus)*, a member of the snapdragon family; whole fields and slopes of pasqueflower *(Anemone patens)*; Indian paintbrush, spring beauty, buttercup, clematis, evening primrose, and wild rose.

Of all the rest, one etches itself in memory as a flash of pale blue in sheltered aspen groves, or in dark ravines. Its flowers bear the colors of the deep blue sky and snowy, glaciated peaks. Delicate but enduring, the blue columbine *(Aquilegia caerulea)*, state flower of Colorado, seems to symbolize nature's carefully developed ecosystems—and their fragility as well.

7. Wilderness of Wonders: The Middle Rockies

The continual roaring of the springs... for some time prevented my going to sleep... and filled my slumbers with visions of waterspouts, cataracts, fountains, jets d'eau of immense dimensions, etc.

Warren A. Ferris,
in *Life in the Rocky Mountains, 1830–35*

When John C. Frémont, who surveyed a great deal of the Far West in the 1840's, rode up the North Platte and Sweetwater rivers, he crossed the Continental Divide without much trouble. It was one of the few places where he could. For in southern Wyoming the great mass of the Southern Rocky Mountains comes to a sudden end, almost completely cut off from other mountain ranges by the Wyoming Basin. Only in the west, where the Uinta Mountains join the White River Plateau, do the Southern and Middle Rocky mountains meet. Even though the passes were comparatively easy to cross, the mountains on either side were in the cordilleran tradition, and not so easy to comprehend. "Around us, the whole scene had one main striking feature," wrote Frémont, "which was that of terrible convulsion."

On the north and east lie sedimentary beds pushed up from below by masses of Precambrian rocks so that they now stand on edge—the Wind River, Owl Creek, Bighorn, and Beartooth mountains. This carries the familiar pattern of Laramide mountain-making in a wide curve that swings toward the northwest and ends with volcanic outpourings of the Absaroka Mountains and Yellowstone Plateau. At the western edge of the province, high ranges have arisen as a result of faults or thrusts, principally the Wasatch and Teton ranges.

In several ways, the center of interest lies in Yellowstone National Park, the first national park in the world, a wild domain of 3472 square miles. Its natural phenomena remained unbelievable to those few explorers who reached it before the 1870's. It has an almost mysterious silence, not quite the same kind one finds in Appalachian, or Andean, or Asian forests. It may be broken by the muffled roar of exploding springs, the bugle call of an elk, or the trumpeting of a swan. And in it man is today confronted with some of the greatest challenges in his relations with nature.

The Coniferous Forest

Like a blanket of green pierced by snow-covered peaks, an almost continuous forest of cone-bearing trees extends along the Rocky Mountains and related cordilleran ranges from Alaska to the tropical forests of Mexico. In Alaska it is a forest primarily of white and black spruce, in British Columbia, Engelmann spruce and Douglas fir, and in Wyoming lodgepole pine *(Pinus contorta var. latifolia)*. Much depends, of course, on latitude, altitude, and exposure; in lower elevations the ponderosa pine becomes a dominant species. But Wyoming belongs to the lodgepole, and vice versa—it is the state tree.

It is easy to see that a smooth-barked tree sustaining a trunk diameter of six inches to a height of fifty feet would be prized as poles for construction of Indian lodges. In some places, individual trees are so closely spaced that a youthful grove of lodgepoles forms a perfect wall; the limbs of each tree interlock with the limbs of perhaps six others to form an effective barrier.

Thermal pools in Yellowstone National Park are colored by algal growths. In certain places microscopic plants thrive even in boiling water. (Bob Clemenz)

When growing densely, lodgepoles prune themselves so that only the upper fifth of the tree has branches. They also thin themselves, and dead snags fall as far as they can, which is seldom more than into the embrace of a neighboring tree. Not all individuals prune themselves so neatly or are clustered and upright, however; a lodgepole by itself grows much less erect and symmetric, for it has space in which to spread out and may be twisted and deformed by weather, landslides, and heavy snows. In crowded stands, the trees are slow-growing; alone or together, they are subject to destruction by fire and the ravages of rust, dwarf mistletoe, spruce budworm, pine bark beetles, pandora moths, and needle miners. Nevertheless, as a pioneering and aggressive species which rapidly establishes itself on burned areas, it covers about a million square miles in the West.

To walk in a lodgepole grove is to experience a softness of footpath and forest floor akin to that of the summits of the Appalachians. Combined with fallen needles are pollen cones, grass in matted patches, sedge, lichen, moss, and an assortment of wild flowers. Strawberries *(Fragaria bracteata)* hug the ground and brighten the shadows with their white petals set beneath a center of numerous yellow stamens. Throughout most of the summer brilliant clusters of purple lupine *(Lupinus sericeus)* may be seen in lodgepole stands as well as on adjacent flats of sagebrush. Very often beside the trail are clumps of harebell *(Campanula rotundifolia)*, pale purple flowers whose corollas have been fused into a bell-like structure that nods from the end of slender stems. Like a number of flower species they are able to grow in dry or moist environments, and thus may be expected in almost any part of the lodgepole forest. At higher elevations, low huckleberry *(Vaccinium scoparium)* is the most common understory shrub.

Honeysuckle, pipsissewa *(Chimaphila umbellata)*, gilia, Oregon grape—the mountain woodland has a number of interesting species. Yampa *(Perideridia gairdneri)* graces meadows and hillsides with its white umbel flowers, much as wild carrot or Queen Anne's lace does in the East. Its heritage in this family is a parsnip-flavored fleshy root, and the yampa has long been dug for food or trade by Indians, explorers, and outdoorsmen. These roots also add to the diet of bears, rodents, and other animals.

Understory plants supply the forage for small animals. Rabbits browse on huckleberry, ruffed grouse on dogwood, hummingbirds on gilia, insects on goldenrod, chipmunks on the fruits of honeysuckle, and beaver, muskrats and birds on sedges. Yet the interior of a lodgepole forest is less rich than its edge. Wildlife abounds in adjoining meadows, where most of the food is, and the animals are able to retreat into the woods when danger threatens.

Wild Animals of the Yellowstone

There can be little question that major interest attaches to the larger animals of the Middle Rocky Mountains. But we must be careful not to detach them from their surroundings. The fact that so many of them remain is due largely to their having been protected in wilderness areas, refuges, and national parks and forests for almost a century. Their ecosystem is dominated, for the present at least, by the lodgepole forest, not crowded out by Douglas fir or other species so aggressive elsewhere in the Rockies. In much of North America forests are far less pure than this, having suffered when men thrust them back as a menace, then cut them and exploited the products, then suddenly saw the forests as a valuable resource to be preserved. In much of western Wyoming, especially that part enclosed in Yellowstone National Park, the forest ecosystem has been fairly well cared for since it was discovered. Protected and uncut, this is a land in ecological repose, free of major man-caused disturbances. How to keep it that way is a national challenge.

If there is one great fact of life in the forest, it is that far more exists than meets the casual, or even the practiced, human eye. So simple a thing as a fallen log contains a well-developed biotic subcommunity that changes with the state of decomposition of the log. There may also be important but hidden benefits. To a fox or raccoon, the problem of shelter is relieved by the discovery of such a log, and perhaps the decomposed products in their finality act as chemical regulators helping to bind the ecosystem together.

But this land has far more than fallen logs. In relatively undisturbed portions of wilderness areas and parks complex natural processes still go on. The time that remains for man to study all parts of these processes, beset as they are by outside influences, may be a great deal less than he thinks. His ability to understand them may not be achieved before they change or disappear. To date, the most elementary and instructive lesson of this kind, the epic of the Yellowstone elk, has been a near disaster.

Though averaging 8000 feet above sea level, the Yellowstone Plateau and Absaroka Mountains are adjacent to still higher country—the Snowy, Gallatin, Teton, and other ranges. Annual precipitation is about twenty inches, and snow depths on the level can exceed six feet. In a severe winter, temperatures plunge to sixty below zero. Despite such extremes—or perhaps because of them, since temperature variations are known to stimulate both man and beast—the Yellowstone country supports a faunal abundance. Approximately five hundred black bears *(Ursus americanus)*, including those of brown and cinnamon colors, live in Yellowstone National Park, and it is these that are so reliably seen. Nature feeds them well, for when they emerge from their winter sleep they dig into burrows for mice, gophers, marmots or ground squirrels, take in ants and grasshoppers when available, or rely on grass, flowers, bulbs, berries and the bark of lodgepole pines. They are also—unfortunately, illegally, and perilously—fed by visitors, a practice that is also obviously quite unnecessary. In Yellowstone National Park the number of personal injuries and amount of

White spray sifts among crags and conifers as the Yellowstone River plunges into a gorge whose yellow, red and golden walls give the river its name. (Hans W. Silvester: Bavaria Verlag)

property damage due to bears each year is often more than in all other national parks combined. In a single year there may be more than sixty bear-inflicted injuries and thousands of dollars worth of property damage. Man, of course, is the intruder, and it is difficult sometimes for him to appreciate the bear's way of life. Almost any wild food is palatable to the omnivorous black bear, so individuals are rarely, if ever, as hungry as they seem. Actually, most of their fattening is done in the fall, and they become more or less dormant between October and April, although the cubs are born in January.

The grizzly bear *(Ursus horribilis)*, large, hump-shouldered, dish-faced, is much more reticent and lives ordinarily at higher elevations. Approximately 250 grizzlies live in the Yellowstone wilderness. Their reputation is based on prowess and size, and even though an exceptional individual may weigh nearly 1200 pounds, grizzlies are on the average smaller than the big brown bear of Alaska and the polar bear of the Arctic. Their diet is much like that of the black bear, and they hardly ever hunt for large animals, man included. But they can be dangerous if surprised, and can be provoked into attacking. Since the adults are not usually tree-climbers, they may be avoided by a climb of ten feet or more, though the chances of a man being approached aggressively by this bear are slight, and depend upon the time of year.

The moose of Yellowstone *(Alces alces shirasi)* are found in marshy meadows along the margins of lakes or streams, where aquatic plants make up the bulk of their diet. In winter many moose migrate to lower elevations while others keep to their ground—or snow, as the case may be—and feed on trees and shrubs, their long legs being as ideal for pushing through snow as for standing in water. The largest of North American cervids, that is, the deer, elk, and caribou family, moose may weigh over twelve hundred pounds, stand seven feet tall, and have an antler spread of five feet, especially in Alaska. Other forms are slightly smaller. For all this bulk, they are excellent swimmers, which

permits them to subsist on a wide variety of aquatic vegetation. Their bulk makes for danger, too, especially if the calves are threatened, in which case the mother makes up her mind to trample intruders into the volcanic soil. She is very well capable of doing it. The female usually bears a single offspring in her first year of motherhood, but thereafter she may be seen with twins and, much more rarely, triplets. The population in Yellowstone seems to maintain itself satisfactorily, and the moose's traditional predator, the wolf, appears to be coming back into the region.

Several herds of bison roam the Yellowstone country, preferring higher and more isolated parts of it in the summer. Like the cervids and bears, they have resisted domestication and do best when not controlled by man. They are formidable animals, with a shoulder height of seven feet and a weight of over 2000 pounds.

The plateau ecosystem is rich in other animals as well—about five hundred bighorn that live primarily on rocky peaks and alpine meadows during the summer, some beaver, abundant coyotes, and innumerable smaller creatures. Approximately 240 species of birds have been recorded in Yellowstone National Park. White pelicans nest on islands in Yellowstone Lake and consume an estimated 300,000 to 450,000 fish per year. They are quite distinct from brown pelicans, which are much darker in color and breed on the Pacific and other coasts. In flight, white pelicans are the epitome of grace, their black-tipped wings beating slowly and with perfect rhythm. "I know of no more magnificent sight in American bird life," wrote the distinguished ornithologist, Arthur Cleveland Bent, "than a large flock of white pelicans in flight." They nest in colonies of hundreds, formerly thousands, in many parts of western North America, laying their eggs on bare ground and relying on remoteness to insulate the eggs and young from enemies. Feeding time, always a spectacle, involves the regurgitation of what amounts to a fish soup into the pouch of the adult. The young bird goes after this greedily. Later a great deal of fish is gathered in the pouch and the growing little pelicans seem almost to climb all the way down their mothers' throats in order to pull out enough to satiate their giant appetites. After a while they are on their own, though unlike the brown pelican they do not dive for fish. They simply scoop up all they can from on or just below the surface.

Ospreys, mergansers, herons, kingfishers, cormorants, gulls and terns make an additional catch of fish, as do bear, mink, otter, fisher and other mammals. Man himself takes about 300,000 fish from the lake each year. Yet the lake is not depleted, park officials seeing to it that the total catch is kept at a safe level, which will protect the equilibrium of life in the lake.

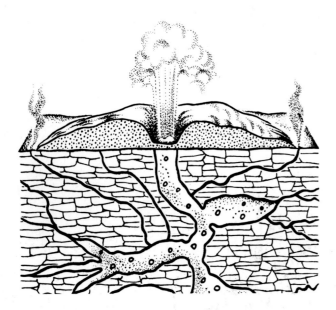

Left: A geyser's underground plumbing system.

Right: Clouds of steam rise from the siliceous cone of Castle Geyser of Yellowstone Park. Every ten hours or so, pressure within the conduit increases enough to hurl hot water as much as a hundred feet into the air. (Hans W. Silvester: Bavaria Verlag)

The Wyoming moose is smaller than its Alaskan relatives, but their habits and habitats are much alike. Moose relish pondweeds, sedges, willows and other plants. (Ed Park)

That all this fishing is harvested from waters where eggs are hatched naturally attests to the immense productivity of lakes and streams in a closed and relatively undisturbed ecosystem. One reason for this is that Yellowstone Lake is the largest and highest of its size. It covers approximately 136 square miles, has a shoreline of a hundred miles, and an average depth of 139 feet. Strangest of all, perhaps, is that nearly all the fish in the lake are of one species, the native cutthroat trout *(Salmo clarki lewisi)*. It is one of the few natural populations of native cutthroat trout that have not had to compete with introduced species. Aquatic biologists have identified fourteen major and twenty-six minor tributaries to the lake, which allows considerable space for spawning runs. However, rigorous physical conditions, such as low temperatures, influence the seasonal productivity of the lake and the biology of the fish. Yellowstone Lake is relatively poor in nutrients, but the depth of production is considerable and there are stable populations of small floating plants and animals, as well as bottom or-

ganisms, on which the cutthroats feed. According to the Bureau of Sport Fisheries and Wildlife, the cutthroat utilizes its available food rather efficiently, its principal diet being *Daphnia schoedleri*, a minute freshwater crustacean that swarms by the millions, and *Gammarus lacustris*, a small amphipod crustacean.

Other waters in the upper Yellowstone basin contain an abundance of aquatic insects, mollusks, crustaceans, and forage fishes, and therefore support an additional fish fauna, among which are the native grayling and whitefish, and the introduced rainbow, brown, lake, and brook trout.

This abundance underscores the dynamic vitality of natural communities properly managed. In the long run, the numbers of organisms in any environment depend not on food that is currently available but on the rate at which it is produced. All or most of the production factors, such as minerals that are used and reused within an ecosystem, still exist in the Yellowstone area. Elsewhere in the West, ecosystems have been impoverished through such actions as the removal of large numbers of trees, with the resultant loss of the minerals that would ordinarily be returned by the decomposition of logs. The quality of Yellowstone ecosystems and the abundance of organisms within them is due in no small part to retention of natural cover, fallen trees, decaying logs, boulders, and mineral soil.

From such a base spring invertebrates that are fed upon by fish that in turn sustain a great many mammals and birds. In this ubiquitous energy chain, nature has her own technique, well-tested by time, of recycling materials, of absorbing, transferring and dispersing energy according to natural laws.

Yet there is also in this land abundant evidence of a defiance of these laws and of things gone wrong. Changes that began with relatively simple acts by man have led to trouble, and have in some instances gone beyond control.

The Elk Problem

Yellowstone's problem with elk (the Indian name *wapiti* is more correct, but that term has still not been widely accepted) is people—too many of them, past and present. Of Yellowstone's three major elk herds, part of the northern used to leave the mountains in autumn and move down the Lamar and Yellowstone River drainages and out of the park to spend the winters; the Gallatin herd moved down the Gallatin River drainage; and the southern herd descended into Jackson Hole. The northern and southern herds each consisted of 15,000 to 30,000 individuals, sometimes more, and apparently the primeval relationships between animal and habitat were harmonious. To early settlers, however, it was intolerable that so much meat should be allowed to remain on the hoof; the elk is second in size only to the moose in the deer family and a good-sized bull can weigh over nine hundred pounds. With its giant rack of antlers it was easy enough to see and its predictable routes of migration, down in winter, up in spring, made it easy to find. The high-powered bugle call of the male, and sometimes even the female, audible for long distances, was something to home in on. Wolves and other predators trailed the herds, harvesting the sick and the lame, or sought out the females with their tender and savory young.

But the elk were rugged creatures. They had evolved in an ecosystem where predation normally and beneficially thinned the population, and where some of the lowest temperatures and deepest snows in the Rocky Mountains culled the herds even more. At mating time the bulls fought savagely; some wounded and killed one another; a few locked antlers, which almost certainly brought on death by starvation. Still, they did have abundant food in the high country every summer so that they could renew their strength. And they could always migrate to lower lands where trees and brush offered a little nourishment in winter.

Or could they? Man the conqueror had arrived and taken up a great deal of the lower land, apparently unaware that it already belonged to the elk. Or else he didn't care; the elk, like the wilderness, was something to be pushed back or eliminated. Despite increasing pressure, the southern herd fared satisfactorily, for it migrated in winter to the Teton Game Preserve, which men, on recognition of the plight of the elk, had established in 1905. But the northern herd had no such winter sanctuary and was therefore subjected to heavy and unrestricted hunting. In addition, men encroached upon the winter range and developed some of the lowland valleys for agriculture and livestock production. This cut off part of the elk migration route and deprived them of their winter home and winter food, which meant that the great beasts simply had to remain in Yellowstone National Park, or near it, all year long. Thanks also to killing by early pioneers, the wolf all but disappeared, and the population of mountain lions was depleted, which gave the elk nearly unchallenged freedom in the park.

With such encroachment outside and disruption of predation inside, elk in the park began to increase in population; by 1914 the northern herd alone reached an estimated 35,300. Whereas the distribution of the herd had in the past been over two feeding grounds, it was now restricted to one, and the brunt of the concentration was borne by the grasses, sedges, huckleberry, bearberry, wild rose, currant, sagebrush, willow and aspen inside the park.

Inevitably the vegetation and soils deteriorated, and the herd did, too, but not enough; 15,000 was still too many for Yellowstone to support in the winter. Accordingly, to prevent this single species from destroying the natural flora and thereby eliminating other animals, elk were herded, trapped, shipped, shot, and otherwise harvested to bring their numbers down to about 5000 animals, the carrying capacity of the range.

The destruction of aspen communities by the elk had already become severe. Long-range tests showed that in some places the change appeared to be permanent. Aspen along certain ponds and streams had been wiped out, and beaver as well, innocent victims of the disturbed ecosystem. "By 1962," says park biologist Bill Barmore, "the status of aspen was at a low point. Some groves had entirely disappeared, others were nearly gone, and most of those remaining were in very poor condition. Aspen reproduction was completely suppressed by overbrowsing, and the bark of older trees was scarred, roughened, and blackened as high as elk could forage. The only age classes present were decadent, overmature trees and young, browsed-off root sprouts. The demise of older trees was probably hastened by disease and insect infestations introduced through elk-damaged bark. A normal, healthy aspen stand could not be found anywhere on the winter range..."

The obvious solution today is to see if the original factors that maintained the harmony of the ecosystem can be restored. This is extremely difficult and time-consuming. If the wolf and mountain lion could be reestablished in their original populations, then man's removal of elk might be replaced by the natural controls of predators. But even if that were done, the original migratory range—the lowlands where the elk once wintered—remains invaded by man.

In the end, the policy most warmly received by the public is that of a minimal amount of wildlife management consistent with the restoration or preservation of pristine conditions. Completely restoring the original, or even determining exactly what it consisted of, is admittedly impossible, but both are goals to which the finest biologists and ecologists in the land have given their thought and study. In any case, the elk is not extinct; a total of about 10,000 animals in three herds remains. But the experience has been an illustrated, historic lesson in the interdependence of organisms and environment. Since man has changed that environment, perhaps to some degree artificial controls over wildlife will always be necessary.

The Trumpeter Swan

Eurasia has three species of swans, Australia one, South America one, and North America two: the whistler *(Olor columbianus)*, and the trumpeter *(O. buccinator)*. Trumpeter swans, like egrets, spoonbills, and other eastern species, are large water birds whose skins, quills, and down were once highly prized by market hunters, and whose meat was a delicate dietary variation in the lives of frontier settlers. They were far more accessible than other birds because they tended to cruise and nest inshore among the sheltering rushes. They were also vociferous, not only because of their wailing, low-pitched, trumpet-like note but because of noisy gatherings in autumn and winter. One could hardly miss their nests either, mounds of plant debris perhaps a half dozen feet across. No doubt also their brilliant white color, their size—they are the largest of North American waterfowl—their brilliance, flight, and down all added to their palatability in appealing to hunters. As a result, trumpeters, which once ranged from Alaska to the Gulf of Mexico, were persecuted and reduced to little more than seventy birds, at which time their extinction was regarded as inevitable. But they won the public concern. Several programs were started to prevent hunting and commercial use and to maintain reserves in which the birds could make a comeback.

Owing to the efforts of the United States Fish and Wildlife Service, primarily at the Red Rock Lakes National Wildlife Refuge, just west of Yellowstone National Park, the attempt has succeeded. The numbers of trumpeter swans have increased to approximately eight hundred in the western United States, with large numbers also in Canada and Alaska. The distribution of the birds is being expanded again, mainly by man; for some reason, trumpeters seem to have abandoned their own original migratory habits.

A Geothermal Wonderland

As rich in geologic phenomena as in fauna and flora, the Yellowstone Plateau is the greatest hotbed of geothermal activity in the world, a wilderness so curious and bizarre that its first explorers withheld the truth about it lest they be charged with lying.

The source of this energy is very likely molten magma at an undetermined depth beneath the crust. We see in cliffs and road cuts abundant evidence that a great deal more than steam has been disgorged from the earth in the distant past, for there are basalt and rhyolite flows, breccias, agglomerates, ash, and welded tuffs—all volcanic materials. So numerous were the eruptions and so heavy the showers of ash that today the remnants of twenty-seven forests of petrified trees are found on Specimen Ridge alone.

Now the time of incandescent avalanches seems gone, or perhaps it has only abated for a while, and the contact of underground water with heat from deep-seated magma chambers creates a pressure that hurls forth various ejecta: hot water, steam, mud, and sand. Hot aqueous solutions contain a great deal of mineral matter, some of which is deposited in and around the discharge vents, the rest being carried away by streams at the rate of nearly four hundred tons per day.

Ground water moves freely in this region, especially through porous glacial gravel deposits. New research suggests that the thermal features result from a rapid upflow of waters through joints and faults. The hot springs are certainly influenced by earthquakes. Estimates of the number of thermal features in the park run as high as 10,000, including 3000 hot springs, and such phenomena as mud pots, boiling pools, steaming cauldrons, and fumaroles. The largest and most beautiful hot spring is Grand Prismatic, in Midway Geyser Basin, which discharges 560 gallons of water per minute.

Geysers

But geysers are the most famous of Yellowstone's natural features. They exist in every imaginable size and shape, from tiny bubbles to massive steam explosions that send hot water three hundred feet into the air. Some discharge only small amounts of water, others as much as a million gallons in a single eruption. Their waters may be boiling hot and issue explosively with a deafening roar. Around the vent of many, a cone composed of geyserite, or siliceous sinter ($SiO_2 \cdot H_2O$), has been formed.

Some geysers are active continually, while a few erupt so far apart in time that man has not been able to record the interval. Some are studies in variables; for example, the most famous, Old Faithful, lifts its waters to heights that vary from 106 to 184 feet, and at intervals that range between thirty-two and ninety-six minutes, a frequency not even closely approached by any other major geyser. It sustains each eruption for a period of two to five minutes, during which it expels between 10,000 and 12,000 gallons of water. Within these variations, wide as they are, Old Faithful has never missed. Nor is it affected by weather. It is as faithful as when explorers named it in 1870—or when it was born, perhaps a century or two before that.

Other geysers are much less predictable and some are far more violent. Morning Geyser used to erupt every morning almost without warning and spout for nearly an hour; it exploded in no fewer than three hundred rapid bursts that sometimes threw out a fan of water sixty feet wide and a hundred and fifty feet high. It has since become dormant. Yet when one geyser sleeps another may wake, suggesting that subterranean interconnections are highly complex. An eruption in one may set off a chain reaction among others.

Amid this temperature and tumult is life, even within the throats of the geysers—relatively simple microhabitats where plants and animals live all year. At the margins of hot sulfur pools and in runoff channels grow sulfur bacteria in yellow strands. Algae occur in various colors that are correspondent to temperature ranges in the pools. Other life in these

Black bears live in nearly every montane forest of North America—and in certain lowlands as well. Their gentle demeanor masks a savage disposition. (Hans W. Silvester: Bavaria Verlag)

miniature worlds includes spiders, brine flies, mites, moss and grass.

Geologists of the United States Geological Survey estimate that there is enough heat stored in the upper six miles of the earth's crust beneath the United States to equal the heat content of nine hundred trillion tons of coal. Outside of Yellowstone National Park, the United States Department of the Interior has classified some eighty-seven million acres of known geothermal energy in five western states as either of "current potential value" or "prospectively valuable." The interest in geothermal resources arises, of course, from possible generation of electric power by releasing steam through drill holes. Such an operation, at The Geysers, in northern California, produces more than 56,000 kilowatts of power, and is said to be capable of producing over a million kilowatts.

Earthquake Belt

There is much else in this wilderness to make it unusual: "poison caves" which the early explorers said con-

tained volcanic gases deadly to mammals and birds; spring-deposited travertine blocks called hoodoos; cliffs of volcanic glass; and, of course, the yellow rock from which the region got its name, a disintegrating rhyolite colored by varying amounts of iron oxide.

The region also is part of an active seismic belt evidenced not only by numerous faults but by occasional earthquakes that do much more than shake the trees. Such a tremor was the Hebgen Lake earthquake of August 17, 1959, very likely one of a series of crustal adjustments responding to movements of magma below. F. V. Hayden, leader of one of the early western surveys, experienced shocks in 1871 and was informed by mountain men that these were common. "I have no doubt," he said, "that if this part of the country should ever be settled and careful observations made, it will be found that earthquake shocks are of very common occurrence."

Subsequent seismic history has proved him right. The Hebgen Lake earthquake, measuring 7.1 in magnitude (the San Francisco earthquake of 1906 measured 8.2), opened rifts, released landslides that created tornadic air blasts, shattered cliffs, set off lake oscillations, tore up trees, caused mudflows and massive slumping, damaged roads and buildings, and killed at least twenty-eight persons. It radically altered a majority of the hot springs along the Firehole River. Although some cooled down and others stopped, the overall effect was an increase in thermal energy and shorter intervals between eruptions. Old Faithful, however, was not affected significantly.

The careful observations that Hayden suggested have been under way for many years, most recently in a comprehensive cooperative program administered by the United States Geological Survey. These studies have included geologic mapping of surface and bedrock, and geophysical research involving gravity, resistivity, magnetism, seismic activity, and thermal systems.

The Grand Tetons

The name *Wyoming* comes from an Indian word that signifies large plains. But Wyoming is a state of mountain ranges, too, the noblest being the Grand Tetons, a solid and serrate range over thirty miles in length and reaching 13,766 feet in elevation. They are among the steepest and most rugged of American mountains, and like the Sierra Nevada were thrust up as a fault block. Unlike the Sierra, they contain little granite, which weathers characteristically into rounded forms. The Tetons are of more durable gneiss and pegmatite. These materials have become serrated by glaciation and stand apart as rugged sawtooth peaks. The topography is also shaped by joints, into which water flows, freezes, expands and contracts until the rock is cleaved and laid open to further attack by the elements.

Because they are steep and comparatively barren of minerals, the Tetons have been spared the scars of road construction. The most magnificent sections still remain largely undisturbed, and hundreds of trails invite the hiker to observe the signatures of ice and the centuries. Classics of glaciation, the Tetons have been engraved or decorated with familiar features: profiles sharpened by glacial sculpturing, cirques scoured out into giant amphitheaters, surfaces grooved and scratched by stones embedded in ice, planes polished almost to a glassy surface, plunging U-shaped canyons lost in shadows, shallow gulches, tarns, moraines, lakes in morainal basins, "Cyclopean stairways" now alive with cascades, hanging valleys, and lakes of a blue-green color—such as Leigh Lake—derived from rock flour suspended in the water.

As a tilted, uplifted fault block, the Teton Range has a comparatively gentle western slope; but the eastern escarpment, soaring above the down-faulted Jackson Hole, represents a profound topographic break. This sharp front is so steep (it rises one and a half miles over a horizontal distance of three miles) that only the eastern face of the Sierra Nevada and the western face of the Wasatch Range match it in the West. It thus represents a master challenge to men; more than four thousand climbers attempt the summits each year, and about three thousand succeed. The hobby is dangerous and strictly controlled by rangers, for it is they who must go to the rescue of climbers in trouble.

Along the streams the sound of a falling aspen or cottonwood signifies that beavers are at work. A willow suddenly begins to shake violently as if it were about to be uprooted; we do not see what is causing this but can well surmise that back in the shadows a moose is at lunch. Almost anywhere on the trails one sights mule deer, and if the hiker climbs high enough he will be able to investigate the habits of the bighorn. Along the edges of meadows or streams a pinpoint of white in the trees gives away the presence of a bald eagle *(Haliaeetus leucocephalus),* sitting at a nest or lookout point. These eagles belong to a coterie of predators and carrion eaters that control the populations of fish in streams and small mammals in meadows and open rocky slopes. Some naturalists regard them as cowards and thieves and observe that their carrion-eating propensities, including a penchant for dead fish, hardly fit them for a role as national emblem. Others feel that they are strong and handsome nonetheless, and despite some of their habits they have a distinguished bearing and noble features. Bald eagles used to occur by the thousands in many parts of North America but have been sharply reduced; if poisoning, shooting, and usurpation of their nesting grounds continues, they may well have to be replaced as a national bird. In Grand Teton National Park at any rate, the eagles are wild and free, safe from human intruders who would harm them.

Canyon and Mountain Flora

South of the Tetons, past an intermontane belt of broken and thrust-faulted ridges, we rise almost to 12,000 feet in the high country of the Wasatch and Bear River ranges of Utah. The wall-like western front of the Wasatch is a fault scarp cut by canyons. The region, culminating on the south in scenic Mount Nebo, is one of many lakes, clones of aspen, forests of lodgepole pine (the most common conifer in the Uinta Mountains to the southeast), spruce and alpine fir at the high elevations, pine, juniper, and Douglas fir lower down. As usual, the species accustomed to cooler habitats thrive on shaded north-facing slopes. A celebrated Rocky Mountain juniper *(Juniperus scopulorum)* over twenty-six feet in diameter is reputed to be 3200 years old.

Wildflower displays are especially handsome in spring. To a considerable degree it is a canyon flora. As you proceed up the deep defiles, beneath fossiliferous outcrops of Ordovician rock, you pass through cool and fragrant groves of box elder and bigtooth maple along the streams. *Clematis* clings to many of the trees, and often on the sheer face of the canyon cliffs a rock crevice provides sufficient anchorage for wild coralbells *(Heuchera rubescens).* Dock and miner's lettuce are frequently encountered but alas the yellow lady's-slipper *(Cypripedium parviflorum),* once quite common, is nearly extinct. Each spring the mountain meadows and slopes burst into wide patches of color: the red of paintbrush, the yellow of buckwheat, mustard, dog-tooth violet and common sunflower, the blue of camas lily and penstemon, the rose of shooting star, and the white of clover. One of our favorites is the low-growing filaree *(Erodium cicutarium),* a member of the geranium family, which in patches of a rich green foliage handsomely exhibits flowers of lilac-pink. Like the mountain mahogany and other plants the filaree bears sharp-pointed seeds with corkscrew tips that coil and uncoil according to available moisture and thus drive themselves into the ground.

A cow elk stays with her young for perhaps a year, then soon gives birth again. If not controlled by predators, herds of elk may multiply beyond the capacity of available forage to support them. (Hans W. Silvester: Bavaria Verlag)

In addition to carpets of flowers, the mountains of Utah possess an extraordinary share of showy individuals such as the nootka rose and Hooker evening primrose with blossoms three inches across, the *Anemone zephyra,* larkspur and monkshood in aspen groves, blanket flower *(Gaillardia aristata),* and mule ears *(Wyethia amplexicaulis)* with its golden-yellow heads four inches in diameter. As in so much of the West, the common mullein *(Verbascum thapsus)* lifts its yellow flowers almost head high. And you would think at first glance that patches of vivid red on shrubs beside a lake were scarlet blossoms, but close inspection reveals instead a cluster of fruit of the mountain ash, not an ash but a rose.

The Bobcat

Mule deer roam these uplands as do mountain lions and smaller predators. Coyotes are coming back, perhaps because they have learned to stay away from poison stations. One of the most interesting mammals of the region and indeed much of the West, is the bobcat *(Lynx rufus),* also called wildcat. This scrappy, crafty feline, different from the Canadian lynx in being smaller, more spotted and having the tail barred rather than black-tipped, can literally lick its weight in wildcats. Though it weighs only twenty to thirty pounds it can bring down prey, such as deer, ten times as heavy, and of course when cornered will fight an adversary of any size, man included.

It does not prefer to do so, however, and concentrates on rabbits, mice, marmots, squirrels, birds, snakes, lizards, and even insects. It thus lives where they do, in open brush country and rocky canyons. Contentious as the bobcat is, one would think it would clash repeatedly with coyotes and badgers that occupy the same domain and pursue the same food sources. But since they have evolved together over the millenniums, the ecosystem seems to hold them all harmoniously. They probably pay little attention to one another.

The bobcat's eyesight is excellent, day or night, and it has the stealth and patience to execute a perfect ambush. Probably most of all it is an opportunist, taking quick advantage of the good luck that comes its way.

Bobcats ramble through nearly all plant communities and life zones from below sea level to nearly tree line, and in most of North America. They even prowl into

towns. Sometimes they use abandoned ranch buildings to raise their litters of three or four kittens, but for the most part life begins in rocky dens. Their hearing is acute, possibly enhanced by tufts of hair on the ears. Daytime sees them holed up to rest, sprawled on a rock ledge or under a bush.

The bobcat does not see as man does the fine distinction between its natural food and the lambs and chickens that have encroached upon its traditional feeding grounds. All are fair game. It therefore harvests a few of these domestic creatures—sometimes a substantial number on a single ranch—even though it ordinarily does not like to get that close to man. Indeed, its consumption of rodents helps to balance the natural ecosystem, a matter of benefit to stockmen, ranchers, farmers and just about everybody.

Nor is there reliable evidence that bobcats are endangering populations of deer or quail—with which, of course, they have evolved. The accusation appears to be statistically false, as determined by cataloguing the stomach contents of hundreds of individuals. Bobcats go much more for ground-dwelling mammals; the quail they get are likely to be old or diseased and their predation may even improve the health of quail coveys.

Nevertheless, bobcats have had a price on their heads in many states for many years, although the bounty system is rapidly becoming obsolete. Thousands have been treed by dogs and trapped or shot by men. With all this hunting, professional or otherwise, it would seem that they ought to be near extinction. Happily, they are not, one reason being that they have almost no natural enemies. An animal so courageous, so skillful and clever as a fighter, so able to survive without man's protection and indeed with a lot of effective enmity, is a source of inspiration in itself.

Cisco and Spermophilus

From atop these mountains one may look down upon Bear Lake, half in Utah, half in Idaho, with its unusual light blue waters—and its mysterious fish. Each January the annual spawning run of the Bonneville cisco (*Prosopium gemmiferum*) takes place along the shores of this lake. Ciscos, flavorful members of the whitefish family, are about seven inches long. Ordinarily, they surface only during a short two weeks of spawning, when they come to shore in such numbers that a strong-armed fisherman can net his limit of fifty in less than five minutes. The rest of the year they apparently

Early explorers used to meet great herds of bison as they rode across the plains toward the Grand Teton Range of Wyoming. (Hans W. Silvester: Bavaria Verlag)

live far down in the two-hundred-foot-deep waters of the lake. Their life cycle and behavior are still imperfectly known.

Alas, "imperfect" describes man's knowledge of the habits of all too many animals, especially those of great importance to the ecosystem, but less often seen than deer, and of little interest commercially. Western universities are making efforts to remedy this lack, an outstanding example of which is the program initiated in 1964 by Utah State University on the Uinta ground squirrel (*Spermophilus armatus*). The studies are not complete, nor are the results known yet, but it is interesting to see what men are trying to find out and how their investigations are being conducted. In this case they wanted to determine whether an animal's behavior has any influence in the control of population density, and if so, how it operates. Working in an unconfined study area of twenty-two acres at about 8000 feet elevation in the Bear River Range, specialists gathered information on approximately seven hundred animals in a natural concentration. Movements, dispersal patterns, parasite infestation, population ecology, food habits, and habitat selection were closely observed.

Between April first, when the animals emerged from hibernation, and about September first, when they retired to their burrows, they were captured, weighed, dye-marked, and released. From seven scanning towers, researchers made daily records of identity, location, and behavior of animals in specific grid areas. Aggressive encounters were analyzed. Sequences of emergence from hibernation, controlled by weather and temperature, were studied in detail. Collar transmitters were used; electrocardiographs and other measurements were made; and physiologic functions, including stress, were analyzed.

With results of these studies recorded, the population was then reduced artificially by seventy-five percent and held at that level for several years. The same types of information were again collected. Finally the restraints were released and the population permitted to return to its natural level. Years will be required to correlate and analyze all the data, and compare them to corollary studies of predation by badgers, weasels, and hawks. Nevertheless such studies have enormous implications in wildlife management and ecological knowledge, and the point we make here is that something is being done about man's woeful lack of knowledge in this field. Ethology, the study of animal behavior, is an infant science. In the critical years ahead, with increasing clashes of man against beast in the West, the information obtained in programs such as that at Utah State is likely to be of utmost importance.

8. Secrets of the Basin and Range Province

Our road the next day was through a continued and dense field of artemisia, *which now entirely covered the country in such a luxuriant growth that it was difficult and laborious for a man on foot to force his way through.*

Lieutenant John Charles Frémont
in *A Report of the Exploring Expedition to Oregon and North California in the Years 1843–'44*

Before going on with the Northern Rocky Mountains, along with the mountains of Canada, we shall turn westward into the Basin and Range Province. We shall enter it from the Wasatch Mountains as did the pioneer geologist, G. K. Gilbert, who traveled in the region in 1871 and 1872. "Short, narrow ranges," he called the mountains, "inferior in altitude to the Sierra Nevada and Wasatch Mountains, which limit the series at the west and east. These ridges are distributed with tolerable regularity and parallelism throughout an extended area."

Regular they are. For a region so large, the Basin and Range Province has a surprising homogeneity of topography. Instead of a jumbled massif, or towering spires, or elongated ridges stretching into the distance, these short ranges—broken, folded, and contorted in almost every conceivable fashion—are generally isolated and parallel to one another. So long and persistently has erosion reduced them and spread out their contents in sheet floods and stream floods that they now lie literally buried in their own debris. The intermontane valleys have almost been filled, and what we see today are only the tops of the major mountain ranges.

The valleys might never have been filled with this debris had there been any other place for the sediment to go. But most of the streams of this region are short and temporary, entering landlocked lakes, sinking into the desert soil, or evaporating. Except for the Colorado, Rio Grande, Klamath and a few other rivers, there is no exterior drainage. When water flows, it transports sediments toward the nearest shallow depression and on arrival possesses little more than salts in solution, the silt and sand and gravel having been dropped along the way. Thus the lower slopes of the ranges have been submerged in alluvium, buried beneath fans that have spread out and coalesced. And in the lowest depressions, at water's end, lie broad deposits of salt precipitated from solution, the familiar desert playa.

Lieutenant John C. Frémont first used the term "Great Basin" when he explored the region in 1843–44. Gilbert extended this to "Basin Range System" and included the entire region, which is now considered to extend from Oregon to Mexico. Most of it lies in the lee of mountain ranges, notably the Sierra Nevada. These western peaks delay the eastward passage of moist air currents from the Pacific, raise them so that moisture is condensed and precipitated in the mountains, and send them on as dry air masses that make this province one of the most arid. In certain localities years have passed without rain; most places have less than five inches a year, and this may fall within a few hours or days. But aridity keeps the region what it is. If more rain fell, the basins might be filled and drainage from them would ultimately spill over into the sea. As it is, the region is dry yet marvelously vegetated, its very appearance denoting natural order. In Captain

Death Valley: after the rain there is a lake, and after the lake a layer of mud that cracks and curls and crumbles. Finally, under sun and wind, there will be only dust. (Bob Clemenz)

Dutton's words, the ranges appear like an army of caterpillars crawling northward out of Mexico. Among them, altogether, are approximately 141 closed basins.

One explanation for the great number of these ranges and basins lies amid the extensive flexing and warping of the earth that occurred contemporaneously with the arching and uplift of the Sierra Nevada. Much of the warping was severe enough to break the crustal rocks into fault mountains that show evidence of tilting and rotation. The large number of faults indicates that crustal adjustments have been occurring for millions of years. Major earthquakes still occur, as in Dixie Valley, Nevada, during 1954, when the vertical displacement was seven feet, and the depth along which the action took place was nearly ten miles.

Evidence also suggests that the whole region has been pulled apart, in somewhat the way that the peninsula of Baja California is presumed to have been pulled away from the Mexican mainland. It is interesting to note that vast "stretches" of the Basin and Range system are being just that—literally stretched apart. Total distention between the Wasatch and Sierra ranges is thought to be about thirty miles, of which the pulling apart must have required many millions of years. This theory is not yet fully developed, however, partly because so much of the faulted area is hidden by sediments. But the evidence suggests that parts of western North America have almost literally been coming apart at the seams.

Great Lakes of the West

Within the basins today there are more dry lakes than liquid ones. During Pleistocene time, when climates were generally cooler and moister and when there were more local mountain glaciers, the number of liquid lakes must have been very large. One authority estimates that of the 141 basins in this province, 119 show evidence of having been sites of lakes.

Fossil mammal remains, such as Miocene elephants, camels, bison, and horses, are found in deposits along the shores of former freshwater lakes. Some lakes apparently contained substantial numbers of fish, judging by relict fish populations today. As the lakes dried up, the species unable to withstand increasing salinity died out. Those adjacent to water sources seem to have thrived. In a spring called Devil's Hole, at Ash Meadows, Nevada, about three hundred individual pupfish (*Cyprinodon*) remain as the entire population of the species. Devil's Hole was protected by addition to Death Valley National Monument in 1952.

Some of the ancient lakes, or chains of lakes, were of very good size. Lake Lahontan, lying chiefly in northwestern Nevada, covered eight thousand square miles. The shoreline of Lake Russell lay 650 feet higher than that of its present-day remnant, Mono Lake, in California. Death Valley itself was long occupied by lakes, the last of which—Lake Manly—measured approximately ninety miles long, from six to eleven miles

A halt to the commercial plume trade saved the snowy egret (Leucophoyx thula), *which now thrives in the West and South. (Bill Ratcliffe)*

The familiar Canada goose flies north very early, often breeding and laying before other birds migrate. (U.S. Forest Service)

wide, and nearly six hundred feet deep. There were numerous lakes on the Mojave Desert, probably connected by streams and fed in part by glacial melt-waters from the neighboring Sierra Nevada. Even if they had an ancient outlet, an abundance of salt was left just the same, precipitated out of solution when the waters dried up. Lake Searles, for example, is now a playa of sixty square miles, much of it composed of evaporites, materials that have been deposited upon the evaporation of saline solutions.

The Salton Sea is not a part of this group of lakes, for it is believed to be a portion of the Gulf of California cut off by flows of sediment from the Colorado River between 1904 and 1907. Yet there is evidence of a much larger body of water, Lake Cahuilla, that once occupied the Salton Trough, covering a good portion of the valley between Palm Springs and the Mexican boundary.

But the largest of all Pleistocene lakes probably was the ancestor of Utah, Sevier, and Great Salt lakes. This prehistoric body of water covered an estimated twenty thousand square miles in what is now Utah, Nevada, and Idaho, and was thus as large as Lake Michigan. G.K. Gilbert's study of it is a classic in western geology; he named it Lake Bonneville, after Captain B.L.E. Bonneville, who saw Great Salt Lake in 1833 and whose account of it was subsequently published by Washington Irving. Gilbert wrote:

"The most conspicuous traces of Lake Bonneville are its shore-lines. At their greatest expanse the waters rose nearly one thousand feet above the present level of Great Salt Lake, and at this and numerous other stages, marked their lingerings by elaborate beaches and terraces. These are very conspicuously displayed on the slopes of the Wasatch range near Great Salt Lake, and on the rocky islands of the lake, and have attracted the attention of every observant traveler from the time of the explorations of Frémont and Beckwith. All the varied products of wave-work, as we know them on modern shores, are represented and beautifully preserved."

Salt Lake City, Ogden, Logan, Provo and other cities are built on these terraces. At one time the lake apparently had an outlet on the north, through Red Rock Pass, into the present Snake River drainage. With the retreat of the glaciers, Lake Bonneville evaporated and shrank to a twentieth its size, becoming the present Great Salt Lake. The water is now eight times saltier than sea water (up to twenty-eight percent) and hence so buoyant that a swimmer simply cannot sink; the experience is almost like swimming in syrup. Most of the lake lacks living organisms, even on the salt-encrusted shores. Yet there is life—halophilic bacteria and salt-resistant algae *(Dunaliella)* that sometimes proliferate to the point of turning portions of the lake green, orange, or red; brine shrimp *(Artemia salina)*, brine flies *(Ephydra)*, and pelicans, gulls, and other birds.

Wings over Bear River

At the mouths of streams flowing into Great Salt Lake there are marshes where the water is less saline and contains a greater variety of animal life. About

150,000 acres have so far been developed as refuges in the Great Salt Lake valley and an equal number are still undeveloped. In these live numerous species of water birds—ducks, swans, geese, and shorebirds—some of which in the early days were shot at the rate of nearly a thousand a day and sold on the commercial market for ninety cents a dozen.

On the delta of Bear River, largest stream in the Western Hemisphere that does not reach the ocean, is Bear River Migratory Bird Refuge, administered by the United States Bureau of Sport Fisheries and Wildlife. It is also one of the few remaining marshlands in the West where ducks and geese nest in great numbers and where fall concentrations of more than a million birds occur. About two hundred species of birds have been recorded on the Refuge. Sixty species nest there, and each year thirty thousand ducks and two thousand Canada geese are born and raised. The most common ducks are gadwalls *(Anas strepera)*, cinnamon teal *(A. cyanoptera)*, mallard *(A. platyrhynchos)*, redhead *(Aythya americana)*, and pintail *(Anas acuta)*, which is the most widely distributed duck in North America.

One may drive along dikes, built to retain fresh water, and observe large numbers of pelicans feeding in flocks. White-faced ibis nest in association with snowy egret and black-crowned night heron. Barn swallows are numerous, as are coots. Whistling swans spend the fall and part of the winter. The refuge also abounds in fish, including carp that reach thirty-five pounds in weight.

One problem at Bear River and elsewhere in the West is a food poisoning known as botulism. It is caused by a toxin formed from the growth of bacteria *(Clostridium botulinum)* in decaying organic matter. Ducks that consume the toxin develop paralysis of the neck muscles and a loosening of feathers. At the turn of the century ducks died by the hundreds of thousands from an outbreak of botulism, and today they are still prey to the disease, though antitoxins are available. Wildlife specialists go out in boats to remove dead birds and treat as many of the living as possible, and in this way they save at least a few directly and reduce the chance of contaminating others.

The Honkers

Call it what you will—honker, brant, cackler, yelper—the Canada goose *(Branta canadensis)* is with little doubt the commonest and best-known wild goose in North America. The familiar sight of a score or more of these birds floating on Bear River and grazing in open fields, or the familiar sound of their honking calls as they fly overhead in long V-strings, brings to

Above: A mother pelican feeds her offspring by regurgitation.
Left: White pelicans nesting near water have at times required protection from the waves stirred up by motorboats speeding too close to them. (Both by Michael Wotton)

mind the words of the great conservationist, Aldo Leopold: "One swallow does not make a summer, but one skein of geese, cleaving the murk of a March thaw, is the spring."

They come by the hundreds on swift and powerful wings, stopping now and then to avoid bad weather or wander in fields and eat, but always obedient to the ages-old compulsion of migration. This carries them home, to Bear River, the Northwest, Canada, the Arctic, wherever good ponds and marshes provide visibility, shelter and food. Though strong of wing they advance rather leisurely and being almost entirely vegetarian they spend much time on land clipping grasses and other plants as neatly as a mower.

Mating is quite a ritualistic process and it would be fascinating to know what all the neck weavings, feather rustlings, head dippings, and vocalizations mean, or at least how they evolved. Pairing of a male and female seems to endure for life, or until terminated by some disaster. Canada geese guard the nesting site with notable steadfastness and noisily drive off any intruder they do not want around. This especially includes those with a taste for goose eggs: crows, magpies, skunks and mink. As a consequence, alertness is the key to successful nesting, and the bird wants its nest high enough to permit an unobstructed view in all directions. Canada geese have good hearing and vision and are so shrewd that they have survived despite the great numbers taken by man. One example of their keen self-defense is the establishment of a sentinel able to distinguish between friend and enemy and who gives the alarm when danger comes too close.

At Bear River Refuge a large percentage of geese nest on the top of muskrat houses, but elsewhere this bird, adaptable in some measure to man and his works, will nest successfully on roofs, tubs, haystacks, wooden platforms, cliffs and in trees. The nest of sticks is lined with down, which helps to protect the eggs against heat as well as cold.

Within hours after the goslings see daylight they are ushered out of the nest, and across the ground, if any, between them and an open watery world which they were born to occupy. It is much safer out there, for no matter how many predators strike from above, the young have only to dive out of sight and swim underwater to safety, something they are well equipped to do almost from the first day of life. But there are other enemies in abundance, so life is seldom entirely secure.

When the young are about half grown the adults molt and thus lose their ability to fly, although they can still swim and dive to avoid predators. This annual molt, a full replacement of feathers, lasts about a month. Afterwards begins migration, the how and why of which are still imperfectly known, though some experiments seem to suggest that birds in migration use the sun and stars for guidance.

At Bear River and a host of other western wildlife refuges, the Canada goose finds protected wetlands

Overleaf: Cathedral Gorge, in eastern Nevada, consists of spires and pinnacles eroded in soft chalky clay.

that are so vital to its continued existence. Driving through in a car will reveal to us many of them, but the pursuit of this great goose has always been a matter of challenge; the ornithologist and photographer alike must apply themselves diligently to creep up on Canada geese. The ultimate assessment comes from Francis H. Kortright, author of *The Ducks, Geese, and Swans of North America.* He calls the Canada goose the grandest of all waterfowl and says: "Sagacity, wariness, strength, and fidelity are characteristics of the Canada goose which, collectively, are possessed in the same degree by no other bird."

Rich Ranges

Utah and Nevada are saturated with labels applied by man to nature's largesse: Mineral Mountains, Mineral Peak, Treasure Hill, Silverado Mountain, Eldorado Valley, Bonanza Hill, Mine Mountain, and other topographic reminders of the riches of the earth and man's impassioned thirst for them. If fur trappers helped to open the West, miners helped to unify it. During the 1848–1880 golden age of metallurgical discoveries, western miners moved on and on, from one find to another, spreading their techniques of extraction and their social habits, and opening the way for progressive technology. Mines and minerals not only supported industrial advances; they helped to determine the location of development of transportation systems and centers of distribution.

The search for pockets and lodes of silver and gold brought the first permanent settlers to much of the Far West at an earlier date than would have been the case if settlement had had to wait for agriculture. Some of the mineral discoveries were *bonanzas,* some were *borrascas,* but either way, they opened the era of the prospector with pick and pan and burro, and the introduction of human social order to otherwise uninhabited terrain.

A casual traveler along Route 50 may find himself compelled by the extraordinary colors and complex contortions of the mountains. To illustrate his report on this region, G. K. Gilbert drew a diagram of what he could see of one of the ranges and the structures were so astonishing that he felt that he must deny any exaggeration; that was the way it was. The formations look as though they had been tilted, folded, broken, beveled, and uplifted a number of times. The rocks themselves, or combinations of them, are in all likelihood the product of several periods of mountain building, and are further complicated by igneous intrusions and basalt flows. Rocks of yellow, orange, red, and brown occur in a crazy-quilt pattern resembling a subdued version of the Painted Desert.

Left above: Few predators are as crafty and skillful as coyotes, which have thrived in spite of intense persecution by men. (Ed Park) Far left: A checkered beetle (Cleridae) blends with a flower as it lies in wait for a passing insect. (Betty Randall) Left: The easy-to-recognize male redhead swims on a western pond. Redheads nest among rushes and cat-tails, and the female may lay more than a dozen eggs. (Joe Van Wormer)

But it is the mineral content that has most captured the minds and energies of men in the last hundred years.

Several miles southwest of Salt Lake City ghost towns crumble in the Oquirrh Range. There in the latter half of the nineteenth century, silver, lead, and zinc were king—and gold a delicate queen much sought after. Digging for copper began in the 1900's, and in Bingham Canyon may be found what Utah residents call the largest single mining project ever undertaken—the Bingham open-pit copper mine. The ore in this pit contains less than one percent copper, which requires highly efficient mass extraction if it is to prove profitable. Nearly two billion tons of ore and waste have been removed, and currently about sixteen thousand tons of refined copper are produced per month.

Directly south are the Tintic Mountains and Eureka, a center of silver mining between the 1870's and 1950's. Continuing past hot springs, disintegrated volcanoes, lava flows, and Antelope Springs with its thousands of Cambrian trilobites and other fossils, we cross range after range and valley after valley, most trending north and south, and a good many endowed with minerals.

One was named Treasure Hill, in the White Pine Mountain area of eastern Nevada. When Clarence King on his survey of the fortieth parallel visited it, one member of the party said that the deposit was probably the most remarkable occurrence of horn silver (silver chloride) on record. A newspaperman descending the mine shafts wrote that "the walls were of silver, the roof over our heads was silver, the very dust which filled our lungs and covered our boots and clothing with a gray coating was fine silver." Miners with pick, gad, and shovel dug up chunks of ore the size of a bucket and valued at $1500 each. There were fissure deposits near the surface, easy to dig out; quartz ledges with blue streaks indicating sulfurets of silver; deposits of gold and silver together; and "immense chambers" of silver-lead deposits in limestone. The ore assayed as high as $27,000 a ton, but, of course, was not everlasting. The White Pine rush has been referred to as probably the shortest and most intense in the history of the West.

Treasure Hill was a discovery of 1867. Before that had been Eureka, and before that the Reese River rush, and before that the Humboldt Mountains discoveries, and before them the Esmeralda. But the greatest in the basin country was the first of them all—the fabulous Comstock.

The Comstock Lode

Lavas, agglomerates, and tuffs overspread a great deal of western Nevada in Oligocene and Miocene time. According to a theory supported by substantial evidence, where igneous activity occurs there is often hot and highly mineralized water circulating among the rocks. This water may reach nearly six hundred degrees Fahrenheit and possess as much as thirty percent dissolved solids. The minerals probably originated in molten magma, were picked up by water and, if the theory is correct, carried through the rock until release of pressure and lowering of temperature caused them to precipitate, that is, to fall from suspension and be collected or concentrated in a richer quantity than before.

The waters frequently follow fracture and fissure systems as paths of least resistance and this may lead them to the surface. If these processes go on long enough, the minerals will be deposited in concentrations that depend on the porosity of the enclosing rock. How such substances as gold are carried in solution is not thoroughly understood, but the belief is that they are carried as ion complexes, meaning that they are associated with atoms or groups of atoms having an electrical charge.

In any case, fissures are filled and veins of minerals formed. Uplift follows. The rich rock slowly begins to disintegrate through erosion. Gold washes out and, being heavy, flows down streams to settle in pockets as placers (from the Spanish noun *placer* signifying a place near a river bank where gold dust is found). Silver, usually combined with other minerals, is not so freely released, and to find a vein of it was therefore a dream of hundreds of thousands of western pioneers.

Unfortunately the waters that flowed into fissures of the Comstock Lode deposited their mineral content unevenly, in what miners called ore chambers, shoots, and branches. But a lode may have immense potentialities, however complex it is. According to Nevada law of the 1880's, a lode was defined as "a continuous body of mineralized rock lying within any

Desert bighorns prefer the untamed wilderness in which their forebears evolved. Though well adapted to arid environments, they depend on water in springs. (Leonard Lee Rue III)

other well-defined boundaries of the earth's surface and under it." In the Comstock Lode the minerals were deposited on walls of fissures and in pockets for two and a half miles. For all its irregularity, it was worth working, and after the discovery of it in 1859 a massive emigration of miners took place from California, where the fever of '49 had begun to dissipate, to Nevada, where new (or renewed) mines and cities burst into prominence: Gold Hill, Virginia City, Washoe, Ophir, Crown Point and Belcher.

Henry Comstock had bestowed his name upon the area, and as many as seventeen thousand claims were staked, most of them worthless. Nevertheless, the first thirty-eight tons of ore taken over the snowy mountains on muleback to San Francisco netted ninety-one thousand dollars. Almost as much gold as silver lay in the Comstock Lode, but as the diggers went deeper the problems mounted. Air temperature increased about three degrees with every hundred feet descended, so that by the time the shafts reached three thousand feet life was virtually unbearable. Even worse, water as hot as 170 degrees was encountered. Then, with the development of dynamite and nitroglycerin, and the introduction of wire cable to haul up ores, mining problems eased—and the earth surrendered to man an enormous treasure. The total yield of the Comstock Lode between 1859 and 1882 was nearly three hundred million dollars. In addition, the metallurgical experience, the refined methods of shoring up subterranean passages, new knowledge of vein structure, and other deep-mining technology gathered along this single lode contributed tremendously to subsequent mining enterprises of the American West.

Gold and Silver

The prospectors had a maxim: "Gold is where I ain't!" But geologically, gold can occur in just about any mineral environment, from auriferous quartz to igneous intrusions of granitic origin, to veins, to placer deposits. Because of its specific gravity of 19.3 it sinks to the bottom among other sediments and on this principle can be separated by panning. Gold is found naturally in the form of crystals, plates, scales, grains (some big enough to be called nuggets), wire (filiform), network (reticulate), and branches (dendritic). Pyrite, chalcopyrite, and mica are often mistaken for gold, but they are not as heavy and lack other recognizable properties of gold.

In nearly every culture where it could be obtained gold has been valued for ornamental purposes to shore up man's vanity or as a medium of exchange or both. More than five hundred domestic producers supply gold in the United States, primarily in Alaska, Arizona, California, Nevada, South Dakota (the mile-deep Homestake Mine produces about 575,000 ounces a year), Utah, and Washington. Millions of ounces are still to be mined on land, and future technology may develop a means of extracting gold from sea water.

Notwithstanding the perennial debate on whether gold is essential to stabilize currencies, the search for gold goes on, but not quite as it always has. Man's techniques are rapidly becoming more sophisticated than they were in the days of prospectors with gold

Bristlecone pines are natural weather-recording stations: their growth rings indicate fluctuations of moisture over thousands of years. (Steve Crouch)

pans. Geochemists of the United States Geological Survey, for example, have developed a cyanide-atomic absorption method of prospecting that can measure concentrations of gold as little as ten parts per billion. With this technique they have located a mass of gold-bearing rock in the Jackson Hole area of Wyoming that may be as large as fifty cubic miles. The gold is in a sandstone and conglomerate, low-grade but workable under new mining and recovery methods.

Large but low-grade deposits also exist in the Cripple Creek district of Colorado, which produced about twenty-one million ounces of gold between 1891 and 1962. The new potential is largely in surface ore which can be readily mined through modern mass-production methods. A deposit near Carlin, Nevada,

discovered in 1962, contained an estimated $120 million in gold, and is considered to be the largest gold discovery of the past half century. Since 1792 the United States has produced more than 307 million ounces of gold. Production is much less then it used to be, but under a Heavy Metals Program, undertaken by the United States Department of the Interior, searches are being made in submerged river-channel deposits in the Bering Sea, conglomerates of the Snake River basin, in volcanic regions, and elsewhere.

California is the leading gold-producing state. The Yukon River basin in Alaska has been a principal placer-mining area, and at Fairbanks are both lode and placer deposits; on the Seward Peninsula lie beach deposits, and productive placers have been discovered in the drainage of the Copper and Kuskokwim rivers. Southwestern Montana gold has immortalized Last Chance Gulch and Alder Gulch. Additional gold localities lie on the headwaters of the Clark Fork of the Columbia River, the Boise Basin of Idaho, and the

By cunning and fecundity, coyotes have managed to hold their own in a hostile world. Their litters may vary from three to ten pups. (Ed Park)

Salmon, Clearwater, and Snake rivers. In Oregon gold occurs in streams that drain the Klamath, Blue, and Wallowa mountains.

Other sources are known in all of the western states, and for the weekend prospector who wishes to try his luck, gold is best sought in or near igneous rocks and along the streams that drain such areas. Chances are, however, that most places have already been tested and panned. The United States Geological Survey believes that the best chance for success in finding gold lies in further systematic study of known productive areas rather than in efforts to discover unknown deposits. Geochemists have developed precise and inexpensive analytical methods of discovery: one mobile chemical and spectrographic laboratory can, in a single summer, make ninety thousand mineralogical determinations.

Since silver occurs naturally in association with copper, lead, and zinc, it is extracted chiefly as a by-product of the mining of base metals. The United States produces about thirty-six million ounces of silver annually, most of it from Idaho, Utah, Arizona, Montana, and Colorado. But even though that is a seventh of world production, it is not enough to meet the demand, for silver is heavily used in rapidly advancing industries such as photography and electronics, and there are as yet no practical industrial substitutes for it. Since 1959, demand has been exceeding supply, compelling the abandonment of nonessential uses of silver. The United States has virtually abandoned silver as a monetary metal, and the next casualty may be silverware on the dinner table. A different solution, of course, is to intensify exploration for more deposits of silver. The federal government encourages domestic minerals exploration by making available loans that are repayable on a royalty basis. In recent years the Office of Minerals Exploration of the Geological Survey has launched silver searches in nearly all the western states. Assorted techniques are being used: infrared prospecting; tunneling along vein systems; crosscutting, drifting, and raising along silicified fracture zones; surface drilling; and underground diamond drilling. Detectors based on a neutron-activation principle are sensitive to as little as a tenth of an ounce of silver per ton of rock, and are capable of locating valuable mineral deposits well below the surface. However, if these devices fail to locate sufficient new ore bodies, the uses of silver may continue to diminish.

Sagebrush Country

There is something immensely appealing about the Basin and Range country—the broad valleys, the volcanic cones, the sand dunes, and thousands of square miles of gently inclined landscape adorned with sagebrush and creosote bush. After a while you get used to this environment and realize that the glare, the dryness, and the stillness are all natural and normal, an integral part of the land. It is a land so wide that it stretches the mind and imagination. It is possible to see a hundred miles or more across it, and the old-timers used to say that a man would get eyestrain looking so far.

Once stirred by the fragrance of the air and the freedom of the open flats, it is easy to comprehend a little of the adventurous spirit and outlook of the Pony Express riders and Overland Mail drivers who used to cross these passes and valleys. From western Utah, throughout most of Nevada, and in parts of California, Idaho, Wyoming, and Oregon, the basins are rich in animal and plant life. Much of the region is cool high desert, but a great deal of the vegetation endures bright sun and high temperature at times. Aridity, of course, is the rule, and prolonged drought always a possibility. Dew may be a greater factor than we think in supplying moisture to desert environments. The formation of dew depends on outgoing radiation and a surface temperature that is lower than the saturation temperature of the air with which it is in contact. Where radiation is strong, as in deserts, dew may form when the relative humidity is sixty percent. It is hard to say how much moisture dew ultimately provides because dew cannot be measured in the same way that ordinary precipitation is. Dew must be weighed, or a tract of ground must be weighed with and without dew and the difference computed. How much is available to roots, how effective dew is in slowing down evapotranspiration, in sum, how much dew benefits the flora directly, is not clearly known.

In any case, desert plants do not have to depend exclusively on dew. The real key to their survival is an ability to become dormant in times when water is unavailable. Geographic distribution of plants also depends upon the soils, which still hold much of their mineral content because of the limited drainage. Alkali on the wide white playas forms a thick saline crust where few or no plants grow. Throughout the Basin and Range Province the floral aspect is one of low-growing, gray-green shrubs, predominantly sagebrush (*Artemisia tridentata*), saltbush, or shadscale (*Atriplex confertifolia*), and greasewood (*Sarcobatus vermiculatus*).

Ironically, sagebrush itself, a member of the sunflower family and possibly the most abundant shrub in western North America, is not very tolerant of alkaline soil and therefore settles principally on alluvial fans and inclined slopes where the soil is porous and the drainage good. But saltbush, greasewood, and winter fat (*Eurotia lanata*), all members of the beet family, Chenopodiaceae, are tolerant of alkaline soils, on which they tend to replace sagebrush. Beneath the sagebrush grow two perennial bunch-grasses, the blue-bunch wheatgrass (*Triticum missouricum*), and sheep fescue

The desert crested lizard (Dipsosaurus dorsalis) *is usually associated with creosote bush but it also eats the flowers, buds and leaves of other plants. (Robert Leatherman)*

(*Festuca ovina*), although where overgrazing has been severe these have disappeared. We also find familiar Indian paintbrush, arrow-leaved balsamroot (*Balsamorhiza sagittata*), several species of lupines, locoweeds (*Astragalus*), phacelia, penstemon, and the sego lily (*Calochortus nuttallii*).

All this makes an ideal environment for animals that are seldom seen because of their burrowing habits: kangaroo rats (*Dipodomys*), mice, gophers, ground squirrels, cottontails or pygmy rabbits (*Sylvilagus idahoensis*) and badger. For these and the black-tailed jackrabbit (*Lepus californicus*), sagebrush means shelter. For the pronghorn, sagebrush means food. For birds, sagebrush means nesting sites, and three birds are especially associated with this community: the sage grouse (*Centrocercus urophasianus*), sage thrasher (*Oreoscoptes montanus*), and sage sparrow (*Amphispiza belli*).

Lack of water is a limiting factor, though to predatory animals the blood of the prey is a source of moisture, and to birds such as quail and phainopepla

127

Sediments eroded from the desert ranges fill the basins, which in most cases have no outlet.

the water in seeds helps to supplement other sources. However, drought, heat, and cold are a constant threat, and it is interesting to note the number of ways in which animals retire from weather extremes in this region. The spadefoot toad *(Scaphiopus hammondi)* digs into the mud and remains there until the rains come. Snakes may congregate in dens of up to a thousand during the winter, and the Nuttall's poorwill *(Phalaenoptilus nuttallii)* may go into hibernation, an act exceedingly rare among birds. The Mojave ground squirrel *(Spermophilus mohavensis)* not only hibernates but it estivates: in the middle of summer it retires underground, its body temperature falls, and it enters a state of lethargy that lasts through the hot, dry summer and autumn, and on through the winter.

Life on the Ranges

Above the basins on rocky hills grow desert tea plants *(Ephedra)*, and above 5500 feet on the higher ranges a pinyon-juniper woodland presides. The pinyon is of two kinds, the familiar two-leaved species *(Pinus edulis)* and the single-leaved *(P. monophylla)*. There are also scrub oak *(Quercus utahensis)*, and mountain mahogany *(Cercocarpus ledifolius)*, which is really a rose, not a true mahogany. West of Las Vegas, Nevada, a traveler rises above the regions where sagebrush and creosote bush dominate and into desert mountains. There he finds a community of juniper, Apache plume, yucca and Joshua tree, single-leaf ash, snakeweed, prickly poppy, cactus, century plant, blackbrush and cottonwood.

In this environment of cliffs, crags, and canyons live the largest mammals of the desert, the bighorns *(Ovis canadensis)*. That animals four feet high and weighing up to two hundred pounds can survive in some of the driest of all ecosystems is due to several evolutionary adaptations in the animal's behavior. Bighorns seem always to be on the move, usually in small bands, nibbling a bit here and there so that an individual plant is seldom overbrowsed. They can subsist on dormant vegetation of many kinds, and even though the moisture from food is scant, it allows these animals to extend their feeding range to considerable distances from waterholes. They need water about once a week; so their routes of travel include familiar springs and other sources, of which there are hundreds, even in Death Valley.

Bighorns are generally free of predators, but their distribution and survival have been influenced by overgrazing of cattle and burros on their range, and the diversion of water supplies to other uses. Man has violated the original ecosystem. But he has also established several national parks where bighorns are assiduously protected. Cattle are removed from these reserves, and where necessary the wild burros, descendants of the days of prospectors, are kept under control. In Death Valley National Monument there are 1500 burros as against an estimated 750 bighorns; yet the judgment of Monument officials is that the number of bighorns is increasing. In the Desert National Wildlife Range in southern Nevada the bighorn population has increased from three hundred to 1500 individuals, and in the Kofa Game Range in southwestern Arizona, established in 1939 to preserve a thousand square miles of bighorn habitat, there are about three hundred bighorns—also increasing. Thus the bighorns are not extinct, and the attention being given to their perpetuation is encouraging. Like the bison and bald eagle, they constitute an irreplaceable part of the natural heritage of North America.

Death Valley

One of the most interesting parts of the Basin and Range Province is a depression that sinks to 282 feet

Mono Lake, California is a remnant of ancient Lake Russell which, as it waned, cut thirty-eight shore-lines in the surrounding basin. (Don Worth)

below sea level, the lowest point in the Western Hemisphere. It seems strange to use the word "interest" in describing this valley; the early emigrant parties knew so much loss and misery in it that their name for it was Death Valley. Now upwards of 500,000 persons visit it every year. With much of the physical hardship of transportation absent, modern emigrants find that it is not only a valley of death, but of life as well.

Geologically, it is a graben, a down-faulted trough between the Panamint and Amargosa ranges. Unlike other parts of the Basin and Range country where such structures are hidden, this valley boldly exhibits such evidence of faulting as truncated ridges, and rock faces polished by friction when they moved against each other. This has all been so recent that erosion has not had time to erase it nor deposits to conceal it. Likewise, the strand or shore lines of old Lake Manly are still visible, and in the northern part of the valley, volcanic craters that exploded a thousand years ago have probably changed very little. Soluble salts leached from the mountains and carried to the basins during infrequent rains still remain. Salt and clay layers may be many thousands of feet deep, for the valley received

So voracious are great horned owls that they may exhaust the rodent supply around their nests and have to move every two or three years. (Ed Park)

a great deal of sediment as it subsided. On the surface of these salt deposits, solution structures take on unusual shapes as crystals are formed and dissolved. Some pools contain high concentrations of Epsom and Glauber's salts, and in days gone by the mining of borax ($Na_2B_4O_7 \cdot 10H_2O$, an ore of boron) was profitable even though the ore had to be hauled by twenty-mule teams to Mojave, 165 miles away.

Death Valley has every reason to appear lifeless. Not only is the soil in much of its 190-mile length forbidding to vegetation, the average rainfall is only 1.65 inches a year at Furnace Creek, and in some years not even a tenth of an inch falls. The average relative humidity in summer is ten percent. The hottest temperature, 134 degrees in 1913, is a record for the Western Hemisphere. That same year, the temperature dropped in the valley to a record low of fifteen degrees. Nevertheless, across pebble-strewn parts of the basin floor the desert holly *(Atriplex hymenelytra),* one of the salt-bushes, offers its rose-tinted white leaves to the sun, and creosote bush finds rootholds. Among the nearly one thousand species of plants that grow in it, half a dozen are unique to this valley, including the Death Valley sage *(Salvia funerea).* The scant supplies of water do not offer much problem. Death Valley plants either grow at springs or have managed to adapt themselves to conserve moisture and reduce its loss, or they enter a period of dormancy until the next rain arrives. With these and other adaptations, a considerable

The hardy grass-eating desert tortoise (Gopherus agassizi) *drinks deeply when water is available. During the heat of the day it rests in communal dens. (Robert Leatherman)*

amount of life, plant and animal, has little difficulty surviving, even when soil temperatures reach 190 degrees. Death Valley, in fact, is not as "cruel" to animals as it used to be to men ill prepared for it and poorly adapted for life in it.

Snails live among the rocks and fish in the waters. Even at Badwater, the lowest point in the valley, there is a pool of salty water that contains an aquatic plant, widgeongrass *(Ruppia),* larvae, young insects and, around the shore, pickleweed *(Allenrolfea occidentalis).* Two hundred and thirty species of birds have been recorded in Death Valley, as well as forty species of mammals, fifteen of snakes, and an undetermined, though large, number of species of insects. A good deal of the animal life is hard to find at midday, but when sundown approaches and the sand dunes turn to a gold as rich in color as any in the Comstock Lode, the observant eye is rewarded. The silence of the valley becomes uneasy. The song of the Gambel's quail is heard. The breeze is touched by a breath of cool air from Telescope Peak or the Funeral Mountains, and creatures begin to move in the diminishing sunlight and then among the evening shadows—cottontails, jackrabbits, wood and kangaroo rats, ground squirrels, coyotes, kit foxes, bats, bobcats, lizards, snakes, spiders, beetles, flies, wasps, grasshoppers, and many others. So it is over much of the Great Basins with the fall of the sun; then valleys of death become valleys of life.

9. Treasures of the High Sierra: John Muir's Range of Light

*The earth blinds you with its light. That
fair contrast we love in lower lands between
bright heavens and dark cool earth here
reverses itself with terrible energy.*

Clarence King
in *Mountaineering in the Sierra Nevada,* 1872

Writing more than half a century ago, John Muir said of the Sierra Nevada: "The Mountains are fountains of men as well as of rivers, of glaciers, of fertile soil.... Of all the upness accessible to mortals, there is no upness comparable to the mountains." Few other mountain ranges have such a combination of extraordinary scenic beauty, animal, plant, and mineral resources, and complex geologic and glacial history. In it are some of the oldest and largest trees in the world, the highest waterfall in North America, and a few of the sheerest and tallest cliffs anywhere.

As an uplifted fault block it resembles neighboring mountains of the Basin and Range Province, but it is higher, wider, and longer than any of them. It ranges from forty to eighty miles in width, extends four hundred miles from the Cascades on the north to the Tehachapi Mountains on the south; and reaches its highest point at 14,495 feet on Mount Whitney. Not only is it a formidable weather barrier, but it is also a barrier to rivers. In all of its four hundred miles, not one river crosses it in either direction.

The Uplifting of the Sierra Nevada

This is all a remarkable change from the Tertiary Sierra Nevada, which was neither as high nor as disruptive to moisture flow as the modern mountains are. Moisture from the sea was carried all the way to the Great Basin area in those days. There it nourished coniferous forests and supplied a drainage system that carried water back through the Sierra to the Pacific. The Sierra was clad in deciduous forests as it slowly arched and rose, and the quiet was disturbed only occasionally by the eruption and flow of rhyolitic lavas. In late Miocene, andesite lavas filled up certain valleys, deranged the natural drainage, and accumulated to as much as a thousand feet in thickness.

Uplift, repose, erosion. This sequence occurred several times as the Sierra was thrust higher into the currents of humid air that fed the Great Basin forests. Little by little the supply of moisture was reduced. Evidence indicates that the coniferous forests in the basin country changed to open savannas as the precipitation diminished. Deciduous forests on the Sierra summits grew thinner as the mountains were raised to nine thousand feet. The Owens Valley, adjacent to the Sierra on the east, subsided and sharpened the contrast in elevation between valley floor and mountain summit.

Earthquakes very likely jarred the range repeatedly, for the faulting that began in early Tertiary is believed to have continued more or less steadily to the present time. The Tahoe basin broke and subsided, later to be dammed by lavas and filled with Lake Tahoe The entire region also rose, thrusting the Sierra even higher, cutting off more moisture to the Great Basin, so that grassy savannas became sagebrush deserts.

All these changes took place before the Ice Age. With its high elevation and a source of moisture, the Sierra was ready for the accumulation and retention of

Undaunted by wind or ice, a Sierra juniper (Juniperus occidentalis) *may cling to the granite crags for a thousand years. (David Cavagnaro)*

snow. Ice caps developed, particularly between the Tahoe and Whitney areas, and glaciers flowed from them as far as sixty miles, scratching and shearing off the granite cliffs, plucking away millions of tons of sediment and boulders, polishing rock surfaces, and scouring out U-shaped valleys.

Under this attack, the Sierra Nevada took on its typical saw-toothed appearance along the summits and was distinctly modified on its lower slopes. When finally the Ice Age passed and the glaciers melted, they left enormous deposits of debris at the mouths of canyons or in the bottoms of valleys. Their shearing action left mountain streams abruptly terminated in hanging valleys so high that waters plunging from them became curtains of spray before reaching the valley floor.

Snow, Drought, and Fire

Today the Sierra Nevada is clothed in a complex forest that reflects its variations in climate and habitat. As is characteristic of the cordilleran forests of the Rocky Mountains there is a general zonation in which plant distribution corresponds more or less to altitude. The rigors of climate are not so pronounced in the oak grasslands of the western Sierra foothills although, of course, all the forests of the region are subject to certain common environmental limits, such as a dry summer. As a visitor rises in elevation he meets the first digger pines *(Pinus sabiniana)*, which introduce the coniferous dominance of higher slopes. At about four thousand feet the ponderosa pine becomes prominent, which in itself suggests the aridity of the Sierra, at least when compared to the fog and rain forests of western Washington and Oregon.

At successively higher levels grow ponderosa, Jeffrey and sugar pine, Douglas and red fir, broad flats of lodgepole pine, then mountain hemlock and finally patches of tundra vegetation. Each of these communities consists also of faunal elements whose distribution is more dependent on suitable food and shelter than upon weather. Some animal species, such as the porcupine, range from two thousand to nearly eleven thousand feet. Others, like the pine marten, are most common from the red fir community up to tree line. Still others, such as meadow mice, occupy specific localities. Since the last glacial period, the present interrelated communities have evolved, and complexly so, into several ecosystems—meadow, forest, wetlands, mountain slopes, and tundra.

Not one but three environmental factors exercise special limiting influences in this domain: flood, drought, and fire. The accumulation of snow in the high country is often extremely pronounced, and careful measurements of it are essential at high elevations in order to estimate runoff and predict floods. In the course of unusually warm periods, augmented by rain, the snow pack is released in quantities of meltwater greater than can be contained by runoff channels. The

At times there is a mood of sky above earth, of granite monoliths ascending to the clouds, of shadow and silence, that renders the Sierra Nevada foothills poetic and incomparable. (Don Worth)

result has been floods that do some damage in the mountains and become devastating to human life and property in the lowlands. With snow pack measurement and refined weather prediction, together with control reservoirs that can be partially emptied in advance to help absorb excessive runoff, the dangers are receding in areas occupied by man. The animals, however, have no flood-control projects. They need none.

Precipitation may end with the last of the winter snows, perhaps as early as February, and it may be November before another drop of moisture falls. Of course, summer rains do occur, and we have seen heavy September cloudbursts that filled the streams and waterfalls. But as a rule, the springs diminish with the last of the meltwater, the waterfalls dry up or are reduced to a fraction of their spring flow, and the grass turns brown and crisp for the summer.

It is also ready to burn. If a "dry" electrical storm moves across the Sierra it can set hundreds of fires which spring up in snags, duff, or patches of grass. These fires may spread far in a very short time, thanks to wind, the dryness and combustibility of the grass and pine needles, and the terrain. Fire may move rapidly upslope, or, making its way through falling limbs and rolling embers, it may extend to lower levels and into remote canyons.

The Sierra Forest

This faces us with a seeming anomaly: how can the forest have become so rich when there was so much fire? It has been the American tradition in forest management to suppress woods fires as soon as possible. Fire has long been considered an enemy of forest, and therefore it seemed logical that the fewer the fires, the better for the forest. Indeed, the operations of the two largest fire-fighting organizations in the United States—the United States Forest Service and the California State Forest Service—have been predicated upon a maximum speed. Now man is coming to realize, on this and other continents, that fire should be considered an ecological factor of the environment, just like soil, temperature, and moisture. Fire may not only be a friend of the forest, it may in some ways be essential.

Such a statement seems treasonous to the natural community, and doubly so in the Sierra Nevada, where the forest communities are so rich. Yet as the ecology of fire is better understood, we realize that the tree distribution has actually become what it is over millenniums of natural conflagration. The Sierra forest has apparently evolved in such a situation. Its trees can withstand repeated fires, or have even come to rely on fire for reproduction. The cones of lodgepole pine, for example, open after a fire and release their seeds, which then have optimum growing conditions in the ash-enriched soil. Lacking fire, the seeds are less able to break free and the seedlings are not as successful as, say, those of spruce and fir, which gradually take over. In the Yellowstone region of Wyoming, man's control of fire may well be contributing to the destruction of one type of forest and establishment of another, a result not intended. We have heard it said that the sugar pine *(Pinus lambertiana)* of the Sierra Nevada might likewise be crowded out some day for lack of

fire to open its cones and release its seeds, although other persons say that this is unlikely, because the cones open well in dry weather.

The Giant Sequoia

And could we, through misunderstanding, eradicate the giant Sequoia *(Sequoia gigantea)* after all the years it has been standing? The big trees have been growing on their Sierra ridges for perhaps three thousand years. They are neither the tallest nor oldest of living things, but the General Sherman Tree is the largest: base diameter thirty-six feet, height 272.4 feet, volume 50,010 cubic feet, and weight an estimated 625 tons. The known age of the Sequoias is exceeded by a bristlecone pine *(Pinus balfouriana)* at about ten thousand feet in the White Mountains, east of the Sierra Nevada; its age was established by tree-ring dating at more than 4600 years. In the Wheeler Peak area of Nevada an even more ancient bristlecone was found to be close to 4900 years old.

Only two species of Sequoia remain, one in the Sierra and one along the Pacific Coast. This number and range is much reduced from a prehistoric distribution that covered a great deal of the Northern Hemisphere. (Sequoias also grow in the Southern Hemisphere, but only where introduced by man.) Their longevity is probably due to the favorable habitat of which they are a part, and to the fact that they are virtually indestructible by storm, disease, and evidently fire.

Sequoias grow more rapidly than other evergreens and are resistant to direct attack by decay and insects. Fire has seared them repeatedly, burned large cavities, and hollowed out whole trunks, but the trees survive and heal themselves. The fibrous bark, up to four feet thick, insulates them from all but the hottest fires.

We may even go so far as to presume that fire is their key to survival: fires burn away less sturdy competitors that might otherwise crowd them out. The process seems simple and natural, but it takes on serious proportions—and portends serious consequences—where man has protected superlative groves of these trees in Kings Canyon, Sequoia, and Yosemite National parks, and thus interrupted the fire regimen. The National Park Service some years ago became concerned about human trampling of the root area at the base of the most popular trees and rerouted visitors in order to forestall possible damage to the great giants. But subsequent studies went beyond mere physical harm to this protected environment, and researchers collected evidence to suggest that, ironically, absence of fire was unfavorable to the reproduction and early growth of the Sequoias. Their experiments indicated that natural fires once cleared out undergrowth and enriched the

Right above: Water-loving Equisetum, *the common horsetail, lives in sandy soils or swamps and multiplies by spores produced on budding rootstocks. Right: The painted lady butterfly, with almost a worldwide distribution, is often found on thistles. (Both by Edward S. Ross) Far right: The scrub jay* (Aphelocoma coerulescens), *one of the West's five species of jays, inhabits scrub oak country. (Robert Leatherman)*

forest floor so that Sequoia seedlings could get a good start in favorable soil and ample sunlight. With no fire, shade-tolerant species, such as white fir and incense cedar, grew up instead. Accordingly, controlled burning experiments were commenced, and as time goes on, these are expected to show just how much fire the Sequoias need. In all likelihood there will continue to be suppression of wild and uncontrolled fires such as have devastated whole slopes almost within the shadows of the Sequoias. But the outlook is that on a lesser scale man will more and more be using fire in ways that nature did—as both a limiting and an expansion factor to sustain the life of the largest living things on earth.

Sierra Seasons

To anyone who lives in the Sierra Nevada, as we did in Yosemite Valley for two years, there are numerous unforgettable aspects of the progress of the seasons; they all compete for recollection. Summer in the wilderness remains the quietest time, when the sky is steadfastly blue month after month, the snowmelt gone, and the waterfalls drained or dripping. The most common summer bird is the junco *(Junco oreganus)*; the Sierra is alive with birds at all elevations: juncos, Steller jays, robins, whiteheaded woodpeckers *(Dendrocopus albolarvatus)*, and creeper *(Certhia familiaris)*, to name a few that are characteristic of the redwood groves.

Unless there is a sizeable storm, summer fades into autumn without much fanfare. In the high country, scattered aspen groves turn color, brightening a vale here and there. The golden-mantled ground squirrel *(Spermophilus lateralis)*, which was so familiar in campgrounds and along roadsides during the summer, is gone; so are other ground squirrels, settled in for hibernation. By September the dry "velvet" of mule deer antlers has been rubbed off and the summer coat is molting.

Down in the valleys the leaves of Pacific dogwood *(Cornus nuttallii)* turn into a cinnamon brown or golden orange as rich and brilliant as any color in nature. The western azalea *(Rhododendron occidentale)* puts forth a few final flowers that seem incongruous in their setting of reddish-brown autumn leaves. The pools along the streams exhibit none of the madness of tumbling spring floods; in the fall they are quiet and barely flowing, their surfaces bearing only an occasional yellow leaf. The waterfalls are dry, or nearly so, and the landscape seems to seek a repose.

Winter in the High Sierra

In many ways, winter is the most exciting season in the Sierra Nevada, for it is then that the great storms come. "I wait for a storm," Ansel Adams, the famous photographer, told us, "for then the mountains are in their most spectacular moods." Great masses of cloud sweep in from the west, envelop the granite domes and shroud the peaks in mist. The white clouds turn to black, and a cold wind bends the pines.

"When the storm began to sound," said John Muir

The steep and ragged stairsteps of the Sierra Nevada's east face glow in the light of a winter sun. (Ansel Adams)

of a winter's gale in December, 1874, "I lost no time in pushing out into the woods to enjoy it. For on such occasions Nature has always something rare to show us." Muir was a Scot who had traveled widely before making California his home, and his writings on long wanderings in the Sierra Nevada, such as *My First Summer in the Sierra, The Mountains of California,* and *The National Parks,* have become classics of their kind. Californians have named more natural features after him than after any other person. To Muir, the pines seemed "the best interpreters of the winds," but as he ran out into the winter's storm in 1874 he was astonished at the different ways in which the trees bent to the winds. He heard trees falling every two or three minutes, he said, because of the strength of the wind and the softness of a rain-soaked soil.

Muir wandered for hours in the gale, listening to what he called its "passionate music," and finally atop a ridge he scaled a Douglas fir that was a hundred feet high. He clung to the top of it for hours, swaying "like a bobolink on a reed," and wrote that he never before had enjoyed "so noble an exhilaration of motion."

Sierra winds can be deadly, and their force often has a direct influence on the forest. For if solar radiation, which we discussed in connection with the Colorado Plateau, is the primary factor in determining local climate, ventilation is next. The topography itself gives rise to differences in temperature and air pressure. These differences constitute an imbalance which in turn gives rise to rapidly moving air currents and an attempt by nature to equalize the pressure. The resultant "mountain winds" are well known, and if there is snow in the mountains, as there usually is in the Sierra, temperature differences are magnified and the effects intensified. These winds come roaring down the valleys with force enough to blow down trees and cause the death of human beings. In the Sierra they are called "Mono winds," but they are not limited to this range. A wind once came out of Cascade Canyon in the Teton Range, Wyoming, and uprooted thousands of trees.

In time the winds abate and the snow begins to fall. For hours it piles up in an atmosphere so still that every leafless oak branch carries a wall of powdered snow. The evergreens take on a hooded aspect, the meadows turn white, and the high country is literally buried.

Night comes and the flakes continue to fall. By dawn the clouds have disappeared and the early sun highlights great banners of snow swirling from the peaks. In the valleys and along meadow fringes trees are bent and nearly smothered, and quiet streams flow beneath masses of snow or among buried boulders. Only the sheerest cliffs lack a mantle of white. The giant Sequoias, their seedlings protected beneath the cover, are weighted by snow, and their massive orange trunks contrast with the white blanket and the evergreen needles. Icicles form on branches and on overhanging ledges. Trickling meltwater starts a journey which may be interrupted many times by freezing before it reaches the valleys or the sea.

Winter Life

While animal activity seems reduced, there is nonetheless life in the forest, and even in the frigid high country. Up in the red fir belt lives the Douglas squirrel *(Tamiasciurus douglasii),* a squirrel active most of the winter. For food it relies on seeds in fir, pine, and Sequoia cones. It has developed the habit of hiding away these seeds under the snow or among rocks and logs—a convenient reserve during times of scarcity or excessively harsh weather.

The snowshoe hare *(Lepus americanus),* sometimes called varying hare because it is brown in summer and white in winter, inhabits high elevations. Although more widely spread in the Arctic, it does occur southward along mountain summits of the Rockies, Cascades, and Sierra ranges.

Many species are well adapted to remaining in the mountains during severe winter conditions through the simple expedients of hibernating or storing food. Chipmunks gather fresh food rapidly, store or bury it, then draw on these reserves when fresh food is unavailable. As spring comes they dig into reserve supplies near the surface of the ground, leaving empty "pugholes." Their evolutionary development has enabled them to transfer and store large quantities of food in elastic cheek pouches. Other species, such as the western gray squirrel *(Sciurus griseus),* lack such pouches and have to eat what and when they can; which means that they must be active all year. Nevertheless, they still may bury acorns, and if such burial plots are forgotten, the seeds may sprout, thus making the squirrel a factor in plant distribution.

Early winter is mating season for mule deer. Mountain quail *(Oreortyx picta)* and red-shafted flickers *(Colaptes cafer)* move down to areas below the level of heavy snow. The chatter of the Steller jay may now and then be heard. The Clark nutcracker *(Nucifraga columbiana)* even begins to nest while snow remains on the ground. Mountain chickadees *(Parus gambeli)* are reliable winter residents, and Cassin's finches *(Carpodacus cassini)* live the year round in the upper forest and subalpine regions.

The Water Ouzel

Many birds besides these are year-round residents of the Sierra Nevada, but few are accorded as much respect as is the dipper, or water ouzel *(Cinclus mexicanus).* John Muir studied the bird intensively and wrote a thoughtful treatise on it. No canyon, he said, was too cold or lonely for this bird, provided there was falling water. For the ouzel is that rare bird with an ecological niche almost to itself: it wades at the edges of streams and, with the aid of its wings, swims and walks under water, hunting aquatic animals, especially mosquito larvae. Its habitat preference is for

Right above: Trees and rocks in the West are commonly patterned with lichens, a mutual-aid association of algae and fungi. They are highly resistant to heat, cold and drought. Right: Bell-like blossoms burst from protective sheaths on the snow plant, a member of the heath family. Far right: This lime-encrusted alga (Calliarthron setchellidae) *is reddish-purple while living, but bleaches when broken off and washed ashore. (All by Betty Randall)*

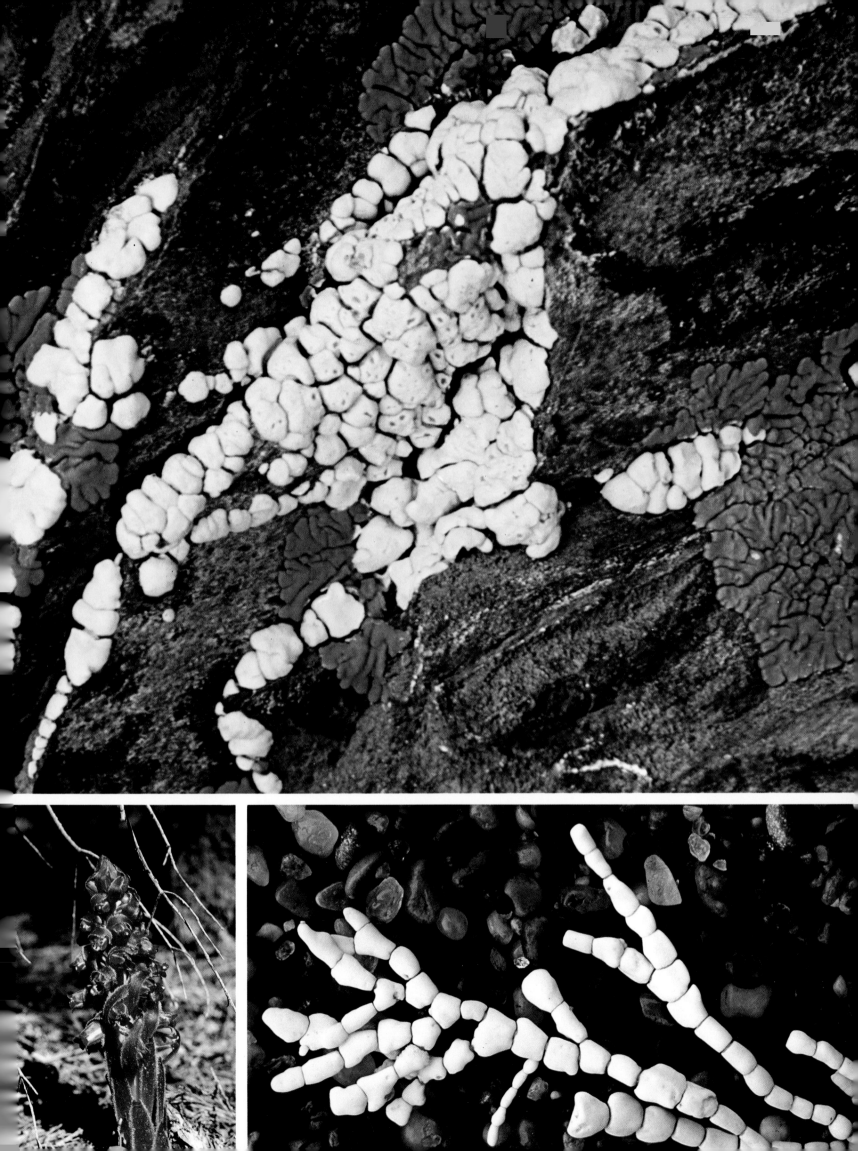

swift-flowing streams and waterfalls. This is not matched by special adaptations, for its feet are not webbed; it is endowed, however, with a dense covering of feathers that sheds water and retains body warmth.

"Among all the mountain birds," Muir wrote, "none has cheered me so much in my lonely wanderings." The ouzel is robin-sized, has a short, stubby tail, and characteristically bobs up and down when alighting on a rock. Muir was impressed with its song—a variable music almost like the sound of falling water—which went on year-round, good weather and bad. "No need of spring sunshine to thaw *his* song," Muir wrote, "for it never freezes."

Ouzels inhabit mountain streams in nearly all of western North America, from Alaska to Panama, and no other bird is so inseparably related to water. It is born in a mossy nest beside the stream and seldom if ever leaves the watery habitat.

The water shrew *(Sorex palustris),* weighing less than an ounce, occupies a similar ecological niche, in and near the rushing mountain streams, in which it swims in search of aquatic insects.

Melting Begins

In due course, the driest stream beds begin to carry waters that drip into them from the slowly, intermittently melting snow. The flow is not great, for winter temperatures usually hold the snow pack tightly to the mountain peaks. Yet the waterfalls begin to trickle, and in the midst of winter, even at night, they send out a spray that fills the air and turns to frozen particles. Some of these bits of congealed spray collect along the face of the cliff, especially at night, in sheets of snow and ice. When morning sun and heat strike these frost-covered cliffs, the slabs of ice crack and collapse, fall away from the rock, and plunge to the base of the cliff with a crash that sounds like the discharge of a howitzer. It is a familiar sound on Sierra mornings and sometimes lasts for hours, each sharp report echoing along the cliffs to distant canyons.

If low temperatures are sustained for a while, these slabs accumulate at the base of the cliff. More spray falls as the streams take on slight increases of water, and after a prolonged period of cold days and nights, when the frozen spray has fallen like snow from the lip of the falls, a "snow cone" develops. This is a pile of frozen white debris that may be over three hundred feet high and contain twenty-five million cubic feet of ice and snow.

During warmer periods, even in January, frogs are heard and insects are seen flying about. As daylight lengthens, more snow melts, so that by noon the waterfalls have picked up in volume and by midafternoon are cascading with nearly full force. Their roaring continues into the night, but diminishes with renewed freezing, and is nearly stilled by dawn.

On certain occasions when the falls are running and the air temperature drops substantially, the waters for some distance downstream from the falls may become choked with so-called frazil ice. This happens when aerated, swiftly moving water becomes so cold that spicules of ice form at its surface. When such crystals accumulate—and air and water temperatures remain

at low levels—a thick slush forms from bank to bank. If it continues to form, and to be swelled by snow in the arriving waters, the frazil ice will expand and pack into a dam that must be broken as an ice jam is, lest it impound waters that threaten to wash out bridges and sections of roads.

Another set of special conditions along the streams causes supercooled water droplets in the air to freeze upon contact with solid surfaces. The result of this is a fragile layer of rime which coats the rocks and clumps of dried grass with a lacework of ice crystals. Such conditions are not commonly seen, perhaps because they are fleeting or because they occur at night or in early morning hours. A more common phenomenon is the freezing of streamside pond and puddle surfaces, which produces geometric designs and patterns. These may be varied by the inclusion of a white granite boulder and several pine needles embedded in the ice—all part of the infinite variation of color and design in a Sierra Nevada winter.

Spring Comes to the Mountains

By March the great snow pack begins to melt in earnest, although deep snows can fall as late as May. The sun warms the steep slopes of ravines, and across these bursts a yellow color that is the most sweeping in the Sierra Nevada. California poppies *(Eschscholzia californica)* bloom by the millions, like golden shawls on the mountain shoulders. This flower has orange petals scarcely two inches wide, and sturdy stems about a foot high. They grow abundantly, along with the greening grass of the slopes, and with other blooming species such as tidy tips *(Layia platyglossa)* and baby blue-eyes *(Nemophila menziesii).*

While the poppies are maturing lower down, the western redbud *(Cercis occidentalis)* is bursting into bloom farther up, as if to announce the upward march of spring. Pacific dogwood *(Cornus nuttallii)* prepares to open its cream-colored bracts under the shade of larger trees. Among the rocks grow lupines of blue, pink, red, and yellow shades. The oaks bloom and leaf out, and distinctive groups of ferns unfold—ultimately at virtually all elevations.

There is likewise a bursting forth of new mammal life. In late winter bear cubs are born. March marks the appearance of mammalian young from wood rat litters in the lowlands to mountain lion kittens in the highlands. Mule deer antlers fall away and new ones begin to grow. In April marmots emerge from upland meadows and tundra. Badger and weasel young are born, and hibernators like the golden-mantled ground squirrel awake to the sun of subalpine meadows and rocky slopes.

Snow Plant

In early April, out of the brown needle layer beneath the ponderosa pines, breaks forth the star attraction of the Sierra Nevada—the snow plant *(Sarcodes sanguinea).* This unusual cluster of bell-shaped flowers rises to a maximum height of eighteen inches; the blooms extend out from a thick stem and between them hang furry bracts that give the cluster a bristling appearance. Nearly every part of the plant is an intense blood red, heightened into vivid scarlet when the sun's rays strike the translucent petals.

The snow plant got its name because it was sometimes seen to bloom at the edge of snow banks. It is a saprophyte, living on dead and decaying vegetation, and has been placed in the heath family because of its structural relation to azalea, rhododendron, and manzanita. The snow plant is unique, however; there are no other members of the genus. Although somewhat sparsely distributed, it is fairly widespread, occurring from Oregon south through the Sierra and east into Nevada. It heralds the coming of spring to the Santa Rosa, San Gabriel, and San Jacinto mountains, as well as to the coniferous forests of the San Antonio and San Bernardino mountains. In later weeks, the specimens at higher elevations—up to nine thousand feet in forests of lodgepole pine—will bloom. Indians are supposed to have used the plant to relieve toothache; Ernst Stuhr, in *Manual of Pacific Coast Drug Plants,* reports that it is said to be poisonous but that in dried and powdered form it was used as a wash for treatment of ulcers and cankers. Like other attractive plants, it is too often picked out of the ground or dug up. Admirers should let it alone, lest we lose what John Muir called "a wonderful curiosity."

A similar caution is advised with regard to the poison oak *(Rhus toxicodendron),* which is not a true oak but a member of the same genus as the familiar poison ivy. It is said to be the most widespread California shrub, occurring from the foothills to five thousand feet in the Sierra Nevada. Its irritating effects are similar to those of its eastern cousin.

Summer in the Sierra

Badgers and weasels bring forth their young, and as spring rises to the summits in May and after, and summer advances from the lowlands, shrews and pikas produce their young, deer fawns are born, and the young of marmots and other species come out of their protective burrows.

A discreet human visitor may enter this complex mountain ecosystem without difficulty, for the John Muir Trail penetrates to the high, wild heart of the range that Muir loved so much. A summer walk along the crest of the Sierra is one of brilliance—white rock, white rapids, bright sun. One is inclined to agree with Muir's description: "After ten years of wandering and wondering in the heart of it, rejoicing in its glorious floods of light, the white beams of the morning streaming through the passes, the noonday radiance on the crystal rocks, the flush of the alpenglow, and the irised spray of countless waterfalls, it still seems above all others the Range of Light."

Along the trail one sees a great deal of the beauty and a little of the drama of mountain life. The Indian paintbrush blossoms at the edge of a snow bank, and a clump of magenta-colored penstemon *(Penstemon menziesii)* strikes a note of contrast as it blooms in a granite crevice. White heather *(Cassiope mertensiana),* and red mountain heather *(Phyllodoce breweri)* hug the rocks or border the icy lakes. In some places one may stroll through whole meadows of Sierra shooting star *(Dodecatheon alpinum),* its pinkish petals yellow at the base and edged with purple. A marmot barks as it sits beside a boulder. Meadows are enlivened by the shrill voice of the Belding ground squirrel *(Spermophilus beldingi),* which perches upright on hind feet and tail to look about for predators.

And predators there are in plenty. As in any ecosystem, the network of life in the Sierra functions efficiently. A great many mechanisms are involved, but some of the natural activities and relationships are seldom seen by man and are thus not clearly understood. The life cycles of burrowing or nocturnal animals, as an example, are difficult to study. Vegetable matter is consumed by cottontails, ground squirrels, chipmunks, beavers, porcupines, bears, and mule deer in the Sierra, and then these animals are consumed by a host of predators. Coyotes, eagles, and hawks capture jackrabbits; martens feed on pikas, chickarees, and birds; snakes feed on chipmunks; skunks feed on insects, and bobcats on rabbits and rodents. Mule deer are the abundant and favorite prey of mountain lions. Mountain coyotes *(Canis latrans)* are common, eating almost everything; gray foxes *(Urocyon cinereoargenteus)* are even more common, especially along the western slope of the range.

All these are but samples of a complex life system, and we risk oversimplification if we do not go further into a few significant predator-prey relationships. Especially interesting is the most ferocious predator of all, the long-tailed weasel *(Mustela frenata).* This beast is about as rapacious and brutal as an animal can be. It is literally bloodthirsty, for it sucks blood from the head or neck of its victims, and is a formidable antagonist. Weasels are built for hunting: small head, short neck, brown coat for camouflage, slender body, and short arms and legs, all designed for the pursuit of prey right into underground burrows. They also climb like squirrels, which renders birds in nests particularly vulnerable. They are fast and nervous and so agile that few other creatures can escape their attack. They do not care how big the enemy is or who gets in the way. Their usual fare consists of rodents, insects, birds, reptiles, and amphibians—in short, about anything that moves. They live and hunt in the Sierra from about four thousand feet to ten thousand, and in winter possess a brilliant white coat, which is another example of adaptive coloration since it makes them virtually invisible against the snow. It is not surprising that weasels are so successful, and so effective a check on other wildlife populations.

At night, weasels permitting, a great deal goes on in the open: pocket mice come out of their meadow burrows to forage, flying squirrels glide from tree to tree; porcupines climb into conifers to get at the juicy inner or cambium layer of bark, skunks engage in the search for insects, and ring-tails and raccoons hunt along stream courses for almost any kind of food.

The Sierra has three species of wild currant and six of gooseberry *(Ribes).* These provide food for birds and mammals, but gooseberry is an intermediate host to the white pine blister rust, which is destructive to all five-needled pines, including the highly valued sugar pine. For this reason, control projects have been undertaken to eradicate infested gooseberry.

Animals in Jeopardy

Quite often countries or states incorporate a common and spectacular native animal as part of an insignia or emblem. Australia's symbol includes the kangaroo and emu, Guatemala uses the quetzal, Trinidad and Tobago the scarlet ibis, and the United States the bald eagle. California became a state in 1850, but before that, frontiersmen had rigged up a red and white flag and chosen the grizzly, largest and strongest animal in California, to be emblazoned on it. These men came to be known as the Bear Flaggers. Their efforts to establish a California Republic came to little, but the bear on the flag endured.

Not so the bear. The grizzly *(Ursus horribilis)* was abundant in the days of the Bear Flaggers, with a California population estimated at ten thousand. Through repeated meat and sport hunting, most intensively between 1849 and 1870, the grizzly was rapidly exterminated in California. It is presumed to have become extinct there in 1924, when the last one was seen alive. But the animal still holds a prominent position on the State Seal of California and appears in the place names of nearly two hundred topographic features and settlements.

Animals now rare in the Sierra Nevada include the fisher *(Martes pennanti)* and the wolverine *(Gulo luscus)*. A few bighorn remain, generally in the high rocky areas of the alpine and subalpine belts.

Two Kinds of Gold

The Sierra Nevada is an exceedingly complex range biologically, geologically, and esthetically. One may experience in a single visit hundreds of memorable sights and sounds: the song of a water ouzel, the call of a coyote, wild grape clinging to oaks and cottonwoods, bell-shaped blooms of manzanita touched by rays of the sun, a lone red columbine *(Aquilegia formosa)* in a mossy setting beside a spring, nights of "moonbows" in the spray of roaring waterfalls; the spectacular Kern River Canyon; the glistening glacial polish on granite domes. Effects like these are likely to be enjoyed for years to come by visitors since they are in such areas of the state and federal domain as Yosemite, Sequoia and Kings Canyon national parks, and Stanislaus, Toiyabe, Inyo, Sierra, Tahoe, El Dorado, Plumas, and Sequoia national forests.

In numerous localities the innermost secrets of Sierra Nevada structure and history lie revealed. The great polygonal columns at Devils Postpile National Monument are among the best examples of columnar basalt in the West. A cooling, shrinking lava flow centuries ago on the east side of the Sierra developed a pattern of cracks, most of them hexagonal, and from this outcrop erosion has fashioned columns as much

Basaltic lava hardens and cools at the Devil's Postpile, cracking into columns up to sixty feet in height and containing "posts" with three to seven sides. (Bob Clemenz)

as sixty feet in height and three and a half feet in diameter. Glacial ice subsequently polished the tops of the columns into a geometrically patterned esplanade.

Complexity seems to have been present in the Sierra Nevada structure from the start. The original bedding and other sedimentary structures of pre-Cretaceous time were severely folded, thrust-faulted, and altered a hundred million years ago. Then great granitic masses—the most common rock type is quartz monzonite—welled up and intruded into these folded and broken structures. Not one, but ten or more such masses have been identified, all collectively called the Sierra Nevada batholith. During the final stages of these intrusions gold quartz veins were formed. Much later, the Sierra was elevated, batholiths, gold and all, as a tilted fault block, and the granitic rocks plus the earlier folded structures were eroded into peaks and domes massively and majestically exposed today. The east face of the Sierra, though steeper than the western, is not a solid wall; rather it is a series of giant stairsteps interpreted as evidence of numerous faults.

Tertiary rivers began to reduce the mountains as soon as they started rising. Streams plucked away some of the gold and concentrated it in placer deposits. Glaciers nearly covered the mountains, and streams made their way down the long Sierra slope, converting the western foothills into one of the richest gold placer regions in the world. Indians sought and found Sierra gold, as did missionaries and settlers. But not until John Marshall's discovery on the south fork of the American River, near the present Coloma, did much come of this knowledge. From the time of the discovery, January 24, 1848, through 1849 the population of California swelled from fourteen thousand to nearly a hundred thousand. Gold seekers spread out on the western slope of the Sierra Nevada.

The farther upstream they worked, the more they dreamed of finding that original source from which the gold must surely have come, the *veta madre* as the Mexican miners referred to it—the mother lode. Yet no single mother vein existed. The gold came from a system of quartz-filled fissures extending along a belt one to six and a half miles wide for a distance of eighty miles northwest of Mariposa. This is the mother lode.

Gold output during 1852 amounted to a sum never again approached on any United States mining frontier: more than eighty-one million dollars. Production tapered off after that, but was sustained at lower levels until by the end of the nineteenth century California had yielded gold to the value of $1,300,000,000.

California's leading mineral product now is oil. But John Muir had discovered the richest treasure of all. In the Sierra Nevada he showed how a trove of natural resources could be "mined" without being destroyed. Today millions of travelers annually take in the natural wonders of the high Sierra, enriching California and themselves in a way that gold could not. If man keeps these mountains unmarred by new vacation resorts and other commercial developments, he will continue to find that the real "mother lode" was not a vein of vanishing gold, but the Range of Light itself.

10. Of Forest and Sea: Exploring the Pacific Coast

*The shores are extremely well wooded...
and as it was now the rainy season, everything
was as green as nature could make it... the
birds were singing in the woods, and great
numbers of wildfowl were flying over our
heads.*

Richard Henry Dana
in *Two Years Before the Mast* (1840)

As we stepped over a row of logs into a forest vale, surrounded by green of a hundred shades, we exclaimed at the richness of the coastal rain forest that surrounded us. We could neither hear nor observe the sea, yet its moisture lay all about, dripping from jeweled maple leaves, glistening on points of hemlock needles, softening the sphagnum moss into which our boots nearly disappeared. Our hands reached out to verify the velvety softness on the logs: a microworld of dozens of species of ferns, moss, lichens and liverworts. In this forest our senses were overwhelmed by a dizzying progression of natural phenomena, some large and some small. It was difficult to believe that a forest could have such an abundance of life.

Yet we were surrounded by it—club moss forming fantastic draperies; shelf fungus that sent its unseen filaments into the interior of slowly decaying logs; avenues of spruce; archways of alder; rivers of blue water dropping over polished stones and gathering in pools that sheltered salmon. And all of it pervaded by the fragrance of decay and of life.

Edge of a Continent

Nowhere in the West is the shape of the land so fully controlled by zones of faulting, or the life upon it so influenced by the sea. Nor does any region possess such a variety of landscapes or sharply differentiated flora. The whole Pacific Border Province, from Mexico to Canada, is a continuous series of stretched-out topographic features, some high and dry, some submerged offshore, broken only by the Transverse Ranges around Los Angeles and by the Klamath Mountains in northern California and southern Oregon.

The region is not without secrets. If we could somehow remove all the sediments that have been carried from the Sierra Nevada westward into the Great Valley of California, we would expose a gorge of enormous proportions. An elongated structural trough, the valley represents a basin three miles deep in some places; in others the bottom has not yet been found. Sediments continue to enter it through the Sacramento River system on the north and the San Joaquin system to the south, and in places these sediments have become richly petroliferous, as in the California oil fields.

But nearly everywhere is one abiding feature of the landscape: mountain ranges related to great systems of earth fractures. Faults are evident in the elongate Peninsular Ranges which extend from Baja California into the United States as far north as Los Angeles. These ranges, like those of the Basin and Range Province, also seem like "caterpillars crawling out of Mexico"; but there is one added feature: these crawl into the sea, continuing westward into the Pacific Ocean for more than two hundred miles. Underwater ranges lie parallel to those on shore, and a few emerge as offshore islands: Santa Catalina, San Clemente, and San Nicolas.

The energies of sun and sea support great tidal ecosystems. Where each organism grows depends upon such factors as the shock of waves, exposure to air, and the nature of the sea floor. (Don Worth) thrown out of alignment. Some of the movements that produced all these may have been gradual, an earth-moving process known as tectonic creep, but the stress and strain on both sides of a fault is sometimes suddenly released, and that is when disaster strikes. Primary, or compression, waves travel rapidly through rocks and sediments of the region, resulting in an audible thud. Secondary waves, also called transverse or shear waves, travel slowly, producing a swaying or rolling motion.

When the dust has settled, many changes in the landscape can be readily observed. In the 1906 earthquake, a road across the head of Tomales Bay was offset twenty-one feet. That seems like a great deal of distance for the crust of the earth to move at once, and it is; but evidence suggests that both sides of the San Andreas fault are offset at least a hundred and sixty miles—a figure that may be surprising but is consistent with a measured average drift rate of nearly two inches every year. Indeed, when we speak of whole mountain systems being uplifted, of great revolutions such as the Laramide that raised the Rocky Mountains, we speak not of sudden calamitous upheavals but rather of slow and persistent changes like that along the San Andreas fault, which over millions of years can build great ranges. Of course, dense populations spread over the large fault systems today make disaster to human life and property a decided possibility with each major crustal shift.

The San Andreas fault is a more or less complex zone of crushed and broken rock a few hundred feet up to a mile wide and with a depth of ten miles or more. Movements along it are variable in energy, and the rocks through which vibrations pass have different densities from place to place. Hence, accurate predictions of earthquakes and the amount of shaking or damage that will ensue are virtually impossible. "No one yet knows how to predict exactly when the next earthquake will occur along the San Andreas fault," says the United States Geological Survey, "but there is every reason to believe that the fault will continue to be active as it has been for millions of years in the past. Another earthquake as strong as that of 1906 could happen at any time."

For a number of years, Geological Survey scientists have undertaken extensive studies at the National Center for Earthquake Research in Menlo Park, California. The objectives of the program are to discover what causes earthquakes, what can be done to minimize the dangers from them, and what steps can be taken to predict the time, place, and strength of tremors. Specialists from many disciplines seek to determine the pattern of earthquake activity in the past few thousand years in order to tell what may happen in the future.

Seismic stations and telemetering networks have been established in several localities, including Alaska, on both sides of the San Francisco Peninsula, along the San Andreas fault, and in the Yellowstone region of Wyoming and Montana. These stations make use of earthquake-sensing instruments such as tiltmeters, strain detectors, magnetometers, gravity meters, and devices to measure electric currents in the earth. Geodimeters, with intense beams of light, detect slow

distortions of the earth's crust—the kind that precede an earthquake. Signals from such outposts are telemetered to the Center for computer analysis. To date, this research has revealed steady slippage along various fault systems. Curiously, computer analyses of continuous readings from about twenty seismographs in and around the San Francisco Bay area show that several hundred small earthquakes occur monthly east of the Bay and south along the San Francisco Peninsula. But along the San Andreas fault beneath San Francisco itself very few earthquakes occur. This could be interpreted to mean that other faults are releasing the strain building up on them, but that beneath San Francisco the pressure is building up for one big shock. When we queried residents of the area about this, they simply shrugged and said: "Well, we've been warned."

The Geological Survey hopes to advance its technology sufficiently in order to predict earthquakes, and plans to extend its automatic seismograph monitoring system throughout the United States and ultimately connect with world networks. The hope is that automatic sensing devices can transmit data to stationary satellites over the northern Pacific basin, which would then relay information to computers at the Earthquake Research Center for immediate analysis. Thus within thirty seconds the world would know where any earthquake had occurred and its magnitude.

New light is being shed on the juxtaposition, even at great depths, of geologic features. These extremely elongated movements of the earth's crust are called transcurrent faults, and geologists are excited about the new concepts and new information arising from studies of them. Both sides of the San Andreas fault, most intensively studied, appear to be offset by at least a hundred and sixty miles and perhaps as much as four hundred and fifty miles. The meaning of this tremendous movement is not entirely clear, but activity appears to have been going on for a long time. Significantly, different parts of the fault have different patterns of movement. Some portions seem to be "locked tight," releasing only occasionally under the strain of a twisting earth, while others are "loose" and their accumulating energy is released more often. Since certain soils shake more intensively than others, buildings on loose sediments tend to vibrate far more than those on bedrock. There is a great deal still to be studied and the goals of earthquake research are long-range ones simply because so much is involved and so little is known.

Inevitably, the question arises: can faults be controlled? Or can pressures along them be released slowly rather than letting nature do it violently? We know already that man can cause earthquakes; the pumping of contaminated water into a 12,000-foot-deep well at the Rocky Mountain Arsenal near Denver in 1962 started a series of small tremors. The Geological Survey planted fifty seismic-wave detectors in the immediate vicinity and cabled the signals to magnetic tape recorders. These showed that from one to twenty microearthquakes occurred daily, centering beneath the well. That raised the question of whether man could initiate minor earthquakes along major faults and keep potentially dangerous stresses from building up. Research has indicated that earthquake control may be possible, but a great many experiments in remote and uninhabited areas are needed before man dares to tamper with earth structures beneath congested areas.

Coastal Highlands and Lowlands

Some of the most tantalizing mysteries of the natural history of the West lie off its shores. The continental shelf, extending seaward ten to twenty-five miles before plunging off the Patton Escarpment to a depth of twelve thousand feet, is far from uniform topographically. Submerged mountains and canyons have been known off California for decades, but only in recent years have detailed echo-soundings and bottom profiles been available. Better yet, in submersible craft and scuba equipment men have gone below for direct observation.

In deep and winding submarine canyons, often found near points where terrestrial streams or valleys come to the sea, explorers have studied cliffs, benches, sediment transport, "waterfalls" of sand, deposits of peat, and concentrations of fish along canyon walls. At the head of Scripps Canyon they found a natural trap where currents carry and deposit sand and plant debris in haystack-like layers, including giant brown algae (*Macrocystis pyrifera* and *Egregia laevigata*) and surf grass (*Phyllospadix torreyi*). In another place they found embedded in clay at seventy-five feet a tree root that radiocarbon dating methods showed to be 8270 years old.

The deepest and largest canyon heads in Monterey Bay. It extends for at least fifty miles to sea and ultimately reaches a depth of more than 9600 feet. In profile it is strikingly, though accidentally, like the Grand Canyon. What seems so strange is that there should be a deep canyon at this locality and none off San Francisco Bay. Evidence suggests that at one time the Golden Gate was not a gate at all, that waters from central California emptied into the Santa Clara Valley and from there cut through the mountains into Monterey Bay.

North of the Columbia River is a continuous series of submarine canyons. Off Alaska, troughs extend from glacial fiords across the continental shelf. Those that follow lines of faults are doubtless structural in origin; others may be valleys eroded on land and later submerged. The truth is that man has only a tantalizing introduction to the facts of these regions; in such localities the unknown exceeds the known. And one more mystery: the average thickness of the earth's crust beneath western North America, thirty-four kilometers, is less than that beneath the eastern half of the continent, forty-four kilometers.

We have seen that the lands submerged off the western coast are an extension of the basins and ranges of southern California. This system of drowned basins, banks, and ridges has been compared to a giant, shallow bowl into which pour waters from the great ocean streams. The Subarctic Current of the North Pacific sends two subsidiary flows toward the North American coast: the Alaska Current, which forms a counterclockwise motion around the Gulf of Alaska, and the California Current, which cools the western coast in summer, and moderates the extremes of winter.

Prevailing northwest winds exert a considerable force which, when combined with the earth's rotational energy, drives some of the surface waters away from shore. These waters are then replaced from below in a process known as upwelling. Off California the velocity of waters moving to the surface is about sixty feet per month, enough to influence life profoundly—on land and in the sea. The rising waters introduce to the surface large quantities of nutrients—soluble inorganic phosphate, nitrate, ammonium, and hydrated silicate ions; these, together with sunlight, support the growth of marine phytoplankton, the floating plants that form the base of the food chain in the sea. For that reason, and for others, the waters off the coast of western North America are among the world's richest in plant and animal life. Whereas the open ocean has a biomass on the order of twenty-five parts per billion by volume, the average inshore concentration of the California current (i.e., within a hundred miles of the coast) is three hundred parts per billion.

The upwelled waters are, moreover, ordinarily colder and denser than the surface waters they replace. If cooler than the moisture-laden air passing over as a result of prevailing westerlies, they may contribute to the formation of coastal fog, especially in summer. And therein lies the story of the "cloud forests" of the Pacific Coast.

A casual introduction might give one the impression that life on the western edge of the continent was either dense rain forest or no forest at all. Actually there is an extraordinary variety of ecosystems and a great many microhabitats, ranging from extremely arid to extremely wet.

Above the tide level lies the coastal strand, an ecosystem of dunes and bluffs, generally arid because the sand has little water-retaining capacity. But succulents grow here, as do sand verbena, picturesque pines, the familiar wax myrtle (*Myrica californica*) and large tracts of handsome yellow lupine (*Lupinus arboreus*). A short way back from shore are the coastal marshes. Those of salt water commonly contain eelgrass (*Zostera marina*), *Spartina*, pickle-weed—the familiar *Salicornia*—and salt grass (*Distichlis spicata*). Those of fresh water possess communities of cat-tail, pondweed, skunk cabbage (*Lysichitum americanum*) and water lily (*Nuphar polysepalum*). Around these marshes may be brushy areas of blackberry, silktassel, twinberry, coyote brush (*Baccharis pilularis*) and various kinds of *Ceanothus*. Since the coast is cooler to the north, and more moist with fog and rain, great forest ecosystems have become established—wooded prairies, hardwoods, and conifers.

As always with vegetation, climate is the major determining factor. In southern California, for example, where the rainfall is scant, many of the promontories are covered with grass, a low scrub chaparral, or scattered oaks. True, in moist and protected habitats, forests of greater density develop, but the southern coastal vegetation, as in the Sierra Nevada, is normally subject to dry summers, high winds, and intensely hot fires. Summer is the dormant season for many plants simply because rain does not come when they need it

California sea lions climb quite well and spend more time on land than do fur seals. From lonely islands or rocky points they often slip into the sea for a meal of squids. (Karl W. Kenyon: National Audubon Society)

most, while winter climate, tempered by the moisture of the sea, encourages the growth of vegetation. It is a turnabout country—as if the seasons were reversed.

Predominant grasses of the Coast Ranges include soft cheat *(Bromus hordeaceus)* and common velvet-grass *(Holcus lanatus)*. The chaparral, in places almost impenetrable, is composed primarily of manzanita, *Ceanothus,* chamise *(Adenostoma fasciculatum),* and scrub oak *(Quercus dumosa).* By contrast, a walk in the open oak woodland and across the savanna, with soft grass beneath your feet, the hills smooth and rolling for as far as the eye can see, and the sheltering oaks growing aloof and widely spaced, is one of the great exhilarating experiences of southern California. The

California Coast Ranges are also particularly notable for their north-south slope plant distribution. In places the north-facing slopes are densely, almost completely, covered with oaks and other species of trees. By contrast, the south-facing slopes are in places completely barren except for grass. On successive ridges for miles into the distance we may see an alternation of forested and barren slopes.

Despite the coast live oak *(Quercus agrifolia)* and blue oak *(Q. douglasii),* there is in places almost a desert aspect, with cactus mixed among the grass and oak. Once in a while one can see a black-tailed deer bounding across the open slopes and, with a little more luck, a smaller animal such as a gray fox, coyote, or bobcat. It should not be assumed that deer in the thick, mature chaparral have plenty to eat. The density of these animals in such habitats is only thirty per square mile—not a large number. But by using certain techniques in the increasingly sophisticated science of wildlife management, that density can be more than

Above left: Twelve feet of rain each year, plus gentle veils of mist, combine to support the coastal forests of Washington's Olympic Peninsula. Above right: Redwoods and rhododendrons are trademarks of the coast. The longevity of redwoods is aided by natural chemicals repellent to insects and fungi, by the absence of fire, and by a strong root system. (Both by Betty Randall) Far left: A delicate carpet on the forest floor is redwood sorrel (Oxalis), member of the geranium family. Left: The California sister (Limenitis bredowii) is found on oaks in the foothill and yellow pine belts of the Sierra Nevada. Right: During migration, monarch butterflies mass by the thousands in trees along their route. (All by Edward S. Ross)

tripled. Wildlife managers simply put ecology to work. They know that through successive stages of growth, one type of plant cover replaces another until a dominant or climax association is reached. This vegetative process is called succession, and it can be held back or suppressed by a single tool: fire. They carefully burn off the brush and within a year small shoots develop from the undisturbed roots. These shoots are a good deal more nutritious for deer than mature chaparral, which contains no more than twelve percent protein; the young shoots have a protein content of twenty to thirty percent. With better nutrition, nearly all of the yearling animals will raise young, and a majority of two-year-olds and older animals will raise two young. Such increases in reproductive rate may raise deer densities to a hundred deer per square mile.

Trees against the Sea

The Coast Ranges are marked by contrasts throughout, especially on their western side, which is subject to fog and invasion by cooler air masses. At higher latitudes there is an increase in conifers, but these are different from all other cone-bearing trees. The Bishop pine *(Pinus muricata)*, for example, has a preference for watersoaked sandy bogs, yet as one of the most sturdy and tolerant of pines it resists the cool gales that blow across the windswept hills near the sea. One of the most impressive groves of it—some stalwart, some pruned by the wind—is in the Point Reyes region and along Tomales Bay, thirty miles northwest of San Francisco.

Monterey pine *(Pinus insignis)* is a short-lived but fast-growing tree. Because of the lumber it yields it has been more widely planted elsewhere than other western conifers; introduced into New Zealand, for example, it has virtually taken over the countryside, invading even where not wanted. In California it is a tree of seacoast slopes and ridges, bathed in fog, lightly draped with lichen *(Ramalina reticulata)*, rooted in shifting dunes. It is native only to a few localities between Cambria, San Luis Obispo county and northern Santa Cruz county, where true to the laws of self-preservation it still hangs on. The tree does much better away from this demanding environment, and is a popular species in ornamental plantings. For reasons still not understood it attracts Monarch butterflies *(Danaus plexippus)*, which year after year gather by the thousands on certain trees.

Perhaps the most arresting tree of this coast is the Monterey cypress *(Cupressus macrocarpa)*. One can almost see John Muir standing admiringly beside it in a salt-filled breeze, observing its tormented form and dramatic setting. Few trees adopt more compelling contortions, its limbs bent, gnarled, and sprawling on the ground, its roots clinging to cliffs, its trunk leaning out over thundering surf, its spreading crown impervious to the violence of wave or wind. Such durability enables it to act as a buffer between the beach and less hardy Monterey pines inland. In its natural state, the cypress is confined to the region of Monterey Bay, Carmel, Pebble Beach and Point Lobos State Park. Elsewhere it is widely cultivated, not the least as a windbreak and as an ornamental. Yet its rugged form, endless diversity of shapes, and the tenacity with which it clings to land and life are all best seen in the limited areas where it grows wild. It is host to a trailing lichen *(Ramalina)* and a filamentous reddish alga *(Trentepohlia)*, both of which add to its strange shapes and forms.

The plant life of the California coastal province reveals a variety of wonders to the discerning eye. Henry A. Gleason and Arthur Cronquist, in their studies of plant geography, refer to it as the most sharply differentiated flora in the nation, declaring:

"The families are in general the same as elsewhere in the country, but many of the genera and especially the species are not found much if at all beyond the borders of the state. A visitor from the Rocky Mountains, or the Great Basin, or the Pacific Northwest will feel reasonably at home in the Sierra Nevada, but let him descend even to the foothills on the western side and he is lost. He will recognize the oaks and pines as oaks and pines, but he will probably not know the species, and many of the herbaceous plants will be wholly unfamiliar."

Consider, for example, the pitcher plant *(Darlingtonia californica)*, the astonishing plant that traps and digests insects. It is found at various elevations from sea level to six thousand feet and also inhabits bog areas. Flowering in early summer, it produces up to a dozen leaves. Insects are attracted to the tubelike leaf openings by nectar or by colorful petal-like appendages at the edge of the opening. Once inside the plant, the insect is confused by many transparent "windows" in the leaf wall and tries to exit through them. Clinging to the slippery inner walls of the leaf is difficult and the intruder is soon trapped by downward-pointing hairs in the lower portion of the leaf tube. After falling into a pool at the bottom, the captive is attacked by digestive enzymes and absorbed as food through thin lower walls. A bog of these unusual and handsome brilliant green plants has been preserved near Highway 101 a few miles north of Florence, Oregon.

Elsewhere along the coast, clinging to precipitous cliffs or covering the gentle open slopes, are conspicuous masses of purple and white foxglove and yellow Scotch broom—both exotic—paintbrush, milfoil *(Achillea)*, fireweed, rhododendron, ferns, daisies, thistles, and both blue and yellow lupine.

The Coastal Forests

From California to Alaska the coastal environment is distinctive. As we go north from San Francisco hardwoods become less prominent; where they grow on old burned-over areas they may dominate for a while, but in the natural process of succession, they finally yield to conifers. Different stages of this sequence may often be found adjacent to one another. The summers are still dry here, but any tendency toward aridity is countered by fog. Atmospheric moisture condenses as it moves inland and rises into the coastal ranges. We thus encounter two water-loving conifers when we leave the sea and enter the forest: the straight and noble Sitka spruce *(Picea sitchensis)*, tallest of the spruces and inhabitant of wet or swampy areas, and lowland fir *(Abies grandis)*, found in moist valleys.

The monarch of the northern coastal province, however, is a tree with no special claim to superlative height or beauty, one that typically nods and droops its leader shoot in an awkward fashion—the western hemlock *(Tsuga mertensiana)*. It is perhaps the most

A sea otter has three meals a day, detaching mollusks from the rocks below, placing them on its stomach, crushing the shells and eating with obvious ease. (Karl W. Kenyon)

common and widely distributed tree of the region, especially along the fiords of Alaska and Canada. It has tiny cones and needles, so many of the latter that its canopy casts a deep, dark shade on the forest floor, allowing few progeny but its own to grow. It creates forests of gentle dignity. Though the value of hemlock in the manufacture of pulp and in the fields of plastics and synthetic textiles has been proved, its greatest value may in the long run be as a haven of tranquility.

Another tree in the fog and rain belt from sea level to six thousand feet has become established over a great deal of northwestern North America. This is the

western red cedar *(Thuya plicata)*, a tree whose narrow conical form may in exceptional cases rise as high as two hundred feet. Sufficient evidence of its durability is the fact that it is the major source of wooden shingles, and that it may lie in water for years without appreciable signs of decay.

Coast Redwoods: Heritage of Time

But the patriarch among western trees, unsurpassed for durability and the sense of serenity it provides, is the coast redwood *(Sequoia sempervirens)*. Sheltered in fogged and misty vales seldom more than thirty miles from the ocean surf, it is scattered in large groves from central California to the southern hills of Oregon. The coast redwood differs from the giant Sequoia in not living quite so long (it reaches a mere two thousand years), in keeping to lower elevations, and in being more slender and taller. One specimen on Redwood Creek, north of Eureka, California, is thought to be the tallest tree in the world, its height calculated at over 367 feet, its basal circumference forty-four feet, and its diameter fourteen feet.

Some coast redwood groves are pure, but the tree also associates widely with a number of other trees, most abundantly the Douglas fir. A visitor among the giant trees in a redwood grove finds at once that his steps are hushed by the soft, rich layers of moss and humus. As in the eastern Appalachians, there are places where the forest floor is overlain with oxalis, here called redwood sorrel *(Oxalis oregana)*. Sometimes, too, the star flower *(Trientalis europaea)* carpets the matted earth with a layer of white to pinkish flowers. Displays of sword ferns, trilliums, wild lilies, Oregon grape, azalea, gooseberries, thimbleberries, bleeding heart *(Dicentra formosa)*, and columbines decorate these cathedral-like groves. Occasionally the deep shade is brightened when California rhododendron *(Rhododendron macrophyllum)*, which grows to as much as thirty feet in height, springs into flower.

With such abundant vegetation, the fauna, too, has diversified. One of the most common food plants in the redwood region, the salal *(Gaultheria shallon)*, a member of the heath family, supplies many birds and mammals, especially bears, with berries. Other heaths occur in plenty, among them black huckleberry *(Vaccinium ovatum)* and red huckleberry *(V. parvifolium)*. Members of the buckthorn family, such as deer brush *(Ceanothus integerrimus)*, provide a staple of diet for deer.

Many forms of wildlife flourish here. Across the moss and lichen moves the bright orange slug *(Ariolimax columbianus)*. Spiders weave their webs among the leaves. Fifteen of the twenty-two species of salamanders in western North America inhabit the redwood area, including the Pacific giant salamander *(Dicamptodon ensatus)*, twelve inches long. Shrews build their runways and moles their hills. When a redwood or other species falls it becomes a "nurse tree," supporting the growth of new vegetation as well as supplying home and food for ground beetles *(Pterostichus vicinus)*, ants, crickets, millipedes and centipedes. And where there are trees there are tree "enemies": beetles, loopers, aphids, sawflies, and borers.

Blue grouse nest in the shadows on the forest floor, and wrens, thrushes, and kinglets in the shrubs. The silence is broken by Steller and, near the California-Oregon border, Canada jays which occur in the coniferous forests year-round. Streams contain rainbow trout, cutthroat, and salmon in season. For black bear we need to go deep into the wilderness woods.

Elk and the Rain Forest

Largest and best known of coast mammals is the Roosevelt elk *(Cervus canadensis rooseveltI)*, named for Theodore Roosevelt. It inhabits parts of California, Oregon, and Canada's Vancouver Island, but the largest herds are on the Olympic Peninsula of Washington. The Roosevelt elk differs from others of its kind in that it has a darker, almost black, neck and is heavier. A good-sized male may weigh a thousand pounds. It also possesses large antlers, which are often put to use in defense of as large a band of females as it can collect and protect. Sounds of battle as well as bugling stir the woods during the September to October mating season. By spring the antlers are shed, though new ones promptly begin to grow. When the young elk are born in June, they enter upon a life of plenty, for on the watersheds of the Rivers Hoh, Queets, Quinalt, Bogachiel, and Soleduck grows some of the richest forest in North America.

This is the Olympic rain forest, a region which in biomass must be comparable to that of tropical forests of the Caribbean, Brazil, and the Fiji Islands. It gives almost the identical feeling of quiet beauty and natural luxuriance as those other faraway forests. But this is a temperate rain forest, receiving in places more than 140 inches of precipitation a year. Above the forest, moisture is lifted to glaciers in the Olympic Mountains where it freezes and falls in the form of approximately 250 feet of snow per year. When they melt, the glacial waters descend into basins of extraordinary beauty. Past wooded banks and into canyons decorated with mosses and ferns, they plunge as falls or rapids, then glide and ripple through the rain forest and beyond to the sea.

Together with a mild climate, all this water helps to produce a dense forest dominated by Sitka spruce, western hemlock, Douglas fir, and western red cedar. Half a dozen species of trees produce their largest known specimen in this environment. Conifers, maples, dead logs, nearly everything is strung with one or more of over seventy species of epiphytes, such as mosses, club mosses, liverworts and ferns, which all depend on a host plant. Of ferns alone there seem always to be half a dozen kinds in view, among them bracken, sword, lady, deer, wood and licorice. Carpets of mosses and liverworts, dependent upon shade and moisture, form a ground cover of some hundred species in the rain forest. Most of the sixty-eight species of lichens grow on trees, and a visitor often will

Coastal rock formations called sea stacks become separated from land by wave action. Between them and the shore are tide pools abounding in marine life. (Ruth Kirk)

find a lettuce-like foliose variety *(Lobaria oregana)* torn from trees by the wind and scattered at his feet. Fleshy fungi abound on logs as well as on living trees and on the forest floor.

Yet it is not altogether a forest of dim vales and misty shadows. The fog frequently thins and evaporates, allowing sunlight to pour into leaves of bigleaf maple *(Acer macrophyllum)*, vine maple *(A. circinnatum)*, red alder *(Alnus rubra)*, and black cottonwood *(Populus trichocarpa)*. The yellow mountain fern moss covers nearly everything. Sphagnum moss *(Sphagnum girgensohnii)*, commonly the peat-maker of bogs, grows on stumps, logs and many another base in this forest; dead plants decay slowly to form thick cushions. Wild flowers and fruits—spring beauty, monkey flower, oxalis, salmonberry—add to the brightness and color. The result is a brilliant mosaic of bluegreen and yellow-green, of soft light invading even the darkest shadows and revealing an unparalleled richness. The visitor sinks into a six-inch carpet of moss, ferns, lichen, oxalis, bedstraw, and dwarf dogwood. Sounds are subdued, and even waterfalls seem muffled by the foliage. Mostly the voice of this wilderness is in its streamside music and the dripping of water from leaf to leaf and tree to pond.

Yet occasionally a shrill, unforgettable voice pierces the rain forest, the bugling call of the elk, a sound that may be heard long distances among the Olympic foothills. Since the elk are shy, this may be the only evidence a hiker gets of them, unless he is alert for tracks, scats, and the remains of branches and small trees ripped or uprooted by thrashing antlers. Elk have ample supplies of food and they evidently prefer to graze in the open meadows where there is an abundance of herbaceous plants. The elk do, in fact, help determine the nature of the rain forest because they also browse extensively on shrubs and tree seedlings, maintaining open areas. Without elk the rain forest would be far more dense than it is. Pacific red elder, for example, cannot stand much browsing and so grows where elk cannot reach it.

Low vales of red alder, on the other hand, are favorite haunts of elk. Evidence can be seen on the alder trunks, where bark has been rubbed by antlers or stripped away as food. Alders serve a further essential function as a pioneer plant that prepares and conditions soil but does not itself become dominant. It builds organic litter and increases soil nitrogen through its root system; small nodules on the alder root are mainly responsible for fixing nitrogen in the soil. The elk can also eat salmonberry, huckleberry, maple and cottonwood, so that it may roam the rain forest at will. Fortunately, winter and summer ranges have been preserved. The Roosevelt elk do not have such distinctive patterns of migration as Yellowstone elk. The herd in Olympic National Park is estimated at five thousand, but it seems to have no appreciable detrimental effects on the vegetation.

As for the visitor who sees no elk in this mountain paradise, he can be entirely content with the rain forest itself, the magnificence of Crescent Lake, the clusters of snow-covered crags topped by Mount Olympus (elevation 7965 feet), or a high-country meadow bursting with thousands of alpine lilies *(Erythronium montanum)*. Little rainfall gets across to the eastern side of the Olympics, where only thirteen inches a year may fall in the "rainshadow" on the lowlands.

A Violent Domain

There is another world of the Olympic country, and indeed of the whole West Coast. This is the ocean strip, where bears come down to the surf at dusk to fish, where deer and elk roam the sandy flats, where raccoons regularly feed on crabs, sea birds nest in the cliffs, and seals and whales move through the offshore waters. Primarily, it is a world of water, the ocean, a complex biome more widespread than all others combined, and by all standards less known.

The Olympic ocean strip and the Oregon coast are famous for their scenic appeal—black sands, rocky promontories, and giant accumulations of driftwood. Some areas, such as the Oregon dunes near Florence, have much light-colored sand, but dunes are relatively rare. Rocky cliffs and headlands are the order of nature—or disorder as it may seem when they break away in landslides and plunge into the sea. These are normal adjustments of a faulted coast, however; many elevated beach terraces are visible, especially in southern California, evidence of movements of land or fluctuations in sea level.

There is no doubt that the edge of the sea is at times a place of extraordinary violence. At Trinidad Head, a promontory north of Eureka, California, storm-borne waves have washed over Pilot Rock, 103 feet high; in one severe storm a lighthouse keeper reported that a wave struck the cliff below the light and water flew up to 196 feet, with spray leaping twenty-five feet or more higher.

Yet Monterey cypress and other terrestrial vegetation exist in the seashore ecosystem, and birds and mammals thrive. Their evolutionary adaptations render them invulnerable to all but the most violent extremes. Food, water, sheltering cliffs, remote islands, coastal forests, and a mild climate (on the Olympic Coast even the coolest month averages forty-seven degrees with a daily temperature range of seven degrees) attract several species of migrant birds. The Pacific flyway is a major migration route, though in some ways of lesser importance than others on the continent because its favorable climate means that certain birds such as Emperor geese *(Philacte canagica)* make only short seasonal migrations. Birds like Ross's goose *(Chen rossi)* migrate from the interior of the continent laterally or diagonally to the West and winter in California. Plovers, terns, and sparrows nest on sandy beaches and among the dunes. Western and least sandpipers may be seen in flocks of a thousand. Gulls, pelicans, and cormorants inhabit most coastal environments, and on rocky shores or cliffs we may see the nesting and foraging sites of murres, guillemots,

Pacific coast redwoods, tallest of living things, develop best in regions of heavy fog. (Ansel Adams: Redwood Empire Association)

and other species. Offshore in summer, great hosts of sooty shearwaters *(Puffinus griseus)* pass by on their route to Tasmania and New Zealand after having migrated north along the Asiatic coast and crossed the North Pacific. One of the most interesting and bizarrely designed species of the coastal crags is the tufted puffin *(Lunda cirrhata)*. Petrels breed on islands off the coast, as do murrelets and auklets. Most abundant is the common murre *(Uria aalge)*, which occurs in large breeding colonies from California to the Aleutians and beyond. Concentrations of such birds are often seen on excursions by boat, though in such places as Point Reyes they may, with prudence, be approached on foot. Although the entire coast is busy with bird life throughout the year, winter is a good time to look for them.

Seals, Sea Lions, and Whales

To certain mammals adapted to life in the water the North Pacific Ocean and the coasts that border it are home. Some, like the whales, have become independent of land, but the "fin-feet"—seals, sea lions, and walruses, together with the sea otter—are tied to the shore or near-shore for at least a portion of their lives. The northern fur seal *(Callorhinus ursinus)*, for example, breeds mainly on the Pribilof Islands, north of the Aleutians and west of the Alaska mainland. As soon as they arrive each year, the females give birth to young conceived the year before. They are gathered into harems of as many as a hundred, bred by the bulls, which can weigh up to seven hundred pounds, and then are free to commence the long migration toward California. The males go little farther south than the Gulf of Alaska, but the females spend the winter off more southerly shores.

Closely related are northern sea lions *(Eumetopias jubata)*, larger—a ton or more in weight—and more broad-shouldered. They range from Santa Rosa Island, California, north to Alaska, their resonant bellows sometimes filling the foggy air in symphony with the pounding waves. Far better known are California sea lions *(Zalophus californianus)*, the smaller, familiar barking animals often seen on rocks off the coast from San Francisco south. Indeed, the celebrated Seal Rocks are occupied principally by sea lions of both species rather than seals.

More widespread though less abundant seals of the Pacific Coast are those with the familiar spotted coat, at home in harbors, bays, rivers, and even inland lakes. These are harbor seals *(Phoca vitulina)*, known in the north as hair seals. Largest of North American seals—and the largest carnivore on the continent—is the northern elephant seal *(Mirounga angustirostris)*. Record specimens have reached approximately eigh-

Even when left alone by man, tide pools are complex natural ecosystems subject to severe environmental changes. Life on the Pacific shore includes anemones, periwinkles, slugs, urchins, chitons, blood stars, and sunflower stars, the latter one of the largest and most active of the asteroids. (Robert Ames; Betty Randall)

teen feet in length and weighed more than five thousand pounds. They used to occur along much of the coast of California and Mexico but so large a bulk was so tempting to men in search of blubber and oil that they were hunted to a low point. They are now protected and making a remarkable comeback. Breeding colonies are found from Guadalupe Island off the west coast of Baja California, Mexico, to Año Nuevo Island off central California.

Sea otters *(Enhydra lutris)* also came near being wiped out, thanks to their fine and highly coveted fur. They are not related to seals, but rather to the mustelids, which include river otters, skunks and weasels. Their webbed hind feet permit good swimming among protective beds of kelp and down to sources of food— sea urchins, mollusks and crustaceans. International protective measures brought the species back from the verge of extinction, and the population is now up in the thousands in the Aleutian Island area; several hundred occur off central California. Limited numbers have been taken in recent years by the government in Alaska. They are to be looked for among kelp beds offshore, floating on their backs, feet up, napping or eating.

Of the numerous whales in the Pacific, most are rarely seen by man, especially from shore. A major exception is the gray whale *(Eschrichtius gibbosus)*. Migration between summer feeding grounds in the Bering Sea and winter breeding and calving waters off Baja California bring gray whales past headlands from San Francisco south, most notably near Point Loma, at San Diego. Between November and February thousands of whales swim past, southward bound, two or three at a time, seventy to eighty a day during peak periods. The return journey, between March and April, is made farther from shore. Altogether, gray whales complete a yearly round trip of twelve thousand miles.

Navigational methods used by whale pods to steer their course are no less mysterious than those used by salmon, birds, or butterflies during migration. Man still understands very little about the impulses behind animal movements. With these great forty-foot whales, such lack of knowledge is understandable because so much of the migration route is hidden within the sea. Even the details of animal migration over land are scant enough. Cliff swallows *(Petrochelidon pyrrhonota)* arrive on or about March 19th every year at the Mission of San Juan Capistrano, north of San Diego, and leave for the south on or about October 23rd; there is a week or more variation in the date of arrival of summering cliff swallows as is true of most species of birds. But the purposes and means of both swallow and whale migration—and all other migration for that matter—have yet to be completely determined. The impulses seem to be reproductive, the timing related to length of day, and the guidance systems possibly dependent on such factors as magnetic fields, the sun and stars, familiar landmarks, and perhaps even the taste or temperature of the sea.

Some whales and sharks prowl off the coast in search of seals and other food. Killer whales *(Orcinus orca)* prey on seals, and in the immense and endless

pyramid of life, the stomachs of seals will be found to contain a quantity of fish, the fish a number of crustaceans, and the crustaceans a supply of plankton.

Ocean and Shore

The function of plankton needs to be clearly understood. Directly or indirectly it is the fundamental source of all ocean life together with a great deal of life that lives above or adjacent to the sea. Plankton is an all-inclusive word that applies to microscopic or near-microscopic floating plants (phytoplankton), minute animals (zooplankton), and such organic miscellany as eggs and larvae (meroplankton). While most members of these groups are tiny and scarcely noticed by human beings, they are nevertheless so abundant that there are countless billions of them and so many different species that it is hard to discover and describe them. The free-floating phytoplankton include mostly minute diatoms and dinoflagellates. These serve the same function in the ocean as grass and other vegetation on land: through photosynthesis they are prime producers of organic matter. This requires sunlight, of course, so the phytoplankton are restricted largely to the upper three hundred feet of water. They serve as food for a considerable proportion of the zooplankton, which includes animals unable to swim effectively against ocean currents, such as crustaceans, foraminifera, mollusks, coelenterates, and giant jellyfish. And far into the depths live creatures that feed on the fallout from above, dependent on organic debris that drifts their way.

Pastures in the sea—the Pacific Ocean has many of these. As a result, life separates more or less into zones, the organisms dividing ecologically according to depth, distance from land, and degree of light penetration. The water itself is called the pelagic environment; it includes an *oceanic* subdivision far out to sea, *neritic* closer to shore, and *littoral* between the tides. Beneath the pelagic environment is that of the benthic, or bottom. The benthic community consists of organisms that live in sediments and those attached to rocks and other surfaces. All this is a three-dimensional world made lively by continuing competition for food, a fluid world of enormous energies where the only certainty is cyclic change.

Strange as it may seem, the western coast of North America is a rich biotic region basically because it is the western edge of a continent. Major ocean currents most influence the land where they flow along shores in the same directions as prevailing winds. Such combinations occur naturally on the western side of continental masses and, as we have seen, produce upwelling ocean waters that bring to surface and shore a supply of cool water and fresh nutrients.

This is one reason why the edge of the sea has a greater diversity of fauna and flora than other ocean environments. Another reason for this diversity is variety of environments; the Pacific Coast has about

The Roosevelt elk is native to the humid Pacific Coast. Lone bulls, or "outriders," patrol the herds at mating time and attempt to lure away cows. (Philip Hyde)

165

every aquatic habitat imaginable: protected rocky coast, exposed rocky coast, open beach, lagoon, mud flat, salt marsh, fresh-water marsh, and submarine canyon. In the shallow waters, phytoplankton production is enormous, resulting in prolific benthic and pelagic ecosystems. Large kelp beds off California have the rich, cool, upwelling waters to their advantage; and abundant pelagic fish—such as salmon—are well known. In this region, where adjustment and adaptation go on endlessly, the most important physical features of the shore are the nature of the sediment or substrate and the temperature and salinity of the water. Some plants and animals occupying shallow waters must be able to withstand fluctuations in water level and salt content as well as short periods of desiccation. Under the constant crash of waves or the pull of currents they must hold fast to the shore, but this is not easy on rocks composed of unconsolidated sediments. More favorable are the hard surfaces of metamorphic, igneous, or compact sedimentary rocks, where such splendid hangers-on as barnacles, chief occupants of the most turbulent parts of the rocky littoral, can survive with ease. In extreme cases, however, namely in arctic waters, the coastal population is comparatively small because the abrasive action of ice tends to remove any species that become attached.

Although the coast of western North America is largely a rocky one, reflecting relatively recent tectonic processes such as faulting, there are a few beaches composed of well-sorted sands. These may contain high density populations of crabs, shrimps, gastropods, and annelid worms, though we do not often see them because of their nocturnal habits.

Altogether, the coastal waters shelter a complex, dynamic ecosystem based upon a ceaseless chain of predation. Certain sponges, clams, and crinoids obtain detritus from overlying waters. Herbivores feed on phytoplankton, larger plants, and encrusting algae. And above these are carnivorous predators and scavengers, including certain fish, starfish, snails, and crustaceans.

Coastal Fishes

In the vernacular of anglers, the waters off the western shores of North America are "loaded with fish." This expert opinion is derived from the presence of warm-water species off southern California, vast numbers of lingcod, rockfish, halibut, and jacksmelt farther north, striped bass and shad, both introduced species, in the San Francisco Bay area, and surf-perches, sculpins, greenlings, and other species. The angler who ventures farther from shore and drops his lures in deeper water is apt to meet with fighting specimens that may weigh hundreds of pounds—bluefin and yellowfin tuna, black sea bass, sharks, swordfish, and striped marlin. Of the sharks, he has a choice of twenty-nine species to give him battle. Off the Washington coast, fishing for alba-

From jagged peaks nearly buried in ice, dark forests descend the Olympic Mountains, ridge after ridge. Down toward the sea are some of the most luxuriant groves in the world. (Don Worth)

core *(Thunnus alalunga)*, a member of the tuna family, has been growing in popularity.

But possibly the greatest stimulus to a western fisherman's pulse is the family *Salmonidae*, the salmon and trout. The thought of tangling with a chinook or king salmon *(Oncorhynchus tschawytscha)* that may reach nearly five feet in length and weigh a hundred pounds is enough to send anglers out in all kinds of weather to all kinds of fishing sites. And if the catch of king salmon does not succeed, there is splendid consolation in a good-sized specimen of red or sockeye salmon *(O. nerka)*, abundant in Washington and British Columbia; pink salmon *(O. borguscha)*, abounding north of the straits of Juan de Fuca; chum *(O. keta)*, found from California's Cape Mendocino to Alaska; and silver or coho *(O. kisutch)*, occurring from San Diego to Alaska.

These species are anadromous, which means that they return to fresh water to spawn. Most of them swim up the rapids and falls of coastal streams as well as major river systems until they find a gravelly stream bed that suits their purpose. A few spawn close to the lower estuaries. The females then excavate shallow nests, and each lays thousands of eggs, upon which the males cast fertilizing layers of milt. Exhausted from the whole ordeal, they go a short distance away to die. The young, depending on the species, hatch and remain in fresh water from a few weeks up to four years before migrating to sea; the principal exception is a subspecies of sockeye, the kokanee, which is landlocked. Trout, on the other hand, may spawn more than once, in fact several times over a period of years. The cutthroat occurs from California to Alaska, and has a sea-run form. The rainbow trout *(Salmo gairdneri)*, with a similar range, also has an ocean-run form, the steelhead.

Such an enormous, but of course not inexhaustible, supply of fish off the Pacific Coast can mean only that the food supply must also be vast. Where there are concentrations of mussels and sea vegetation an abundance of fish may be found, both in numbers and species. It would take pages to list and describe the forage fishes that sustain larger predatory species; among the most common are anchovy, sardine, smelt, herring, and killifish.

Other species attract attention because of their extraordinary habits. The California grunion *(Leuresthes tenuis)* is a small and slender fish that swarms on sandy beaches at night during high summer tides. This and another species of *Leuresthes* in the Gulf of California are the only fish to spawn on land. Females choose just the right swell following high tide after a full moon, dig holes in the sand and partially bury themselves. Immediately the eggs are deposited, a thousand or more at a time. Waiting males wrap their bodies around the females and release their sperm, which filters down to fertilize the eggs. With the next high breaker the fish are washed back to sea, but the eggs remain where they are, the embryos developing until another high tide two weeks later. Then they, too, are washed away, whereupon the larvae hatch and head for deeper water. This process continues for four or five nights after each high tide, and may be observed between March and

September. Neither predatory birds nor fish can attack during the mating process because it is conducted on land and at night. Nor are the buried eggs molested to a great extent.

Fishing for surf smelt *(Hypomesus pretiosus)* is a popular sport, engaged in with nets and fish rakes. When schools of smelt come ashore to spawn, usually heralded by swarming gulls offshore, they deposit their eggs in sandy or gravelly shallow-water areas near the limit of high tide, a process that goes on between April and October.

The flatfishes—sole, halibut, sanddab, turbot, flounder—undergo a metamorphosis during which one eye moves over to the other side. Some flatfishes are right-eyed, others left-eyed. The eyeless or "blind" side is kept down as the fish swims horizontally or rests flat on the ocean floor. Some flatfishes may be gigantic in size. The female Pacific halibut *(Hippoglossus stenolepis)* weighs up to five hundred pounds and produces two and a half million eggs. This species occurs from California to the Aleutian Islands and seems to be increasing in abundance, especially in the northern part of its range.

Life Between Tides

Discovering life between tides is like discovering another world. Or several worlds. As with ecological communities on land, those in the sea have different zones occupied by specific groups of plants and animals. Each group has, during thousands of years, become associated with a certain habitat and each individual of the group has become adapted to the environment and to other organisms sharing it. Along the Pacific Coast, which in reality is not very pacific at all, both wind and current combine to hurl some forceful waves against the shore, and such species as the starfish must be equipped with tube feet and vacuum cups to avoid being washed away by wave impact. Offshore islands may break up this impact, or sandspits moderate it, so that there are protected bays, coves, and estuaries. But in each of these environments—violent or calm, rocky, sandy, muddy, grassy—life depends on depth, light, aeration of waters, exposure between tides, salinity, food and other factors.

The uppermost zone of rocky coasts, which is seldom wetted or even sprayed, contains a snail *(Littorina planaxis)* so well adapted to its environment that it may be an example of a marine species evolving into a land species. A few sand fleas, flatworms, limpets, and barnacles also cling to life. Barnacles *(Balanus glandula)*, among the most abundant coast animals, attach their homes to the rocks and feed only for a short time when high tide comes. They are crustaceans, not mollusks, and are more closely related to crabs than to clams. So hardy are they that they can exist in almost any environment, dry or wet, rough or calm. Likewise, limpets—which are gastropods—cling so tightly to the rocks that neither wave nor man can pry them loose without using great force. The common limpet *(Acmaea digitalis)* occurs in immense colonies from California to Alaska.

In the next lower level, water remains a longer time and consequently life is far more varied and abundant.

Exploring the tidal pools, we find aquatic plants providing "nurseries" for such animals as periwinkles. Or we discover under rocks the fragile and sometimes beautiful brittle-stars *(Amphipholis pugetana)*. Barnacles grow larger and limpets more varied. We follow a hermit crab *(Pagurus samuelis)* as it hunts for snail shells in which to make a home.

Below this environment is one of still greater diversity, one regularly covered by high tides, and which we are not as easily able to enter. But in the clear waters we can see the most abundant coastal anemone *(Bunodactis elegantissima)* waving its paralyzing tentacles and taking in almost any kind of food that comes within reach. The richness of tide pools needs to be closely studied to be grasped fully; a few of the most common types of lower animals are starfish, sponges, nudibranchs (snails without shells), chitons, corals, worms and shrimps. Unfortunately, this section of the surf is a favorite collecting locality; as a result, starfish of red, yellow, or purple coloration have been much reduced except in tidal pools that are difficult for human beings to reach. Some animals, such as crabs, occupy bare rock; others live among rockweed. Hermit crabs and other organisms are adapted to thrive in several of the shore habitats.

There is little waste in this community. What appears complex and confused has a definite organization and order. For example, debris is gleaned by so many different organisms that it is constantly used up, a true economy of natural ecosystems. On the other hand, there are times when this orderliness seems to be disrupted—and the result is wholesale natural slaughter. Excessive multiplication of certain noxious dinoflagellates, a form of plant plankton, causes mass mortality and renders the meat of clams and other organisms poisonous. At such times, specific beaches may be quarantined to forestall digging and consumption by human beings. Although these "red tides" are known in many other places around the world, the conditions that bring them on are little understood. It may be that availability of nutrients combines with unusually favorable physical conditions to encourage the growth of offensive plankton. Disturbance of the upwelling current, temporary stagnation of water, and rise in ocean temperature may likewise be contributing factors.

The lowest tidal environment of the rocky coast is seldom exposed to air, and contains what may well be nature's most abundant treasures of the sea. The clusters and associations are remarkable; one might almost term them tiny ecosystems, some developed among rocks, others in the folded arms of algae. The great green anemone *(Anthopleura xanthogrammica)*, up to ten inches in diameter, is the one most often seen by human visitors to this water environment. What may be the largest known starfish occurs here, the sunflower star *(Pycnopodia helianthoides)*, with up to twenty-four arms and a diameter of twenty-four inches. One of the most beautiful of all mollusks, the red abalone *(Haliotus rufescens)*, lives on the undersides of rock ledges and crawls about to feed on algae. Iridescent colors of the shell have long made abalone popular; as a result of collecting and commercial use it has been depleted, but is now protected by California law and cannot be shipped or otherwise taken from the state. Its greatest development is attained along the Monterey coast; abalones inhabit other parts of the world but only in the Pacific do they attain large size. In some cases, they may grow to be twelve inches long.

The largest chiton in the world *(Cryptochiton stelleri)*, up to thirteen inches long, occurs from California to Alaska, excellent evidence of the high productivity of this marine life system. And among the other inhabitants of rocky tide pools are sea cucumbers, sea urchins, hydroids, sponges, tunicates, bryozoa, shrimps, spiny lobsters, and a small species of octopus that is popular among gourmets as a source of food.

Out on the open rocky coast, currents are more powerful, and organisms need to be equipped with attachment devices that enable them to resist the tremendous energy of the surf. Inhabitants of this agitated region include mussels, anemones, goose barnacles, and starfish. In contrast are the quiet bays and estuaries, protected from heavy surf, home of still another community of marine animals. One of the coast's best examples of a sheltered environment is Puget Sound. A few familiar organisms of rocky areas, such as barnacles, limpets and crabs, are found in this environment; the edible mussel *(Mytilus edulis)* grows in tremendous congregations from Puget Sound north. Most of the inhabitants have become adapted to life in quiet waters: certain species of snails, anemones, starfish, and chitons, plus hydroids, bryozoa, and masses of oysters and scallops. On sand flats gather concentrations of sand dollars *(Dendraster excentricus)*, dark-colored when alive but conspicuously white after they have died and their round skeletons have washed up on shore. They are urchins despite their lack of long spines; evidence is in the five-pointed design on the back, somewhat lopsided itself and set off center. Razor clams *(Siliqua patula)* are much sought by human diggers on the sandy beaches of Washington, but speed is essential; this clam can bury itself in less than ten seconds.

In some places along the coast, beds of eelgrass also harbor distinctive communities of organisms, including snails, hydroids, shrimps and worms. Mud flats lack the customary attachment surfaces that would be found on rocks of the open coast, so there are few or no starfish, sponges, chitons and the like. But the specialized fauna does include fiddler crabs and many snails, clams and worms. The largest clam on the coast is the geoduck *(Panope generosa)*, a deep-burrowing species; its shells may be more than eight inches long.

In these pages we have touched only a few highlights of the complex marine world at the edge of the continent. We could go on to describe phosphorescent flatworms, clams that jump, mollusks that bore into rocks, nudibranchs that walk on the underside of the water surface, or snails and oysters that are born male, become bisexual for a while, then turn into females. But this is enough to suggest how enormously complex is life along the Pacific seashore. Added to the biologic makeup of the cypress forests, redwood groves, elk and condors, and to the geological makeup of glaciers, mountain ranges, and faults that extend for hundreds of miles, it is clear that the Pacific coastal province possesses a natural treasury of immense appeal to students of science and to those who appreciate the outdoor heritage of western North America.

11. Volcano Country: North to the Cascades

And out of that hill breaketh fire with brimstone, as it were in hell.

Bartholomaeus Anglicus
in *De proprietatibus rerum,* 1470

As we approached the great lava fields of the southern Cascades, ascending slowly from Red Bluff, California, there seemed little to show for what must have been tremendous disruptions of the earth's crust and vast outpourings of molten rock. For mile after mile we crossed over reddish and brown expanses of lava covered by grass and scattered oak trees. At an elevation of a thousand feet came the diaphanous silhouettes of sparsely branched digger pines, and at three thousand the outriders of the vast ponderosa pine forest of northeastern California. None of this gave warning of what we were about to see.

As far as most of the world is concerned, the Cascade Range is simply a 1200-mile line of towering volcanoes of calendar-picture familiarity: Mount Hood, Mount St. Helens, Mount Rainier, Mount Baker, Lassen Peak and others, most of them with snow and glaciers, usually surrounded by picturesque lakes and ponds, all with some degree of vegetation and animal life on the lower slopes. Often this is all that many travelers see; they do not realize that the snowy peaks are portals not only to scenic grandeur but to some extraordinary hidden facets of the Northwest.

Foothold in the Sky

The farther we went in this basically black landscape, the more unusual the country became. The clear air at five thousand feet bore a scent of pine and sagebrush. Earlier that morning the streams at lower elevations had been lined with elderberry and willow, but now the aspect was an arid one in which it seemed that neither stream, pond, nor even a hidden seep could exist; on these porous lava plateaus rainfall must certainly sink into the ground and drain away directly rather than run off in streams. One almost expected, by extension, that wildlife would be rare, that those names along the trail—Quail Spring, Grouse Mountain, Deer Hill and Badger Well—were not to be trusted. Yet there in the open woods grew grass and browse plants sufficient to sustain a good animal community. Furthermore, the Indian wheat *(Wyethia mollis),* large and leafy, indicated at least some moisture; so did the pine and sagebrush. And so, as in a dry land at almost any elevation, there was obviously an ecosystem composed of organisms well suited to their environment and to other organisms.

As the day progressed and the temperature rose, a high haze overspread the sky. All those clouds that had been wisps along the horizon in early morning developed into thunderheads, and these in turn made way for other wisps that rose, expanded, coalesced and broke off to form their own storms. Along the horizon grew a line of rising clouds, as if a white forest were burgeoning. Barely discernible in the distance was one sharp-pointed "cloud" that did not move or change its shape: the master eminence of Shasta, fifty miles away and almost liquid in the disturbed reflections of heat

Above the meadows along King's Creek the crags of Lassen Peak are silent and peaceful. But in 1915 there were molten lava, searing steam, and devastating floods of mud. (Ken Wheeler)

and haze. There could be no question of its command. As nature had split the Rocky Mountains into three divisions, so had the Cascades been separated into south, middle, and north components, and of the southernmost section, Mount Shasta stood master at 14,162 feet. Long ago it had magnetically attracted early explorers. Clarence King, the Survey geologist of fortieth parallel fame, climbed to the ice-clad summit in 1870 and later wrote: "Once upon the spiry pinnacles which crown the crater rim, a scene of wild power broke upon us. The round crater-bowl, about a mile in diameter and nearly a thousand feet deep, lay beneath us, its steep, shelving sides of shattered lava mantled in places to the very bottom by fields of snow." Shortly after King's ascent, John Muir climbed the mountain twice. "I held my commanding foothold in the sky for two hours," he wrote, "gazing on the glorious landscapes spread maplike around the immense horizon, and tracing the outlines of the ancient lava-streams extending far into the surrounding plains, and the pathways of vanished glaciers of which Shasta had been the center." Muir felt at home among the plants and animals of this region, and spoke of lilies, violets, and larkspurs in rich confusion, of golden sunbeams streaming through the pines and cedars, and of birds, squirrels and other fauna.

We soon arrived in the heart of the lava and cinder country, the youngest part of it, where we might have expected only black jagged lava, barren and forbidding, as yet uncolonized by advancing vegetation. Indeed, on the freshest flows life had had little chance to become established. The California lava beds were not unlike other sites in western North America that possess lava flows and cinder cones so recently erupted that they seem Hawaii-like. One example, Sunset Crater, in northern Arizona, erupted within the present millennium. Another, the so-called Modoc Lava Beds of northern California, had been our destination this summer morning and we were not disappointed to find that a great deal of the region lay strewn with lava flows so recent and devoid of life that like the eruptions of Sunset Crater they must be very young. In any case, no soil had obliterated the smooth contours of the taffy-like pahoehoe lava, which seemed to be sealed in a sugar glaze. No grass had softened the vicious-looking jagged material that Hawaiians call *aa* and Mexicans refer to as *malpais,* meaning bad country. The lavas had originated from a subterranean mass of molten

basalt, and had been in places viscous enough to flow for miles and cover a wide area before cooling enough to harden and come to a halt.

In other places, more violent and explosive in origin, globs of lava had been hurled into the air, where they broke apart, cooled and hardened into porous cinders that fell around vents to form cinder cones. We could easily picture the spectacular "curtains of fire" that must have been responsible for the crater complexes because such fountains are familiar in Hawaiian eruptions of historic times. Red-hot spatter had been disgorged in formless masses that cooled and draped over one another like heaps of mud. Some lava flows, both old and new, were crossed by cracks and canyons, and spotted with driblet cones supplied through tubes going into the earth a hundred feet or more. The lava and cinders even had colors—yellow, gray, brown and red.

But life? We soon discovered that a great deal more of it existed, and in greater variety, than met the eye. Growing directly on the lava itself, for example, and among the first to get established on a barren lava flow, were green and brown pads of moss, withered in the summer heat but capable of revival by occasional rain. Small fibers penetrated cracks in the rock, anchoring the plant. Lichens, likewise pioneer plants, hugged the rough surfaces, and displayed a wide range of colors: black, gray, red, orange, yellow, and chartreuse. Throughout the lava hills grew rabbitbrush (*Chrysothamnus* sp.), which in late summer and fall explodes in a ball of golden-yellow flowers.

Nearly everywhere we saw the Sierra juniper *(Juniperus occidentalis)*, an aromatic evergreen that reaches scarcely half the height here that it does in more favored localities. In places it was decorated with a handsome green lichen. To our delight, the farther we went into the lava beds, the greater the floral and faunal complexity became. Patches of tumbled black rock quite literally sheltered a multitude of rose gardens. The fernbush *(Spiraea millefolium)*, which we had known at the Grand Canyon, grew singly or in groups on even the recent flows; its yellow and white sweet-smelling blossoms lured busy flurries of butterflies and nectar-loving insects. Another member of the rose family was the bitterbrush *(Purshia tridentata)*, another the bitter cherry *(Prunus emarginata)*, a diminutive shrub with glossy, even sticky, leaves, new orange stems and old gray ones; and another the mountain mahogany *(Cercocarpus ledifolius)*. All these left little doubt that there was animal life among the lava beds: such palatable leaves, fruits and seeds would be a temptation to many species.

Life on the Lava Beds

To see many animals that might inhabit the lava beds we rose before dawn for nearly a week, and by the time the sun flooded the lava with orange light, we had hiked halfway up Schonchin Butte, gone far out along Black Lava Flow, or made our way down to the edge of Tule Lake. The evening hours could have produced somewhat the same results, but mornings were definitely to be preferred. They were quiet and the air was clean; the breezes, if any, remained gentle and fragrant, and the dew. sensible if not visible, helped to alleviate the dryness of the land.

Cottontail and jackrabbits, conspicuous though silent, moved among the sage and sagebrush. Deer fed on shrubs in a scattered pattern, though most of the resident herd, less than two thousand in all, had migrated for the summer to mountains farther south. Even though the ground was broken by craters and crevices, quite obviously an impediment to a fast getaway, pronghorns lived on the lava beds. Chipmunks and golden-mantled ground squirrels ran furiously along the fallen logs of pines. California ground squirrels hunted for seeds, fruits or roots. Yellow-bellied marmots stretched out in the sun. As the final traces of night were being dissolved, even a casual glance would reveal either the big brown bat *(Eptesicus fuscus)* or the Townsend's big-eared bat *(Plecotus townsendii)*, the presence of both suggesting a good supply of flying insects. Earthbound insects were controlled by at least five species of shrews, the most common being Trowbridge's shrew *(Sorex trowbridgii)*; we did not see these—few people do—because they are small, largely nocturnal, and wary, their lives divided between hunting smaller creatures and escaping the talons of marauding owls.

It seemed quite logical that in such a thriving community of marmots, shrews, rabbits, hares and conies, predators other than owls would be at work to balance the population. Hence the sight of a coyote, its gray fur reddened by sunrise, seemed a perfectly normal part of the scene. There would have been nothing unusual about seeing a bobcat either; it might have been watching the terrain intently from a juniper tree or waiting beside some black rock crevice for the appearance of a careless rodent. The human visitor might be pardoned for wondering how, with so many crevices and escape routes in the lava beds, the bobcat got a living. But, of course, the key to bobcat survival lay partly in overabundance of animal life, a situation dependent on good times or bad; also, the bobcat relied on a cunning usually superior to that of its prey. The difficulty may increase when many of the rodents hibernate, but to the wily bobcat this is not a major obstacle.

It is easy to become lyrical about the lava beds and their inhabitants, yet we find most memorable the things that were relatively simple. A remarkable sight was that of two large yellow swallowtail butterflies drinking at a small pocket of water in the rough lava surface; their brilliance contrasted so with the dark surroundings that we can still see them drinking, flying up, fluttering around, landing, drinking again.

Another advantage of rising early is to hear the call of the canyon wren, as we did from the side of Schonchin Butte. In the ponderosa pine forest one morning we tape-recorded the "wheezing" note of the rufous-sided towhee *(Pipilo erythrophthalmus)*, then later replayed it at one-eighth the original speed, which revealed musical notes and nuances we had never dreamed of, and which are ordinarily indistinguishable to the human ear. The forest was full of sound: a woodpecker's drilling echoed through the trees like the tattoo of a drum. A red-shafted flicker shouted as it flew into the branches of a tall pine. Pinyon jays chattered and swooped in pairs from tree to tree.

Some of the larger animals that once inhabited this region were gone—the camel and mastodon of prehistoric times, the bear, wolf, and mountain sheep of historic times. With luck a visitor may still sight a mountain lion. He may come across a badger, and efforts are being made to reintroduce bighorns. If the hour is right and his patience endures, he may witness the antics of a kangaroo rat, or see a porcupine ambling along the trail. Such is morning life on the lava beds; what seems at midday to be a hot and forbidding environment devoid of animal life is simply a smoothly working and highly complex life system all but asleep.

Subterranean Surprises

There could hardly be a wider contrast than that between the ice-walled peaks of the high Cascades and the somber flows of Lava Beds National Monument. It seemed to us, as we stood on Black Craters and surveyed the sharp jumbled ridges roundabout, that a visitor to the Cascades constantly met such contrasts and encountered the unexpected—from wildlife as well as human history. For example, it might occur to any student that the basaltic ridges and clefts qualified as prime terrain for fights between Indians and soldiers, that the overhangs and half-collapsed craters made ideal council chambers, and that rocky points served superbly as ridges from which to watch for approaching enemies. All this actually happened. In these lava beds, the Modoc Indian War of 1872–73 was fought. So well did the Modocs know this confusing territory and so well entrenched were they that the battle was quite likely the most costly Indian campaign ever waged by the United States. A few dozen Modocs, with the help of their natural resources, held the United States Army at bay and inflicted some stinging losses. The soldiers won, eventually, but at enormous price. They were, after all, fighting not only Indians, but lava as well.

For any combatants who wished to use them, the lava provided secret tunnels. We knew that lava flows characteristically leave behind air pockets, large and small. In some cases, long moving tongues of lava cool and harden on the outside while the molten interior flows on, spends itself, and leaves a tunnel that resembles a subway tube. What surprised us was the concentration of these. Lava Beds National Monument, which at 46,238 acres is just a fraction of the lava beds region, preserves some three hundred known caves, the largest 96 feet in diameter. Many lava tubes, moreover, run for miles beneath the surface.

As we explored one after another of these caves, we found them to possess some of the most interesting subterranean formations in the West. For one thing, their nearly level floors, composed of congealed lava, exhibited distinctive designs that showed up weirdly in the light of our lanterns. We could well imagine the temperatures that must have prevailed in these natural tunnels when the lava flowed to a stop. The degree of its viscosity determined, in fact, the contours of the floor; thin lavas left almost a boulevard-like pavement, thick lavas a broken billowing surface. It reminded us of the mixing phase in making fudge when the surface is stirred and left in arrangements of curves and ridges. In some places the floors had remained in a three-dimensional checkerboard pattern; in others, there were "frozen" rapids, falls, and eddy currents. Where the level of lava fluctuated while the flow diminished, it left behind a series of terraces. Where the rate of drainage varied, it left shelves or even caves on several levels.

More than once we had to bend over to avoid colliding with sharp-pointed lava stalactites. There a mass of lava had pulled away and flowed on down the tube; the ceiling dripped red-hot lava that solidified in the form of icicles called lava-cicles. Their endlessly varied patterns provide some of the most fascinating designs in nature. Furthermore, there is more color in these dark passages than one expects; in the Golden

Pintails, a surface-feeding species, depend for food on roots or shoots of aquatic plants and on snails and minnows. (Allan D. Cruickshank: National Audubon Society)

Dome cave the ceiling and lava-cicles have a rich yellow coating of sulfur compounds.

These features give some idea of what conditions must have been inside a lava flow, where shapes and colors grew literally out of fire and brimstone. But now there was no heat—only icy cold. Since expansion of gases had left millions of tiny vesicles in the lava, it possessed precisely the properties of insulation used by man in picnic "ice chests," which hold in cold and slow down melting. For centuries, rainwater sank into the lava beds and came to rest in certain caves and tubes where the temperature seldom rose above freezing.

This residual cold apparently comes from winter air that settles into caves and seldom, if ever, mixes with warm summer air—which rises rather than settles. About a hundred of the known caves in Lava Beds National Monument contain ice or water or both, and in some the ice has accumulated to a depth of six feet or formed in "frozen rivers" hundreds of feet long. In many cases the ice is clear and transparent; one ice pendant measures twenty feet high and four to six inches thick. Other caves contain abundant crystals of ice.

Pintails by the Million

Perhaps the greatest of unexpected pleasures is something one would hardly expect in a land of dry lava beds and waterless cinder cones. This is the largest annual concentration of waterfowl in North America. A combination of natural circumstances has made the Klamath Basin, on the dividing line between Oregon and California, an avian health resort and a breeding ground par excellence. So attractive to waterfowl are the marshes, ponds, and islands, that incredible numbers of birds using the Pacific Flyway turn inland and settle for a time on five national wildlife refuges within a fifty-mile radius of Klamath Falls, Oregon. One, the Lower Klamath Refuge, was established in 1908 by Theodore Roosevelt as the first national wildlife refuge devoted primarily to the protection of waterfowl. The site of greatest concentration is in the Tule Lake National Wildlife Refuge, which borders the northern edge of Lava Beds National Monument. Tule Lake gained its protected status in 1928, and includes about 37,000 acres of ideal waterfowl habitat. Here nest thousands of eared, western, and pied-billed grebes. Most abundant of the nesting birds is the redhead (Aythya americana), a species that requires large marsh areas of a kind that is rapidly diminishing over much of the continent.

Gadwalls breed here also, as do mallards, teals, ruddy ducks, shovelers, scaups, and canvasbacks, altogether a recorded 160 species nesting within the refuges. Through extraordinary foresight, the United States Fish and Wildlife Service has provided grainfields beside the refuges so that a good portion of the birds will get their fill on refuge land and not encroach so heavily on privately owned fields in the region; moreover, such good eating in autumn delays migration long enough to allow Imperial and Sacramento Valley farmers to harvest their rice or lettuce crops before the birds continue southward.

Pelicans, terns, gulls, cormorants, herons and egrets also nest among these refuges, but the greatest spectacle occurs in October when birds by the million converge on the lakes and marshes, darkening the sky with their wings. Hundreds of thousands each of mallards, American widgeons, and white-fronted geese gather here, though by far the most abundant is a bird that happens to be also the most widely distributed and one of the best-known North American ducks, the pintail (Anas acuta). It has collected here in concentrations of five million.

The pintail's name comes from pointed, elongated central feathers of the tail, but the pintail is also memorable for the male's dark head, elegant white stripe along the neck, and clean white front. These characteristics, plus its rapid, graceful flight, distinguish it from the tropics to the Arctic. Moreover, it is a hardy duck. The cold of winter does not impair its migratory drives and it may arrive in northern Alaska breeding grounds as early as April. That signals the start of nuptial affairs—expanding chest, softly uttered notes, rapid pursuit—which in turn heralds the time of nesting. Though a water bird, the pintail builds its nest on land, often well away from water, either on islands or in fields. In the nest the female lays six to a dozen eggs, and few water birds are as fearlessly defensive of these or, three weeks later, of the young; some naturalists have referred to the pintail as the most devoted of all ducks in this respect. But courage has also led to capture and subsequent slaughter of the birds. The newly hatched must walk before they swim, which may mean a prodigious overland trek to water. Once there, they enter upon their search for food: insects, aquatic animals, the roots and shoots of water plants, seeds of land plants, and other assorted

edibles. Pintails are primarily vegetarian, however, consuming mostly pondweeds.

As Aubudon said, few birds exhibit more graceful motions on water than the pintail. "Its delicately slender neck," he wrote, "the beautiful form of its body, and its pointed tail, which it always carries highly raised, distinguish it from the other species with which it may associate." Being a surface feeder, it is also often observed in a somewhat less than dignified posture—upended, feet paddling, tail high, its long neck invisible beneath the water, its bill searching the shallows for food. On the wing, pintails are fast and powerful, able to maneuver skillfully and migrate swiftly once the urge to head south comes upon them. Their "racy lines" permit them speeds of well over sixty miles per hour. Peak populations of ducks arrive at Tule Lake and the other Klamath refuges during the first half of October, and the sight of thousands of pintails in the air especially delights photographers. For the rest of the winter, pintails spread out from Florida to Hawaii.

Tule Lake is not to be thought of solely as a bird sanctuary; its shores are also a favorite gathering place for mink, muskrats, and striped skunks. Not far away, at the Modoc National Wildlife Refuge, near Alturas, California, large flocks of whistling swans gather during migration. Thus, the Lava Beds region, though generally deficient in water as far as man is concerned, does have its ponds and lakes, and on these live a splendid variety and sometimes surpassing abundance of animals in a wetlands ecosystem.

The Great Eruptions

For as far as the eye could see over the lava beds, everything was volcanic. And beyond this dramatic landscape lay others, over the horizon and even beyond the continent. All land areas fringing the Pacific Ocean are replete with volcanoes, fault scarps, and associated phenomena. There are thirty-six active volcanoes in the Aleutians and a continuous string of them down through Japan, the Philippines, the East Indies and the South Pacific to New Zealand. It is now believed that the floor of the Pacific Basin contains tens of thousands of volcanoes, which suggests an eruptive violence far more intense than has ever been produced on continents. That the Cascades, a part of this volcanic family, should have had some stirring cataclysms at one time or another is not surprising. Perhaps the best example is Crater Lake, now a tranquil caldera, or volcanic basin. This crater was once a mountain like its neighbors, evidently adorned with glaciers because glacial sediments now lie interbedded on the slopes of

Right above: Mount Rainier is made up of lava layers and of rock debris explosively ejected—a contrast to the delicate fields of summer flowers. (Bob Clemenz) Right: Yellow corolla-like spathes of skunk cabbage open early in a swampy swale on the side of Mount Rainier. (Ann and Myron Sutton) Far right: Mountain bluebirds (Sialia currucoides) *lack the reddish tints of other bluebirds and are found at higher elevations—up to twelve thousand feet. (Ed Park)*

the caldera. Toward late Pleistocene the mountain either exploded with a spectacular blast or, as seems more likely because there appears to be too little blown-out debris to equal the bulk of the missing mountain top, collapsed upon itself, probably after ejection of molten material from within. Crater Lake, at 2177 feet in depth, is the deepest terrestrial lake in North America. To many admirers it is also the bluest and most beautiful.

Throughout the Cascades there is ample evidence of explosive forces at work, and the line of volcanoes so striking today is but the most recent in a long series of volcanic events. Igneous materials poured out onto an Eocene plain to initiate the evolution of the Cascade Range; then after a period of mountain folding came some of the greatest outpourings of lava anywhere, the basalt plateaus of what is now the Columbia River basin; after that, there was more folding in Pliocene time, and finally the birth of the present generation of volcanoes. Since then, the mountain contours have been modified by glaciers.

The Cascades contain shield volcanoes such as Shasta, in which the cone was built up, probably rather quietly, of overlapping and interfingering lava flows. This mountain is believed to have had volcanic activity as recently as 1786 A.D. In a few cases there are plug domes, where viscous lava accumulated in a domelike mass over and around a volcanic vent. The North Cascades, in north-central Washington, differ in that even though Mount Baker and Glacier Peak are volcanic, the neighboring peaks are granitic, their summits almost plateau-like, as in the Sierra Nevada. The North Cascades are also marked by long, deep valleys, some with sizeable bodies of water. Lake Chelan, for instance, lies in a glacial trough that is 8500 feet from bottom of lake to top of crest. It once held a glacier that may have been more than eighty miles long. But the rocks are basically very old rather than very young, which underscores the many contrasts in the Cascade Range. Today the North Cascades possess the greatest concentration of glaciers in the United States—with the exception of Alaska.

Have the Eruptions Ended?

Have the eruptions ended or is this merely a quiescent period? No one knows, but all the evidence suggests that volcanic activity has not by any means subsided. There are still steam vents in the lava beds region and many thermal phenomena around Lassen Peak, eighty miles south of Lava Beds National Monument. Lassen, in fact, is Yellowstone all over again. The great geysers are missing but the mountains are grander, jumbled crags and barren summits from which a wisp of steam now and then issues. Farther downslope and away through the forest comes the faint but unmistakable odor of sulfurous gases. Boiling lakes lie shrouded in veils of heated mist. We investigate the hissing sound of escaping steam, and enter a valley of desolation partly hidden by clouds of vapor. A hollow bellowing sound emanates from the throat of a steam vent, sounding as though it came from some subterranean boiler chamber. From mud pots globs of red mud are thrown out of a porridge-like mass that seethes at two hundred

degrees Fahrenheit. Spatter cones, fumaroles, ghost forests killed by migrating hot-spring activity, cinder cones, lava flows—all this is evidence that internal heat still remains beneath the Cascades, and that this particular geothermal complex seems to be biding its time until once again it can blow up as it did between 1915 and 1917. Perhaps Lassen Peak will send another column of smoke five miles into the air, another lava flow down the side of the mountain, or another cloud of steam and gas horizontally like an exploding jet to devastate the forest. Altogether the Cascade Range extends much farther north than Lassen Peak and the Lava Beds, almost 1200 miles if you consider Hoodoo Mountain, in British Columbia, the northern terminus of the range.

But there is a great deal more to the Cascades besides flows of lava and caves of ice. Each of the major stratovolcanoes erupted almost entirely from central craters, one outpouring of lava issuing on another, cones coalescing, layers of basalt and basaltic andesite piling up one by one, until peaks higher than anything now existing in this region were achieved. This round of activity commenced about the beginning of Pliocene time, and while there may have been violent activity, by and large the issuance of lavas was probably quiet. Afterward the big volcanoes received invading, upsurging masses of granodiorite and diorite. Presently the mountains seem subdued, but subdued does not mean finished. As with Lassen Peak, there is every evidence that the mountains are only waiting. Mount St. Helens did in fact erupt in the last century, and there are enough warm springs and steam vents to foretell a little, at least, about the future.

Highest of all the Cascade peaks is Mount Rainier (14,410 feet), which typifies the volcanic structure and awesome natural beauty of these mountains. It has been about five hundred years since Mount Rainier heated up enough to cause any rash activity, and that was little more than a flow of debris. But volcanologists know that Mount Rainier's history is one of long quiet periods punctuated by action. Eruptions of pumice, steam, or lava are possible, and mudflows big enough to travel forty miles could be generated. The latter might well reach a thickness of seventy feet, as did the Osceola Mudflow five thousand years ago; on this mudflow the cities of Enumclaw and Buckley, Washington, have been built. Nor would it take much heating up of the summit crater or cone of Mount Rainier, which is still warm, to cause substantial melting of snow and ice. The United States Geological Survey says that although it has been about two thousand years since the last major eruption, a new one could occur at any time. A small eruption of pumice occurred sometime between 1820 and 1854. Mount Rainier, too, is a mountain waiting.

A Paradise of Flowers

Meanwhile, Mount Rainier's "inside story" has been exposed by centuries of erosion, glaciers scouring deep canyons on the flanks of cones, or landslides and mudflows hauling away millions of tons of debris. Perennially capped with ice and snow, Mount Rainier lies in the path of tons of moisture lifted out of the Pacific and carried on rising air masses to the mountain slopes. Paradise Ranger Station, in Mountain Rainier National Park, has long enjoyed the reputation of having some of the heaviest snowfall in the country: 575 inches (about fifty feet) annually, with accumulation some winters of nearly twice that. This snow compacts into glaciers above seven thousand feet. No other mountain in the conterminous United States has such a system of them. There are nearly thirty glaciers covering over thirty square miles.

But it is grandeur, solitude, and the animal life that make Mount Rainier most memorable. Even the glaciers, curiously enough, possess their own life forms, for insects, chiefly thysanurons, a group that includes the silverfish, live on them, as do certain worms *(Mesenchytraeus)*; and it is colonies of bacteria *(Protococcus nivalis)* that produce "red snow." On the lower slopes, Mount Rainier possesses flower-strewn meadows that are unquestionably among the finest in the world, "a perfect flower elysium," John Muir called them. When in June the snow retreats from forests or melts away to expose large areas of soil to the sun, butterbur or coltsfoot *(Petasites speciosus)* and yellow-flowered skunk cabbage *(Lysichitum americanum)* burst into bloom as harbingers of the floral pageant to follow. The skunk cabbage is particularly conspicuous, its yellow corolla-like spathes being larger and showier than those of eastern varieties. This plant often masses in swamps or bogs, where the casual visitor finds that the odor it imparts well earns its descriptive name. On open meadows the snow may not have disappeared before avalanche fawnlily *(Erythronium montanum)* and western anemone *(Anemone occidentalis)* burst into flower. With a short season, nature seems almost desperate to complete the reproductive cycle before winter returns. When the mountain meadows become filled with white marsh marigold *(Caltha leptosepala)*, spiraea, lupine, red, white and yellow heather, shooting star, blue gentian, phlox, paintbrush, penstemon, bluebells, and daisies, it seems as though every species were trying to bloom at once. The annual tenure of these gardens being brief, and the ecosystem in which they grow being highly fragile, we can be thankful for the fact that the mountain is a national park. The Act of Congress which established the park in 1899 emphasized its "natural curiosities" and "wonderful objects," and clearly specified that "all hunting or the killing, wounding, or capturing at any time of any wild bird or animal" is prohibited and that the Secretary of the Interior shall provide "for the protection of the animals and birds in the park from capture or destruction, and to prevent their being frightened or driven from the park...."

This provision has been enforced, so that a hiker who takes the ninety-mile Wonderland Trail around the mountain is sure to see a great deal of plant and animal life in a wilderness setting. Raccoons may well be the first animals to be seen since they occupy the few places where man himself comes into the park. But pikas inhabit the rock slides and the hiker may come upon Douglas and golden-mantled ground squirrels, marmots, chipmunks, blacktail deer, elk, beaver, porcupine, snowshoe hare, fox, coyote, bob-cat, and cougar. One of the most likely, and perhaps most stirring, encounters for those who hike the high country, whether here in the northern Cascades or in the Northern and Canadian Rockies, is that with the agile, almost unbelievable mountain goat.

The Goat That Is an Antelope

A speck of white against the cliff, little different from a multitude of snowbanks, is how most people see a mountain goat *(Oreamnos americanus)*, and even then they may have to use powerful binoculars to make out details. Occasionally humans reach the domain of the mountain goat, which in many places requires crampons, rope, carabiners, pitons and all the other accoutrements of climbers in high places.

The mountain goat has none of these, only feet that are two-toed and blunt for traction and equipped with sharp-edged, pliable, non-skid pads which, according to Stewart Brandborg, who studied the life history of the mountain goat in Idaho, allow the animal to display greater nimbleness on rough terrain than any other large animal species in North America. Men who watch this broad-shouldered ponderous beast (it may weigh up to three hundred pounds) negotiate narrow ledges, pull itself up steep slopes, and cross the face of cliffs, may be astonished at its fine sense of balance and inclined to think that the animal never slips, stumbles, or falls into the depths below. It appears almost to be careless, leaping and dashing when necessary, or ambling amiably and possibly even drowsily on nearly vertical terrain. Yet the mountain goat does lose its footing. It does get trapped on ledges and have to turn back. It does slip on cliffs. And it undoubtedly falls.

The mountain goat occupies high peaks from the northern Cascades and Northern Rockies north through the Canadian Rockies into Alaska. From man's point of view this environment may seem entirely lacking in food and utterly hostile, although, of course, men like Sir John Franklin have survived in the Arctic for a month on little more than lichens. In summer, on the high ranges, the mountain goat is generally content with the foliage at hand but does exhibit preferences, mostly grasses in summer and shrubs in winter. Much depends on what is available, and winter food shortages are sometimes serious. Water is little or no problem but sometimes mountain goats will travel miles to a salt lick. If weather becomes too severe or forage too scarce the mountain goat can descend into a more equable climate where a better supply of food awaits it; migration between summer and winter ranges, often not far apart, is common. Still, the mountain goat's food is that of high places, and with several inches of fine fur beneath a shaggy outer coat there are few extremes of cold that the animal cannot endure.

Living remotely and being adapted to such an environment has saved this species from exploitation, but human hunters still chase the mountain goat into its home grounds. The number and distribution of the animals may well be about what they were in earlier times. In a few places, such as along the upper Salmon River in Idaho, construction of roads into high places introduced hunters and miners to the mountain goat's habitat, with the result that some herds were depleted.

The beneficial role of the red-tailed hawk (Buteo jamaicensis) *in natural ecosystems as well as agricultural areas has been well established.* (Ed Park)

In a few places, the mountain goat hunting season had to be closed. The uncontrolled use of helicopters may prove an even more serious threat. Even airlines may be causing damage; pilots hoping to titillate passengers sometimes fly low over mountain meadows. At the swooping approach of an airlines flight near Juneau, Alaska, we have seen herds of forty or more mountain goats racing frantically across alpine meadows.

For the present, mountain goats seem to be holding their own with what tranquillity remains to them. They breed in the fall, then move during winter from one patch of tundra to another where winds have blown the snow away, and give birth in spring to one or two kids. Evolution has worked remarkably well and the kids are born with an ability to jump; in less than an hour after birth they not only stand but can leap short distances. And apparently from the beginning they have a coat that shields them against subzero temperatures.

Play time is vigorous, but ends all too soon as adulthood approaches. For most of its life, all the mountain goat needs or wants is a little space in which to roam and hunt for food, a place in which to bed down—and peace. Usually reticent, it is entirely able to butt intruders, men included, off the mountain if trapped into doing so, or can climb out of reach of wolves, grizzly bears and mountain lions, though not man. The horns, worn by both male and female and never shed, are seldom more than a foot long, yet a sharp upward jab of them can inflict serious injury. But the mountain goat is no match for, and has little defense against, a horde of more insidious enemies that share the wilderness with it: fleas, ticks, lice and tapeworms, plus diseases like pneumonia and peritonitis, the latter an ailment that may result from goring during mating battles. Just what toll avalanches take is hard to determine, but the loss is believed to be substantial, and may be even greater than mortality from other causes.

As with so many animals of the West, this one has been misnamed. It is not a goat. That may seem hard to believe because the beast looks so much like a goat. But take away the beard, remove a few inches of shaggy coat, slenderize the shoulders a little, color the animal brown—and you have an antelope. The mountain "goat" is the only North American antelope (remembering that the pronghorn is not an antelope but rather is in a family by itself) and is more closely related to the European chamois, an inhabitant of the wooded heights of the Alps and adjacent mountain chains. William Berryman Scott, in his *History of Land Mammals in the Western Hemisphere,* calls it a peculiar and aberrant form of the chamois subfamily of antelopes and suggests that it was a Pleistocene migrant from Asia. In any case, on the upland tundra of North America, where the white-tailed ptarmigan feeds on dwarf willow, and where the water pipit and gray-crowned rosy finch construct their nests, the mountain "goat" has become adapted to a special environment.

Mysterious Giants

In the Cascades, and indeed throughout the western half of North America, we may in time become accustomed to bigness, to scales and dimensions unlike those with which we are usually familiar. Some men measure the West in terms of its deepest canyons, highest mountains, largest trees, and so on; in the upper Columbia River basin there are none of these. The general image of northern Oregon and eastern Washington is one of broad plains and lava bluffs, quite often somber rather than colorful, and where few monoliths, mountains, or tracts of tall trees manifest giantism in the usual sense.

But the Columbia Intermontane Province, which includes the Snake River basin, is quite otherwise, and possesses some features of incredible size, some so large that they are, of all things, nearly impossible to see. Before, during, and after the Miocene Epoch, the earth opened up evidently along large fissure systems and extruded some of the greatest floods of basaltic lava in the known geologic history of the earth. Pouring out evenly and horizontally, individual flows became as

Sagebrush stretches across a portion of the vast volcanic Snake River Plain of Idaho. (Ernst Peterson)

thick as a hundred feet and some traveled as far as a hundred miles. Altogether they covered nearly everything in sight for 200,000 square miles in what is today Washington, Oregon and Idaho, and piled up lava to a depth of at least 11,000 feet. In places great cliffs of "flow upon flow" structure extend for miles along the walls of canyons in northeastern Oregon. How many thousands of cubic miles of basalt poured out from these eruptions is still a mystery because the greatest depth is nature's secret and the original topography over which the lavas spread remains imperfectly known. The common estimate, however, is 35,000 cubic miles.

What happened afterwards is another secret. The Columbia River basalts cooled and hardened. Climates changed. Glaciers advanced, remained for a while, and then began to melt. At this point the picture blurs because the clues are of such extraordinary size that man has had little or no experience with them. There are the coulees, for example. "Coulee" apparently comes from the French *couler*, to flow, and literally means lava flow; but in the Northwest it denotes a steep-sided gulch or water channel. Numerous coulees contain no streams, but they must have contained water because something, and most probably running water, gouged them out in the first place. Grand Coulee itself measures fifty miles long and nearly five miles wide; near the head it is close to a thousand feet deep. In one place there is a cliff that could only be an abandoned waterfall—but the size of it! These "dry falls" must once have been roaring with cascades of water four hundred feet high and something like three miles wide, making them twice the height and five times the width of modern Niagara.

Even this is only part of a 2000-square-mile area known as "scablands." That name refers to "scars" in the landscape—coulees and other channels—made by running water, and to places where vast floods laid bare certain tracts of basalt. Judging by the land now, those inundations must have been far greater than anything man has ever seen. The source for such floods was doubtless glacial meltwaters, but these usually issue in streams that are not very large. To account for a waterfall three miles wide we need to imagine a whole lake draining within a few days time, a lake perhaps as huge as one of the present Great Lakes. Geologists disagree on the details, but they have some impressive evidence to support a theory of giant floods. For one thing, coulees are interlocked and cut into a maze of scabland channels. For another there are midchannel buttes with sheer cliffs, which would have worn away under conventional water erosion. From the air we get splendid views of objects difficult to distinguish on the ground: huge potholes, lava sections peeled off whole rather than abraded slowly by "normal-sized" glacial streams, huge gravel bars, and giant ripple marks some twenty feet high and three hundred feet from crest to crest. Whatever made those was hardly a small or gently rippling stream. Somehow the water was introduced abruptly, perhaps by the giving way of an ice dam. Those who venture a postulation say that an advancing ice sheet dammed the Clark Fork of the Columbia River, creating what is called Glacial Lake Missoula; then when the ice retreated and the dam

began to melt, waters poured under the dam to gouge out Lake Pend Oreille. Finally the dam broke and the lake emptied in what may have been the West's greatest flood, sweeping across Washington and down the Columbia River Gorge. Geologists have attempted to estimate the flow required and have suggested that for a few days at least there was a surge one hundred times the volume of flood stage on the lower Mississippi, or nearly two thousand times the average flow of the Colorado River. Given that kind of force, it is not difficult to explain the coulees, scablands, and other giant features of Columbia lava country.

Fossils of the John Day Basin

The lava plains are generally arid, and the scablands do not even have a permanent stream. By contrast, sedimentary rock layers between the lavas show evidence of a moist climate differing entirely from that which prevails today. Along the John Day River of central Oregon lie strata that belong in a class with the finest fossil-bearing outcrops in the West. There are not a great many of these. The Bridger Basin of southwestern Wyoming has been called the most complete sequence of early Tertiary mammalian faunas known anywhere in the world. The Green River shales, not far from the Bridger, contain the most perfectly preserved freshwater fish skeletons ever discovered. In South Dakota's White River badlands occur the world's best exposures of Oligocene mammals. And we have seen how perfectly preserved were the fauna and flora, especially insects and spiders, during a moment of Oligocene time in the Florissant fossil beds of Colorado. Here in the John Day Basin, however, we have more than a window opened to a single chapter of earth history; this is a flashback through successive periods of geologic time. In the words of Dr. J. Arnold Shotwell, Director of the Museum of Natural History of the University of Oregon, "the John Day Basin offers an entire book." No region of the world, he observes, has a more complete sequence of Tertiary land populations, both plant and animal.

The John Day Basin holds records of life over roughly the last 37 million years, a time during the Cenozoic Era when profound changes took place in plant and animal life around the world. During such a long period there have been many deposits, from layers of volcanic ash to flows of Columbia River basalt to sands and gravels of lake origin. Lowest of the group, the Clarno formation, Eocene in age, contains fossilized remains of a subtropical biota. Laurel and palm families are well represented; there were breadfruit, cinnamon, fig, avocado, pecan and walnut. With so many trees we find animals adapted to life in forests or swamps: crocodile, tapir, peccary, and oreodont, the latter a common creature that may have looked like a pig. The familiar story of the evolution of the horse was beginning with the four-toed *Eohippus*, about the size of a modern sheep. A group of running rhinos somewhat paralleled the horse in evolution; and another group of rhinos, more squat and heavy like the ones we know today, seems to have been water-loving and swamp-dwelling, and had we entered the Eocene forests of the time we would probably have seen them mostly along river banks. It seems a little strange to talk of ancient Oregon in terms of humid subtropical swamps, or to think of a land that now has some sharp winters as having no frost whatever. But all the evidence points to some kind of latitudinal shift, and from the record that remains it is apparent that warm and moist climates spread throughout all middle latitudes in Eocene time. The ancient forests of central Oregon have been compared to rain forests in Central and South America, even as far as having vines and tree ferns. The rainfall is estimated to have been eighty inches a year.

In late Oligocene and early Miocene, the humidity decreased, although dawn redwoods *(Metasequoia)* and bald cypresses seem to have been dominant along lowlands and streams. The John Day formation, a colorful combination of red, green, and yellow sediments about a thousand feet thick, contains a flora of a kind somewhat more familiar to us: oaks, elms, sycamore, chestnut, basswood, birch, and maple. These indicate a warm temperate climate with about fifty inches of rain a year. There seem to have been no mountain ranges between this interior region and the sea; not even the early Cascades blocked off the inflow of moist winds from the Pacific. Nevertheless, grasslands had become more prevalent, replacing some of the forests. And as might be expected, certain forest animals were replaced by species adapted to grasslands.

More than 120 kinds of fossil mammals are known from the John Day formation and while their names sound like a roll call of modern forms—dog, rabbit, beaver, opossum—nearly all bore only a remote resemblance to their current forms. Oreodonts were still the most common; rhinos remained, as did tapirs, and there were camels, sabre-toothed cats, and giant pigs. The next step in the evolution of the horse is found in the three-toed *Miochippus,* which measured six hands high at the withers.

The Miocene Mascall formation, deposited in the John Day region when lava flows were pouring out elsewhere, contains floral and faunal elements that signify mild, humid climates—the gingko and swamp cypress, for example. Fossils in this formation include the three-toed horse, *Merychippus,* estimated to be about the size of a modern pony. Had we wandered across this terrain we might have come face to face with mastodons, bears, giant pigs, sabre-toothed cats, dogs that were huge and bearlike, and dogs that were the ancestors of the modern wolves. Some of the carnivores resembled modern raccoons and mustelids. An elklike member of the deer family *(Dromomeryx)* had curved horns that looked like clubs.

Finally, the Rattlesnake formation, composed of Pliocene sands and gravels, was deposited as the first Cascades volcanos began to erupt. In a warm temperate climate there was a great deal of grassland, with trees and shrubs largely along stream courses, the landscape resembling that of the high plateaus today. In due course, the rising Cascades would cut off a great deal of moisture that had for so long come in from the Pacific. There is a dearth of Pliocene plant life in central Oregon, but not of animal life. The horse had now become the one-toed *Pliohippus,* and there was additionally a side-branch *(Neohipparion)* that was destined to

die out. Both mastodons and mammoths lived in Oregon until a few thousand years ago, becoming extinct, ironically, after having survived the rigors of the ice age. The John Day Basin contains some of the last rhinos to be found in North America, for they disappeared shortly after that time. Camels, very large ones, were still to be seen, as were the bearlike dogs, and an early form of coyote, antelopes, peccaries, rabbits, squirrels, and cats, but the oreodonts and *Dromomeryx* had disappeared. One of the fossil bears of this region has a close similarity to one in Asia, and a fossil ground sloth here resembles another in South America, implying that land bridges had been formed to those continents and that mammalian migratory routes had been established.

Thus it is that few places in the world have a richer endowment of fossils or cover a greater sequence of this planet's biological history than the beds of the John Day Basin, so close in time and space to the great eruptions of the lava plateaus.

Among the Craters of the Moon

And then, finally, in going east we come back, as it were, to where we started. Out on the Snake River plains of Idaho lies a chaotic jumble of lava, cinder cones, tubes, tunnels, and spattered vents that recall the lava beds of northern California. Like those, these lavas are "fresh" and "new," being possibly less than two thousand years old.

In Idaho, the High Lava Plains are flatter and less modified by erosion than those of the Columbia River basalt series, and are sufficiently younger so that not very much soil has had time to accumulate on them. Water from rainfall consequently sinks into the lava, and in a few places emerges in considerable quantities. The Thousand Springs, between Twin Falls and Bliss, Idaho, have a combined flow of nearly forty thousand gallons per second, and eleven of the springs rank among the largest in the United States.

Along the Snake River, naturalists and adventurers may find nearly all they dream of. As the river winds around the Grand Teton Mountains it is a translucent green, gliding swiftly over gravels, or pausing in pools that reflect the forests and snow-covered peaks above. On a float trip down this river you pass the nests of osprey and of bald eagle, the grazing grounds of moose, and rich green meadows dotted with beaver ponds. Working its way westward, the Snake passes through small canyons. Generally it has not had enough time to dissect the lava plains very deeply, but two hundred miles downstream from Boise, the river enters Hell's Canyon, which for a distance of forty miles has an average depth of 5500 feet. The river flows northward between the Seven Devils Mountains of Idaho and the Wallowa Mountains of Oregon, and in places has exposed as much as six thousand feet of basalt.

Still, the general character of the Snake River plains is one of utter flatness, built of lava that welled out quietly and profusely. But there was explosive action, too, with outpourings in the Hawaii style and lava erupting violently at two thousand degrees Fahrenheit. In one particular area of about three thousand square

Short but powerful legs move the mountain goat over rough terrain. Specially constructed hoofs give dependable traction. (Leonard Lee Rue III)

miles near Arco, Idaho, this built up a lava surface that looks as though it had been imported from the moon. Eighty-three square miles of black dunes, cinder crags, and jagged lava have been set aside as Craters of the Moon National Monument; there one may find the remnants of thirty-five cones and vents and thirty different lava flows. Far less vegetation covers these than the Lava Beds, yet it should come as no surprise that even here on the barest cinder slopes, nature presents at times colorful and dramatic living spectacles.

While cinder deposits are porous and soak up most

of the rain that falls on them, they have an interesting capacity to hold some of this moisture for a time, perhaps as close to the surface as a few millimeters. Very likely the insulating properties of lava help to reduce evaporation, which in turn encourages the growth of seeds that blow in and settle among the bits of basalt. As you approach the Craters of the Moon you see what appear to be snowballs evenly spaced across the black dunes, a stark contrast if there ever was one. These white tufts are not snow at all, but clumps of pioneering dwarf buckwheat (*Eriogonum* sp.) that venture to sprout on the fresh surfaces almost before any other plant except lichens. This gives the dunes a speckled, mottled appearance. Of course, even insulating cinders cannot hold water forever in this arid region, so sometimes these plants have to sink roots deeply for the moisture they need; buckwheat roots may go down as much as forty-eight inches.

Investigating the lava features more intently we discover that in sheltered cracks of even the freshest flows may be found the mock orange or syringa *(Philadelphus lewisii)*. There are occasions when nature turns the black cinder landscape into a dazzling reddish purple with the simultaneous blooming of thousands of dwarf monkey flowers *(Mimulus nanus)*. Penstemon and bitterroot bloom in June and July, and over a good part of the lava beds enough time has elapsed to permit the forming of some soil and the growth of large limber pines *(Pinus flexilis)*. But since limber pines have shallow roots, and the competition is keen for moisture, they grow in a scattered fashion.

Sagebrush and cactus cover the Snake River lavas, and a massive display of rubber rabbitbrush *(Bigelowia dracunculoides)* turns the scene a brilliant yellow in August and September. Fernbush thrives here as it does on the California Lava Beds. So does the bitterbrush, attractive to deer. Seeds of limber pine sustain the yellow-pine chipmunk, golden-mantled ground squirrel, and bushy-tailed wood rat. These and yellow-bellied marmots find in lava holes and crevices at least some refuge from their perennial enemies, the red fox, coyote and bobcat. Overhead, the circle of life is completed by such birds as the violet-green swallow, Clark's nutcracker, rock wren, flicker, phoebe, mourning dove, and mountain bluebird, each of which thrives on its choice of vegetation or invertebrate animals or both.

And so at the Craters of the Moon we have come full circle from the Lava Beds. In both places, under heat and cold and drought, complex life systems have become established at the mercy of volcanoes and in obedience to ecological laws.

12. Hidden Trails in the Northern Rockies

The mountains which we crossed to-day were much more difficult than those of yesterday; the last was particularly fatiguing, being steep and stony, broken by fallen timber, and thickly overgrown by pine, spruce, fir, hacmatack and tamarac.

Lewis and Clark
in *History of the Expedition,* 1814

Out of the Pacific Ocean, into the Columbia River, past Portland and the Dalles, up the Snake River, and far inland to the headwaters of the Salmon River in central Idaho, they drive themselves resolutely. For sixty-nine nights and days, without stopping, resting, or eating, they force themselves through rapidly moving water. Against all riffles and rapids, and leaping up roaring falls, the chinook salmon move onward and upward at an average speed of over one mile per hour, probably equivalent to a swimming speed of three miles per hour, depending on the force and speed of the running stream. High falls may hold them back. Artificial reservoirs may confuse them. Some are lost to men or other animals. But the survivors manage to maintain an average daily progress of twelve miles and come at last to a canyon with sheer and colorful walls, open slopes adorned with grass and sagebrush, and side ravines supporting stands of aspen and Douglas fir. It is a long and exhausting journey—828 miles from the ocean, not counting inevitable detours required by currents and obstacles—and a rise in elevation of nearly six thousand feet. But to the chinook salmon there is no other destiny, no other ultimate aim in life. This is home.

The Mystery at Indian Riffles

Many a stream in the Northern and Canadian Rockies receives an annual spawning run of salmon, one of nature's most mysterious miracles. The upper sixty miles of Idaho's river named for the fish itself—the Salmon—is a prime location for the playing out of this immemorial and dramatic ritual. Here the Salmon River measures about a hundred feet across. The water, pure and nearly silt-free, sifts through willow and cottonwood roots, races over beds of boulders, breaks into rapids, divides into channels that isolate islands of willow and heaps of gravel, or flows in a straight line that resembles a long, wide avenue. Over the river terraces fly robins, ducks, and doves, and, in virtually every habitat, black-billed magpies, so great in number that the Salmon Valley might well be renamed Magpie Valley. The river could easily be called All-American River, too, because it flows through forests, badlands, canyons, fertile valleys, upland deserts, and other environments widely encountered across North America. Cliffs of orange, yellow, red, green and brown line the river course. Some slopes are torn by landslides old and new, as though a giant hand had clawed the rocks, leaving them raw and bleeding. Animal trails crisscross the hills. In open places only lonely pines or junipers interrupt the pattern of sagebrush. Then, with rising elevation, we glimpse, through notches in the nearer walls, some heavily forested peaks in the distance. Before long the river narrows to seventy-five feet and seems to flow more swiftly than below. It runs through deeper and more restricted canyons, and beneath steeply pitching slopes of Douglas fir and quaking aspen. In this milieu we arrive at Indian Riffles.

On an autumn day the life of many salmon begins in

A picturesque old log disintegrates into organic-rich dust near Trapper Peak in the Bitterroot Mountains of Montana. (Ernst Peterson)

Roaring rapids and plunging waterfalls are among the major obstacles to be surmounted by salmon on their way to spawn. The journey is so exhausting that each fish has little margin for error. (Ruth Kirk)

the shallows at this site, in conspicuous light-colored patches on the floor of the stream: the spawning beds. After a trip of more than eight hundred miles upstream, the female salmon begins to clean the rocks by vigorous swishes of the tail and body, thus preparing a suitable nest for eggs. Boulders in the river bottom normally have a yellowish color, but where the salmon clean them they are nearly white. A dozen or so salmon, facing upstream, swim over or beside these beds. Most are large and distinctly the worse for wear, owing partly to battles that even now erupt beside the beds and result in long and lightning-fast pursuits upstream.

With the help of the current, the female digs a nest, called a redd, four to eighteen inches deep and so arranged that it receives a steady flow of fresh water. She deposits three thousand to eleven thousand eggs, which are fertilized by the males and left to fate. Although the adults then die, they have yielded up a

progeny in numbers commensurate with the dangers the new generation will face at sea and on inland streams. For example, at a counting weir above Indian Riffles, records show that four thousand adults come upstream in a successful season and forty thousand juveniles go down the following year.

Deep in the gravel nests, the eggs remain until mid-winter, when they hatch. For a year the young remain near home, then make their journey to the sea, at which time they are less than six inches long. One to three years after roaming the Pacific and growing up to almost five feet long and a weight of possibly a hundred pounds, they find the mouths of the Columbia, Snake and Salmon rivers with mystifying accuracy, and complete their once-in-a-lifetime spawning run. The capacity of the salmon to know which rivers and tributaries to choose during their thousand-mile trek may be due to a keen sense of smell. Experiments have suggested that different streams have different odors, that young salmon become conditioned to these odors before they go to sea and that they remember them as they grow into adulthood. Their remarkable homing behavior may simply be instinctive reaction to specific odors and other conditions which their ancestors have

A grizzly can drag off moose weighing nearly a ton—but agility counts much more in capturing fish. (Leonard Lee Rue III)

been reacting to for unknown centuries. If all this be true, the remarkable fact is that although the odors characteristic of Indian Riffles become mixed and diluted a thousand times over on their way to the sea, the right one can be sensed and selected by the salmon.

Equally astonishing is how the salmon can make so long and grueling a trip. The margin of success is slim at best, and evidently does not allow for tampering by men. Salmon need unpolluted, free-flowing streams and apparently a current to follow. Man has attempted to install fish lifts and ladders to help salmon get around dams, but what about the lakes behind the dams? Lacking a current in the reservoirs, the fish, it has been found, get confused and lost. Some may never find their way out. One dam that impeded anadromous fish runs where a million-dollar fishing industry was at stake, had to be dynamited. In some cases, where the dams remained, fish runs ceased. All told, according to the Idaho Fish and Game Department, the number of

fish now spawning in Idaho is only a fraction of what it used to be. Aquatic biologists say that salmon are lost in tremendous numbers for reasons which are different for nearly every dam so far designed.

In chemical and biological studies of sockeye salmon, specialists have attempted to determine how much energy the migrating salmon expends and what is the metabolic basis of its extraordinary endurance. For one thing, the fish requires cool streams so as not to overexpend its energy, which means that thermal pollution of inland waters is a constant danger. For another, the salmon is capable of increasing its metabolism and sustaining a high output of energy. The racehorse does this, too. Researchers working in Canadian streams found that after the female salmon had completed its journey and spawned, it had used up 96 percent of its body fat and more than half of its protein reserves. During their travels the fish expended energy at the rate of eighty percent of their maximum capability, leaving little for emergencies. This is remarkable for any organism. If man can learn to duplicate and better this, as he has done with the power of his flight as compared with that of birds, he will have unlocked useful secrets in the production and use of energy.

Above Indian Riffles the chinook share spawning grounds with related species. We may trace the course of the Salmon River to Redfish Lake, well named because it is the home of the bright red kokanee *(Oncorhynchus nerka kennerlyi)*, a subspecies of the sockeye. The landlocked kokanee, which averages seven to fourteen inches in length and three ounces to a pound in weight, spends its entire lifetime in fresh water. Like other sockeyes, it dies after spawning.

A Tangle of Peaks

Redfish Lake and the upper Salmon River may be the end of a difficult journey for fish, but it is only the beginning of trial and trouble for men who go beyond. For there on the horizon, sharp as the teeth of a saw, rise the granite spires of precipitous glaciated ridges. These are the Sawtooth Mountains, so severely plucked at by glaciers that they are a thoroughly rugged combination of sheer cliffs, leaning crags, Matterhorn-like spires, lake basins, plunging talus slopes, moraines, and glacier-polished patches of rock. Glaciation is indeed the master sculpturing hand throughout the Northern Rockies because here the snow-line lies much lower on the mountains than in the Middle or Southern Rockies. And glaciation has laid bare or cross-sectioned enough of the uplands to show that the Northern Rockies have little unanimity of structure, and little in common with some of their counterparts in the cordillera. This jumble of mountains, with few distinct ranges, is as confused and confusing as the southern Appalachians. There are granite intrusions into folded rock that make up the Okanogan Highlands, west of Spokane. There are structural valleys and uplifts along the Rocky Mountain and Purcell trenches, to be described in the next chapter. There is a gigantic mass of granitic rocks called the Idaho batholith. Folds and faults occur in abundance, resulting in topography similar to that of the Basin and Range Province. There are mountains domed from the intrusion of laccoliths, as in the Little Belt Mountains. And there are rock slices that have been broken and thrust across one another like shingles on a roof, especially in the northern Montana "Disturbed Belt." In this diversity of mountains we do find a few slender threads of constancy and grasp them in an effort to understand the Northern Rockies. As well as any, the Sawtooth Range typifies the entire group.

This range is carved from an enormous mass of granitic rock, the Idaho batholith, that covers some twenty thousand square miles. It should be borne in mind that batholiths, largest of all intrusive bodies of igneous rock, rise from deep-seated molten material and harden beneath the surface of the earth. Where they have been injected into crustal rocks and then uncovered by erosion we can see what they look like. The West has a number of batholiths, most often small and localized ones like that at the Granite Dells near Prescott, Arizona; but by far the three largest are the Idaho, Sierra, and the most massive of all, the Coast Ranges batholith of western British Columbia. The Sawtooth Range is only one of several mountain groups—Bitterroot, Coeur D'Alene, Clearwater, and Salmon River mountains—eroding out of the Idaho

batholith, and has been faulted, lifted, and tilted so that it is complex in its own right.

As in much of the Northern Rockies, overthrust faulting is prominent. Rock strata of the region were folded in a normal manner at first, but the pressures continued so long that the folds were overturned. Reaching their limit of strain, the strata broke. Still the folding continued, thrusting old strata over younger, reversing the natural sequence of sedimentation. More sheets of land were broken and thrust over others like slices of bread, and some of these were themselves folded. Most famous of these broken and displaced folds is the Lewis overthrust, an enormous slab of the earth's crust some 350 miles wide that extended from Montana well into Canada. As the slab moved slowly to the east it crumpled and crushed the soft rocks it was overriding, and broke into several faults itself. Inch by inch, century after century, overcoming all resistance, the great mass moved forty miles or more to the east. Erosion has since dissected and worn away some of the slab, leaving resistant portions standing alone as outlying mountains. Chief Mountain, just south of the Canadian border, is a classic example of this. It is composed of resistant strata of extremely old Precambrian rocks lying directly on a pedestal of younger, softer Cretaceous shales. The Mountain is not only an anomaly because of its reversed rock sequence but it is literally a mountain without roots. The strata from which it was torn must now lie at least forty miles to the west and an undetermined depth beneath the surface.

All these changes in the tangled mass called the Northern Rockies are bound to have produced a variety and abundance of minerals. Idaho is sometimes called the Gem State, partly because of its magnificent star garnet (almandite), but there are extraordinary deposits throughout the Rockies and the West. Gems—beautiful, durable, rare—may be either single minerals or complex combinations of several. They occur in every western state, and eighty-seven percent of those produced commercially in the United States come, in order, from Oregon, California, Texas, Nevada, Arizona, Washington, Wyoming, Utah, Colorado, and Montana. The sapphire beds of Yogo Gulch, Montana, are extremely valuable gem deposits. The principal gem of Wyoming and Alaska is jade; Texas topaz is among the finest in North America; some of the most beautiful lapis lazuli in the world is found in Gunnison County, Colorado; and California is said to possess more kinds of gems and other minerals than any state, including the world's most important source of tourmaline. New Mexico leads in turquoise, a hydrous copper aluminium phosphate found mostly in

Right above: Almost any hole in trees, rocks or stream banks is acceptable to the mountain bluebird as a nesting site. (Eliot Porter)   Right: The lower portions of beargrass flower clusters open first, initiating a long and colorful season. (Bob Clemenz)   Far right: The fairy slipper (Calypso bulbosa) *is a mountain orchid widely distributed but not abundant in the Rockies. (Ernst Peterson)*

volcanic rocks of arid regions. Nevada is one of the centers for opal hunters. Agates of numerous types—banded, plume, moss, blood, botryoidal, circle, rainbow—may be sought on gravel bars along the Clearwater River in Idaho, or the banks and tributaries of the Yellowstone River between Miles City and Billings, Montana, or terraces and bottoms of the Big Horn and Sweetwater Rivers in Wyoming. British Columbia contains a number of agate deposits, but most of them are difficult to reach.

As for precious metals, Idaho and Montana have meant "pay dirt" for miners since the 1860's when gold was discovered. There have been gold rushes to the Boise Basin of southwest Idaho and to various sites in Montana: Bannack, Alder Gulch at Virginia City, Last Chance Gulch at Helena, and Butte. Most of these held out for a few years, then declined, but at Butte gold gave way to the extraction of silver. Because it was a base, not a precious metal, copper was at first unappreciated, and it would not have been profitable to transport large quantities of it. But in time a narrow-gauge railway arrived, and it was soon discovered that Butte had one of the richest copper deposits in the world. Ordinarily, copper occurs in various geological environments. Porphyry deposits, those in which the copper is uniformly but sparsely distributed throughout the rock, result from mineralization associated with the intrusion of igneous rocks. In other cases, water removes copper and redistributes it at water-table levels, creating a rich deposit. And where copper minerals fill fractures and other openings, the quantities are rarely as large as those at Butte.

Finally, another group of minerals, those enriching the soil, produces a different kind of riches—great forests that fill the valleys and clothe the lower mountain slopes. Unlike the gems and precious metals that are removed and not replaced, soil minerals are constantly renewed, sustaining a perpetual yield of trees and a perpetual supply of nests, burrows, insects, seeds—in fact, life itself. Within this ecological circle the vegetation and wildlife of the region flourish.

Land of the Larches

It is easier to find similarities than differences between the forests of the Northern Rocky Mountains and those of ranges to the south or north. Alpine tundra in these mountains, with its pikas, ptarmigans, dwarf willow and birch, bears some resemblance to the Arctic tundra of Alaska and the Yukon. Upper montane forests are dominated by Engelmann spruce and sub-

Left above: A hiker who meets a grizzly on the trail may well attest to the claim that it is the largest flesh-eating mammal in the world. Grizzlies range from Mexico to Alaska. (Leonard Lee Rue III) Far left: Beavers in the Northern Rockies subsist primarily on the bark of aspen, willow and cottonwood. They also use these trees for building sturdy lodges waterproofed with mud. (National Film Board of Canada) Left: The white-tailed ptarmigan, a small grouse, is the only permanent bird resident in certain high reaches of the Northern Rockies. (Robert Belous)

alpine fir just as forests in parts of Canada, and in them wander bears, mountain goats, and porcupines. Lower montane forests of hemlock, cedar, pine, and Douglas fir, reminiscent of coastal ranges, shelter an abundance of wild animals. The lowest zones, almost prairie-like, contain open stands of ponderosa pine mixed with aspen, a common feature of mountains in the Southwest and Mexico.

But there are distinctive trademarks of this forest, and while they may occur in other places, we remember them most vividly from our walks along the streams and hidden trails of the Northern Rockies. The black hawthorn *(Crataegus douglasii)*, with its sharp brown spikes, abundance of delicate white blooms, and clusters of shiny black fruits, is one of the few hawthorns to grow in the West. We saw it first in the Bitterroot Range of southwestern Montana, along a sunny streambank which it shared with aspen, cottonwood, dogwoods, willows, and lodgepole pines, the latter draped with yellow lichens. In and out of these thickets darted flycatchers, plying their trade between the stream and their protruding perches on the haws and willows. In this community, the hawthorn grew in beds of wild roses, currants, asters, daisies, goldenrods, and purple thistles. And there is the bitterroot itself *(Lewisia rediviva)*, with a conspicuous pinkish bloom. It was first collected by Captain Meriwether Lewis in the Bitterroot Valley, and later named in his honor. Though the root is bitter, Indians, mountain men, and probably even the members of the Lewis and Clark expedition used it for food; the bitterness can be reduced by cooking.

Perhaps the most distinctive trademark of this forest is a tree that can be told from others in an instant—a conifer that violates nearly all the rules, the western larch *(Larix occidentalis)*. Other names for it are hackmatack (a word of Algonquin Indian origin) and tamarack, both of which Lewis and Clark knew; however, it should not be confused with more eastern and northern tamarack *(Larix americana)*, or introduced tamarisk *(Tamarix gallica)*, the saltcedar of arid regions. In the Northern Rockies the larch is a tall and stately tree recognized by its slender bole with yellowish-brown plates of bark. It ignores the rules that require conifers to be somber and dark in color and to hold their leaves all winter. The larch has yellow-green needles that stand out strikingly against the clear blue sky of the Northwest, as well as in the dark green forests. The branches issue from whorled clusters on the trunk and not only they but the needles that grow from them are sparse, giving the tree an open aspect. Straight as a flagpole, the larch rises out of the forest 150 feet or more. It is sturdy and able to withstand fire; like the lodgepole pine it comes into burned-over areas, seeds itself well, and gets established rapidly. Then in late summer the real uniqueness of the larch becomes apparent. Its soft, flat needles, which grow in bundles of fifteen to thirty along the branches, begin to turn a golden yellow. On a forested hillside you can pick out groups of larch immediately because they are the only deciduous conifer and therefore the only ones that drop their leaves. Throughout the winter they present no more than naked trunk and limbs to the sky, unlike the general pattern of conifer life. The closest relative, sub-alpine larch *(Larix lyallii)*, grows at a higher elevation but is smaller.

In the Realm of the Grizzly

The Northern Rockies contain some of the most magnificent hiking country in all of North America. There are thousands of miles of trails, not only trails for walking but wild-animal trails used by moose, deer, sheep, coyote, mountain goat, mountain lion, elk, black bear, grizzly bear and many another resident. The opportunity to see such animals, sometimes in congregations, is a compelling lure of these mountains. Trails cross open ridges in view of enormous mountains, towering cliffs, and glistening glaciers, or become hidden passageways through forests that contain waterfalls, springs, and luxurious gardens of wild flowers. To know the silence, to hear the music of falling water or songs of birds, and to meet the animals on their own terms, it is almost essential to go on foot. Some travelers would never think of entering such a "dangerous" area. But a wilderness feared is a wilderness lost. A little knowledge of how to act while in the domain of wild creatures not only reduces fear but engenders respect and admiration.

There is little doubt that the animals most respected in these mountains as well as in the Canadian Rockies and Alaska are the bears. They are wild creatures, and they may indeed be dangerous to man, depending on what man does to them. If he feeds or teases them, or threatens a mother with cubs, he almost certainly exposes himself to attack and injury. Bears like to be left alone; one authority says they are shy and that they run first and find out later what they are running from. But they are simply unpredictable and can move with a speed thoroughly unexpected in such a sluggish-looking creature. We did not entirely believe this until we once analyzed a motion picture film that showed how quickly a black bear *(Ursus americanus)* could move from peaceful browsing along a road to attack on people in an open car. The driver had the engine running and his foot on the accelerator; he pulled out in a shower of gravel and the occupants escaped without injury, but there must surely have been claw marks on the side of the car.

The bear is well equipped to defend itself. Nature has placed at its disposal some sturdy and well-built claws, good teeth and strong jaws, powerful muscles, and a clever brain trained in the laws of the forest—which is to say survival of the fittest. Some men believe that pound for pound the bear is the most powerful animal alive. Though weighing only ten ounces at birth, the black bear grows steadily through the rollicking cub stage into adult life where weights of five hundred pounds are not surprising and record weights are in the area of seven hundred pounds. Yet measurements have

Black bear cubs stay with their mother for a year or more, swimming, playing, hunting, digging, scurrying up trees when endangered, and learning to fend for themselves. (Hans W. Silvester: Bavaria Verlag)

shown that in spite of this bulk, bears can run at a rate of twenty-five miles an hour.

Beyond this, black bears are almost indefinable. Color is not diagnostic, for they range from black to brown to cinnamon to gray to white. They have no special food habits; nearly everything tempts them and they can be seen pawing over the bones of dead animals, digging up rodent burrows and ant hills, peeling off conifer bark, and munching berries or tasting the tops of thistles, parsnips and other plants. About the only reliable descriptive index is the bear's similarity to a dog, especially when viewed in profile. Bears originated from about the same evolutionary source as wolves, coyotes and others of the canines. But bears are a bit more accustomed to standing on their hind legs and climbing trees, and some of their bitter mating brawls are conducted in an upright position.

The black bear has good hearing and keen smell, but poor vision. It spends the winter more or less asleep, its temperature and heartbeat remaining near normal. Like man and a few other mammals it is plantigrade, walking flat-footed with heels on the ground. Several dozen species of parasites and various diseases decimate the bear, and its other enemies include, where their ranges overlap, the mountain lion, wolf, and grizzly bear.

Altogether there are three kinds of bears in North America. The black bear, most abundant and widespread, occurs in some eighteen subspecies, and inhabits the cordillera from Mexico to Alaska and many areas in eastern North America. The polar bear *(Thalarctos maritimus)* is distinctly an inhabitant of ice floes and Arctic shores. The grizzly *(Ursus horribilis)* lives in the United States and Canadian Rockies as well as much of western Canada and most of Alaska. A well-known subspecies, the big brown bear *(Ursus middendorffi)*, largest of all terrestrial carnivores, inhabits the coastal areas of southern and southeastern Alaska.

Whatever respect we accord the black bear we must double for the grizzly. It is wilder, shyer, and higher ranging than other bears, preferring open tundra rather than open forest. Some people are convinced that it is meaner and grumpier, too. Grizzly fur can be light or dark, but is distinctive for the light-colored ends of the hairs, which produce a grizzled, i.e., grayish, appearance. The animal is further distinguished by pronounced humped shoulders and by a general tendency of the nose, as seen in profile, to turn slightly up, while the tip of the black bear's nose points slightly down. If you are able to discern this difference with the naked eye, you may be too close. There is little doubt that the great bulk of that mass beneath the fur is composed of solid and usable muscle. From nose to tail the grizzly measures about nine feet, more than twice the equivalent measure of man; it has a seventy-inch chest and a forty-inch neck, and may weigh as much as one thousand pounds. Perhaps because of all this the adult grizzly lacks the ability to climb trees—but there may be few trees in its habitat anyway. With its strength, the grizzly need be little concerned about its relatively poor eyesight. A high intelligence plus a good sense of smell and hearing suffice to give warning of its one mortal enemy, man, from whom it usually flees at a gallop.

Life begins in winter, though there is not much life to begin with since the newborn grizzly weighs only a pound and is utterly helpless. The mother customarily gives birth to twins. In April or May the animals leave the den, and from then on much of life is spent in rooting, rummaging and digging in a search for food. Although grizzlies are omnivorous they prefer small mammals. The big brown bear is well known for its skill in fishing for salmon along Alaska streams, but it uses mouth, not paws, to get the fish out of the water. Open grassy meadows are preferred, but the grizzly will go into forests or anywhere to find food, since it needs a great deal of nourishment to keep such a huge bulk fueled and active. As for neighboring animals with whom the grizzly shares its environment—moose, deer, mountain goat and so on—the motto seems to be, "live and let live," even though the grizzly can conquer and carry away these creatures if necessary.

The grizzly stands on its hind legs to view the countryside or to scratch and bite trees, but does not charge in this position, nor does it hug its enemies to death. It really has little to fear except man and possibly the wolf, and it seems to be aware of the perils of skunks and porcupines. For sleeping quarters it digs small shallow basins in the ground. When winter comes it may or may not dig a lair and enter into long periods of sleep. This depends, among other things, on where the bear lives and how much winter food is available. For some grizzlies, perhaps most, half of life is spent asleep, the animal's metabolism sustained by its supply of fat.

The cubs remain with their mother until they are yearlings, and in some cases until they are more than two years old. After casting them off, she is free to take up with a male and repeat the process. For the young, life beyond mother is often solitary and their existence may seem like one of aloofness until the first mating period, although some researchers have picked up evidence that the grizzly is, after all, a social animal. Sexual maturity arrives in three to five years; mating occurs in summer, and after a gestation period of six months the cycle of life begins again.

The grizzly range is now much reduced from its original extent and the bears have been eliminated from so many areas that some states are taking urgent action to protect them. Altogether, in the United States and Canada there are probably tens of thousands of bears remaining, but in several places they are still being legally shot at the average rate of five hundred or more a year. Chronicles of what man has done *to* the grizzly in times past make grim reading. Yet what man has done *for* this animal, the pains he has taken to learn about and protect so brutal a beast, gives evidence that he is maturing in his relationship with wildlife. The public conscience has begun to reduce man's inhumanity to beast, although it is probable that as man expands his territory, especially in Alaska, the range and numbers of the grizzly will be further reduced.

Finally, considering that hundreds of thousands of hikers have entered these wilds on foot and not even seen a grizzly, the chances of being attacked seem very small. Only a few attacks have been recorded and even fewer fatalities, but those have been enough to give the grizzly an ugly reputation. Perhaps the most interesting testimony comes from persons who have photographed or studied grizzlies almost to within touching distance. "I have never been charged," says one. The grizzly is defensive, not aggressive, said the great naturalist, William T. Hornaday. Of course, man may not always be sure that he is provoking grizzly attacks; certain odors such as hair spray, deodorants, cosmetics, and domestic dogs may do this, and women pregnant or in menstruation should avoid grizzly territory. Adolph Murie, the great naturalist of Alaska, said that he always burned garbage and cans that contained food so as to destroy food odors, and thus had very little bear trouble. Public officials recommend that if an attack comes, a person should drop to the ground, draw his legs up to his chest, clasp his hands over the back of his neck, and play dead. The assumption is that grizzlies are not after human intruders as food, but as potential enemies whom they wish to repulse. Bears should never be fed. Hikers should make noises so as not to come silently upon a grizzly and startle it. Fear, however, should never restrict human lovers of the wilderness. There is, in fact, a certain challenge in entering, respectfully, this wild domain. As Adolph Murie said, it is a way to add zest to living.

On Glacier Trails

There are numerous places in the Northern Rockies where the land and wildlife can still be found more or less in its original state. The Selway-Bitterroot Wilderness Area in southwestern Montana covers over a million acres. The Waterton-Glacier International Peace Park, two adjoining national parks in Alberta and Montana, offers opportunity to examine and understand the natural features in detail through wayside exhibits and naturalist programs. Perhaps most memorable are self-guiding trails that lead to waterfalls, lakes, forests, and alpine meadows. Nearly everywhere is the beargrass *(Xerophyllum setifolium)* which thrusts its head of creamy-white flowers into the June winds long before winter snows have melted. Actually, it is not a grass but a lily, and there seems to be no reason why Meriwether Lewis named it after bears. It grows abundantly on open, dry slopes and in open forests at all elevations; on higher terraces it blooms until the end of September.

To man, the climate at times may seem severe. It certainly varies from place to place. In some high basins the precipitation may average over a hundred inches a year. More than seven inches of rain may fall in a single day. By contrast, certain lower slopes get less than twenty inches of rain a year. Summit temperatures in January may fall to fifty or more degrees below zero, and you may hear of the mythical fur-bearing fish that inhabits high mountain lakes. The winter's peace may be disturbed by warming chinook winds blowing over a hundred miles an hour. But summers are cool and pleasant, a delightful time to be out on foot.

Glacier trails lead where the water ouzel dips into foaming, zigzag cascades; where larch and spruce and Pacific yew gather with other trees to form a rich, luxuriant forest; to western redcedars nearly six feet in diameter; to moss-covered springs or "weeping rocks" where trillium grows; past hanging gardens ablaze with flowers; to roaring waterfalls; along the shores of lakes; beside geologic displays of enormous dimensions; and through the rarefied atmosphere of the high country where the only bird that lives year-round is the willow ptarmigan *(Lagopus leucurus)*. The ptarmigan will not be easy to see, summer or winter. Its brown and black summer plumage blends splendidly with the mottled shapes and colors of rocky terrain. In winter the bird takes on an entirely different plumage, an all-over white that renders it nearly invisible against the snow. Moreover, its slow movements keep it inconspicuous. Farther downslope is another animal that changes color, the snowshoe hare *(Lepus americanus)*. Its brown summer coat becomes mottled with white in the autumn and then changes to almost a pure white for the winter.

There is no end to the changing patterns of life, color, and form in the Glacier-Waterton region, or for that matter in all the Northern Rockies. A larch standing tall and straight, a thrush singing, a mountain spray clinging to crags and tossing its flowers in the wind, a sideways-sliding cascade tumbling over shelves of tilted strata, a wild hollyhock lighting the shadows with its pinkish blooms are all parts of a special signature by which nature reveals its infinite variations, and grants to the mind a sense of wonder, freedom, and peace.

13. The Badlands: "Hell with the Fires Out"

The Bad Lands grade all the way from those that are almost rolling in character to those that are so fantastically broken in form and so bizarre in color as to seem hardly properly to belong to this earth.

Theodore Roosevelt
in *Hunting Trips of a Ranchman*, 1885

A few miles west of Dickinson, North Dakota, past green wheat fields and rolling terrain, the landscape drops away as suddenly as at the edge of a lunar crater. With an abruptness unusual even for the West, there is all at once a world of eroded cliffs and stark red ridges as far as the eye can see. Dry washes filled with gray-green Rocky Mountain juniper *(Juniperus scopulorum)* curve among the jumbled hills, but despite the grassy patches here and there, the change is of such a magnitude that one almost cries out—what bad lands! And badlands is exactly what they have been called for generations. The Dakota Indians referred to them as *mako sica*, the French explorers as *mauvaises terres*, all with the same intent to derogate. But they are not as bad as they seem, and in some ways this name "badlands" as applied to the sharply eroded "breaks" of the Missouri Plateau is a misnomer. Ninety percent of these "bad" lands are covered with vegetation and are utilized by a diversity of animals on, above and below the surface. The majestic ponderosa pine grows in this region, and there are nearly forty species of reptiles and amphibians. Even an early epithet, "hell with the fires out," is doubly incorrect; it is not hell and the fires are still burning.

Understandably, on a cold winter night the badlands may have little to recommend them to man or beast. But the annual rainfall is fourteen inches, which is the same as Salt Lake City and Los Angeles, and on a summer day with the sky pure blue and the big sand grass *(Calamovilfa longifolia)* waving five feet tall, this country is more like paradise than badland.

Theodore Roosevelt was certainly moved by his experiences there. "In spite of their look of savage desolation," he wrote, "the Bad Lands make a good cattle country, for there is plenty of nourishing grass." When he arrived in the 1880's a little of the original fauna remained. Bighorn, grizzly, elk, wolf, and black-footed ferret were either going or gone, and the slaughter of bison was almost over. But enough other species remained to please his passion for hunting. He wrote that there were few sensations he preferred to that of galloping over these rolling, limitless prairies, "or winding my way among the barren, fantastic and grimly picturesque deserts of the so-called Bad Lands."

Origin of the Badlands

What impressed Roosevelt, and what impresses visitors today, aside from the quiet and solitude, is the variety of form and color to be found within this region. Considering the kinds of sediments that have washed into, or fallen upon, this land, it is no wonder that the colors run the chromatic scale from black to white. Since these beds were laid down in the Cenozoic Era, which gives us so much of what is delicate and fragile in the landscapes of the West, we might have expected this scene.

In contrast to the Central Lowlands, most of the strata of the Great Plains are composed of relatively

Rich prairies of buffalo grass alternate with eroding hills in the Badlands of South Dakota. (Esther Henderson: Rapho Guillumette)

younger rocks—Mesozoic and Cenozoic in age. Beneath the surface of the plains, as we approach the mountain provinces, are three giant basins in which many thousands of feet of sediments were deposited by ancient oceans, or by streams from adjacent uplands. Southernmost of these is the Delaware Basin of Texas and New Mexico; north of that is the Denver Basin; and northernmost, near Williston, North Dakota, is the Williston Basin.

The latter covers approximately 130,000 square miles, including parts of Saskatchewan, Manitoba, Montana, the western two-thirds of North Dakota and the northeast quarter of South Dakota. Not a great deal could be told about its interior structure, except in general terms or through inferences made by associations of rock strata, until 1951, when oil of commercial value was discovered in the heart of the basin. Since then many holes have been drilled, and rock samples brought up, analyzed and correlated. Almost every kind of sediment imaginable washed into this basin, or formed in it, resulting in sandstones, limestones, radioactive shales, salt, volcanic ash, and beds of coal. Among these sediments is the Tongue River formation, now being dissected by erosion into the badlands.

From almost any viewpoint, this group of rocks offers curious contrasts, scenically and scientifically. Fine sediments of shale and clay, in subdued tones of gray to brown, seem to match the grays of the sagebrush and the brown of the grass along the slopes. The sandstones approach a buff and tan, even yellow-orange, and lead up to the blue of the sky and the white of the clouds. There is not a jarring color or an inexplicable shape; rain has sculptured, wind has polished, the chemistry of the past has touched the beds with pastel hues, in contrast to the more pronounced coloration of the Painted Desert in Arizona.

Like the Painted Desert, the Tongue River formation contains an abundance of bentonite, or volcanic clay. This material is non-marine, deposited and re-deposited by water on an alluvial plain and perhaps reworked by wind. Eruptions from volcanoes in the distant Rocky Mountains threw an enormous amount of ash and cinder into the sky and it settled to earth miles away, much as volcanic material ejected from the 1912 eruption near Mount Katmai in Alaska dropped on Seattle, Washington, 1600 miles away. Repeated eruptions, perhaps over many years, laid down ash that has now decomposed to a blue clay and forms one of the most striking features of the badlands.

The Big Blue Bed, as it is locally known, is an excellent example of bentonite, and has a special capacity for absorption of water. When wet it swells and turns into a sticky mass, sometimes even flowing down the side of a cliff or causing blocks of the earth to slump.

Here and there in this deposit are spherical concretions and petrified stumps and logs. Waters carrying sediment from the ancestral Rocky Mountains poured into swamps; with the passage of time these became stagnant, received organic debris, including snags of fallen conifers related to modern Sequoias, and after chemical and physical changes over the millenniums, compacted into peat, and then into low-grade lignite.

Today North Dakota and Montana lead the world in lignite production, but the natural influence of unmined lignite on the landscape is one of the most compelling features of the badlands. The long black bands define and sharpen the outlines of the layers and provide a sense of stability to the scene, but the lignite beds are actually undermining the landscape and rendering it unstable.

When erosion by rainfall and by streams tributary to the Little Missouri River uncovers a bed of lignite, or even the edge of a bed, the soft, combustible rock "slacks," or loses its moisture and crumbles as a result of exposure to atmospheric influences. Other conditions being right, oxidation sets in, the temperature within the mass increases, and unless lightning or some other outside force ignites the bed, it may undergo spontaneous combustion. This produces a burning coal vein.

When that happens, three special aspects of the landscape result. One is a pouring out of smoke and fumes from rifts in the ground, forming a brilliant natural "furnace" that glows like a volcano among the rocky crevices. Another is the collapse of overlying rocks when a lignite seam is reduced to ashes. Cracking and crumbling of upper strata make the surface treacherous to man; in Theodore Roosevelt National Memorial Park, near Medora, a sign that interprets the geological nature of the burning vein has been installed on skids so that it can be pulled back with the advance of the collapsing ground.

The third aspect produced by subterranean fires is the baking of adjacent rock formations into an orange-red stone resembling slag or clinker from a smelter. This bricklike rock resists erosion and provides a protective cap for otherwise friable ridges, accounting for some of the most conspicuous and pleasing coloration of the badlands. Such rock is locally known as "scoria," which confuses it with true scoria, a rock of volcanic origin. But as a color of the badlands, it leaves in the mind of the visitor an indelible impression of a landscape being burned by fires that are still aglow beneath the surface.

Last Stand of the Prairie Dog

So rich are these badlands, contrary to the stories about them, that it is fascinating to wander among them at random. We have done so for hours and days, pushing through the tall grasses, walking along the washes, crossing the undulating hills, and it never palls. There is simply too much to see. Herds of American pronghorns catch the eye, and by waving a handkerchief from a hidden position, one may be able to draw them remarkably close. With a little luck, deer may be seen, or a coyote loping across a grassy swale. Bison have been reintroduced, and are frequently observed as they graze on the hills or proceed in single file across the sun-dried grass—a small but sharp reminder of what the West was like a century ago.

Life also flourishes along the Little Missouri River, where there is abundant evidence of old post-glacial river courses. At the water's edge and high on the cliffs are terraces of the ancestral river which, in Pliocene time, joined the Missouri River and emptied

Badlands often consist of volcanic ash compacted into a clay called bentonite, which may possess many colors. It has a marked ability to absorb water and expand. (Paul Caponigro)

into Hudson Bay rather than the Gulf of Mexico. The present river bank is lined in places with groves of plains cottonwood *(Populus sargentii)* which, in the course of ecological succession, eventually yields to ash and boxelder. These cottonwoods also shelter a considerable variety of bird life, including towhees, sparrows, goldfinches, red-shafted flickers, western and eastern kingbirds, and various warblers. In the adjacent cliffs a golden eagle or great horned owl may nest, or a rock wren may chatter and break the silence of the river scene. All forms of life are protected in the memorial park by federal regulations.

That is very fortunate for the prairie dog—which is not a dog but a rodent. It has sanctuary here from a world of hostile ranchers who claim that it competes with cattle for food and that many a horse has broken a leg by stepping into a prairie dog hole. The West has a history of poisoning with intent to exterminate this creature and the effort has largely been successful; a few thousand pounds of strychnine have helped to destroy millions of animals. In Theodore Roosevelt Memorial Park there are more than thirty separate colonies; and in the Beef Corral colony alone live an estimated 720 individuals. If this sounds like a large population, it should be remembered that less than a century ago one town in Texas is said to have held 400 million prairie dogs and covered a surface of 25,000 square miles. That almost all of the original towns are gone is not the fault of the badger or the black-footed ferret, which in the natural scheme of things controlled the prairie dog population. Ironically, the prairie dog is not extinct, but the ferret—which preyed on it—almost is; the ferret has been called the rarest mammal in North America.

At the Beef Corral prairie dog town, located appropriately near a place called Peaceful Valley, one of the world's largest remaining colonies is protected by United States park rangers as if it were a national treasure. The animals pay little attention to automobiles at the parking turnout, but if human visitors advance too deeply into the colony, a barking eruption occurs and the nearest animals disappear from sight as though they had vanished in thin air.

But each has vanished only into an underground chamber, or more correctly, into an elaborate system of chambers leading from a central shaft dug by sharp front claws to a depth of ten or more feet. Directly beneath the surface is a chamber that functions as a listening post, a kind of second bastion of observation. Beneath or beyond that is the bedroom, lined with grass or other fibrous material. There may be a toilet chamber where droppings are deposited and later removed. Usually there are old rooms or loop hallways or sealed-off passageways adjacent. All in all, the earth-moving prairie dog influences its environment by transporting, aerating and enriching the soil, providing homes for burrowing owls and other creatures, and making an ideal dry wallowing ground for bison.

The whole badlands community, as this arrangement suggests, is an intricate network of organisms and mechanisms. Interdependence is obligatory. What one animal does is bound to have a chain effect on what other animals do or upon the plant life and, by extension, upon the fluted hills and upon the rivers that erode them. We say this glibly, for man has accumulated a great deal of evidence. Nevertheless, as a noted biologist has said, the vast interplay of plant and animal species and climatic and geological factors is still inadequately understood. This is certainly true of the West; like his knowledge of medicine and space, man's mastery of ecology, the study of the relations of living things to one another and to their environment, is still in a primitive state.

Two species of prairie dog inhabit the West. The black-tailed *(Cynomys ludovicianus),* characterized by a black tip on its tail, occurs on plains, badlands and foothills from Mexico to Canada. The white-tailed prairie dog *(Cynomys leucurus)* is found in higher country west of the badlands, along the Rocky Mountains south to Arizona and New Mexico.

"On a sunny day," says the distinguished ecologist Durward Allen, known for his prairie studies, "we can spend an hour among the prairie dogs and nearly always see something new." It is a fast-moving, nervous animal; with so many enemies prowling about and ever ready to pounce, speed is essential for survival, and any relaxation is likely to be punished by the talons of an eagle or the jaws of a coyote. The prairie dog does not have much defense, however, against a badger that pursues it into its tunnel.

These rodents have quite strong social relationships. They primp endlessly and groom themselves and other members of their immediate family, and join in the common defense of burrow and colony. The town indeed seems to be divided into individual plots, each occupied by a male and several breeding females. In April or May the young are born and by September are weaned and ready to take on life alone. Curiously, it is not the young that are expelled from the burrow; rather the adults depart, leaving the diggings to their offspring. The adults construct new

Prairie dogs come in litters of up to ten. Their traditional enemy, the black-footed ferret, has become rare, but badgers, bobcats, coyotes, eagles and snakes have not. (Leonard Lee Rue III)

burrows at the edge of the colony, or reoccupy abandoned ones. Such habits produce a very stable community which, but for man, would probably last indefinitely.

South Dakota Badlands

Nearly every area of western North America contains some form of badlands; there are the Painted Desert of Arizona; Bryce Canyon, Cedar Breaks and the Uinta Basin in Utah; Cathedral Gorge in Nevada; Death Valley and the lower Mojave River in California; Hell's Halfacre on the headwaters of the Powder River, Wyoming; and Lignite Creek, Alaska,

to name a few. Among the best known are the White River Badlands of South Dakota. The eroded rock through which the river flows is fluvial, deposited by streams, or lacustral, deposited in lakes, and today remains soft and relatively unconsolidated. Running water thus wears the terrain into slopes so steeply pitched that vegetation seldom gets a chance to establish itself. Only fifty percent of the South Dakota Badlands are covered with vegetation.

Yet within the beds themselves are rich deposits of another world and a different way of life. It was here in 1849 that Dr. John Evans, under the direction of Dr. David Owen, geologist of the General Land Office, explored the strata and collected fossils. "From the uniform, monotonous, open prairie," said Evans, "the traveller suddenly descends, one or two hundred feet, into a valley that looks as if it had sunk away from the surrounding world, leaving standing all over it thousands of abrupt, irregular, prismatic, and columnar

masses, frequently capped with irregular pyramids and stretching up to a height of from one to two hundred feet or more...." The valley was suffocating, but, the explorer declared, the fossil treasures in it "well repay its sultriness and fatigue.... Embedded in the debris, lie strewn in the greatest profusion, organic relics of extinct animals. All speak of a vast freshwater deposit of the early Tertiary Period, and disclose the former existence of most remarkable races...."

Owen's report, with fossil descriptions by Dr. Joseph Leidy, is one of the earliest significant studies of vertebrate paleontology in the United States. After that, the Badlands were a focal point for students, scientists and collectors. In 1929 Congress authorized the protection of these areas.

It is not surprising that the beds are so rich and interesting. They are a product of the Oligocene Epoch, a time about thirty million years ago when this region was occupied by early forms of the camel, horse,

Gregarious, social and colonial, bison roamed the West—and East—in great herds from Mexico to Canada. They wandered erratically, grazing on grass, a few herbs, and perhaps some leaves of shrubs. (Pete Balestrero: Western Ways Features)

saber-toothed cat, rhinoceros, and dog. Sediments were transported from the Black Hills and spread out by streams that slowed down enough to allow them to settle. The situation may have been analogous to that of the Nile, where for centuries the flood plain was enriched by periodic deposits of river silt.

In the South Dakota Badlands the result has been much the same as in the North Dakota badlands. The color of these hills is mostly tan, but with bands of red, pink, and brown.

A Treasury of Fossils

Nothing is simple, however, about the life that lived on those ancient river deltas, banks, and swamps, the evidence of which lies buried in these beds. Streams that brought in mud carried a few skeletal fragments

as well, and in the Brule and Chadron formations of the South Dakota Badlands is found an extraordinary fossil assemblage of developing mammalian life. There are also tortoises, several kinds of lizards, and hawks, grebes and ducks. An almost perfect skeleton of an alligator was uncovered. But mammals are the most abundant. Altogether, more than two hundred and fifty species of vertebrate animals have been recorded from the Badlands.

Earlier in the Cenozoic Era, when mammals gained pre-eminence, a number of species underwent considerable evolutionary development, and by Oligocene time substantial advances had been made. Among the most common mammals were the oreodonts, who roamed the ancient meadows in what must have been enormous herds, so abundant are their fossils today, especially in the Badlands. We have little way of telling what they looked like because they have long been extinct and nothing like them seems to have survived. They grazed and browsed, chewed their cud, had teeth like camels, had an even number of toes, and grew to about the size of a goat.

The saber-toothed cat, now extinct, roamed this

region, and so did hyenas. Both probably fed on the less spectacular but almost certainly more abundant smaller animals whose remains are associated with theirs: opossums, dogs, pigs, weasels, and rodents.

Most of the fossil remains are those of artiodactyls, a division of the hoofed mammals, or ungulates, that have an even number of toes, such as deer, antelope, and peccary. "In the White River genera there is every reason to think," said William Berryman Scott, eminent paleontologist, "that we have the actual ancestors of all existing camels and llamas."

Of the perissodactyls, ungulates with an odd number of toes, there where tapir and rhinoceros. These fossil deposits illustrate the development of the North American rhinoceros; some rhinos later migrated to the Old World, where they survive today, but the rest of the group had become extinct in North America by the end of Pliocene. The horse went on to greater size, but other species, such as the brontotherium and archeotherium, were later reduced or eliminated.

No one knows, of course, what will be exposed in beds not eroded, or whether there were delicate animals of Oligocene time that were rarely, if ever,

fossilized, such as bats. Even so, almost an entire regional fauna is here in fossil form, preserved down through the millenniums.

The Circle of Life

In a land so seemingly hostile and so devoid of vegetation, one might expect an absence of animal life. The precipitation is variable and may not come in sufficient quantities when growing plants require it most. Or when it does, it may be in the form of devastating hail or heavy downpours that wash out roots or even whole plants. Chilling, desiccating winds prevail on the plains at times, increasing evaporation and intensifying the loss of whatever moisture the plants do have. Under such extremes, trees and shrubs must be well adapted to survive, or must establish themselves in depressions with some degree of protection from the elements and where a little moisture is likely to accumulate in the soil.

In this environment the greatest numbers of animals are those that burrow, and in their burrows they are usually protected from the harsh effects of weather. Surface-ranging creatures, such as deer and bison, have been adapted by evolutionary processes to living where temperatures fall well below zero or rise above 100 degrees F. The other prominent animal of the grasslands province, the pronghorn, is also adapted to live on the plains and prairies. In these wide-open spaces where predators and prey can be seen for miles, the ages have given the pronghorn keen eyesight, an elaborate system of warning reactions, and a high running speed.

Here, as in all large natural environments, or biomes, there is not only plant life but a well-regulated animal community dependent upon it, and an equilibrium—though always a fragile one—between the organisms and their environment. The badlands lie, in fact, within the largest single biome in North America, the prairies and plains, with vegetation characterized by needle and grama grasses. This community extends well into Canada from as far south as central Mexico, and from the Midwest to the Pacific Coast. It varies from place to place; parts of the region are drier than others, parts are lower, and in some areas entirely different ecological associations are interspersed among the grasslands. Yet the two major grassland genera, *Stipa*, needlegrass, and *Bouteloua*, grama grass, are about as ubiquitous as any North American species, and are found in wet places and dry, hot and cold, high and low.

In the Badlands, as in so many other places, the two most common species are blue grama *(Bouteloua oligostachyra)* and needle-and-thread *(Stipa comata)*. Blue grama, a native perennial with curling, bunching, narrow leaves, is recognizable by the cluster of curved seed heads on stalks ten to twenty inches high. For the animals that feed on it, blue grama has features that may mean life or death. It endures extreme climatic variations and after droughts recovers rapidly. The withered stalk retains a good deal of its nutritive value, preserved in the natural curing process.

Needle-and-thread grass gets its name from the seed, which has a pointed head resembling a needle, to which is attached a long and twisted threadlike awn. In the Badlands, it combines with grama grass to dominate the high ground. At lower levels, other species such as little bluestem, wheatgrass, and the familiar buffalo grass *(Buchloe dactyloides)* mingle in the association.

So much grass, in such variety, has for milleniums supported foraging animal life. The seeds, leaves, roots, or stems of grasses, and of the broader-leaved plants, however scarce, have provided sustenance to hordes of birds and mammals in the Badlands, from rats and mice to rabbits and raccoons, squirrels, goldfinches, sparrows, and meadowlarks. Insects, too, have fed upon the plant life, and in turn have been fed upon by such insectivorous predators as swallows, nuthatches, bluebirds, skunks, and lizards. It is the same today. On successively higher levels of predation the badger digs prairie dogs, mice, and ground squirrels from their burrows. Snakes pounce on gophers, and are pounced upon by hawks. Coyotes feed on rabbits. Non-predatory animals—bison, bighorn, deer, pronghorn, and porcupine—subsist more directly upon the vegetation.

The Black Hills

One cannot approach the edge of the plains without a sense of wonder at the first spectacular outliers of the Rocky Mountains. Long before the westward traveler sees the Rockies, while the Front Range is still 250 miles away, he encounters in western South Dakota and northeastern Wyoming a place where the land tilts up suddenly. Not far from the White River Badlands, this mountain complex rises out of the plains, its towers and pinnacles reaching 7242 feet at Harney Peak. Since the Black Hills were formed during the same Cretaceous period of mountain-building that lifted the ancestral Rocky Mountains and other western structures, e.g., the Laramide Revolution, they are thus linked more or less structurally and chronologically to uplifts farther west.

They are, in fact, the erosional remnant of a giant domelike structure raised about sixty million years ago. Pressures from within the earth slowly thrust up a 60-by-125-mile area some 9000 feet, though erosion probably kept the actual altitude relatively low. The basement complex of the Black Hills, a series of rocks fundamental to the structure of the region, is composed of folded Precambrian schists interlaced with masses of granite, and now lies grandly revealed along the highway from Deadwood to Custer. At Mount Rushmore in South Dakota the granite is sufficiently uniform and weather-resistant to justify sculpture on a gigantic scale, and the figures carved by Gutzum Borglum on the mountainside are likely to endure for centuries.

Like all rock, granite weathers in different ways and its surface appearance is often related to structural weaknesses that have developed in it over the ages. Along vertical planes of fracture, erosion has reduced the outcrops sometimes to narrow spires or pinnacles, and hence "The Needles." Also grandly revealed, and adding a great deal of interest and variety to this region, are volcanic materials that have welled up into other rock along the northern end of the Black Hills uplift. These intruding lavas are largely nepheline syenite or phonolite. The conspicuous volcanic neck of Devils Tower is made up of a porphyry, a handsome grayish-brown igneous rock with black and white crystalline inclusions. At Lead, South Dakota, an intrusive dome-like structure includes the celebrated Homestake gold mining district.

The original sedimentary layers overlying this region were peeled away by erosion, except for remnants flanking the Black Hills uplift. There they lie steeply tilted, as seen on the eastern side of Red Valley, near Rapid City. That valley is red because it is cut in the reddish Spearfish shales, deposited during Triassic time and now bent up and exposed to the forces of erosion. The ridge, known as a hogback, forms an almost continuous rim around the Black Hills.

Wind Cave and Jewel Cave

Between this rim and the central core lies a plateau of Paleozoic limestones, in which abundant fractures permit the percolation of ground water. Through combination with gases from the surface, the water became slightly acid and over many years has dissolved out numerous passageways. Best known of these are Wind Cave and Jewel Cave, in the Pahasapa limestone. Wind cave, so named because of the rush of wind in and out of the natural entrance—a characteristic of many caves—may be explored on trails that descend 326 feet beneath the surface. About a tenth of the known cave system is open to visitors. It is famous for its delicate boxwork—ceiling cubicles formed by lime deposits from ground water dripping from a network of cracks. Jewel Cave, a few miles to the northwest, is named for its crystals of calcite, a form of calcium carbonate which occurs here in sharp-pointed rhombic crystals known as dogtooth spar.

Above the caverns, the limestone plateau supports an open forest of ponderosa pine, a tree which the pioneer conservationist, John Muir, said gave forth the finest music to the winds. Few other trees, so ubiquitous, so stately, could provide as appropriate an introduction to western vegetation; the ponderosa, or western yellow pine, is among the most common trees of the West. Mountain mahogany grows here, too, and mariposa lily, mallow, lupine, fireweed, and other members of a characteristic western flora. Mammals associated with this upland forest may be seen along the trails and highways of the Black Hills, principally deer, elk, a few bighorn, and the reintroduced bison at Wind Cave National Park and Custer State Park.

In reality, the Black Hills are a faunal and floral crossroads, where life forms of east and west, north and south, plains and mountains meet. The mountains support a mixture of vegetative forms from three provinces: the grasslands out of which they rise; the eastern deciduous forest; and the boreal, or northern forest, of western mountains. The species most prominent, however, are those of western mountains, and the Black Hills are considered to be outliers of what is called the Cordilleran Forest Province. This means that the conifers preside over all other plants, but there are elm and bur oak from the east, cactus and cottonwood from the south, and juniper and pine from the west. Needlegrass and grama rise from the surrounding plains, and on the forest floor grow attractive flowering plants such as phlox, shooting star, and pasqueflower *(Anemone patens),* state flower of South Dakota. With this kind of shelter and food, it is only natural that the mountain ecosystem also consist of well-developed animal communities—buffalo, prairie dog, badger, and meadowlarks on the open meadows; deer and elk at the forest edge; raccoons, chickadees, woodpeckers, grouse and many other life forms among the trees.

Once he leaves the Black Hills, heading westward, the traveler sees soft green landscapes change into snow-topped mountain peaks, deep red canyons, and hot deserts. He feels the sun burning in a cloudless sky, the bite of dust on the spring wind, or the sense of entrapment as the cliffs close in around him. There are also pleasant things: the scent of the pine, the sky-wide colors of sunsets such as he has never seen, and the howl of coyotes at night. The only constant is change itself, change that is sometimes violent, sometimes gentle. But the traveler has had a glimpse of the burning beds of the badlands and the wild cliffs of the Black Hills, and is partly prepared for the grand experience of the Rocky Mountains.

14. *In the Wilds of Western Canada*

The dark green forest, rushing streams, purple peaks, silvery ice, a cloudless sky, all combine to form a perfect alpine paradise.

The Reverend William Spotswood Green
in *Among the Selkirk Glaciers*, 1890

The Rocky Mountains of Canada seem larger, higher, and more complex than any mountains on earth, but they are none of these. They seem so because they are breathtaking, their structure is often grandly revealed in a complex pattern, and access by road, rail, and trail permit us to travel in them for hundreds of miles in nearly any direction. If there is a phenomenon that distinguishes the Canadian Rockies, we think it is their illustration of earth movements. Nowhere else in the West or the world, not even in the Basin and Range Province or the Andes, have we seen more splendid illustrations of tectonic processes on so large a scale.

The naked cliffs and warped valleys expose clear and unmistakable evidence of upfolds (anticlines), downfolds (synclines), overthrusts, fractures, and the work of glaciers. One overthrust after another characterizes these mountains, and after traveling in them for days, seeing upturned, folded, pitched and broken strata in nearly every direction, an observer gets an overwhelming sense of the surging forces of the earth.

West of Calgary or Edmonton the traveler enters foothills of folded strata that introduce the great mountain front lying beyond. Then he passes over or through range after range of the Canadian Rockies, all parallel and trending toward Alaska for a thousand miles.

Of Trilobites and Emerald Lakes

The eye perceives in these mountains part of an enormous thickness of sediment turned to stone. Rock layers in the Bow River Valley, if stacked in one place, would exceed twelve thousand feet. The oldest are thinly bedded shales that form the tree-covered lower slopes of the mountains. Higher up, between strata of durable limestone that form spectacular cliffs, lie fossiliferous shales that open for us the life and times of the Cambrian world. One of the most significant North American fossil discoveries was made on Mount Stephen, near the village of Field, British Columbia, nearly a century ago. Almost two thousand feet up on the mountainside lie slabs of shale and limestone imprinted with thousands of Cambrian fossils, chiefly trilobites, the most common being *Ogygopsis klotzi*. Other identifiable animals of Cambrian seas include jellyfish, sponges and worms. The miracle is that they were preserved at all. Such soft-bodied creatures were usually dissolved into oblivion or consumed by predators. Though now little more than carbonaceous film, like ink on a page, they exhibit the delicacy and details not only of external appendages but sometimes of viscera as well.

Before their discovery and description, life in Cambrian seas was very imperfectly known. These slabs of Burgess shale held evidence that life in the Cambrian period was well established and flourishing in a variety of forms, a knowledge that considerably advanced man's studies of the principles of evolution. Shortly after the turn of the century, these fossils were brought

Mile-high Maligne Lake, in Jasper National Park, is the largest glacial lake in the Canadian Rockies. (Byron S. Crader)

to the attention of C. D. Walcott of the Smithsonian Institution, a leading authority on Cambrian life in North America. He devoted the next twenty years to studying the site and its fossils, most of which were new to science.

These mountains likewise constitute a monumental tribute to the rest of the Paleozoic Era. The cordilleran trough, once of continent size, received sand, silt, gravel and lime, which were converted to rock and then severely compressed. The strata were literally wrinkled, the Canadian Rockies thus constituting an excellent demonstration of how mountains are born and raised. Castle mountains, for example, consist of limestone and quartzite beds with softer strata between, much like a layer cake. Erosion of less durable beds causes the hard rocks to break off in cliffs. A splendid example is Castle Mountain, now renamed Mount Eisenhower, in Banff National Park. When elevated at one end or the other, the mountain may sometimes look like a sinking ship, as in the dramatic case of Mount Rundle, which soars above the village of Banff, Alberta.

A Columbian ground squirrel stands alert near one of its many burrow exits. At a hint of danger, it races from one doorway to another and emits a piping note of alarm. (Ann and Myron Sutton)

A second type, sawtooth mountains, results from erosion of upended sediments. Dogtooth mountains remain as conspicuous pinnacles from erosion of up-turned resistant beds, while another type of spire, more closely resembling a pyramid or obelisk, is the Matter-horn-like Mount Assiniboine, at the edge of Banff National Park; it is a remnant of a peak from which glaciers have swept away rock on all sides.

Perhaps most striking are the mountains based on folding and faulting. Downfolds of resistant strata isolated by erosion and left high and dry become synclinal mountains, of which Mount Kerkeslin in Jasper National Park is an extraordinary example. Upfolds result in anticlinal mountains, and in the Canadian Rockies we find combinations of these and other types, complicated by faults, broken loose and perhaps thrust over one another. Of these creative, almost bizarre, works of natural engineering the eastern portion of Jasper National Park provides an enormous outdoor museum, almost a giant sculpture garden.

Superimposed upon all this are the effects of glaciers, which vastly altered the landscape. Only much-reduced remnants of former ice masses exist, but if you examine the seemingly fresh and clean rock in the vicinity of a glacier you may be able to see almost exactly where and how much larger the glacier was. Robson and Athabasca Glaciers are prime exhibits of this phenomena, but in both Canada and Alaska one frequently observes the polished swaths of recent ice. Long ridges of sand, gravel, and ground-up rock were left from the deposition of a glacier. These terminal or lateral moraines come in assorted shapes and sizes and constitute a significant part of the Rocky Mountain scene. Many boulders caught in the moving ice cut and scratched the mountains over which they moved, and they in turn were cut and scratched in the process. Now they serve as vivid evidence of how glacier-held materials became the tools of erosion.

Nearly everything here that went on in the past is still going on today. But the glaciers, though still advancing, are now melting at a faster rate than they are moving forward, with the result that most glaciers and ice fields are diminishing. Athabasca Glacier, for example, flows forward fifty feet a year but melts back at three times that rate, resulting in a net retreat of about one hundred feet per year.

Waters melting from the Columbia icefield flow into three great oceans via the Fraser, Athabasca and North Saskatchewan rivers. Gray silted streams gush from the front of Athabasca glacier at a temperature in summer of about thirty-three degrees. Most such streams are decidedly murky at their source and for a considerable distance downstream are little more than flowing mud, sand and boulders. As soon as they spread out and lose some of their velocity the heavier contents of the load drop out. On these rock-strewn flats the stream divides, rejoins and splits, crossing and recrossing itself, forming what is known as a braided stream. There is hardly a watercourse in the northern glacier country that doesn't exhibit some kind of braided pattern before it leaves the mountains.

The farther downstream these waters flow, the more of their load is left behind until at last they transport only finely divided sediment that represents the most intense pulverization of rocks by glaciers. Like the suspension of lime and sugar in a limeade, the water maintains a fairly constant light green cloudiness. Emerald, Peyto, and O'Hara lakes are of this type, their pale green waters reflecting the massive mountains and dark green forests that rise above them. No doubt the most famous is tranquil Lake Louise, located in a forest of Engelmann spruce and alpine fir. It is a mile long, over two hundred feet deep, and measures fifty degrees at the surface in summer. Around its shores grow dwarf dogwood, parsnip, thickets of alder and willow, and generous layers of moss and lichen. As for aquatic life within such glacial lakes, there is usually minimum productivity, the lakes being deep, cold, and almost lifeless, or oligotrophic. Those that are characteristic of plains and lower elevations are eutrophic and produce more food. Our favorite stream in these mountains, a twisting, surging avenue of bluish white, is the Kicking Horse River, but the Bow River and others have similar color and charm.

High mountain lakes, or tarns, which occupy glacier-gouged bowls, called cirques, may be observed intimately only by those with strength and stamina to hike in these rugged mountains. Spectacular ice falls also reward the hardy explorer. Great glacial masses cling to the cliffs in a frozen state of animation, such as Angel Glacier on Mount Edith Cavell. Athabasca Glacier has a three-step ice fall, and another is appropriately named Crowfoot Glacier. More liquid and active falls abound, also, and quite often the wide-flowing rivers are, like the Nile at Murchison Falls in Uganda, confined to narrow gorges. Examples of this are the thundering Athabasca, Wapta and Sunwapta falls. Or the water plunges from valleys left hanging by glacial action, such as Takakkaw Falls and Twin Falls, both in the classical pattern of California's famed Yosemite Falls.

In a fair number of places the plunging streams have dug themselves so deeply into the limestones that they have nearly disappeared. The Maligne River narrows, for example, have cliffs so overlapping that observers on either rim find it difficult to see the river, although they can hear it roaring 152 feet below. Potholes and other evidence of abrasion show the power of running water moving at a gradient of four hundred feet per mile. There are also rivers that sink out of sight, and lakes with no apparent outlet, both indicative of complex underground drainage. Sometimes water that has gone deeply enough comes in contact with heated masses of igneous rock, is warmed by the internal heat of the earth and resurfaces as hot springs. Radium Hot Springs, in Kootenay National Park, British Columbia, emerges from shatter zones in the Jubilee limestone. Miette Hot Springs in Jasper National Park pours out 125,000 gallons a day and one of its springs, at 126 degrees, is the hottest in the Canadian Rockies. Several miles away, near the Athabasca River, a cold sulfur spring emerges at a temperature of forty-five degrees.

But all is not the peace and quiet that springs and lakes and inspiring mountain vistas seem to indicate. Avalanches, for example, roar down the mountains with splendid indifference to the works of man, so

Clark's nutcracker, symbolic of the western mountains, prefers the cool woods just below tree line. It feeds on nearly anything the spruce-fir forest offers, including seeds, fruits and berries. (Ann and Myron Sutton)

snow sheds of reinforced concrete have been installed along routes of travel. The mountains are literally scarred with landslides. One of these dammed the outlet of Moraine Lake. Another roared off Turtle Mountain, Alberta, in 1903 and into the town of Frank, leaving an awesome scar that is visible for dozens of miles across the plains. In approximately one hundred seconds the mountain flank, an estimated ninety million tons of limestone, fell and flowed nearly three miles across the valley, climbing five hundred feet up the opposite wall. No one knows how many persons were killed; some estimates run over seventy-five. Today the slide scar seems as fresh as though it were made only yesterday, and boulders still on the mountain seem tottering and ready to fall. But a little soil is forming and a few small plants are trying to grow, though the wound will take thousands of years to heal, if it ever does. It is the most recent and dramatic evidence of Canada's mountains on the move.

On the Mountain Tundra

Amidst the clattering notes of a Clark's nutcracker, the variable call of the gray jay and, when you can hear it, the singing of wind through Engelmann spruce and alpine fir, Bow Pass offers a lively introduction to life in the Canadian Rockies. From the shoulder of the mountain a splendid view of Peyto Lake and the Mistaya Valley unfolds, a bit dizzying at first because the mountains in the distance seem to be leaning backward and falling away on both sides of the valley. However,

With webbed feet, dense fur and a fish diet, river otters have become well adapted to aquatic life. They build riverbank slides for easy access to the water. (Leonard Lee Rue III)

the valley is simply a great arch or anticline of Cambrian rock from which water and ice have exacted their toll, and the mountains on either side are what remains of the flank of the arch. Peyto Glacier, a tongue of the Wapta ice field, comes down from the left, frozen almost in silence. Its waters discharge into a lake that is normally dark blue but turns to a magnificent green when finely ground "rock flour" pours in and becomes suspended in the water.

On a July day most of winter's severity—the raging wind, the flaying ice crystals, the bitter cold—are gone. So is the heavy snow pack. For a few weeks nature suspends its attacks and withdraws its annual mantle of snow. The sun pours warmth into the ground. Globe flowers *(Trollius albiflorus)* and spring beauties *(Claytonia lanceolata)* burst up and bloom through the final wetness of the melting snow. Where life a few weeks

before might have seemed hopeless, now the mountain tundra comes alive with color, form and motion.

In the background, the conifers seem always to have been there. By the time the montane forest of the Mistaya Valley reaches this elevation, even the sturdiest trees have become misshapen and scrubby. Engelmann spruce *(Picea engelmanni)*, elsewhere a slender and stalwart spire a hundred feet tall, does well to grow a quarter of that height here. The bushy green appearance, thick quota of reddish-purple cones, and vociferous populations of jays and nutcrackers nevertheless give it character. Alpine fir *(Abies lasiocarpa)* survives in a somewhat different way. When lower branches are pressed against the earth by heavy snow they establish root and grow in a candelabrum around the mother tree.

No matter how high or low the forest, it and the mountain tundra make up complex ecosystems containing numerous animals—including the bighorn, hoary marmot, mountain goat, chipmunk, pika, golden-mantled ground squirrel, ptarmigan, golden eagle, and occasional moose and bear. Certain snow-fleas or springtails, small black scorpion flies *(Boreus californicus fuscus)* and primitive craneflies *(Chionea alexandriana)* may even be found on the surface of snow. Clark's nutcracker, named for Captain Clark of the celebrated expedition, hops through trees or on snow and ground in a perpetual search for nuts and anything else it can find. With a beak like a crowbar, this member of the crow family has little difficulty extracting seeds from cones, or food from picnic tables. Neither this, nor the raids on other birds' nests, nor the crackling voice endear it very much to human observers, yet its abundance, prominence, and place in the ecosystem should win it respect. Clark's nutcrackers occur in most of western North America, though they prefer the mountains, where many remain throughout the winter. What might be cold and miserable to human beings in such an environment apparently makes no difference to the nutcracker, even during nesting. Early in the year four or five eggs are laid in a nest of dry twigs, not much protection against late winter storms and subzero winds. But the diligent female is rewarded in three weeks, though the young are naked and do not become fully feathered for several weeks after birth.

Away from the forest and out on the mountain tundra grow trees even less imposing than the conifers, among them three kinds of willow: rock *(Salix vestita)*, alpine *(S. nivalis)*, and Barratt's *(S. barrattiana)*. The heathers, conspicuous with their blossoms, come in three colors—red *(Phyllodoce empetriformis)*, yellow *(P. glanduliflora)*, and white *(Cassiope mertensiana)*. Another heath, the alpine bearberry *(Arctostaphylos rubra)*, gathers in mats on ledges and slopes.

Nothing in this environment, however, is quite as colorful as the summer-long display of ground-hugging alpine flowers. Whatever the eye surveys seems ablaze with orange, scarlet and pink paintbrush, all forms of *Castilleja miniata*, whose colorful bracts envelop its less conspicuous flowers; moreover, at this and lower elevations, we come across the yellow paintbrush *(C. occidentalis)*. In the lily family greenish-brown

Two pine martens fight for possession of a red squirrel.
(National Film Board of Canada)

flowers of the diminutive, retiring bronze bells *(Stenanthium occidentale)* and the graceful white camas or green lily *(Zygadenus elegans)* nod gently on slender stalks that sway with the slightest breeze. We found ourselves particularly drawn to the fringed grass-of-parnassus *(Parnassia fimbriata)*, resident in moist and mossy places; not only are its green-veined flowers conspicuous but its cluster of glossy leaves adds to the luxuriance of the mountain flora.

Two members of the figwort family, which includes snapdragons, are the alpine lousewort *(Pedicularis contorta)* and speedwell *(Veronica alpina)*, both venturing well above tree line. Strangest in shape among the upland flowers of this prolific family is the elephant head *(Pedicularis groenlandica)*. A tiny two-lipped corolla, lavender to maroon in color, resembles an elephant's head complete with trunk, ears and tusks. This species may most successfully be sought in upland bogs, patches of moist grass, and soil beside a lake or stream. Mountain sorrel *(Oxyria digyna)*, a wild buck-wheat, adds a touch of red that softens the rocky landscape.

To the sunflower family the mountain tundra owes a great deal for its remarkable color and variety. Most common are alpine goldenrod *(Solidago multiradiata)*, purple aster, yarrow, ragwort and pussy toes. Few flowers are as welcome as the golden fleabane *(Erigeron aureus)*, a low-growing perennial with clusters of bright green hairy leaves. There are indeed more flowers than we realize, some hidden in the shadows like columbine, some far out on exposed sites like the avens. There is literally a rainbow of colors—fireweed, anemone, strawberry, arnica, vetch and cinquefoil—and the combination of soft green forest, shining glaciers, emerald lakes, and deep blue sky reinforces Ruskin's dictum that mountains are the beginning and the end of all natural scenery.

Along the Alaska Highway

Not so long ago the Yukon and Northwest territories seemed to be at the ends of the earth, and pictures conjured up in the public mind were of frozen wastes where only polar bears lived. Now with access by air and road, a more varied picture is emerging, and men are realizing that there is much more to this land than formerly met the eye. One of the central reasons is improvement of overland transportation, chiefly the 1523-mile route completed in 1942 between Dawson Creek, British Columbia, and Fairbanks, Alaska. It is called the Alaska Highway, though four-fifths of it lie in Canada.

From Dawson Creek it passes north across the Alberta Plateau, cut here and there by tributaries to the Peace and Liard rivers. This first three hundred miles offers little in the way of mountain views, the road being enclosed in a dense mixed forest. But we found every mile along the highway interesting. Along this section, particularly, the northbound traveler enters a fascinating biome that stretches almost without interruption around the world—the taiga, a broad belt of forest just short of the treeless arctic tundra. Cottonwood, aspen, and lodgepole pine vie for space, but most persistent and successful is the white spruce *(Picea glauca)*. A great deal of activity goes on in the forest—warblers extracting insect larvae from leaves, grouse setting up low-frequency pulsations with wing beats during drumming, and high-hopping spittlebugs secreting masses of sticky substances on twigs to protect hatching nymphs. It is interesting to note how different are conditions beneath stands of aspen, which allow much solar energy to pass through their canopy, and stands of spruce, which do not. With more warmth and light we may expect more flowering plants and perhaps more animal life. On the other hand, each autumn's blanket of fallen leaves beneath deciduous trees all but precludes the beautiful carpets of moss expected in coniferous stands. The fallen aspen leaves are devoured by detritus-feeders whose wastes are removed by such consumers as bacteria and earthworms. This drama is heightened when the aspen and spruce are mixed in different proportions. Thus the universal circle of flowing energy operates as efficiently in this taiga as on the tundra and in the tropics.

Chickadees, jays, and hawks are as much a part of the scene as birches and foxtail grass. Flocks of ravens often fly noisily overhead or search for carrion. The road is repeatedly crossed by arctic ground squirrels *(Spermophilus parryi)*. Bighorn ewes traverse the highway with their lambs, and moose browse in the forests alongside it. When wind and rain sweep out of the sky, they force on the trees a thrashing violence, but at other times the forest lies quietly beneath a soft and gentle mist.

We looked in moist places for the brilliant shrubby cinquefoil *(Potentilla fruticosa)* and nearly always found it there, glittering yellow against the differing shades of green. Daisies and goldenrod line the highway, and along stream banks or deep in thickets of birch grow the rich green horsetail *(Equisetum* sp.). Fireweed and yarrow grace the highway from end to end.

After nearly four hundred miles, the traveler enters the Stone and then the Sentinel ranges. Suddenly he is in the heart of the Rocky Mountains, surrounded by massive cliffs of shale, slate, limestone and marble, a catalog of rocks from Precambrian to Jurassic. This confused mass has been intruded by igneous rock folded and thrust-faulted almost beyond recognition, but it is a thrilling experience for persons who have come across hundreds of miles of prairie and enveloping forest.

Farther on, the Liard River comes into view, a massive blue river flowing through spruce and lodgepole pine that seem of lesser stature as the road goes northwestward. Stretches of lodgepole, all about the same age, signal the fires that once swept the region. A thirty-five-mile section of the highway paved with coal, clay, shale, and assorted gravel has a blue-black appearance. Liard Hot Springs, a British Columbia Provincial Park, issue at about 120 degrees, and nourish a botanist's paradise, with rich growths of mosses, mushrooms, ferns, alder, cottonwood, spruce, aspen, birch, larch, cinquefoil, bunchberry, parsnip, wild rose, and a host of other species made accessible by a board walk.

The Alaska Highway ranges in elevation from a thousand to over four thousand feet, and from parts of it can be seen the Saint Elias Range, which contains Mount Logan, 19,850 feet, second highest peak in North America. The traveler crosses picturesque white rivers composed of volcanic ash deposits. Eskers, curving ridges of till deposited by glacial streams, may be seen from the highway, as may hill-sized deposits of glacial material called drumlins, as well as balanced rocks, erosion pillars, waterfalls, and a succession of rivers and lakes. Any fisherman will make very slow progress along the highway if he tries out every opportunity to wet a line for lake and rainbow trout, arctic grayling, Dolly Varden, and kokanee. From time to time the traveler can stop and with binoculars scan the barren peaks for bighorn, locally called stone sheep, mountain goat and bear, but his closest association with wildlife is apt to be the unwanted companionship of mosquitoes, midges, craneflies, horseflies and deerflies. Particularly exasperating to man and beast are the blackflies, which considerately inject an anesthetic before drawing blood, but leave an intensely irritating aftereffect. Even so, the pleasures outweigh the hardships, and two things about the Alaska Highway stand out most vividly—fires and fireweed.

Yukon Fires and Fireweed

White spruce is the essential tree of the Yukon, and indeed of much of the arctic north, where it marches to the northern limit of trees with its sturdy companions, black spruce *(Picea mariana)* and larch. Although the white spruce attains its greatest height and grandeur farther east and south, it still counts as the principal lumber tree of Yukon, even against great odds. With a shallow root system it is at the mercy of the winds. Temperatures in this region can sink to the lowest in Canada; the record is eighty-one degrees below zero at Snag, Yukon. Only twelve inches of rain fall annually, a desert-like amount. Under these conditions the land is especially susceptible to burning which, of course, is not without advantages. Nutrient materials released in the ashes produce favorable beds for seeds, and the subsequent plant growth attracts various animal populations. But the spruce itself is slow to regenerate. Because the ecosystem is based so much on continuous fire, mature forests in the Yukon exist chiefly along moist river banks and bottoms.

Notwithstanding the cold and aridity in this Land of the Midnight Sun, there is no lack of summer thunderstorms and scarcely an acre of Yukon Territory has not been burned at one time or another. Storms ablaze with lightning sweep the territory from northwest to southeast, leaving a trail of fires (one hundred in 1966) that may burn for months or smolder for years. In few places are the results so evident as between Mileposts 928 and 960 on the Alaska Highway. For thirty-two miles the traveler sees burned black remnants of trees stretching to every horizon, the consequence of three fires that coalesced in 1958. Altogether that year, one and one-half million acres of the Yukon burned, and in 1966 an Alaska-Yukon fire consumed five hundred thousand acres.

Such trails of burgeoning fires are often too much for human resources to handle, and when there are not enough men to fight them the fires simply have to burn. The Yukon Territorial Government has established protected zones around all communities, highways, and major bodies of water, where fires will be suppressed with all possible means. This is a sensible step for a much-abused land that was steadily cut and burned by man during the Klondike Gold Rush and the construction of the Alaska Highway. Just to fuel steamers plying the Yukon River between Whitehorse and Dawson required an estimated 300,000 cords of wood between 1898 and 1950.

The Territory has hundreds of thousands of acres of arable land but natural resources seem destined to afford a richer yield than agriculture. These resources include scenery, forests, water power, wildlife for hunting and fur trapping, and such metals as gold, silver, lead, zinc, cadmium and copper. In Whitehorse a giant copper nugget weighing 2600 pounds is on display, but gold made the Yukon's history most lively. Just before the turn of the century, miners poured into Skagway, Alaska, on the Pacific Coast, crossed the mountains inland to Yukon Territory and Whitehorse, then floated in one way or another down the Yukon River north to Dawson. There, between 1896, when gold was struck on Bonanza Creek in the Klondike region, and 1904, more than a hundred million dollars in gold were extracted from river sands and gravels.

Now a more enduring kind of gold is being mined. As the Superintendent of Forestry of the Yukon Forest Service told us in Whitehorse: "It is generally accepted that tourism in the Yukon has tremendous potential, and its dollar value may eventually equal or surpass that of the long-established mining industry. Whatever the result, the Yukon is magnificent tourist country with its mountains, lakes and historical centers and in all of these cases, the beauty or appeal is enhanced by the forests."

Part of that beauty is the fireweed *(Epilobium angustifolium)*, floral emblem of the Territory. Flowers of this genus, which has a hundred species worldwide, cover a great deal of Yukon and Alaska, and ornament the entire Alaska Highway. Whereas we think of evening primroses as white or yellow, this one is pink,

lilac lavender, or magenta, its four-petaled flowers an inch across. The lower ones bloom first, so that the long raceme or flowering stalk may bear blossoms and seed capsules while still crowned with buds preparing to open. The leaves being narrow and lance-shaped have given to the plant the alternate name of willow-weed. Though it may seem incongruous beside stumps of charred and blackened trees, the ash-enriched soil seems to be highly suitable for fireweed, which is often the first to sprout and bloom in a burned-out forest; hence its name. Grizzly bears consider fireweed good to eat. So do deer and elk. The plant grows over five feet tall and may occur in masses wherever the forest canopy has been opened to sunlight. Its striking color against black snags, green tundra or white snow is enough to make a traveler remember Alaska and the Yukon not as landscapes of barren gray or white but of living green and magenta.

Great Rift Valleys

There are two other ways to approach Alaska, one by air, which reveals the grandness and majesty of the land as a whole, and the other by sea. Going by sea allows more time to observe the wildlife, and permits a trek across one of Canada's most beautiful provinces, British Columbia.

All the mountains of western Canada are not Rocky Mountains. In fact there is a specific demarcation line between the Rockies and the uplands to the west. This is a great rift of the same kind as those of Africa, the Rhine, the Red Sea, and the mid-Atlantic Ocean. It is a structural valley five or ten miles wide and a thousand miles long, from Montana to the Yukon, a more or less linear feature in a region so otherwise disorderly. But there it is, the Rocky Mountain Trench, a tree-filled interlude between mountains, a basin drained not by one river but by parts of eight: the Columbia, Kootenay, Fraser, Canoe, Kechika, Fox, Finlay and Parsnip. Its southern end is in southwestern Montana; Flathead Lake and Kalispell lie in it, and perhaps the Bitterroot Valley is a part of the Trench. Not far above the international boundary the Purcell Trench branches off to the west and follows the lower course of the Kootenay River to a point near Lake Coeur D'Alene. Other long, straight valleys, such as the Tintina and Shakwak of the Yukon, seem not to be connected with the Trench, but are suspiciously in alignment with it.

Whatever the seeming simplicity of its surface arrangements, the Rocky Mountain Trench apparently has a complex structure of faults and variously dipping rock strata. In some places it is sinuous. In others it is uneven in cross-section, with the east wall higher than the west. The broad-floored valley indicates considerable erosion along a fault line, and also shows evidence of massive glacial erosion during Pleistocene time. The Trench may well be of block fault origin, but a landscape feature so huge requires a great deal of study which, in this case, has only begun. In the words of geologist Philip King, no explanation of the origin of the Trench can be proved in the present state of our knowledge. Nevertheless, exploitation is a different matter—and thereby hangs the tale of the North

American Water and Power Alliance, or Nawapa. Nawapa, based on the supposition that Canada's abundant fresh water ought to be shared with other countries, was proposed in 1964 by a Los Angeles engineering firm and envisions the storage and distribution of water on a scale that staggers the imagination. It involves some fifty diversion and control works such as dams, canals, tunnels, and reservoirs, and includes a dam twice as high as any yet constructed. For a cost of a hundred billion dollars, the project would deliver Canadian water to the United States and Mexico, generate electric power, open new lands to irrigation, and allegedly flush polluted wastes from lakes and streams.

The project calls for damming headwaters of major rivers in Alaska, Yukon, and British Columbia and diverting their waters into enormous reservoirs—including the Rocky Mountain Trench. This would produce North America's largest man-made lake, which at an estimated 518,200,000 acre feet would be sixteen times the capacity of Lake Mead. Huge canals and pumping systems would carry the water from the Trench into Idaho, Utah, and the Southwest, where enormous aqueducts would spread it further. Other systems would link the Saint Lawrence Seaway with the Pacific Coast and tie into the Great Lakes and Mississippi River for good measure.

Proponents of Nawapa have assumed that such a system is needed to meet America's coming water shortage, though hydrology experts do not all believe that there is going to be such a shortage now or in the future, a matter discussed in Chapter 16. Even if water were scarce, better means of getting, keeping and moving it are or soon will be available: desalinization, depollution, increased use of ground water, modification of weather, evaporation control, and the undersea transfer of water.

Although various communities and historic sites would be inundated, as well as major surface transportation routes, the greatest dangers inherent in the Nawapa proposal might be natural. What would happen to the underground structure of western Canada, for example, if the Rocky Mountain Trench were filled with water? Experience elsewhere, on a lesser scale, suggests that earthquakes could be one of the first results. If water storage warmed up regions of permafrost and, as it were, melted the soil, what havoc would landslides play? A wholesale redistribution of surface water in North America might affect climates and ecosystems so profoundly that no one could say what adjustments would have to be made, or whether man would have initiated an uncontrollable sequence of events.

In the final analysis, Canadians are not likely to part with what they consider their most priceless resource, free-flowing fresh water. Nor are they apt to disturb the magnificent scenery and wildlife that can yield many more benefits, both economically and esthetically, than dams and reservoirs. The era of massive technological solutions to massive human problems also may be a thing of the past. But in passing it is interesting to note how man, still unaware of nature's secrets, has the courage—or perhaps fool-

Agile and quick, the golden-mantled ground squirrel has become adapted to mountainous regions of the West. (Ruth Kirk)

hardiness—to suggest alteration of half a continent, and to propose filling up the Rocky Mountain Trench, a thousand-mile avenue through some of the most beautiful wilderness in the world.

Wildlife of British Columbia

Seeing only a few animals at a time in the wilderness, it may be difficult to realize how many there are and how closely associated each is with the other and with the world in which they live. Each must be self-sufficient, yet each is dependent, too, in compliance with natural law. All, of course, are directly or indirectly dependent on vegetal matter. Of the lower animals, tent caterpillars defoliate aspen and long-horned borer beetles feed on conifers. Some insects form galls on leaves or needles, cones and roots. Some bore channels into bark and sapwood or etch geometric designs in leaves. Most destructive are the bark or engraver beetles which hollow out galleries between wood and bark. A tree in good health can extrude enough pitch to drown the hungry beetle larvae, but dead and weakened trees yield to their attack—a kind of natural thinning process. Thus the role of insects is a dynamic one, but they are not indestructible. Parasites and viral, bacterial, and fungal diseases prey on insects even when the ever-attentive birds, shrews and moles do not.

The whole sequence of events is exceedingly intricate, for insects, like fire or wind, may fell a tree, then attack the trunk and reduce it to soil. This helps regenerate vegetation and that helps support animal life. In fact, where there is an abundance of vegetation we are likely to find an abundance of vegetarians. One species which occupies a variety of ecological niches, especially grassy meadows surrounded by coniferous forest, is the abundant Columbian ground squirrel *(Spermophilus columbianus)*. Since it feeds on seeds and shoots it constitutes a primary consumer, the basic first-echelon transfer of energy from plants to plant-eaters. Neighboring members of this echelon—mice, chipmunks, squirrels, pockets gophers, and other herbivorous rodents—make up a vast food resource for larger animals.

The Columbian ground squirrel, chiefly colonial, occupies burrows and earth mounds linked with interior and exterior runways. If you approach one opening the animal barks and disappears only to pop up a few seconds later at another. The squirrel spends all summer in getting fat and as early as August it begins to hibernate even though a month's good weather may remain. It is out again in April, playing host as usual to parasites that include the spotted fever tick *(Dermacentor andersoni)*, and, if careless, providing a meal for such predators as badgers and golden eagles.

In the predator fraternity, the weasel family also contains several members that are ferociously predatory on small mammals, and because of this their fortunes are tied to the fortunes of herbivores and insectivores. The Richardson weasel, or ermine *(Mustela erminea)*, takes squirrels, grouse, rabbit, anything it can find and conquer, its powers of creeping up undetected enhanced by a coat that changes from summer brown to winter white. Martens *(Martes americana)* consume squirrels, mice, chipmunks and birds, and go one step further in the ecological cycle by occasionally making their homes in the abandoned nests of pileated woodpeckers. Fishers *(Martes pennanti)*, also members of the weasel family, thrive on a similar diet (though rarely on fish as their name implies), and are among the few animals that can get away with killing and eating a porcupine. Wolverines *(Gulo luscus)* are fierce and fearless, able to dispatch a moose or caribou if they happen to find one mired in mud or snow. Attempts to transplant Atlantic lobster to the Pacific Coast have been hampered by the voracious mink *(Mustela vison)*, a semi-aquatic short-legged weasel that feasts on fish, muskrats, frogs, insects and other food of the water habitat. Otters have become almost fully aquatic and subsist on a similar diet.

In addition to the weasel family, the wild dogs also make great inroads into the populations of herbivores, small as well as large. Timber wolves prefer to bring down deer and elk, but rodents are sometimes likely to be more abundant and available. Red foxes *(Vulpes fulva)* use their intelligence to outwit small mammals, but foxes are only secondary consumers in the food chain and if they don't watch out they may become food for tertiary consumers such as wolves, eagles, fishers and lynxes.

Lynxes and the other cats—bobcats and mountain lions—likewise rely on mammals for food. In particular, the secretive Canada lynx *(Lynx canadensis)* shares its habitat with snowshoe hares, its main source of food. Lynx populations have been found to rise and fall in ten-year cycles more or less coincident with the abundance or scarcity of hares. But like the bobcat, a member of the same genus, the lynx will also take small rodents, birds and other fare.

The Moose

It might well be called king of beasts in North America, or at least co-ruler with the grizzly bear. The moose *(Alces alces)*, largest of living antlered mammals, measures as much as eight feet in height. It has a massive head and neck and a high shoulder hump; its weight may approach 1800 pounds. Even so, a moose can tiptoe silently away from enemies, though if you startle one on a lonely trail it is likely to go crashing through the woods like an elephant.

Mixed forest is its usual habitat, and although the moose is not a wanderer like the caribou it does drift up to tree line in summer and old bulls are sometimes seen on alpine tundra. During winter, the moose seeks lower elevations, and tends to favor dense brush in extreme cold. Customarily, it inhabits weedy lakes or swamps, the edges of ponds, shallows of sluggish streams, and the muck of bogs, where it feeds on aquatic vegetation. After dipping its head deep into the water in search of succulent greenery, it may come up with tendrils of water lily clinging to the antlers.

A moose eats willow leaves mostly, but also dines on leaves of other deciduous trees and shrubs, especially those that come into burned-over areas. During winter the moose may have to rely on conifers, buds, twigs, and bark. With autumn, however, food takes second place to sex. The antlers, designed to reinforce the male's demand for the female, begin to grow in summer, nourished by a velvet covering that ultimately dries and falls away or is rubbed off on the trunk of a fir. Thus unsheathed, the heavy palmate antlers are ready for duelling. The rutting season takes place between September and October, and while the monstrous moose ordinarily is quiet and reserved, now the woods may be filled with roaring, barking and grunting. "The peculiar, hoarse bellowing of the bull moose in the mating season," says J. Dewey Soper, a well-known Canadian biologist, "is a memorable, far-reaching sound fraught with tingling qualities of the primordial. While deep-throated and raucous to the human ear, it doubtless broadcasts haunting and seductive overtones to the patiently waiting adventuress in the woods."

That adventuress certainly has a prominent viewpoint from which to watch proceedings. Fierce battles between males rarely erupt, but when they do the ground may be torn up, trees broken, and shrubbery trampled. In head-on clashes the males can break their necks or antlers, or the antlers can get locked so that the animals subsequently starve to death, a rare occurrence. Blood may be scattered freely, but after a little of this the losing combatant clears out. In due course, the antlers separate from the skull and are discarded. The following year, when the female gets ready to produce her new offspring, she casts out any young still around her, and perhaps on a remote island bears her new calf.

The world of the moose is a pleasant enough place in which to be born, but the perils of life begin at an early age. Although good swimmers, moose sometimes get exhausted and drown or become so impossibly mired in muck and mud that they cannot extricate themselves. They are especially sensitive to scent and sound, but with age the alertness dims. At best, life is one plague after another. Hordes of flies and mosquitoes gorge themselves on moose blood. The primary predator is man, but mothers must protect their young from wolves, mountain lions and bears as well. Ultimately the end comes from disease or degeneration, and the remains are soon disposed of by wolves or carrion eaters.

Evidence shows that the moose is rather new to North America in the geologic sense, apparently being a Pleistocene immigrant from the Old World. It is shy and retiring and in fact withdraws before the onrush of civilization, which suggests that it needs wilderness more than does the deer. It has diminished in numbers and distribution since the advent of men, though remote wilderness areas still appear to be well populated with moose. The immense size of the animal, combined with the immensity of British Columbia's mountains, give it a kind of regal aura, and the sight of it still alive and master of its domain, as nature intended, is both thrilling and inspiring.

Canada's Coastal Forests

British Columbians define their mountains as monoliths of granite, and well they may. The Coast Ranges little resemble the Canadian Rockies, being neither layered nor cut into castles; their peaks are dome-shaped with giant plates of granite peeling from sides and tops, Sierra Nevada style. For a thousand miles from the United States to the Yukon they rise above the interior plateau, culminate in peaks that have been sharply glaciated, then plunge with dramatic suddenness into the sea. More than a hundred million years ago the rocks welled up toward the surface of the earth in a giant batholith that has since been exposed to erosion by water and ice. Glaciers have grooved the coastal mountains deeply, forming channels that rival in grandeur the fiords of Norway, New Zealand, and South America. Some inlets measure half a mile to two miles wide and over a hundred miles in length. Some have water half a mile deep, or summits as much as eight thousand feet above sea level. Landslides have severely scarred the steep slopes and torn away vegetation. In other places the forests are interrupted by roaring cascades.

Beaches are scarce in this vertical land, but life is not. In addition to the abundant kelp (Nereocystis luetkeana), bladder wrack (Fucus furcatus), and eelgrass, the sea supports a splendid fauna. In fact, the northern Pacific Coast is said to have more kinds of starfish than any region in the world, among them the rose, purple, red, blood, pink-skinned, mottled, leather, sun, and sunflower. At Miracle Beach, on Vancouver Island, nineteen species of shells have been classified as common, including clams, oysters, mussels, cockles, snails, limpets, and periwinkles. Shore crabs scavenge under boulders and along the rocky shore. Chitons cling to the rocks and flatfish rest in the waters, confident of their camouflage. Where sand collects in sufficient quantity, sand dollars (Dendraster eccentricus) grow by the thousands, reaching four inches in diameter. Whelks prey on clams and oysters, drilling neat holes in the shells, playing out in their own way the universal drama of predation and energy transfer.

Out of the water and into the forest we find cathedral groves that resemble the Olympic rain forests, though here the conifers seem more erect, the maples less prominent, the oxalis absent. A robin flies up into the branches of a hemlock, where chickadees live and wrens sing. Brown creepers (Certhia familiaris) have a great deal of trunk area to explore because in these forests the soil and climate nurture Douglas firs up to eight hundred years, allowing them to rise to heights of 250 feet and a diameter of more than nine feet. The inevitable Steller jays seem to object to everything, while flocks of juncos move with much less noise among the blueberry thickets.

In this mild climate, moderated by the moisture of the sea, there is little or none of the violence, especially wind, that in parts of the Canadian Rockies controls the lives of anything that walks, crawls, flies or grows; here are no "chinook" winds that raise or lower temperatures forty degrees in ten minutes. Much of this forest has obviously never been disturbed by such events, for the hemlock, spruce and cedar reach great dimensions and the dark green of the vertical forests is spotted with the white bleached stems of dead but standing trees. To step on the forest floor is to sink into hemlock needles, bunchberry, moss, lichens, liverworts, fern moss, more than half a dozen kinds of ferns—a resilient bed of live and decaying material that is the distinctive essence of rich rain forests.

The visitor does not walk through a great deal of this forest, he must fight his way through, and that can be painful if he tangles with the bulky, brutal devil's club (Oplopanax horridus), which bristles with spines. Closely associated is the notorious skunk cabbage (Lysichiton kamtschatcense), believed to have the largest leaves of any native plant in British Columbia; we see it in sheltered marshy areas of the coast, where the leaves, sometimes a dozen to a single plant, grow three feet long. And the richness is further enhanced by patches of horsetail and running club moss (Lycopodium clavatum).

This mass of green is punctuated along the coast with ubiquitous shrubs of ocean spray (Holodiscus discolor), a member of the rose family and quite likely the most abundant flowering shrub in British Columbia. Its foamlike clusters of creamy white flowers decorate exposed ridges, open meadows, and deep forests. And as is so often the case in northern forests, red berries add conspicuously to the decoration. At various times of year the eyes are dazzled by mountain ash, wild cherry, kinnikinnick, bunchberry, cranberry, strawberry, baneberry, arbutus, hawthorn, twinberry, soopolallie (Shepherdia canadensis), and squashberry

Western Canada and Alaska are brightened nearly everywhere with patches of fireweed (Epilobium). *(Willis Peterson)*

(*Viburnum edule*). But among the most pronounced are red-berry elder *(Sambucus racemosa)* which graces the gloom to which it utterly contrasts, and the salmon-berry *(Rubus spectabilis),* a fruit that varies from yellow to maroon.

All this is just a sampling of the natural phenomena to be found in the wilds of western Canada. Thrushes sing repeatedly in the forests, and tape recordings of their voices reveal a complicated song structure; even when played at one-eighth normal speed there are still apparently notes so high that the human ear can scarcely pick them out. Anxious to keep their natural treasures intact, from bird songs to sand dollars, British Columbians have begun to set aside wildlife habitats and superlative landscapes as provincial parks. The appeal of their scenic and scientific resources should outweigh all others, commercially and esthetically, for centuries to come.

Right: On Vancouver Island, nature presents an extravagant floral display, including the lavender harebell (Campanula rotundifolia). *(Ann and Myron Sutton)*
Left: Bison live not only on open plains or in temperate zones. Some are adapted to shadowy boreal forests and to the temperature extremes of northern Canada. (J. Allan Cash)

15. By Fiord to Alaska, Nature's Last Frontier

The very thought of this Alaska garden is a joyful exhilaration.

John Muir
in *Travels in Alaska,* 1915

The farther north the ferry goes, the higher our spirit of adventure rises. The days grow longer, the air cooler. Yesterday, glaciers clung to the high mountain peaks, today they plunge directly into the sea, launching fleets of icebergs that drift along the shores of the Inside Passage. Clouds curl into rolling fronts and flow over the snowy peaks, opening one or another of them to the sun. The very sea on which we sail changes from a dark blue to a translucent green, suggesting infusions of glacial powder. The water surface is liberally sprinkled with sea birds, and the air pierced by clusters of bald eagles, flying white specks against the dense forest walls of these ocean channels.

The environment grows younger and fresher with every mile; it seems to generate a sense of anticipation —the scenery still to be seen, the animals to be discovered, the opportunities unfolding in a still-primitive land. If there is a place to feel like pioneers, it is Alaska. Of the many remaining frontiers—space, the ocean, the wilderness, the mind—Alaska encompasses them all: Arctic vastness so lonely as to seem like an outpost of Jupiter; ocean trenches little known but of enormous depth; wilderness as rich as any; and as for peace and solitude and exhilaration, sourdoughs themselves say that Alaska is a state of mind. There is little doubt about it being a land of promise, or vast natural resources and scenic splendor.

It is also a place of violence, which begins with the mammals of the sea. Ahead to starboard, wisps of spray rise above the waves. There is a commotion in the water. A slender fin, more erect and vertical than that of a shark, breaks the water surface. In slow motion, a smooth black back rolls out of the deep and settles again. We are being escorted by killer whales, scourge of the sea.

Killer Whales

They have been described as notorious predators, cutting, slashing and gulping prey both large and small, dining on fish, swallowing seals, wounding other whales which die from loss of blood. Such tales surround the killer whale *(Orcinus orca)*, commonly seen along the Alaska coast in wide bays sheltered from the surface fury of the Pacific. The tales of the whale's exploits are not all legends. They will attack almost anything, traveling in hunter packs, surrounding and herding porpoises, seals, sea-lions, and even walruses. The young of prey are preferred, probably because they are tender and delicious and easier to take. The stomachs of these voracious whales have been found to contain more than a dozen each of porpoises and seals. They possess sufficient capacity to swallow a man, but there does not seem to be a record of their having done

Alaska coastal glaciers meet the sea and discharge icebergs of infinitely varied sizes and shapes. (Willis Peterson)
Overleaf: Johns Hopkins Glacier descends from the Fairweather Range into Glacier Bay, Alaska. From a summit of over fifteen thousand feet the elevation drops to the sea in a horizontal distance of fifteen miles. (Austin Post)

Sea birds such as gulls utilize icebergs as observation posts. (Josef Muench)

so. They do seem to kill for pleasure, though, a habit that they seem to share with such other animals as men and weasels.

Like other seagoing mammals, killer whales are intelligent (they have been taught tricks in captivity) and they practice the principle of mutual assistance. When a whale is in distress, its comrades converge from many directions. Killer whales may grow to a length of thirty feet, and such a bulk tends to keep them away from surf and shallow rocky shores. That may be part of the reason that seals seek refuge on rocky ledges and floes of ice. Killers that pursue them too far and too fast into the surf may get stranded. Like cattle and bison, whales are subject to panic. Whatever may frighten them—storm, shallow water, temperature changes—the panicking herd instinct grips them and they may actually run aground. However,

mass strandings are not very common, as far as is known. The trouble is that much too little is known about the life of this "sea wolf," respected and feared wherever it cruises.

In the distance, gleaming white glaciers—Sumdum, Taku, Mendenhall—discharge their waters into or toward the sea. Past Juneau we curve around Admiralty Island and into Icy Strait, heading for one of the greatest concentrations of giant ice rivers in Alaska—Glacier Bay. Two hundred years ago there was no Glacier Bay as we know it today, only a massive white sheet that buried the present rivers, islands, shores and valleys in up to four thousand feet of glacial ice. So deeply covered was the coast during Captain George Vancouver's passage through Icy Strait in 1794 that he did not even mention the site.

Since Vancouver's day the mantle of ice has retreated as much as sixty-five miles, revealing one new inlet after another. Everywhere the trimline, denoting the highest level reached by the early glaciers, now lies far up on the mountain slopes, all rock below it scraped clean by the vanished ice. Nowhere else in the world has such a rapid recession of glaciers been recorded. Every stage of growth has developed on the newly exposed landscape, from dense forests at the mouth of the bay, where the ice has been absent longest, to the barren soil opened only yesterday. As a classic sample of natural succession, and because its towering peaks rise from sea level to the top of 15,320-foot Mount Fairweather, Glacier Bay is in effect a summary of the beauty, mystery, and variety of Alaska.

In Glacier Bay

A visitor learns very early that wild Alaska, on land and sea, hums with activity and is alive with sound and color. If a killer whale's fin is not cutting the surface like a periscope, a humpback whale is leaping out of the water, or a trio of harbor porpoises prowls the coves. In this brilliant land of green sea, blue ice, brown cliffs and white waterfalls birds abound. As we advance up the bay, we see them streaming in all directions. A flash of orange with rapid wingbeats is the tufted puffin *(Lunda cirrhata)* speeding from the cliffs out over the sea. A visitor is likely to note that the glaucous-winged gulls *(Larus glaucescens),* the most conspicuous and common gull here, is also the most noisy, especially at the Marble Islands, a group of rocky outcrops occupied by nesting gulls, guillemots and pelagic cormorants *(Phalacrocorax pelagicus).*

Sometimes the water in this area is covered by hundreds of thousands of northern phalaropes *(Lobipes lobatus),* their location dependent upon where the greatest amount of marine life is brought to the surface by currents. Or the water may be blackened by hundreds of surf scoters *(Melanitta perspicillata)* and white-winged scoters *(M. deglandi),* both of which remain during the winter. In Glacier Bay, the most common of the alcids, short-tailed pelagic birds that come ashore only to breed, is the chunky marbled murrelet *(Brachyramphus marmoratum).* Seemingly the least functional, it looks like an airplane with a fuselage too large for the wings to carry; when it first becomes airborne it falls back to the surface and bounces across the water like a glancing stone before at last sustaining flight. Or failing to flee in time, it simply plunges into the water and vanishes like a sinking stone.

Proceeding, we see the clouds separate and let in rays of the sun, as though a skylight had been opened in a gallery of marble sculpture. The fronts of the glaciers, broken into spires, cracked, layered, or nearly smooth, are wide and high and shine with a blue that seems to radiate from within. The face of Muir Glacier, one of the most active, rises 250 feet above water. The bay echoes with the booming thunder of ice cracking and falling away, and of the roaring of the calving bergs as they tumble down the crystal cliff and crash into the sea. Or, without warning, an ice mass deep within the water breaks away and shoots up to the surface. With that, the bergs already collected at the front of the glacier grind against each other and the sound of popping, lapping waves increases in tempo and volume as the swell moves down the bay and washes the rocks on either shore. Before this sound

fades, another boom is heard, and the echoes once again reverberate from the white mountain peaks to the green waves. In the background is the roar of silt-laden streams that break from beneath the glaciers and cascade to the sea in a cloud of spray.

As the fog burns off, the land grows brighter, and as we enter the limits of the upper bays, the waterways become narrower, the glaciers larger and more numerous, and the mountains higher. One glacier clings to a cliff in an enormous ice fall, one terrace after another of broken ice. Others hang high on cliffs, from which loose bergs plunge thousands of feet. Along the valleys gravel lies heaped in glacial moraines. Mountain goats amble across the scree, and if we step on shore we may see the tracks of coyotes, wolves and grizzlies. Birds that frequent the upper bay include water pipits, golden-crowned sparrows, snow buntings, redpolls, and hermit thrushes.

Kittiwake Country

We are escorted by hair seals *(Phoca vitulina),* which surface from time to time around us. The quantity of icebergs and the infinite shapes of them—T-shapes, goblets, bridges, platforms—increase and we must soon thread our way carefully among their green, blue and white masses. At certain times of year this can be dangerous, as John Muir found in 1890, during one of his trips to study the glaciers of Glacier Bay. He wrote:

"Paddling and pushing to right and left, I at last discovered a sheer-walled opening about four feet wide and perhaps two hundred feet long, formed apparently by the splitting of a huge iceberg. I hesitated to enter this passage, fearing that the slightest change in the tide-current might close it, but ventured nevertheless, judging that the dangers ahead might not be greater than those I had already passed. When I got about a third of the way in, I suddenly discovered that the smooth-walled ice-lane was growing narrower, and with desperate haste backed out. Just as the bow of the canoe cleared the sheer walls they came together with a growling crunch."

Icebergs serve as perches for gulls, cormorants, and even eagles. At times it is possible to see hundreds of red-throated loons *(Gavia stellata)* on islands in this area, and some loons nest on ponds in glacial outwash areas. Mew gulls *(Larus canus)* cruise above the shore, uttering their harsh shrieks in association with the rapid chattering of the Arctic tern *(Sterna paradisaea).* The tern nests in two cycles during the summer, then resumes its annual migratory journey that may be more than twenty-two thousand miles each year, not counting the twistings, turnings, and circlings that must mean hundreds of additional miles en route to the Antarctic. With the longest known migration route of any animal, Arctic terns have the distinction of seeing more sunlight during a year than any other living creature.

The music of the wild, rocky shores is punctuated by the piping voice of the black oystercatcher *(Haematopus bachmani).* Since there is little or no shrubbery for shelter, the oystercatcher has become a master in the art of deception, luring away intruders from its nest and even sitting on nonexistent nests. The eggs are laid in a nest of barren rocks, and these as well as the young birds are so well camouflaged as to defy discovery. Far more wary than the oystercatcher is the beautifully colored harlequin duck *(Histrionicus histrionicus)*, which keeps watch from rocky points along the shore, or swims in the fiord waters; it is very shy and flies away when an intruder tries to creep up on it.

Near Margerie Glacier a colony of black-legged kittiwakes *(Rissa tridactyla)* occupies the cliffs. More than a hundred nests have been counted here, fitted to the merest ledges and crevices. As an oceanic bird and one of the commonest gulls of the Bering Sea, the kittiwake dines on what it can glean from the water, plunging in a powerful dive when prey is sighted. It also follows in the wake of whales to see what their disturbance of the sea turns up; at Margerie Glacier they hover over the roiling sea when a berg has calved, dipping into the waters for food brought to the surface.

If sea life is sufficient to sustain so many birds, then it must explain the presence of seals as well, which congregate by the hundreds on bergs and floes. So far,

however, little study has been made of the upper bays. Fresh waters from the glaciers hold scant life. They unload into the bays a great deal of silt, thus making the sea floor soft-bottomed. Plankton is probably an important key; at times so many plankton concentrate that the water takes on a greenish-brown hue and looks like soup. Where fresh water enters the bay and flows over salt water, plankton is likely to be found several meters below the surface. Life in those levels includes shrimp and a species of cod, both largely bottom feeders and scavengers, but there is bound to be some link between them and the plankton, an intermediate food echelon of which little is known. The seals know a great deal about it, however, because when you see them sound, surface, and sound again, you can be virtually sure that they are feeding. When not diving they lounge in comfortable ease on the ice, appetites obviously sated.

Elsewhere in Glacier Bay, and along the Alaska coast, the great chain of life goes on. Algae are consumed by small animals that are food for fish or birds which are in turn food for larger predators. Finally the killer whale exacts its toll, but it has parasites preying on it, and those parasites must have their own parasites until at last all life decomposes into minerals and nutrients—which the algae consume. Thus the energy transfer never ends, and the rich cold waters contain an abundance of life, from shipworms to king crabs to whales.

They call it "the old man of the sea," but at breeding time the tufted puffin leaves the sea and comes ashore to nest. (Karl W. Kenyon: National Audubon Society)

The common loon (Gavia immer) *prefers the solitude of the wilderness. It returns to the same nesting locality year after year. (Michael Wotton)*

Red Squirrels and Sitka Spruce

If we return by land to the mouth of the bay, we will observe a prime example of natural ecological succession. Immediately upon deglaciation, some kind of life begins, and on the rocky slopes beneath the towering glacier fronts we discover mats of mountain avens *(Dryas drummondii)*. One of the first plants to develop, avens grows in patches that cover sand, gravel, and boulder beaches or slopes. Small yellow flowers turn into knots of twisted seeds and eventually heads plumed like a dandelion, two inches in diameter. In common with other pioneers it spreads its seeds on the wind. As time goes on, the seeds of other species—dwarf fireweed *(Epilobium latifolium)*, willow and alder—collect and germinate, and mosses and horsetails are propagated.

Thus started, the forest becomes well established. Halfway down the bay, where the absence of glaciers has allowed the vegetation to make good its conquest of the land, a visitor may fight his way through growths of Sitka alder *(Alnus sinuata)*, Sitka spruce and cottonwoods, the latter containing bald eagles' nests believed to have been in use for at least thirty-five years. Of all the trees, spruce is the most successful at germinating beneath a canopy of alder leaves, so it becomes abundant, crowds out the others and assumes a dominance that gives the mouth of Glacier Bay some of its richest and

most luxuriant forests. In time the dominance may give way to hemlock, approaching the make-up of most of the forests of southeast Alaska and western Canada. Even so, the spruce may live seven hundred years or more, rise in excess of two hundred feet, and approach fourteen feet in diameter.

The Sitka spruce forest is poor in number of species as compared with the rich rain forests of the Olympics, and has few common perennial herbs. It is more open, has fewer windfalls, and a traveller is not compelled to cut his way through brush as dense as in other parts of Alaska. You may come upon heaps of spruce scales and dozens of holes in the forest floor, all made by the red squirrel *(Tamiasciurus hudsonicus)* and locally called "squirrel kitchens." The red squirrel is more abundant here than in mature forests probably because these young spruce trees are vigorously putting out seed stock. In this ecosystem the red squirrel is dependent on spruce, which makes it dependent on the quality of cones produced. Some years the spruce produces abundantly, some years poorly. The squirrel takes whole spruce cones into its holes, which evidently connect in an elaborate storage system. As you walk along the soft forest floor you can hear the squirrel's loud persistent chatter and see it sitting on a spruce limb, flaking off cone scales and eating the seeds on the spot. At other times the woods are noisy with the thud of falling cones nipped off and let fall for subsequent removal to storage. Thus the relation of red squirrels to this ecosystem differs a trifle from that of their cousins in drier forests, where mushrooms are gathered by the squirrels and dried for the winter.

In this forest, the annual rainfall amounts to eighty inches a year; winter snow may accumulate to six feet in depth and the temperature drops to about seven degrees below zero at the coldest. Several kinds of lichen hang from the trees, among them *Usnea*, the common "beard moss." Early blueberry is by far the most common shrub, but in time this understory will become thicker and more complex. It will include the devils club *(Oplopanax horridus)* which we find abundant in the fiord forests farther south, and which already is making its appearance in these two-hundred-year-old woods. On the forest floor of ferns, fern moss, and other species is an orchid conspicuous for its abundance, the twayblade *(Listera cordata)*, of which the greenish or purplish flowers are very persistent and cling to the fruits until about the end of August. Among the other plants of the area are Nagoon berry *(Rubus stellatus)*, Nootka lupine *(Lupinus nootkatensis)*, Kamchatka lily *(Fritillaria camschatcensis)*, and red and yellow paintbrush. Where the forest meets the sea, beach pea *(Lathyrus maritimus)* and beach ryegrass *(Elymus mollis)* grow. Curiously, there is also a small pond which, if it followed the normal regimen of ponds, would be filling with soil. Rather it is enlarging, due probably to the influx of organic materials which clog permeable gravels, cut off drainage, and raise the water level, thus drowning spruces at the edge.

In spring the forest resounds with the hollow booming of blue grouse *(Dendragapus obscurus)*, and in July the mother with chicks wanders among the shrubs with royal dignity and aplomb. Black-tailed deer also roam through the woods, though they are uncommon in the new forests.

That this is a forest in flux can be readily seen because the before-and-after elements of the transition are evident. For one thing, *Equisetum* still grows here, though it was one of the first plants to occupy gravels exposed by melting glaciers. It is one of the few pioneer species that can persist through the successional sequence all the way into the spruce forest. Another is the *Phyllodoce*, a heather that John Muir mentioned perhaps more than any other Alaska plant. It may not bloom in the Sitka spruce forest, however, just as the *Equisetum* fails to produce spores—both plants hanging on vegetatively from former times. By contrast, there is a great deal of hemlock rising under the spruce canopy. Ultimately seventy to eighty percent of the stand will be hemlock, and after that some of it may evolve into muskeg, a moist meadow-like habitat dominated by mosses, sedges and small trees, and in which may grow the tiny insectivorous sundew *(Drosera rotundifolia)*. Thus the spruce will decrease, but for the present it forms a forest in transition, floored with orchids, filled with the chatter of red squirrels, and possessed of the delicate aroma and gentle charm of Alaska's coastal forests.

Pingos and Other Puzzles

The concept of Alaska having two seasons—winter and the Fourth of July—makes a good joke. The facts are otherwise, for there are extremes of heat as well as of cold. There are also extremes of height, offshore depth, and natural beauty. Few localities in the world seem to infect their inhabitants with such loyalty and affection. "All that night time down south gets on our nerves," one family in interior Alaska told us. "Here we have a winter night but it is never black. There is always something to see and do, and we'll never see it all."

One reason for this is Alaska's sheer immensity. It is as long and wide as the "lower forty-eight" and has a great diversity of environments. The fourteen highest mountains in the United States are in Alaska, with Mount McKinley exceeding twenty thousand feet, while offshore the Aleutian Trench drops 25,000 feet below sea level. Alaska has five times the tidal shoreline of any other coastal state—33,904 miles. It has also served as a significant land bridge over which plants and animals (including man) have emigrated from the Eastern Hemisphere.

Much of Alaska is on a grand scale—the mountain arcs, the rivers, the lowlands bejewelled with lakes and clothed with marshes, the deltas, the offshore islands. It is perhaps as difficult to pick the most beautiful place in Alaska as to pick the most beautiful of diamonds. Some say it is Glacier Bay or Mount McKinley; some choose the area of the Alatna-Kobuk Rivers in the Brooks Range; others have utmost praise for the Wood-Tikchik region three hundred miles west of Anchorage. All these have one common denominator: their beauty is based on mountains.

The cordillera in its steady trend northwest from Mexico through Canada turns abruptly in Alaska, almost at right angles to itself, and heads toward the southwest. The Alaska "panhandle," or Ketchikan-Sitka-Juneau area of the Inside Passage, is known as the Alexander Archipelago, a coastal range of granitic rocks containing evidence of faults and other structural features. The greatest of these is a single fiord, Chatham Strait and the Lynn Canal, 250 miles long.

From Glacier Bay to the northwest rise the Saint Elias Mountains, which have been described as probably the most spectacular mountain range in North America. The range is so difficult to reach that few people know its wonders firsthand. Since these mountains range from sea level to more than nineteen thousand feet in less than fifty miles, they are second only to the Andes for abrupt rise from the coast. A great deal of moisture blows in from the sea, rises, condenses to snow and falls heavily in the mountains; hence glaciers abound, from one, ninety miles long, to another, the Malaspina, which covers 850 square miles.

Westward, the Wrangell, Chugach, and Kenai mountains thrust clean white caps and ice fields into the sky. They can be approached more closely by automobile and thus are probably better known—the image of an incredibly scenic state. They are volcanic, containing shield and composite volcanoes, and some are active. The Alaska Range, with a highly complex structure, is arcuate like the others, but it reaches higher elevation than any. The "seagoing" Aleutians are famous for their nearly eighty major volcanoes, almost half of which have been active at some time during the last two centuries. Novarupta Volcano, near Mount Katmai, hurled more than seven cubic miles of volcanic ejecta into the atmosphere in 1912, and Buldir

Black-legged kittiwakes come ashore only to nest. This cliff at Glacier Bay shelters an active, noisy colony. (Ann and Myron Sutton)

Caldera, an ancient and now submerged basin that measures thirteen by twenty-seven miles, may be the world's largest volcanic crater. This section of Alaska, as well as the southeastern panhandle, are particularly subject to earth movements, such as that of 1964, which originated in Prince William Sound, damaged a number of Alaskan cities, and left fifty feet of vertical uplift in some places. Another tremor produced the world's highest wave. In the coastal section of Glacier Bay National Monument an estimated ninety million tons of rock broke loose and fell into Lituya Bay on July 9, 1958. Water surged up to 1740 feet on the opposite wall of an inlet and generated hundred-foot waves that moved at a hundred miles per hour down the bay and wiped out shore forests for miles around it.

This southern portion of Alaska is characterized by relatively mild temperatures, without extremes, the averages being on the order of twenty-eight to fifty degrees from coldest to hottest. Interior Alaska is the reverse—and in places great extremes have been recorded. Fort Yukon, on the Arctic Circle, has records of seventy-five degrees below zero and a hundred degrees above zero. The northern arctic region of the state does not get as cold, but periods of low temperature are more prolonged. Other elements go to make up the "chill factor"; arctic winds, for example, can transform relatively mild periods into bitter freezing weather.

Nor does one find more glaciers the farther north he proceeds. Only three percent of Alaska is covered by glaciers. The reason is simply that glaciers require much moisture and wind circulation as well as cold temperatures, and along the southern quarter of the state, roughly the broad arc around the Gulf of Alaska, the annual precipitation rises in some places to more than 220 inches a year. This gives rise to mountain glaciers and enormous coastal ice masses such as Bering, Guyot and Malaspina glaciers. Inland, the amount of rain and snow tapers off substantially. The northern quarter of the state has less than forty inches annually, and therefore fewer and smaller glaciers.

The profile of western Alaska is like the profile of a man: a long thin goatee is the Aleutian chain, the chin being the broad delta region of the Kuskokwim and Yukon rivers, the nose the Seward Peninsula, the eye and ear about where the Arctic Circle crosses, and the forehead where the Brooks Range comes to the sea. The mountains of interior Alaska are mostly of lesser elevation than those to the south, and are surrounded by lowlands filled with lakes and rivers. A great deal of the interior lies above or beyond tree line and lacks a complete forest cover. The most spectacular section is that between the Wood and Tikchik rivers, an area of fiord-like lakes glacially scoured to well below sea level. This chain of fresh-water fiords and interconnected lakes is not duplicated in the United States and has long been recognized as an area of outstanding natural beauty. The names of some of the lakes—Upnuk, Nishlik, Chikuminuk, Chauekuktuli, Nuyakuk—add to the otherwordly feeling one gets among these forested vales and towering granite cliffs.

Equally spectacular is the Brooks Range, which, at nine thousand feet, is the world's highest mountain range north of the Arctic Circle. Its geology is still imperfectly known, but there is evidence of folding, faulting and thrust action. From the Brooks Range north stretches a gradually descending Arctic Slope, hilly to flat, frozen, dotted with lakes that are strikingly oriented in the same direction, as mysterious and inexplicable as the famed Carolina Bays on the eastern coast of the United States.

Beneath the mantle of surface soil most of Alaska consists of permafrost, permanently frozen subsoil; only the southern shores and islands are entirely free of it. In central Alaska, permafrost is sporadic or discontinuous, but in the northern third of the state is continuous. Beneath the Arctic Coastal Plain it is believed to be at least a thousand feet thick.

Permafrost, and the alternate freezing and thawing of water in gravels and soils overlying it, very much decide the configuration of the landscape. Not only does loose material resting on the surface thaw in summer but often a bit of permafrost beneath, with the result that a great deal of the state is swampy and impassable to human traffic in the summer. When all this water freezes in winter the ground heaves outward or upward, producing interesting, if not completely understood, phenomena. The following spring, while thawing, the surface layer slowly settles and moves downhill, a process known as creep. Some soils, saturated with water, flow downhill like sludge, a process known as solifluction. These two types of land movement produce a diversity of surface features, and where they bypass outcrops of resistant bedrock, these soon stand out as steep-sided knobs, called tors, conspicuous above the surroundings.

Freezing and thawing also rearrange the soil constituents in interesting patterns, notably polygons of stones in an intricate network, each with a silty or clayey central mound. Other features of this icy land include rock glaciers, where accumulations of rock are held together by ice, and frozen muck, which consists of vegetable and animal remains mixed with windblown silt that may be several hundred feet thick. Throughout much of interior and Arctic Alaska may be seen mysterious conical, oval, elliptical or irregular mounds up to a hundred feet high and twelve hundred feet in diameter. These are called pingos. They form possibly as a result of hydraulic pressure of moving ground water; the water is trapped and frozen in a ball or blister of ice that elevates surficial material. If the ice core melts and the summit of the pingo collapses, the result is a ringlike mound or cratered pingo. Should this happen in a water-filled muskeg, a lake may form in the crater, but the sides of the pingo are sufficiently drained to support a mature birch forest.

In Alaska Gardens

"Out of all the cold darkness and glacial crushing and grinding comes this warm, abounding beauty and life..." So said John Muir of the profusion of flowering plants at Glacier Bay. Now we enter the taiga of interior Alaska, an ecosystem different in many ways, yet similarly endowed with beauty. To the Russians, *taiga* meant "land of little sticks," which referred to stunted subarctic forests. Trees of the taiga reach moderate height where protected, as in ravines. Even then they are subject to the heaving of unstable ground and doomed to topple unless they can spread roots widely. In the ground above permafrost, trees get twisted, pulled and carried along as the saturated topsoil slips across buried ice. The result is a "drunken forest" whose trees tip over in all directions.

Yet the black spruce *(Picea nigra)* is not everywhere a "little stick." It can grow to a height of a hundred feet farther south, but does well to reach as much as forty here; a tree two inches in diameter may be a hundred years old. It seems to thrive in saturated soils, and we see it most often invading muskeg. A taiga forest, however, is not black spruce alone, which often mingles with quaking aspen, larch, balsam poplar, white spruce and Alaska paper birch *(Betula papyrifera)*.

Life, though hazardous, is rich. Grasses bind the soil and furnish food for sparrows, voles and grizzlies. Porcupines girdle spruce, but porcupines and spruce have lived together successfully for many years. Grayling thrive in lakes, sandpipers search for insects around the shores and beavers cut their way into aspen patches. Mosquitoes drive even the moose, monarch of the forest, to distraction. When not escaping to ponds for a respite or dining on aquatic plants, the moose finds twigs of willow suitable for fall and winter food while catkins and leaves are fare for spring and summer. To keep its vast bulk going, a

Mount McKinley, the highest mountain in North America, rises above a lake-dotted tundra rich in flora and fauna. (Willis Peterson)

Above: On swift and graceful wings the long-tailed jaeger (Stercorarius longicaudus) *hovers over lemmings, its favorite prey.*
Left: The barren ground looks scarcely able to support them, but caribou once migrated in herds of up to fifteen thousand, eating whatever lichens they could find. (Both by Charles J. Ott: National Audubon Society)

moose must eat about fifty pounds of shoots a day, which leaves in the taiga a legacy of broken, twisted, misshapen willow. Yet the trees grow quickly, and have evolved harmoniously with the moose in this ecosystem.

Beneath the trees is a layer of shrubs composed in part of cranberry, blueberry, Labrador tea *(Ledum groenlandicum)*, kinnikinnick *(Arctostaphylos uva-ursi)* and other heaths. Hugging the taiga floor are bunchberry, or ground dogwood, and the familiar lichen, *Cladonia*. A splendid place to see this array of vegetation, and to learn about it, is Mount McKinley National Park, where protection and proper manage-ment of fragile ecosystems is paramount; marked trails and museums, as well as naturalists on duty, explain the intricate interrelationships of the taiga system.

As the visitor rises above the taiga to tree line, he enters the alpine tundra, a world of its own. If he expected barrenness and lack of life he sees how mistaken he was, for nature endowed the tundra with abundant wildlife and extensive natural gardens. So luxuriant is it that the walker sinks up to his knees in sphagnum moss, a fibrous yellow mass that merges, perhaps many feet below, into a black muck, and that may contain small mushrooms of a bright bronze color. In such a soft carpet trails soon become channels several feet deep. The tundra also consists of dwarf shrubs, low matted grass, sedges and mosses. One of the most common shrubs is scarcely recognizable as a birch, having blunt leaves that are wavy-margined as though they were some exotic squawbush; yet this is dwarf birch *(Betula nana)*, which associates with blueberry. There are also shrubby cinquefoil, copses of low spruce trying to reach great heights where they

Dall Sheep are the only white-haired bighorns in North America. Their range includes Alaska and western Canada. (Charles J. Ott; Leonard Lee Rue III)

cannot, and a matting of lichens, mushrooms, grass and *Equisetum*. Beneath this surface vegetation, layers of permafrost block the downward movement of water so that we have soft spongy hummocks. With better drainage, as on upland ridges, the tundra takes on a drier aspect.

Low temperatures and a short growing season are the factors limiting life in this environment. While conditions may be rigorous for man, the warm-blooded animals that live here are well-adapted to them, or if unable to withstand the cold they simply avoid it. There are no large trees, but the beaver is here, inhabiting lakes and building dams of earth to maintain deep water. It relies on grasses, sedges and willows for food and it stores provisions in autumn because several feet of ice may seal its pond during winter. Decay is slow simply because reduction of vegetation by bacteria does not proceed as rapidly as in warm temperatures.

The transfer of energy still goes on, though subject to substantial oscillations. When lemmings, small reddish rodents, reach a peak of population they produce a marked effect on the tundra by consuming large quantities of vegetation. Owls and jaegers enjoy a feast of lemmings and so breed abundantly. But then the number of lemmings decreases, and the birds become scarce; their breeding may be delayed until better days.

Small mammals such as voles occupy an ecosystem of their own—a small air space between snow and soil where the temperature may be eighty degrees warmer than on the surface. The vole, with its thin fur, is no more adapted to cold than certain desert mammals are to heat; both groups thrive because they inhabit a microenvironment lacking temperature extremes. The willow ptarmigan nests on the open tundra and is also important food to other forms of wildlife. Hudsonian curlews or whimbrels *(Numenius phaeopus)*, long-legged curve-billed sandpipers, come to the northern tundra from their homes in South America. Many birds thrive in central Alaska, from black-billed magpies to sandhill cranes, and the delta of the Kuskokwim River is one of the largest waterfowl nesting areas in North America.

The rolling tundra is typically home for the omnivorous grizzly, which can often be seen rummaging vigorously among shrubs or in the grass and soil, or strolling across the open slopes with an awkward-looking sideways motion of the hips. People used to get out of their cars and try to approach grizzlies in the Sable Pass area of Mount McKinley National Park, with the result that the grizzlies soon began to move elsewhere. Park authorities then restricted human visitors to the road. Now the grizzlies have come back so well that a visitor can be fairly sure of seeing one or more from the highway.

With sharp eyes he can also see Dall sheep (Ovis dalli), a white species of the bighorn, feeding high on the green slopes of dry alpine tundra and treeless ridges. As he watches, one of them may bound down the mountain at breakneck speed, and he is apt to conclude that, since no enemy is apparent, the animals are simply having a good time. Life is not always so carefree, however, because sheep must be alert for wolves, bears and, outside parks and refuges, men. There are no mountain goats here, or anywhere in Alaska except for the southeast corner.

As for tundra flowers, they lack little in variety and color. All summer there are successive displays of them as each snowbank melts and opens another patch of south-facing slope to twenty-four hours of light. In both tundra and taiga, monkshood (Aconitum napellus) lifts its intricately arranged deep purple blossoms in nearly all environments from mountain slope to rushing stream. White-flowered avens (Dryas octopetala) blankets exposed mountain slopes. A field of Richardson's saxifrage (Boykinia richardsoni) covering a steep slope exhibits long stalks of white and maroon blossoms over a bed of rich green leaves. The nodding head of Lessing's arnica dangles in the tundra breeze. You cannot wander very far without passing a clump of bluebells, or the small forget-me-not (Myosotis alpestris) with its blue and yellow blossoms. A hardy member of the honeysuckle family, the twin flower (Linnaea borealis), hangs its pink petals from trailing evergreen shrublets. Step after step, through dock, daisy, phlox, harebell, bistort and—as always—the ubiquitous fireweed, we are reminded that Alaska's greatness lies not only in giant things but in the small and delicate as well. To match the snow-covered peaks, there are vast spreads of cotton grass (Eriophorum), which is actually a sedge. When its envelopes of silky bristles break open along the edges of beaver ponds or lakes, the tundra glows with brilliant touches of white and pale yellow, as though great snowbanks had fallen from the sky. This scene endures in the mind long after summer passes, as does the conviction that Alaska's wild and fragile gardens are treasures to be cherished forever.

The Wolf and the Caribou

With so much mountain greenery, it is little wonder that animal life is abundant and widespread. Even on approach roads, where Arctic ground squirrels dash by the dozens, where porcupines wander among the spruce, and gulls fly over the tundra, it is evident that the productivity is high. Where you see a wolf or grizzly intently digging into the ground, you can be fairly sure that the prey is a ground squirrel, for these are a tempting side dish in carnivorous diets. They stand at their holes and give sharp warning calls, or slip underground at the approach of danger. If a grizzly digs at one entrance, the ground squirrel pops out another, but it had better be fast, for the grizzly can clutch with lightning speed.

Another source of food for the flesh-eaters of the tundra is the caribou (Rangifer arcticus), crucial not only to wolves that bring it down, but to foxes and other animals that eat those portions of the carcasses wolves leave behind. Caribou, as defined by the field naturalist Adolph Murie, who studied the behavior of Alaska wolves and caribou, are circumpolar deer adapted to life in the Arctic. They are cousin to deer, elk and moose, and are among the most gregarious of animals. They spend their lives in search of lichens, blueberry, cranberry, fungi, horsetail and other vegetation, which keeps them on the move over a territory of hundreds of square miles per herd. Travelling sometimes in bands of thousands, they cut deep trails in the tundra. By wandering across open ground, through taiga forests, along gravelly braided streams and over mountain passes, they find a variety of herbaceous food in summer, but it is the winter availability of lichens and other forage that is the weakest link in their chain of life. What with pestering flies, mosquitoes, internal parasites, and wolves, life is sometimes miserable, yet it has obviously been successful, for caribou were once more widespread and numerous than any other large mammal of Alaska. Given a good supply of food, the reproduction rate is more than adequate to sustain the species and a female may produce half a dozen offspring in her lifetime. In fact, without some check, or population control, caribou would increase beyond the carrying capacity of their range.

The bulls clean the velvet from their antlers each fall by thrashing them among small willows or spruce trees. They are then ready for the rut, and are splendid specimens indeed. The male battles to conserve a harem or secure additions to it and sometimes these battles are bloody and fatally deadlocked. Caribou are not particularly intelligent, though they have a good sense of smell and are excellent swimmers. They panic easily, and often seem uncertain of what to do when danger threatens unexpectedly. Still, the sight of a handsome bull on a promontory overlooking a herd below has all the elements of drama that could be wanted in the wilderness.

The evolution of so majestic a creature has been partly the work of wolves, which have for centuries culled from caribou herds the sick, the slow, the clumsy, the ill-formed and retarded, and some of the young. Keeping the herd fit and within the feeding limits of its range, wolves have thus maintained the quality of the herds and pruned the weak as efficiently as weather and disease could do it. But pioneer men, who saw no pattern in this natural selection process, visited upon the head of the wolf such devastation as few other wild animals have ever endured. This is especially ironic because wolves improved the caribou herds while men—prospectors, trappers, settlers, sailors—have been most responsible for reducing the numbers of caribou. Where these animals once occurred in the millions, they now are numbered only in thousands, due to commercial introduction of reindeer that overgrazed and ruined natural caribou pastures, and to man-caused fires (over and above natural fires) that burned off eighty percent of Alaska's white spruce forests and took the lichens with them.

A rodent with its head above the tundra, watching for enemies, is apt to be the Arctic ground squirrel. (Helmut Heimpel: Bavaria Verlag)

The introduction of several hundred Siberian reindeer *(Rangifer tarandus)* just before the turn of the century was intended to sustain those Eskimos whose caribou and other wildlife resources had been wiped out by non-native immigrants. But the reindeer increased to more than 600,000 animals by 1932. This eliminated lichen forage in western and northern Alaska, and as a consequence the reindeer population collapsed in the next twenty years to less than thirty thousand animals.

In any case, the wolf *(Canis lupus)* has been subjected to continuous persecution, not least because it was supposed to be a threat to man and his domestic animals. Stockgrowers in southerly climes substituted cattle for bison and pronghorn, which were the wolf's normal food in those regions, and then removed the wolf when it preyed on cattle. Now a preponderance

of men begins to ask for some of the original nature back, and by extreme good fortune there are wolves still left with which to reconstruct it.

Wolves vary in color from black, usually with a white spot on the chest, to white, the latter living in the Arctic. Alaska subspecies are variable in color, from gray to black. Wolves of western mountains tend to be gray and brown. The wolves of northern North America are the world's largest, the record being a 175-pound specimen trapped in east-central Alaska. For the most part, however, wolves weigh less than a hundred pounds.

Murie's field observations in the Mount McKinley region have given us many insights into wolf social behavior. Theirs is not a lazy life, he found, because they must work hard and travel long distances to capture food; but he believed that they enjoyed their nightly excursions to hunt. After all his work with wolves, he said that the strongest impression that remained with him was their friendliness. This is evidenced by gregariousness largely at the den, which may be a cave, rock shelter, tunnel, or the remodeled burrow of some other animal. Life there is usually

A red fox chasing a snowshoe hare. The fox's fame for outwitting other animals comes from a cunning widely recognized in wild dogs. (National Film Board of Canada)

relaxed and rather social, mostly a matter of the comings and goings of food-gathering members of the group. They depart in the evening, hunt all night and return in the morning, and even the mother will go along if another female is available to stay with the pups.

The father is solicitous of the young and even helps in raising them; in fact, several males may reside at the den. There are demonstrations of affection, such as hugging, tail wagging, and nose touching. Play is common, but there can also be viciousness in driving from the vicinity an unwanted wolf. The young are born in the dens in spring, and so closely knit is wolf society that if something should destroy the parents, the young may be cared for by other wolves.

Being social, wolves collect in packs in which lines of dominance and subordination are clear. Hunting in packs, they demonstrate a talent not too common in the animal world—cooperation in the pursuit of other creatures. They are well designed for attacking and tearing prey to pieces, so nearly all their food is raw meat, principally caribou, but also deer, moose, beaver,

mice and other animals. Wolves may eat as much as twenty pounds of meat in a single day, or if not that hungry they will bite off portions of a kill and either bury them in various locations within a few hundred yards, or transport meat to the den for pup food. Sometimes a wolf will swallow meat, carry it many miles to the den, then regurgitate it for the pups.

If the opportunity arises, wolves will readily ransack caches of other animals, but the fox, for one, gets back by ransacking caches to which a wolf has dragged spare meat. Foxes are great followers in the Arctic, and may trail wolves as well as other animals to feast on a carcass when the hunter gets sated. Adolph Murie credits the wolf with being able to alter its route of travel for the express purpose of deceiving pursuers. To do so, he says, the wolf apparently backtracks, jumps off the trail, walks through water or wet tundra, traverses island sand bars, travels in a circuitous path, and finally hides the food beneath a covering of gravel, lichens or snow. He tracked a fox that was following such a wolf trail, and not once did the wolf's puzzling peregrinations throw the fox off. When Murie arrived at the wolf's cache he found it torn open and saw a fox trotting away with something in its mouth, probably a portion of the wolf's kill.

Thus wolf caches are enormously important in the ecosystem. Without them bears, foxes, eagles, and other carnivores might have a more difficult time surviving. Even Eskimos used wolf-cached meat when necessary. Cache robbery does little or no harm to wolves; the cache itself is a sign of abundance, while in times of scarcity most of the captured prey is consumed without being stored away.

Wolf life is not all hunting and eating, and when exhausted or hot—even in Mount McKinley National Park the temperature may approach ninety degrees—wolves rest in whatever cool spot they can find. Disease and danger are always near: rabies, distemper and other afflictions transmitted by immigrant dogs, poisoning, trapping, hunting from aircraft, starvation. Grizzlies are big enough, of course, to crush wolves with ease, but there are few accounts of wolf-bear battles.

When caribou give birth to their young, wolves will travel twenty miles each night, if necessary, to get to the calving grounds. In each band of caribou there is likely to be one individual weaker than the rest by virtue of age or health, and this is the one that soon falls behind in a chase. The wolf is very efficient; one well-placed slash of the stomach may be enough to end the hunt. Wolves also snap at head, neck and flanks as opportunity provides. A pack may surround the prey, or start it running and keep it moving until it collapses from exhaustion. Other strategies are also used. Unless rabid or crazed, wolves apparently do not

The weasel's winter coat helps it to blend against the snow. This is the "ermine" of the fur trade. (Charles J. Ott)

kill wastefully, as is often assumed; if they fail to consume an entire carcass, this may mean only that they were not very hungry.

Ever since the Three Little Pigs and Little Red Riding Hood, the wolf has been cast as public enemy number one in the wilderness. It has long had a reputation for attacking human beings, but does it really do so? Men have been challenged by wolf packs under conditions favorable to the animals—but challenge does not equal attack. Russell Rutter and Douglas Pimlott, in their study of the world of the wolf, say that North American wolves have never posed a real threat to man, and that in fact the wolves do not consider man as prey. There seems to be only one authentic record of wolf attack on man in North America and that was in Ontario by an animal that was probably rabid. The wolf is so wary of men that the risk of being attacked by one in the wilderness is infinitesimal compared to the risk of getting to the wilderness in the first place. Adolph Murie once crawled into a wolf den and extracted some of the pups for research purposes while the adults barked nearby. No reports of wolf-caused deaths have been substantiated on this continent.

Man, of course, wants to harvest surplus caribou rather than let wolves do it, so there have been efforts to shoot, trap and poison wolves. Two distinguished biologists, A. Starker Leopold and F. Fraser Darling, warned some years ago, however, that control of wolf predation should be an integrated part of a total wildlife management program. "Deer irruptions all over the United States," they pointed out, "attest to the

fallacy of closely regulating hunting and predation without reference to range limitations."

Much research is under way, for there is a great deal yet unknown about the wolf. In the meantime, men have begun to think of the animal, as Rutter and Pimlott do, as "an exceptionally interesting part of our wildlife heritage and an outstanding representative of that wilderness which we are belatedly trying to preserve."

On Snow and Ice

By good fortune and foresight, a number of extensive national parks, forests and wildlife refuges have been established to maintain certain Alaska habitats. The setting aside of such reserves is still incomplete, and battles to stave off construction of dams, testing sites and other public works goes on. Nearly all of the Aleutian Islands are encompassed in a National Wildlife Refuge. Katmai National Monument is the largest unit of the National Park System and Tongass National Forest the largest national forest. The Kenai National Moose Range protects 7500 moose in a splendid mountain wilderness of 2500 square miles. Perhaps it is most significant that the country's largest unit of the wildlife refuge system is the Arctic National Wildlife Range, in the northeastern corner of Alaska, which preserves habitat for caribou, polar and grizzly bears, Dall sheep, and other animals. Mount McKinley National Park serves as an extraordinary study area because it is unhunted; it is being used for scientific comparison purposes.

There is indeed a great deal in the Arctic worth preserving. The northernmost third of Alaska lies within the Arctic Circle, much of it fragile ecosystem of wet or frozen tundra, bordered by ice-filled seas or barren mountain ranges, sunless most of the winter when average temperatures hover at seventeen degrees below zero. This and parts of adjacent Canada are the home of the Eskimo and other northern Indians, who long ago learned to live in harmony with polar environments. They made, among other things, mats and mukluks of sealskin, parkas from the bellies of ducks, bows of whalebone, fishnets of moose sinew and snowshoes of caribou hide.

The walrus (Odobenus rosmarus) figured in their hunting expeditions because it was valued for its meat, blubber, hides, intestines and ivory tusks. Among marine mammals, walruses, which may exceed three thousand pounds, are outweighed only by whales and elephant seals. As much as any sea-going creature, the walrus may appear to some observers as something out of fantasy. The vast bulk of blubber, the wrinkled hairy pink hide, the ivory tusks of up to three feet in length, the thick, whisker-like vibrissae, and the wart-like tubercules all contribute to what Victorian sailors called an unearthly and demoniacal look. Walruses inhabit the pack ice and prefer to haul themselves out on drifting floes, but sometimes crowd together in spectacular concentrations on land. The site has to be safe from stalking polar bears and the young must be sheltered from possible attacks by killer whales.

Each summer walruses migrate north from islands off the western coast of Alaska through Bering Strait into the Chukchi Sea, where they can be near ice floes and clam beds. They eat some fish and other marine life as well as grasses and algae, but their main fare is molluscan fauna, chiefly clams (Mya truncata and Clinocardium nuttalli). They dive steeply to depths of as much as three hundred feet and feed for perhaps ten minutes, standing almost on their heads to gouge out molluscs with probing tusks. In one day's eating a single walrus may consume the feet and siphons of more than three thousand clams. With the approach of winter, walruses move south, keeping to the edge of the pack ice, mostly in the region of St. Lawrence and Nunivak Islands, off the Alaskan coast.

Some authorities say that the solicitude of a cow walrus for her calf is unsurpassed among mammals, and there are numerous reports of frantic maternal efforts to shield the young against intruders. This appears to coincide with the habit of walruses to care for injured comrades—and there have been many injuries. The walrus custom of hauling out on beaches in densely massed thousands proved almost to be the downfall of the species. They were killed in droves by commercial hunters, and some persons believe that had they not retired each summer to inaccessible parts of the Arctic ice pack they would be extinct. About 125,000 walruses survive in the world, most of them in the Bering and Chukchi seas.

A singular, and perhaps surprising, fact about western natural history is that the farther north one goes, the larger the animals become. On the face of it, this seems incongruous, since large Arctic mammals do not seem particularly fitted to avoid the cold—neither migrating to warmer latitudes nor entering a comatose state of hibernation. It is in fact interesting to examine the reasons why they prosper in lands so cold, where indeed an animal's hide and fat may have to separate temperatures as far apart as 150 degrees. For one thing, a large animal's bulk allows it certain safety margins between production and loss of heat. For another, it grows a thicker and more effective coat. Resident smaller animals, such as birds, must compensate for these abilities by furious activity and enormous fuel consumption, while voles and lemmings seek protection in runways beneath the snow. Northern seas are rich in nutrients and never colder than twenty-seven degrees; hence seals and whales need not submit to the wide extremes encountered on land.

Heavy snow is a help as well as a hindrance. Moose move through it easily with their slender legs, though when the surface freezes they may get badly cut and leave trails of blood. Lynxes, snowshoe hares and ptarmigans are well equipped to walk on the surface of

Right above: The porcupine's defense is virtually passive—but effective. Its quills may enter and work through the bodies of other animals and inflict considerable damage. (Charles J. Ott) Right: The spectacled eider (Lampronetta fischeri) used to be more common in the Aleutians but was decimated by hunters. (Michael Wotton) Far right: With chicks well hidden, a mother blue grouse takes bearings from a log in the Sitka spruce forest at Glacier Bay. (Ann and Myron Sutton)

snow. One disadvantage of snow is that it covers food supplies, including lichens. But caribou dig and small animals tunnel. Birds can't dig, so they and certain herbivores must migrate or else transfer their appetites to twigs, bark, buds, leaves and seeds—about the only food remaining. These things may not be as welcome as berries and fresh green leaves, but the Arctic offers little choice. Wolverines, on the other hand, have quite a choice because they are able to conquer a great many other mammals of the north. As the most powerful member of the bloodthirstiest tribe—weasels—wolverines attack all except their largest neighbors, and even these are fair game if ailing. There are few examples of greater hatred between man and beast than that between trappers and wolverines, for the wolverine sometimes wantonly destroys furbearers caught in traps. In all fairness, however, the wolverine is not to be faulted for exercising its natural habits; man, in fact, has undertaken a senseless extermination of the wolverine in parts of the West, and that is a habit that hopefully is changing.

Left: A walrus herd on Round Island, Alaska. Between active periods walruses haul out on rocky shores or ice floes to rest. Their hides insulate them to − 50° or colder. (Karl W. Kenyon: National Audubon Society)
Below: These whisker-like bristles, called vibrissae, may serve important functions in the food-getting process. (Jeanne White: National Audubon Society)

The Polar Bear

If polar bears *(Thalarctos maritimus)* are like other bears, it is hard to imagine what there is in this world of ice and snow to eat. But polar bears are not altogether like other bears; they live primarily on seals, and for this reason occupy regions where seals abound —the pack ice with open channels of water. In North America they are most likely to be found off the icy northern coasts of Alaska and Canada. They range as far south as the Pribilof Islands, Japan, Hudson Bay and even inland a bit, but they are principally a coastal species resident north of the Arctic Circle.

It is a noisy environment, with ice cracking, floes grinding over one another, ice rising up in ridges, or storms blowing savagely over land and sea. Obviously it was all made for the polar bear, which has such a splendid coat of insulation that subzero temperatures seldom restrict its ramblings. The polar bear is nomadic, but its wanderings have not been thoroughly studied; they must range over hundreds of miles, however, judging from known facts.

Life is busy at times, for a great deal of food is required to keep these thousand-pound brutes alert and active. Despite the weight and bulky build, polar bears are as agile as other bears and can outrun a pack of huskies. The hair-covered soles of the feet, together with the gripper claws, can dig into ice for a fast getaway whenever the usual shuffle is insufficient. On snow the bear is aided by its own built-in showshoes— paws that measure thirty-four inches in circumference

For insulation the coat of the polar bear consists of guard-hairs, underfur, and spongy skin over layers of subcutaneous fat. (A.W. Ambler: National Audubon Society)

—but it prefers hard ice, and is able to scurry up cliffs with ease. One bear, being pursued by dogs, is said to have climbed to the top of an iceberg, leaped from a fifty-foot cliff into the water and started swimming toward shore, twenty-two miles away.

Thus it is an excellent swimmer, but almost helpless while doing so; if attacked by a walrus, which is larger and better designed for the fluid environment, the bear may have little chance. Even seals may gang up on a swimming polar bear and nip its hindquarters. That is distinctly the reverse of usual seal-bear relationships, for the bear is almost always on the hunt for seals, and does not venture into water except in dire emergencies. When approaching seals relaxing on an ice floe it swims furtively, sometimes with only the nose above water, sometimes completely submerged. At the proper

moment it literally springs out of the water to capture its quarry. Elsewhere, polar bears wait at the edge of a seal's hole in the ice, aware that seals must surface and breathe periodically. The bear grasps the seal with teeth and claws the instant it appears and pulls it bodily out of the water, thoroughly crushing it in the process. Polar bears also stalk seals on land, sneaking up to within a few feet, lying low when necessary, advancing by the merest movements, then catapulting forward in a lightning bound to strike a stunning or fatal blow. Failure may produce an emotion akin to rage; one observer saw a bear so angry at missing a seal that it slammed its paw on a rock—and broke every bone in the paw, as determined when the bear was shot.

After a successful hunt, polar bears may gorge. One investigator reported finding 156 pounds of walrus in the stomach of a bear. Fifty seals a year seems to be the average intake, in addition to shellfish, crustaceans and such carrion as the carcasses of whales, seals and walruses. Summer's vegetable diet must be a welcome change from blubber and carrion, for the bear dines on moss, berries, grass, seaweed and other fresh foods. In this delicate ecosystem the bear's abandonment of a partially eaten carcass helps to support other animals. Foxes are dependent on the remains of bear kills if they are unable to capture hares or lemmings for themselves.

When the time comes to do battle, polar bears slash out viciously with claws and teeth. A great many have hide wounds. Mating is in spring, usually April. By autumn, when the sun has disappeared and the snow blows across the land, pregnant females search for drifts in which to den, give birth and raise their young. The she-bear stays resolutely within, nourished by reserves of fat, no doubt sleeping much of the time. The young are born in the midst of the long polar night.

Because they are nomadic it is difficult to count polar bears and to determine accurately any trends that may be developing in their pattern of survival. Some persons estimate the world population at around ten thousand, but quickly add that polar bears are being killed by man in numbers exceeding natural losses. If the population is, in fact, less—say around five thousand—then, as one author has observed, the polar bear is a dying species. The Soviet Union claims to have stopped the killing of polar bears in its Arctic realms. Elsewhere, the situation appears to be more lax, and the killing of bears is highly efficient when hunters in spotter planes can land within stalking distance. Hopefully, international protective measures will increase and thus prevent extermination of the "tiger of the ice."

In this review of Alaska, we have seen the richness and variety of its natural resources. Today, Steller jays still fly in the coastal forests where the first naturalist of Alaska, Georg Wilhelm Steller, discovered them in 1741 on Vitus Bering's last expedition. What Steller saw remains a magnificent wilderness, and indeed most of Alaska still possesses in reasonably undisturbed condition the wonders, wildness, and wildlife that made it famous. These should make it richer on a nonconsumptive tourism-recreation basis than all the oil on the Arctic coast.

16. Prospects for Nature in the West

We endeavor, by our various operations in this world, to make, as it were, another nature.

Cicero
in *Tusculan Disputations*

In recent years, public dialogue on the natural environment has increased greatly, and with advances in audiovisual education the notion has spread that man is not only threatening wildlife but the entire ecosystem of which he is a part. To be sure, he has made quite an impact on the environment he originally found. "Had General Wolfe waded ashore at l'Anse-aux-Foulons in the summer of 1968," began a lead story on water pollution in the Canadian edition of *Time,* "he would have emerged on the Plains of Abraham covered with something besides glory." Ray Dasmann has chronicled *The Destruction of California.* William O. Douglas has said *Farewell to Texas.* The Sierra Club has documented the demise of river canyons and mountain valleys. There would seem to remain one question. At what cost has the West been won? To this we would add another. With what success is it being saved?

The most obvious wounds are large ones, chiefly damage to water, air and land. Air pollutants have expanded beyond the limits of urban areas and risen into mountain valleys once free of contamination, as in the case of desert communities. A cross-section of biomedical scientists, all members of the University of California at Los Angeles medical faculty, issued a statement deeming it their "collective responsibility" to warn of health hazards and suggest that all persons move away from the smoggiest parts of metropolitan areas. The smog problem may be solved in ten years or so, they said, but they questioned whether human beings could survive that long.

More fundamental may be the changing quality of air itself. By paving hundreds of thousands of acres of grasslands every year man is indirectly removing oxygen from the air that would otherwise have been put there by plant processes. If the rate of combustion ever exceeds the rate of photosynthesis, the oxygen content of the atmosphere will decrease. Were nitrogen then to break down it could be replaced by poisonous ammonia.

Esthetic principles are involved in the expansion of visible air pollutants. For many years there have been calls in the West for limitation of jet flights over scenic areas because a sky full of jet trails tends to detract from the natural beauty of a region. On occasion, these vapors have even expanded into cirrus bands that obscured the sun. We saw this over Crater Lake, Oregon, one morning and aside from the frustrations that thousands of photographers must have felt we thought of the long-range effects of reduced solar radiation on western ecosystems. Another aircraft-connected effect, the sonic boom, has set up sufficient vibrations to dislodge portions of cliffs; a Navajo Indian in Canyon de Chelly, Arizona, heard such a boom and then watched tons of rock fall into and destroy a prehistoric Indian ruin.

Poisonous materials washed into water from agricultural, municipal or industrial sources are taken in by plankton, the poisoned plankton are fed on by fish, and so on through the established system of energy transfer. Overuse of nitrogen fertilizers, for example, is beginning to affect foods and cause illness. Scientists see in this a disruption of the natural nitrogen cycle which man may have to balance by returning to organic fertilizers. The dumping of hot water into lakes and streams helps to release dissolved oxygen in the waters and thus restricts that environment for aquatic forms. River modification has become quite advanced, even in relatively pristine areas. The city of Whitehorse dumps refuse into the Yukon River and according to the Yukon *Daily News,* it is now often called the most scenic dump in Canada.

As for oceanic pollution, the West very probably has its share of oil, sludge and industrial wastes being pumped into the sea, but in few places is the discharge of refuse so obvious as on vessels plying the Inside Passage to Alaska. While passengers watch the changing patterns of forest, glacier and fiord, great heaps of garbage are flung over the rail—in addition to unseen discharge of sewage wastes from plumbing systems below water. Added to that is the refuse presumed cast from the blanketing network of fishing vessels scattered across the water. British Columbia Ferries at least collect dry refuse and deposit it at dockside.

Transmission lines have done a great deal to mar the scenery of the West. They cut indiscriminately across inlets, valleys, canyons and wide-open plains. Parts of the White Sands area are covered with a spider web of overhead wire lines in a region where underground installation should have been comparatively easy. One line passing over the highway has seven crossbars on each pole. In other places forests have been shaved in wide swaths from hillsides to admit parallel sets of transmission lines, each supported by double rows of posts painted red, white and green. Conspicuous redball markers on wire lines decorate fiords, rivers and canyons that would otherwise be scenically attractive.

All this demonstrates that in certain places the environment is being substantially altered. Often what begins as a simple experiment magnifies disastrously, as with the introduction of exotic flora and fauna. The tamarisk or saltcedar from the Mediterranean has seeded readily in the West and although it may be beneficial in some places, it also interferes with waterfowl habitat and reduces ground water through evapotranspiration. There is a demand by ranchers for the introduction of large African and Asian ungulates and other animals, and on large ranches of Texas this has taken place, but this may also have introduced blood parasites to which native animals such as the white-tailed deer have not evolved an immunity. Barbary sheep brought into New Mexico are aggressive breeders while resident bighorns are barely holding on, which leads to speculation that some day the foreign breed will replace the native.

Another method of modifying the environment is through dams and reservoirs. The first result is to drown wilderness, as John Muir pointed out in his unsuccessful efforts to save Hetch Hetchy Valley in the Sierra Nevada. A dam across Canada's Peace River is an engineering marvel, but in the words of an Alberta columnist: "Something has died along the Peace. Gone forever is the grand waterway which carried early explorers to the outposts of the north. For 200 years, it has been the 'Mighty Peace.' Now it is like a caged animal."

Among the subtle and surprising effects of damming may be the loss of ocean beaches. Seashore sands along parts of the Pacific Coast are being transferred by natural currents into submarine canyons; if the sand was derived largely from sediment-carrying streams, and those streams have now been dammed, then replacement sands are being deposited not on ocean beaches as before but in reservoirs far inland. Razor clams seem to prefer basalt sands washed down to the seashore by the Columbia River, but not much sand will be washed to the sea when the river is fully dammed. The future of chinook salmon in the Columbia River system is not entirely clear. Even with fish-passage facilities around dams, the fish experience delay and confusion, and it is well known that salmon travels and timing are executed with scant margin for error.

The reduction of marshlands and use of pesticides have been so fully discussed that they need not be reviewed here. Other direct and indirect attacks on wildlife are being sustained as a result of commercial trapping, hunting and fishing. Poisoned bait, distributed through several carriers, may have effects more widespread than intended; the poison could be transferred from coyotes to magpies and other carrion-eaters, substituting a chain of death for the chain of life. Mating calls and devices that imitate the distress sounds of small mammals such as rabbits have proven effective in luring coyotes, bobcats and other predators within rifle range. Western farmers have broadcast oats coated with a poison strong enough to kill crop-destroying mice but allegedly too mild to hurt other animals.

The sale of wild animal meat and hides is still prevalent in the West. Alaska offers canned whale meat and seal sausage. Canadian tourist shops sell skins of fox for thirty dollars, Dall sheep for thirty-five, coyote for fifty-six, and wolf, mountain lion, and black bear skins for $280 each. Some fear has developed that two or three species of salmon may be overwhelmed by the sheer number of pursuers, or reduced by having to swim through industrial wastes, insecticides and detergents on journeys inland to spawn. Sea lions are being heavily persecuted in Alaska because they follow boats and take bites out of fish being hauled from the water, rendering the fish unmarketable and infuriating fishermen. "It is a reflex action on the part of just about every fisherman in southeast Alaska," one naturalist told us, "to pull the trigger the minute he sees a seal." Apparently all that saves the harbor seal is the value of its pelt, whereas failure of commercial attempts to utilize sea lions rob those creatures of even that much consideration.

As a result of all this combined attrition, the survival of several animal species has been imperiled, among them the wolf, wolverine, black-footed ferret, gray whale, Eskimo curlew, California condor, Gila monster, and various starfish. With stringent measures, rescue of some species may be possible, but not easy; because of the marten's peculiar disposition, for example, restoration of that animal over large parts of its former range may well be impossible.

Nor are mineral resources exempt from exhaustion. Gem deposits of good quality, such as jade, have been

The habits of human beings are contradictory. People appreciate the out-of-doors yet mar it; they strive for cleanliness yet throw away litter; they care for natural wonders yet overwhelm them. Our dilemma is to decide whether we shall satisfy this generation and possibly the next, or enforce self-restraint and have at least a little natural beauty for all people for all time. (All by Rondal Partridge)

thoroughly picked over. Of the valuable metals, the demand for silver and mercury is exceeding the supply. The Western Hemisphere is notably deficient in chromium, though there is a low-grade deposit in Montana; ninety-eight percent of the world's known reserves of high-grade chromium rest in Rhodesia and South Africa. Ninety-nine percent of the nickel used in the United States is obtained from Canada, though Oregon has one small mine. Tungsten production in North America is negligible. There is iron in quantity, but its conversion to steel takes manganese, of which there is little. Either the steel-making process needs to be altered, or sea-floor sources of manganese nodules developed, or foreign relations kept friendly. Altogether, says the United States Geological Survey, the worldwide picture is one of impending shortages of many important minerals.

The Human Tide

There is not much doubt any more that the greatest challenge to the natural environment is man, but he is also, by necessity if nothing else, an agent of improvement. The very nature of the West—its wide-open spaces, colorful landscapes and recreation opportunities—has attracted a flood of tourists into the wilder-

ness even though they are often insulated from it. They are so eager to see wildlife that they trample the grass on which animals feed, so persistent in photography that they chase wild animals out of valleys or destroy birds in the nest. Unmindful of the consequences, they feed bears, dig up cactuses, break off cliffrose limbs, and ride horses into pristine valleys where horses never were and where alfalfa brought to feed the horses escapes and competes with native plants. Specialists in outdoor recreation have determined that walking for pleasure is the number one outdoor pastime, but in improperly managed parks and other wilderness sites, hiking and camping have proved disastrous to natural ecosystems.

The very appeal of natural objects contributes to their destruction. Irreplaceable deposits of petrified wood are subject to continuing petty theft. Unknown thousands of stalactites and stalagmites have been removed from caves. A colorful starfish *(Patiria miniata)* on the Pacific Coast can no longer be found in the great concentrations that formerly existed. It was even necessary to prohibit the collecting of stones at Pebble Beach State Park, California. A delicately scalloped border that once edged Morning Glory Pool, most famous and most heavily visited hot spring in Yellowstone National Park, has been removed by souvenir hunters. Elsewhere in the national parks, the sheer tide of humanity has threatened the purposes for which the parks were set aside. Summit climbs of Mount Rainier have increased by over five hundred percent within the last decade and well over two thousand persons now reach the top each year.

Such is the state of nature in the West today, but there is another side to this story, and a careful consideration of the remedial forces at work suggests an attitude of cautious optimism. The indications are that

man is beginning to discipline himself, and to make some encouraging strides toward restoring or improving the natural environment. Steps have been made toward the establishment of wild sanctuaries and the control of human access to them. Perhaps most significant has been the development of ways for industrial objectives to be achieved without severely disturbing the natural scene. To reduce the need for dams and reservoirs man is well on the way toward desalting sea and brackish water. To modify the desire for hydroelectric dams he is generating power by nuclear and geothermal means. To eradicate overhead transmission lines he is developing new cables that will endure underground. And as one long-range antidote to air pollution he is experimenting with steam and electric automobiles.

Under certain circumstances hunting is a bona-fide wildlife management tool to reduce surplus populations. But the opportunities for hunting do not grow at a rate proportionate to the growth of population, if only because the amount of land producing wildlife is diminishing. Hunting pressure can therefore be distributed only in accordance with the capacity of various animal species to withstand removals. As a form of relaxation, hunting has become a declining fraction of overall recreation land use. Simultaneously, there is increasing interest in other uses, such as nonconsumptive outdoor recreation, which is stimulating management and research into these fields. Also, certain forms of wildlife control, such as poisoning, trapping and shooting, have become less acceptable in the public mind. One possible solution, where wildlife control is mandatory, may be the humane use of diethylsilbestrol ($C_{18}H_{20}O_2$) which, if used just as breeding begins, causes the female to abort.

The debate over pesticides has stepped up research

for other biological pest controls, and the outlook is encouraging. Certain hormone-like chemicals have proved to be selective on one species of insect at a time, doing no other harm than sterilizing the females or perhaps preventing pupae from molting into adults. Fully developed, this might mean the end of crop pests, flies and mosquitoes, but that, of course, raises the question of how seriously the absence of specific insects would affect the natural ecosystem. "Nature has set us so well in the center," said the French philosopher Blaise Pascal in the seventeenth century, "that if we change one side of the balance, we change the other also."

Even the intensity of man's efforts to eradicate wolves is abating. This is no doubt due first to increased public enlightenment and an interest in salvaging threatened species, and second to a flow of advice and recommendations for legislators at all levels. Informed public opinion forthrightly given has done more for the cause of conservation than can be adequately measured. Indeed, as the Washington *Post* observed, the time has long since passed when public officials could impose their preconceived ideas upon the country's land, water, parks and wilderness. The United States Fish and Wildlife Service has under way a massive program to care for endangered animals and ease them back, if possible, from the brink of extinction.

Adequate Alternatives

Men seem to be meeting the challenge of vanishing minerals, too. Even though the richest lodes have been exhausted, it is possible with new detection instruments to find deposits previously unknown or with new mining methods to utilize sources passed over before. Metals such as zinc have good prospects. The

new technology of aluminum extraction is making possible the use of high-alumina clays as a substitute for bauxite. The demand for minerals scarce in North America, such as tin, is expected to ebb and flow with the development of substitutes. For mercury, however, there are as yet no adequate alternatives and this may be one of the first metals to come under government allocation. A new electrical cable composed of sodium metal core with a plastic sheath is under test and if developed successfully may influence requirements for copper. Removing lead from gasoline in order to reduce environmental pollution, or using fuel cells to replace storage batteries will conserve the supply of that mineral.

If nuclear reactors are to be used for power generation, desalination plants, and the propulsion of sea, air, and space craft, attention will focus on uranium and other fissionable materials. The largest United States reserves are in New Mexico and Wyoming, though Canada has the bulk of the world's reserves. However, deposits now known are not expected to supply the demand, so man may have to place his hopes in nuclear fusion, which produces fewer contaminants than nuclear fission, and in thorium as a prime energy source. Development of such sources could reduce combustion of coal and other fossil fuels. Then coal could conceivably be used as food for microbes that help produce high-protein food supplements. The losses that the electric car would mean to the petroleum industry might be balanced by increased uses of petrochemicals.

In his new role of enlightened dominance of the world ecosystem, man can at least regulate some of the inevitable changes. If we are to believe Thomas Edison, what man's mind can create, man's character can control. The thermal pollution of rivers, for example, may adversely affect fish and wildlife, water potability and industrial usage; but the United States Geological Survey is studying rates of dissipation in heat loads imposed in streams, attempting to determine what factors affect heat transfer to and from streams.

Some minerals may be diminishing in supply, but fifty to seventy new minerals are being discovered every year, and the electron microprobe allows grain-by-grain analysis of the content of rocks. Research at ultra-high temperatures and pressures takes us into a world as unfamiliar as space itself.

Since agricultural fertilizers and pest control methods have drawn the public ire, it may be well to examine plans under way by the Japanese to establish "farms" on the sea floor and raise dozens of varieties of fish and crustaceans. Pollution abatement has become a determined effort from the household to the international level, and the control of noise, particularly sonic booms, is under study by scientific leaders

Air particles failing to dissipate clog the sky, blot out the sun and impair public health. (Rondal Partridge) Overleaf: In much of the West, as in the Monashee Mountains of British Columbia, men share with other life forms a rich and delicate natural world too fragile to bear abuse. (Don Worth)

and government officials. Resource surveys have been vastly accelerated by observation from space stations. National and state park and forest systems as well as wildlife refuges are not only being enlarged but are being managed with increasingly sophisticated data and techniques.

The West is often said to be short of water, but this is not so and never has been. It has a specific, normally fluctuating supply of moisture, to which a complex biologic community has become adapted. Statistics show that neither the climate of the West nor the hydrological cycle has changed significantly in the last century. There is so much water, in fact, that ninety-five percent of it is flowing out to sea. The problem is, rather, the abundance and distribution of water-users.

Even on the most pressing of problems—the abundance of human beings—the science of birth control seems to be advancing with increased popular support. But we should never forget that large numbers of people can also be a positive and helpful force, and it is largely through their gratifying experiences in the West that remarkable systems of national parks and equivalent reserves have been established, and endangered wildlife rescued. Tourism, cited by the United Nations as the largest single item in world trade, seems almost certain to replace mining, lumbering, and stock-raising as the number one industry in western states and provinces. If it remains nonconsumptive, is held within bounds, and does not damage natural resources, tourism should continue to be the key that unlocks the West's great potentials for human inspiration and rejuvenation.

Sometimes, of course, this is a personal, even a solitary, process. The distinguished biologist and conservationist, Stanley A. Cain, once observed that "there is a saturation point beyond which the wilderness experience cannot be had, beyond which a campground is no longer a pleasant place. Parks need to apply the familiar rangeland concept of carrying capacity. Innumerable people cannot enjoy solitude together." So succinct a recognition of the problem is a measured step toward its solution. Public confidence can be sustained through the opening of large scenic recreation areas for high-density use, simultaneously with the restriction of wild areas for use by persons who can meet and appreciate the wilderness on its own terms. This opens up management problems of a different kind, but their solution is the challenge of our times.

Discipline is a human trait. Smoke-filtering devices have been increased, sewage treatment plants expanded and sanctuaries augmented. Populations may even be stabilizing. Some day our present efforts will seem primitive, but hopefully they will also prove successful. And it is tempting to speculate that with the maintenance of western ecosystems in as natural a condition as possible we shall be able to carry wildlife and other research to undreamed-of conclusions. Perhaps some day we shall even be able to answer that eternal question posed by an Alaskan Indian: "Have wolves souls?"

Thus almost every sign points to man's rise from his predicament, so that we may be witnessing a landmark

change in human habits from selfish exploitation to an almost selfless retrieval of what has been taken away.

Far-sighted Alaskans have proposed a policy for the future based on the simple assumption that the dominant Alaskan resource is the wilderness itself. They have recommended that all development be pursued only if it would not depreciate wilderness resources or would in fact augment the wilderness status of the land. If that sort of wisdom prevails in the government circles of states and provinces, and in national government planning, then the land and wildlife are secure. If a love of nature prevails in the hearts of men and they hear in the voice of the crane an echo of the past and a song of the future, those men will have approached the kind of maturity that stewardship of the land requires. And if by listening to the music of a mountain stream and the gentle rustle of cottonwood leaves they find their vision enlarged and their burdens lifted, then the West has been won and its greatness will endure.

Topographical Maps

Overleaf: The Southern Regions

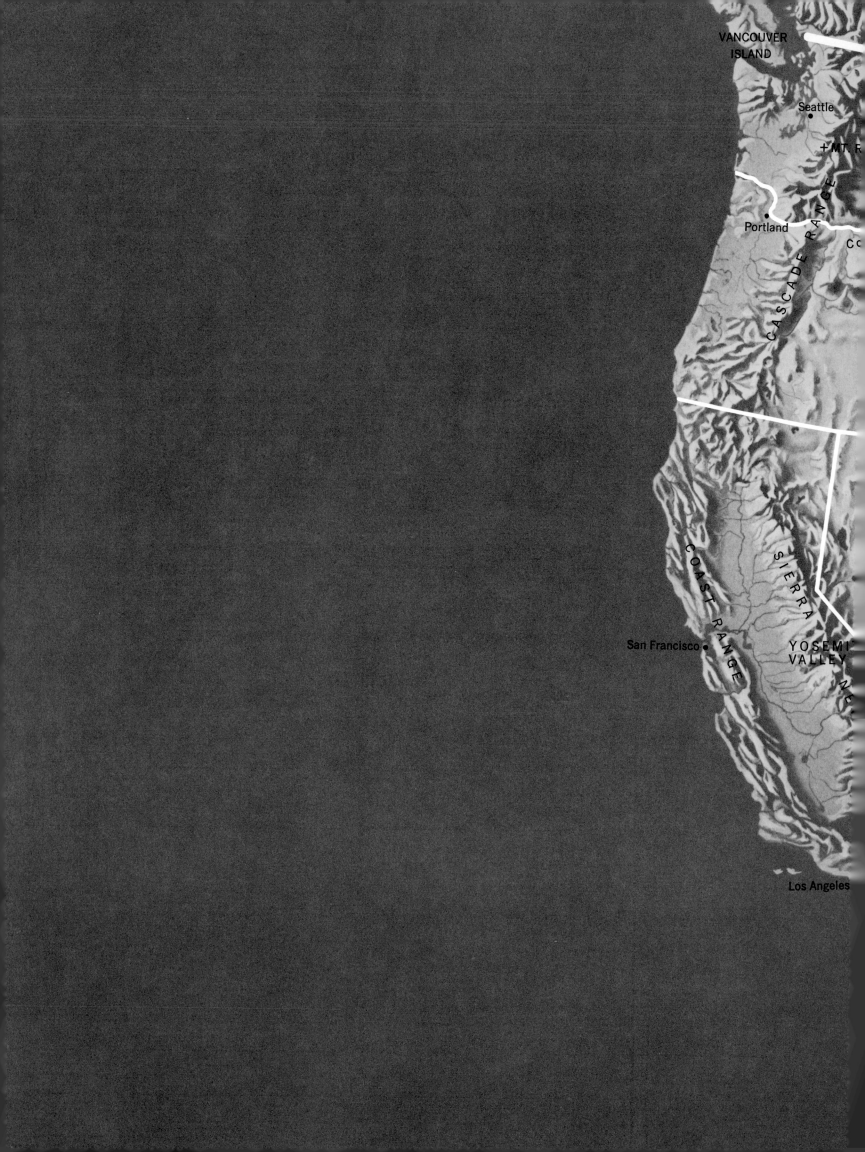

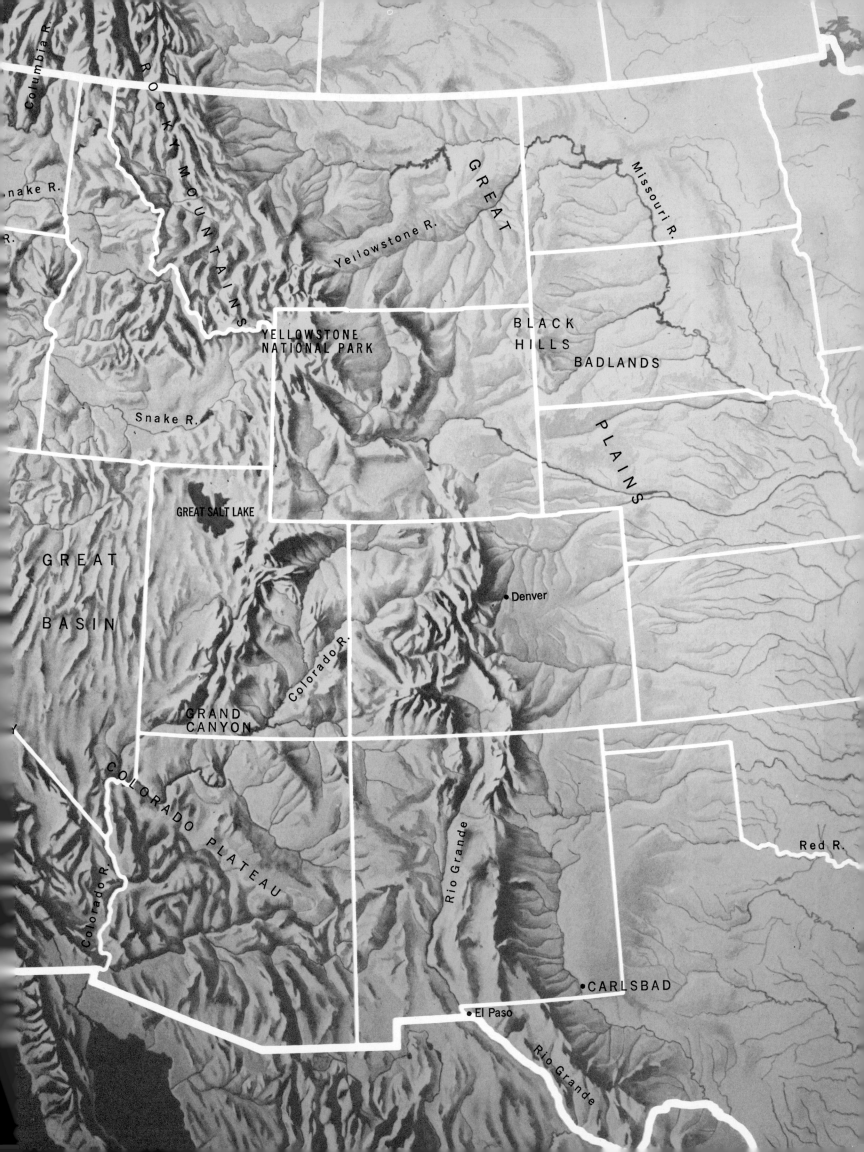

Overleaf: The Northern Regions and Alaska

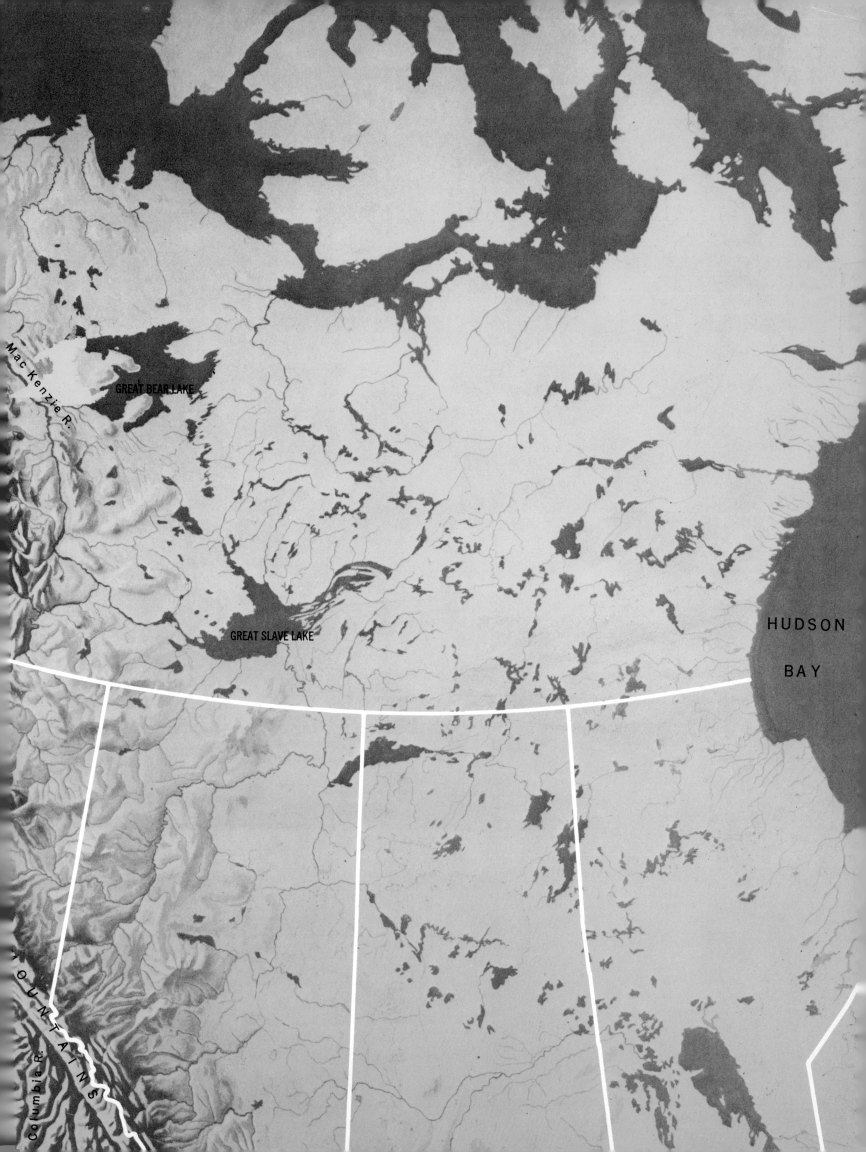

Bibliography

Allen, Durward L., *The Life of Prairies and Plains*, 1967, McGraw-Hill Book Company, N.Y.

American Heritage, Editors of, *The American Heritage Book of Natural Wonders*, 1963, American Heritage Publishing Company, Inc., N.Y.

Amos, William H., *The Life of the Seashore*, 1966, McGraw-Hill Book Company, N.Y.

Anderson, J.P., *Flora of Alaska and Adjacent Parts of Canada*, 1959, Iowa State University Press.

Baldwin, Ewart M., *Geology of Oregon*, 1964, University of Oregon Press.

Bartlett, Richard A., *Great Surveys of the American West*, 1962, University of Oklahoma Press.

Berrill, N.J., *The Life of the Ocean*, 1966, McGraw-Hill Book Company, N.Y.

Brockman, C. Frank, *Trees of North America*, 1968, Golden Press, N.Y.

Brooks, Maurice, *The Life of the Mountains*, 1967, McGraw-Hill Book Company, N.Y.

Bullard, Fred M., *Volcanoes: In History, In Theory, In Eruption*, 1962, University of Texas Press.

Burns, William A., (Ed.). *The Natural History of the Southwest*, 1960, Franklin Watts, Inc., N.Y.

Cahalane, Victor, *Mammals of North America*, 1967, The Macmillan Company, N.Y.

Cormack, R.G.H., *Wild Flowers of Alberta*, 1967, Alberta Department of Industry and Development.

Craighead, John, and others, *A Field Guid to Rocky Mountain Wildflowers*, 1963, Houghton Mifflin Company, Boston.

Crampton, C. Gregory, *Standing Up Country: The Canyon Lands of Utah and Arizona*, 1964, Alfred A. Knopf, N.Y.

Darling, F. Fraser, and Milton, John P., *Future Environments of North America*, 1966, The Natural History Press, N.Y.

Eardley, A.J., *Structural Geology of North America*, 1962, Harper and Row, Publishers, N.Y.

Farb, Peter, *Face of North America: The Natural History of a Continent*, 1963, Harper and Row, Publishers, N.Y.

———, and the Editors of LIFE, *The Land and Wildlife of North America*, 1964, Time Inc., N.Y.

Flawn, Peter T., *Mineral Resources*, 1966, Rand McNally and Company, Chicago.

Geiger, Rudolph, *The Climate Near the Ground*, 1965, Harvard University Press.

Gleason, Henry A., and Cronquist, Arthur, *The Natural Geography of Plants*, 1964, Columbia University Press, N.Y.

Hardy, W.G., *Alberta: A Natural History*, 1967, M.G. Hurtig, Alberta.

Hastings, James Rodney, and Turner, Raymond M., *The Changing Mile*, 1965, University of Arizona Press.

Hunt, Charles B., *Physiography of the United States*, 1967, W.H. Freeman and Company, San Francisco.

Jaeger, Edmund C., *The North American Deserts*, 1957, Stanford University Press.

King, Philip B., *The Evolution of North America*, 1959, Princeton University Press.

Kortright, Francis H., *The Ducks, Geese and Swans of North America*, 1953, Wildlife Management Institute, Washington.

Mather, Kirtley F., *The Earth Beneath Us*, 1964, Random House, N.Y.

Matthiessen, Peter, *Wildlife in America*, 1959, Viking Press Inc., N.Y.

McCormick, Jack, *The Life of the Forest*, 1966, McGraw-Hill Book Company, N.Y.

Niering, William A., *The Life of the Marsh*, 1966, McGraw-Hill Book Company, N.Y.

Odum, Eugene P., *Fundamentals of Ecology*, 1959, W.B. Saunders Company, Philadelphia.

Paul, Rodman Wilson, *Mining Frontiers of the Far West*, 1963, Holt, Rinehart and Winston, N.Y.

Peattie, Donald Culross, *A Natural History of Western Trees*, 1963, Houghton Mifflin Company, Boston.

Peterson, Roger T., *A Field Guide to Western Birds*, 1961, Houghton Mifflin Company, Boston.

Powell, John Wesley, *The Exploration of the Colorado River and its Canyons*, 1895, reprinted in 1961 by Dover Publications Inc., N.Y.

Ricketts, Edward F., and Calvin, Jack, *Between Pacific Tides*, 1968, Stanford University Press.

Robbins, Chandler; Bruun, Bertel; and Zim, Herbert S., *Birds of North America*, 1966, Golden Press, N.Y.

Scott, William Berryman, *A History of Land Mammals in the Western Hemisphere*, 1937, reprinted in 1962 by Hafner Publishing Company, N.Y.

Shelford, Victor E., *The Ecology of North America*, 1963, University of Illinois Press.

Shelton, John S., *Geology Illustrated*, 1966, W.H. Freeman and Company, San Francisco.

Shepard, Francis P., and Dill, Robert F., *Submarine Canyons and other Sea Valleys*, 1966, Rand McNally and Company, Chicago.

Soper, J. Dewey, *The Mammals of Alberta*, 1964, The Hamly Press Ltd, Edmonton, Alberta.

Stebbins, Robert C., *A Field Guide to Western Reptiles and Amphibians*, 1966, Houghton Mifflin Company, Boston.

———, *Amphibians and Reptiles of Western North America*, 1954, McGraw-Hill Book Company, N.Y.

Sudworth, George B., *Forest Trees of the Pacific Slope*, 1967, Dover Publications Inc., N.Y.

Sunset Books and Sunset Magazine, Editors of, *National Parks of the West*, 1965, Lane Magazine and Book Company, Menlo Park, Calif.

Sutton, Ann and Myron, *The Life of the Desert*, 1966, McGraw-Hill Book Company, N.Y.

Thornbury, William D., *Regional Geomorphology of the United States*, 1965, John Wiley and Sons, Inc., N.Y.

Usinger, Robert L., *The Life of Rivers and Streams*, 1967, McGraw-Hill Book Company, N.Y.

Woodbury, Angus M., *Principles of General Ecology*, McGraw-Hill Book Company Inc., N.Y.

Index

Asterisks indicate pages containing illustrations

Planned and produced by Paul Steiner and the staff of Chanticleer Press
Editors: Milton Rugoff and Constance Sullivan
Design: Ulrich Ruchti   Production Coordination: Gudrun Buettner

48141770